£12.99

The Russian Revolution 1917–1921

A Short History

James D. White

Lecturer in Russian History,
Institute of Russian and East European Studies
University of Glasgow

Edward Arnold
A member of the Hodder Headline Group
LONDON NEW YORK MELBOURNE AUCKLAND

© 1994 James D. White

First published in Great Britain 1994

Distributed in the USA by Routledge, Chapman and Hall, Inc.
29 West 35th Street, New York, NY 10001

British Library Cataloguing in Publication Data
Available on request.

ISBN 0 340 539097 (HB)
0 340 539100 (PB)

Typeset in 10 on 11pt Palatino
by Hewer Text Composition Services, Edinburgh
Printed and bound in Great Britain for Edward Arnold,
a division of Hodder Headline PLC, 338 Euston Road,
London NW1 3BH by Biddles Ltd, Guildford & King's Lynn.

Contents

List of Maps

Preface

With the collapse of the Soviet regime, the continuity between the events of 1917 and current politics has been broken, and the Russian revolution has passed into history. It is now clear that the entire Soviet period was no more than an episode in the life of the country, one which had a beginning in 1917 and had an end in 1991. This knowledge provides a new perspective from which the Russian revolution can be studied and evaluated.

In the last years of the Soviet regime, policies introduced by Mikhail Gorbachev made possible the publication both of fresh historical materials and the republication of earlier works which had been suppressed. The failed coup in 1991 and the subsequent measures taken against the Communist Party led to the removal of any remaining prohibitions on the study of the Russian revolution.

The new perspective, and the new source material which has become available, provide an opportunity to re-examine the subject and investigate the nature of the event which more than any other shaped world politics of the twentieth century.

This book sets out to give a concise chronological account of the revolutionary period. At its most basic level, it tries to answer the question: What took place when? It traces the sequence of events covering the antecedents of the revolution, the collapse of the tsarist regime, the establishment and overthrow of the Provisional Government, the Civil War and the first years of the Soviet State. It tries, as far as possible, to do this in an unbroken sequence, to show the links leading from one event to the next and, in particular, to reveal the continuities. Besides chronological integration, the narrative tries to bring together the various aspects of the subject – political, economic, social, military and ideological – of which the Russian revolution presented a rich interplay.

How the succession of events and processes came together to form the totality of the revolution is treated here as a subject for research in its own right. Accordingly, the sources used have been, wherever possible, primary ones, though a variety of monographs has also been drawn upon. The latter include the work of Western and Soviet writers as well as that of authors writing in German, Polish, Latvian, etc., which deserve to be better known.

Dates up to 14 February 1918 are given according to the Russian calendar, which was 13 days behind that of the West. Thereafter all dates are given according to the Western calendar, though in cases where ambiguity might arise they appear in both styles.

Russian words and names have been transliterated in a simplified form of the Library of Congress system, though exceptions have been made in the text where other forms of transliteration have become familiar, e.g. Trotsky rather than Trotskii. Non-Russian names have been given in the modern spelling of the languages to which they belong. Thus, 'Vācietis' rather than 'Vatsetis' and 'Dzierżyński' rather than 'Dzerzhinskii'.

Towns and cities are referred to by the names they had in the period in question, e.g. 'Vilna' rather than 'Vilnius' and 'Reval' rather than 'Tallinn'. The capital of the Russian Empire, St Petersburg, was renamed Petrograd in August 1914 to give it a Russian- and not a German-sounding name. Most Russian socialists, however, refused to pander to the chauvinist sentiment that had brought the change about, and continued to use the city's old name. For than reason, both 'St Petersburg' and 'Petrograd' were current in the revolutionary period, and will be encountered in the pages which follow.

Thanks are due to Alec Nove, Bill Wallace, Tauno Tiusanen, Ian Thatcher and to Christopher Wheeler of Edward Arnold Publishers.

1

Russian Social and Economic Development before the Revolution

The Russian Empire

The Russian Empire, as it existed in 1917, was the product of the territorial expansion Russia had undergone between the sixteenth and nineteenth centuries. Russia's initial and greatest area of expansion had been in the East, in Siberia. The way was opened by Ivan the Terrible's conquest of the Tatar kingdoms of Kazan and Astrakhan in the 1550s. By the first decades of the seventeenth century Russia controlled western Siberia to the river Enisei; by the middle of the century it had reached the Amur river, the conquest of eastern Siberia to the Pacific taking place in the second half of the seventeenth century. Further progress in the East was halted after the Qing dynasty came to power in China. After he had completed the pacification of the country, the Emperor Kang Xi turned his attention to securing his Manchurian frontier. The Treaty of Nerchinsk, concluded in 1689 and giving China the undisputed control of the Amur basin, settled Russian and Chinese spheres of influence in the East.

In the West, much of Russia's territorial expansion had taken place from the time of Peter the Great onwards. Peter had annexed most of the Baltic coastline from Sweden at the beginning of the eighteenth century, giving Russia its 'window on the West'. His successors completed the conquest of the Baltic territories and added the Western border lands of the Ukraine, Belorussia, Lithuania and Poland through the Partitions of Poland (1772, 1793 and 1795) and the settlement at the Congress of Vienna (1815). Finland was conquered by Russia in 1809, and Bessarabia was annexed three years later following the war with Turkey in 1812.

The Transcaucasian territories of Georgia, Armenia and Azerbaijan were also acquired by Russia in 1812, though they were not completely assimilated until the end of the nineteenth century. The Kazakh and Kirghiz steppes as far as the rivers Alma-Ata and Syr-Darya were occupied between the 1830s and the 1850s. In the second half of the nineteenth century Russian forces conquered the central Asian khanates of Khiva and Bokhara. Russian domination was then extended further south with the annexation of the city and territory of Merv in 1884, when the territorial expansion of the Russian Empire virtually ceased. By that time the area of the empire covered

The Russian Empire c.1885

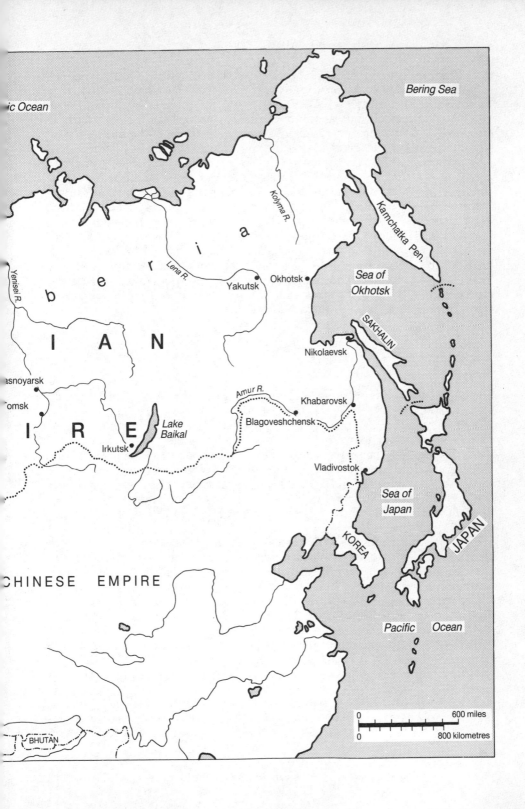

Bering Sea

ic Ocean

Kolyma R.

Kamchatka Pen.

b e r i a

Lena R.

Yenisei R.

Yakutsk

Okhotsk

Sea of
Okhotsk

I A N

SAKHALIN

asnoyarsk

omsk

Amur R.

Nikolaevsk

I R E

Lake
Baikal

Khabarovsk

Irkutsk

Blagoveshchensk

Vladivostok

Sea of
Japan

JAPAN

CHINESE EMPIRE

KOREA

Pacific   Ocean

BHUTAN

0   600 miles

0   800 kilometres

over 21 million square miles and had a population of over 178 million people.

With the expansion of territory Russia acquired a population with a very mixed national composition. The Baltic territories, for example, were populated by indigenous Latvians and Estonians, as well as by the German-speaking land-owning and merchant classes. The lands of the former Polish Commonwealth were peopled not only by Poles, Lithuanians, Belorussians and Ukrainians but also by Jews, who formed a major part of the urban population of the towns in the Ukrainian and Lithuanian provinces. The conquest of central Asia had considerably increased the numbers of Turkic-Tatar peoples in the empire, making them the second largest national group. They numbered 18.9 million in 1913, constituting 10.6 per cent of the population. The largest contingent were the Russians who, together with the Ukrainians and Belorussians, totalled 116.8 million, representing two-thirds of the whole. The third largest national group in the empire were the Poles, whose 11 million represented 5.8 per cent of the population.[1] Of course, far from all of the peoples incorporated into the Russian Empire in various ways were entirely willing subjects of the tsar.

The Peasantry

The Russian Empire on the eve of the revolution was overwhelmingly an agrarian territory. Eighty per cent of the population was composed of peasants living for the most part in scattered villages with poor communications between them. To the Russian peasant, the village was for all practical purposes the world. The word *mir* in Russian signified both 'village community' (or 'commune') and 'world'. The workings of the *mir* are of cardinal importance for understanding Russian society both before and after the revolution, for these determined the attitude and outlook of the vast majority of the people who composed it. To a large degree Russian society *was* the *mir*.[2]

It is significant that in Russian the word *mir* meant not only 'the world' but also 'peace': because the Russian peasant commune incorporated the two principles of self-sufficiency and harmony into the way it operated, both internally and externally.

The *mir* acted as a self-sufficient unit with regard to the outside world. It tried as far as possible to regulate the affairs of its members without recourse to governmental authorities. In fact, the peasants came into very little direct contact with the agencies of the tsarist government and only then through representatives of the *mir*. On the other hand, the fact that the *mir* was a self-governing entity simplified central government's task of running such a vast country.

The officers who acted as representatives of the *mir* to the outside world, the elder or *starosta* and the clerk (*pisar'*), were elected by the heads of households at the village assembly or *skhod*. The assembly also decided on

[1]   A. Suvorin, ed., *Russkii kalendar' na 1916 g.* (Petrograd, 1916), pp. 83–88.
[2]   In fact, *obshchestvo*, the other word in Russian for the peasant commune, also means 'society'.

all other matters which affected the members of the commune as a whole, and which lay outside the competence of the peasant family. The family's relationship to the *mir* was like that of the *mir* to the outside world: it tried to deal with all matters involving its members without recourse to outsiders. Responsibility for ensuring the discipline and well-being of individuals fell first of all on the head of the family, who acted as the representative of the family in relation to the rest of the *mir*.

In accordance with the principle of maintaining peace and harmony, the *mir* tried to divide equally among the peasant community the obligations it had to fulfil and the assets it had to dispose of. In this first category, until the abolition of serfdom in 1861, were the labour services and the payments in money and kind due to the land-owner. These had been imposed on the *mir* as a whole and what each particular family had to contribute was decided by a meeting of the *skhod*. The existence of the *mir* had thus been of considerable benefit to the land-owners and had ensured its continued survival.

The sharing of resources was a major source of the *mir*'s strength and resilience. The peasant commune acted as a mutual-aid society for its members. If any of them suffered adversity or disaster, the rest would rally round and give moral and material support. Help would be given to the poor, the ill, orphans and old people who had no family to support them. Hospitals, churches and schools were maintained at the expense of the *mir*. Major enterprises such as the building of a house would be undertaken collectively, and commune members would help each other at harvest and other times when extra labour was required.

The feature of Russian peasant communes which seemed most remarkable to outsiders, and was first described to a foreign audience by the German traveller August von Haxthausen in the 1840s, was the way in which they periodically redistributed the land among their members.[3] This preserved social cohesion by maintaining a rough economic equality in the community. By no means all peasant communes were repartitional, however. In the central Russian heartland the repartitional type of commune was dominant, but in the western Ukraine and the Belorussian provinces the non-repartitional type was characteristic. In areas where there was abundant land for cultivation, communes were less likely to carry out redivisions than in provinces where land was scarce and congested.[4]

In order that each family should enjoy the same chance of prosperity, it was necessary that good and bad soil, stony or marshy ground, should be apportioned in equal measure. Consequently the land in the three fields which commonly surrounded the village was first of all classified according to quality, and each of these areas was marked out with turf dykes. Each area was then divided into narrow strips, and these were assigned by lot to heads of households at a special meeting of the *skhod*.

The population of the peasant commune might change; some families might grow, while others might disappear altogether. There was an infinity of ways in which inequalities might arise. These could be corrected by redivi-

---

[3] A. von Haxthausen, *Studien über die innern Zustände, das Volksleben und insbesondere die ländlichen Einrichtungen Russlands* i (Hannover, 1847), p. 124.

[4] V. P. Danilov, 'K voprosu o kharaktere i znachenii krestianskoi pozemel'noi obshchiny v Rossii', *Problemy sotsial'no-ekonomicheskoi istorii Rossy. Sbornik statei* (Moscow, 1971), p. 348.

sions of the land. How often this would take place depended on local custom, but general redivisions were rather infrequent, perhaps every decade, while partial redivisions were more common.

From a purely economic point of view the repartitional commune had two severe disadvantages. The first was that since the strips of land were subject to periodic redistribution it was not worth while for any peasant cultivator to spend money or effort in an attempt to improve the land he currently worked by, for example, the application of fertilizer; for in time the advantage would be enjoyed by someone else. The repartitional commune, therefore, did not encourage advance in agricultural technique.

The second disadvantage arose out of the physical configuration of the repartitional commune. A great deal of its area was taken up with boundary dykes marking off the allotments and this was entirely lost to agriculture. Moreover, the multiplicity of intermingled strips made cultivation difficult. Even if the peasants could have afforded machinery, the smallness of the strips would have effectively prevented its use. It was also inconvenient and time consuming to move between strips located in different parts of the fields.

In reply to the charge that the peasant commune was not economically efficient, it must be said that it was not meant to be efficient: it was meant to ensure fairness and justice. It was designed to maintain the peace and harmony, the equality and solidarity of the agrarian community. Economic considerations were subordinated to the ethic of the *mir*.

The Agrarian Economy

The framers of the legislation which emancipated the serfs in 1861 believed that the long-term consequences of their efforts would be the creation of a Western-type market economy. They imagined that gradually the peasant communes would dissolve and give way to individual ownership of the land, just as had happened in Western European countries. The legislators intended, however, that in Russia's case the process should not be accompanied by any social upheaval. They therefore took measures to ensure that things should proceed smoothly if slowly.

When the legislation was being prepared most land-owners expressed the preference that the peasants simply be given their personal freedom but that they, the land-owners, should be allowed to keep the land. This had been the pattern in the Baltic provinces between 1816 and 1819. It had been advantageous to the land-owners because the freed peasants, being without any means of supporting themselves and their families, had to continue working for the land-owners in return for the hire of a piece of land to cultivate. By changing in this way from serfdom to hired labour the land-owners suffered no substantial loss.[5]

Alexander II and his advisers, however, were unwilling to agree to this policy because of its social consequences. It uprooted the peasants from the

[5] A. Rikhter, *Istoriia krest'ianskogo sosloviia v prisoedinennykh k Rossii pribaltiiskikh guberniiakh* (Riga, 1860), pp. 22–66.

land and left them to find employment as best they could. It created a propertyless and rootless class of people, a proletariat, which might cause social and political instability – as had happened in 1848 throughout Western Europe. The 1861 legislation was framed in such a way as to prevent the creation of a proletariat. This was the consideration which underlay two important provisions of the 1861 statute. One was that the *mir* was to be retained, and the other was that the peasants were to be freed with land.[6]

But if the peasants were to be given land to maintain themselves, what incentive would they have to work on the land-owners' estates? This problem was one which greatly exercised the land-owners prior to the emancipation. One method of solving this problem was to provide for a transitional period of nine years during which the peasant would be 'temporarily obligated' to his former master, and would provide labour and other services as before. A more long-term solution was that although the peasants would be given land, it would be insufficient to provide for all their needs. They would have less land after the emancipation than they had formerly cultivated.

The tracts of land which the peasants had formerly been able to make use of but which were now unavailable to them – except for payment – were called *otrezki*, literally 'pieces cut off'. These were now reserved for the land-owner. Often they consisted of woods, streams and roads, all of which had been regarded as the common property of the commune.

But the chief method by which the 1861 legislation proposed to ensure peasant labour for the land-owners was by making the full freedom of the peasants conditional on the purchase of an allotment of land from the land-owner. The sum necessary to purchase the land would be advanced to the land-owner by the government, and the peasant would repay the money plus the interest to the government in annual instalments or 'redemption' payments. This procedure had two advantages for the land-owner: it meant that the peasants, being in need of ready cash to meet their redemption payments, would be forced to work for the land-owner; and, secondly, it would provide the land-owner with a considerable sum of ready money to use in paying the wages of his hired workers and for purchasing any agricultural equipment he might need.

The emancipation Act of 1861 was a well thought-out piece of legislation, which was designed to ensure a smooth changeover from serfdom to contractual, market relations. In the event that is not what took place, and the objective of a Western-type economy was not achieved. Besides this, the emancipation legislation had some social consequences which its liberal framers had not foreseen.

Although the Russian government took all possible measures to safeguard the interests of the land-owners, it was in the long term unsuccessful in this endeavour. One reason was that the Russian aristocracy had no tradition of running its estates in the businesslike way required by the new arrangements. Secondly, the money the land-owners received from the government was often much less than the inflated amounts they had charged the peasant purchasers. For the government deducted from the sum it gave to the land-

[6] N. A. Tsagolov, *Ocherki russkoi ekonomicheskoi mysli perioda padeniia krepostnogo prava* (Moscow, 1956), pp. 282–84.

owners any moneys they might owe to the exchequer. This was often quite considerable because, prior to 1861, land-owner estates had been heavily indebted. Thirdly, the land-owners were paid in government bonds, which soon depreciated. Consequently, in the years after the emancipation, land-owners suffered from a severe shortage of credit to run their estates.

The second half of the nineteenth century and the first decades of the twentieth saw a precipitous decline in the fortunes of the Russian nobility. The amount of land in its possession decreased steadily. Before 1861 the land-owners had in their possession 84.9 million hectares of land. By 1887 this had shrunk to 79.8 million and by 1905 it was only 58.1 million. The revolution of 1905 caused massive land sales, and between 1906 and 1910 over 7 million hectares passed out of the nobility's ownership. By 1917 the land-owners had just over a half of what they had possessed in 1861.[7] After 1905 one-third of landed proprietors were peasants or merchants by origin.[8] In these circumstances the land-owning class looked increasingly to the government for financial support. In 1885 the government established the Nobles' Land Bank. This provided aristocratic land-owners with cheap credit and, by its indulgent treatment of its clients, gave them a hidden subsidy to keep possession of their estates. When the nobles did lose their land, they could expect the tsarist government to provide them with a livelihood by giving them posts in the army or the civil service. This economic dependence tended to cement together the interests of the land-owners with the tsarist government, an identity reflected in the political attitudes of the land-owning class.[9]

But the decline in the nobility's land-ownership was not uniform through-out the empire. It was most rapid and severe in the central industrial and northern provinces, whereas the nobility's hold on the land was most persistent in the Baltic and western provinces, where even by 1905 the land-owners still retained 80 per cent of their pre-1861 holdings. In these provinces the land-owning class was either Polish or German, and the emancipation of the serfs had varied from the pattern laid down by the 1861 statute. In the Baltic provinces of Livland, Estland and Kurland the peasants had been liberated without land during the reign of Alexander I, so that in this case the terms had been more favourable to the German nobility. In the western provinces of Vilna, Kovno, Grodno, Vitebsk, Minsk, Mogilev, Volhynia, Kiev and Podolia, the provisions of the 1861 legislation had been modified following the outbreak of the 1863 Polish rebellion. There the peasantry had been given more generous allotments under more favourable terms in order to deprive the local nobility of their support and to strengthen the peasants' allegiance to the Russian government. A number of measures were enacted to restrict Polish and encourage Russian ownership of land. The restrictions on the freedom to buy and sell land in these provinces had the effect of ensuring that despite the change in nationality of the land-owner, estates remained in the nobility's ownership.

The nobility's political influence had also been reinforced by the system of

[7]   S. M. Dubrovskii, *Sel'skoe khoziaistvo i krest'ianstvo Rossy v period imperializma* (Moscow, 1975), pp. 94–95.
[8]   V. S. Diakin, *Samoderzhavie, burzhuaziia i dvorianstvo v 1907–1911 gg.* (Leningrad, 1978), p. 12.
[9]   Diakin, *Samoderzhavie*, p. 16.

local government which had been established in 1864, the *zemstvos*. By the end of the 1870s *zemstvos* had been established in 34 provinces but there were none in the Polish, Lithuanian, Caucasian or central Asian provinces. Over the years the *zemstvos* became centres of liberal and constitutional ideas. The *zemstvos* engaged numerous professional employees, the so-called 'third element', who worked among the peasants as doctors, schoolteachers, veterinary surgeons, agronomists and statisticians. Their contact with the common people and their predicament often made these *zemstvo* workers politically radical.[10]

As far as the peasants were concerned, the measures to prevent their becoming economically self-sufficient worked only too well. In order to raise money to pay the redemption dues and the poll tax, they were forced to sell the grain they produced, work for the land-owners or more prosperous peasants, or find employment in industry.

The more prosperous peasants, who were able to employ their poorer neighbours to work for them, lend them money at high rates of interest or take over their allotments of land, were considered to infringe the *mir*'s egalitarian ethic, and were referred to opprobriously as *miroedy* (*mir*-eaters) or *kulaks* (tight-fisted characters). The possibility of their accumulating land had been increased by the 1861 legislation because this had stipulated that a general redivision required a two-thirds majority of those entitled to vote. (Formerly a simple majority had sufficed.) The poorer peasants, who would have most benefited by a general redivision of the land, however, were the ones most likely to be absent when a vote was taken, since it was the poorer peasants who left the village to work in industry.

Whereas those peasants who left to work in the towns were anxious to keep a portion of land in their native village to act as a kind of insurance policy against unemployment, those who stayed behind often tried to pressure industrial workers into giving up their shares completely, as the villagers would then have more land at their disposal. No one who contemplated returning to his native village would relinquish his land willingly. For once a peasant had done this he lost the right to determine how the land belonging to the commune was apportioned. Landless peasants, like village schoolteachers, priests and women tended to be excluded from *skhods* at which the division of the land was decided.[11]

Two factors operated to make pressure on the land more acute in the post-emancipation period. The first was that the peasant population increased rapidly. Between 1863 and 1879 the agrarian population of European Russia rose from 55 to 81 million.[12] The second factor was that, following the emancipation, the number of peasant households grew by the division of existing households. Whereas formerly it was common for Russian peasants to live in extended families with as many as three generations under one roof, now married sons took advantage of the new freedom to set up house independently, claiming their own share in the communal fields. The process resulted in plots of land becoming ever smaller and more difficult to cultivate

[10] N. N. Pirumova, *Zemskoe liberal'noe dvizhenie* (Moscow, 1977), pp. 28–29.
[11] J. Pallott, 'The northern commune', in R. Bartlett, ed., *Land Commune and Peasant Community in Russia: Communal Forms in Imperial and Early Soviet Society* (London, 1990), p. 56.
[12] A. M. Anfimov, *Krest'ianskoe khoziaistvo Evropeiskoi Rossii 1881–1904* (Moscow, 1980), p. 11.

effectively. Whereas the average peasant allotment in 1860 had been 2.52 hectares, 40 years later it was only 1.43 hectares.[13]

Some peasants resorted to purchasing additional land, and to help them do so a Peasants' Land Bank was established in 1883. Some rented more land, and some emigrated to less populated areas of the Russian Empire – to Siberia or central Asia, where the land was less congested. In central Asia Russian settlers occupied land traditionally inhabited by nomadic Kirghiz and Kazakh peoples. They also displaced some of the Moslem peoples who had made permanent settlements. The process served to sow the seeds of national conflict.

Industry

Peasants, especially those outside the black-earth region of Russia, did not spend all their time in agriculture. During the long winter months they produced articles of everyday use such as textiles, crockery, cutlery, leather goods or carts. These local handicraft industries traditionally provided most goods peasant families were likely to need. Due to the fact that some areas had a ready supply of iron ore, clay, timber or other raw materials, there developed a considerable degree of specialization in peasant handicraft industries.

Local specialization of this kind of course required that there be some mechanism by which manufactures could be exchanged. This was complicated by the vastness of the country and the inadequacy of the communications. Considerable rewards awaited anyone who could convey goods from where they were produced to where they were in demand. The process, however, was costly and prolonged. Goods were brought once a year to conveniently situated towns from where they could be distributed round the country by hawkers and merchants. Several towns in Russia had annual fairs at which peasant handicraft workers could sell their produce to merchants and purchase items made in other areas. The biggest of these fairs was the one at Nizhnii Novgorod, which was held throughout the month of August. Not only merchandise from all over Russia was bought and sold at Nizhnii Novgorod but also goods from China and central Asia as well.[14]

Due to its central location in the country and its proximity to several areas of handicraft specialization, Moscow had always been an important pivot of the handicraft trade. The merchants of that city consequently came to occupy an important place in the country's economy. In the course of the nineteenth century the Moscow merchant dynasties – the Riabushinskiis, the Tretiakovs, the Konovalovs, the Guchkovs – grew in self-confidence and influence to become an indigenous financial and industrial oligarchy.

The transition from merchant to industrialist was easily made. Once a merchant had found a regular market for handicraft goods he tried to make sure that these products were in constant supply. To that end he might

---

[13] A. Leroy-Beaulieu, *The Empire of the Tsars and the Russians* i (New York, 1902), pp. 498–99.
[14] Haxthausen, *Studien* i, pp. 425–28.

provide the handicraft workers with raw materials and give them orders to fulfil. He might even rationalize the situation by having the workers work for him on a regular basis in a factory. The manufacture of cotton fabrics in the first half of the nineteenth century encouraged this process, because cotton was originally imported and passed through the merchants' hands. These distributed some of the cotton yarn to the villages which had traditionally produced woollen fabrics, but much of the production of cotton cloth took place in large factories constructed by the merchants.[15]

One such example was described by Haxthausen. While in Moscow he visited the textile factory run by the Guchkov brothers. This was equipped with 800 looms, though weaving was also done for the firm 'in the villages'. The Guchkovs, who were, as Haxthausen noted, Old Believers, impressed the German traveller by their wealth and taste. The Riabushinskii, the Khludov and the Morozov textile firms also began by trading in handicraft goods before establishing factories in the mid-nineteenth century.[16]

Only part of Russia's industry, however, was of indigenous origin: the greater portion came from abroad. Foreign involvement in Russian industry dated back to the first half of the nineteenth century. In 1839, for example, Nicholas I invited Murdoch MacPherson, a Glasgow shipbuilder, to come to Russia and build yachts for him on the Neva. When MacPherson's shipyard was established it employed over 70 workers from the Clyde, who settled in St Petersburg with their families. In 1874 MacPherson gave up his share in the business, which was taken over by the Russian Admiralty. It was renamed the Baltic shipyard, the name it bore in 1917.[17]

The introduction of mechanical cotton-spinning was largely due to the German entrepreneur Ludwig Knoop. Knoop set up his first spinning mill near Moscow, but his business expanded rapidly so that he was able to establish 122 cotton factories throughout Russia. Knoop's success became legendary, giving rise to the proverb: 'Gde tserkov' – tam pop: gde fabrika – tam Knopp.' ('Where there is a church there is a priest: and where there is a factory there is a Knoop.')

The founding of a modern iron industry in the Ukraine owed much to the Welsh ironmaster John Hughes. In 1869 ironworks were set up in the Donets basin to make rails for the new railways. Twenty years later a town had grown up round the plant. It was called Iuzovka after its founder. The rise of Russia's oil industry was largely due to the Swedish firm, Robert and Ludwig Nobel.

The construction of railways was particularly important in the development of Russia's economy in the last decades of the nineteenth century. The first railway in Russia, that between St Petersburg and Tsarskoe Selo, had been built in 1838. Between 1860 and 1879 20,000 km of track had been laid, often for strategic reasons. To promote the grain trade, railways were built from the grain-producing areas in the interior to the main population centres and to the ports on the Baltic and the Black Seas. Railway construction

[15] V. V. (V. P. Vorontsov), *Sud'ba kapitalisticheskoi Rossii* (St Petersburg, 1907), pp. 13–15; P. G. Ryndziunskii, *Krest'ianskaia promyshlennost' v poreformennoi Rossii* (Moscow, 1966), pp. 140–45.
[16] Haxthausen, *Studien* ii; J. A. Ruckman, *The Moscow Business Elite* (Northern Illinois University Press, 1984), p. 50.
[17] F. L. Maclaren, 'From Clyde to Neva', *The Scots Magazine* xliii (July 1945, no. 4), pp. 249–54.

dominated the industrial upsurge of the 1890s. Between 1890 and 1900 the length of track expanded from 30,596 to 53,234 km. In 1891 work on the greatest railway of all – the Trans-Siberian Railway – began. Railway construction stimulated other branches of industry, such as metal-working, engineering and construction.

Raising loans for railway building and the importation of rolling stock resulted in constant problems of budget deficits in the 1880s. In order to solve the balance-of-payments problem, the government tried to raise revenue by imposing duties on imports. In 1877 a duty was levied on the import of locomotives and rolling stock. In 1891 the then Minister of Finance, I. A. Vyshnegradskii, established a high tariff barrier for foreign imports. This, it was thought, would not only improve Russia's balance of payments but would also accumulate gold to service foreign debts.

In the event the Russian government's protectionist policy did not operate in the manner expected. The reaction of foreign firms was to get round the high cost of importing by setting up branches of their companies inside the country. They might give these branches Russian-sounding names and appoint a board of directors composed of Russian dignitaries. The process began in the Baltic provinces, where German business had a traditional foothold,[18] but subsequently the practice spread to the rest of the country, and companies from Britain, France, Belgium, Sweden and the USA joined the Germans in setting up business in Russia. The advantage of doing this was that once behind the tariff barrier the foreign enterprise was then in a position to benefit from it. Labour in Russia was plentiful and cheap, and there was a good return on the investment.

German business was involved in several key sectors of the Russian economy, such as metal-working, machine construction, the manufacture of electrical equipment, chemicals and banking. French and Belgian entrepreneurs were mainly interested in the metallurgical and mining concerns in the south of Russia. The French were also involved in machine construction, metal-processing and commercial banks. The Belgians concentrated on municipal services, primarily the construction of the tramway systems in the capital cities. Telephone equipment was manufactured by the Swedish firm, Ericsson. British firms were involved in such branches of the economy as the textile industry, oil-refining at Baku and shipbuilding at Odessa.

American companies supplied Russia with locomotives and agricultural machinery. The Singer sewing machine company was able to sell its machines to the Russian peasants by introducing the method of hire purchase. The method proved to be successful and was later to be adopted by many other firms elsewhere.

Foreign investment in Russia was not distributed evenly throughout the country but concentrated in several important centres. The chief of these was St Petersburg, a traditionally Western-orientated city. (Moscow on the other hand remained the domain of native Russian capital.) The south of Russia, the Ukraine, the Urals and Baku, were oases of foreign investment.

When Count Sergei Witte became Minister of Finance in 1892 he made the unforeseen effects of the tariff policy into a consciously formulated economic

---

[18] J. Mai, *Das deutsche Kapital in Russland 1850–1894* (Berlin, 1970), p. 60.

strategy. He believed that the introduction of foreign capital into Russia brought the country considerable benefits. In 1897 Witte introduced the gold standard to make Russian currency more stable and so encourage foreign investors. He tried to make doing business in Russia less hazardous for foreign entrepreneurs by offering them subsidies and seeing to it that the State Bank would come to their help if difficulties arose.

Despite the solicitude of Witte, foreign entrepreneurs found the business environment in Russia difficult to operate in. They had to contend with a maze of restrictions, red tape, dilatoriness and official corruption. Although there was a minimum of regulations enacted for the protection of the workforce, they found them excessive and irksome. Financial support from the government was found to be grudging and inadequate.

There was, moreover, considerable resistance to Witte's economic policies. This came first of all from the nobility, whose economic survival was increasingly threatened as the country became more committed to a free-enterprise system. There was also the important consideration that subsidies spent on encouraging foreign capitalists would not be available to subsidize their estates. In their opposition to Witte's policies they were supported by the Ministry of the Interior, which was the department of government most committed to the defence of the land-owning class. In this way Witte's Ministry of Finance and the Ministry of the Interior frequently found themselves at odds.[19]

There was opposition to Witte's protectionist policy from the *zemstvo* liberals. They believed that the high tariffs were produced by the industrial lobby, and that the high prices they brought about impoverished the peasantry. They also thought that Witte's fiscal policies placed the tax burden on the poorest sections of the peasantry, and that the existing system of indirect taxes should be replaced by an income tax levied on all sections of the population.

Opposition to foreign firms in Russia also came from the indigenous Russian capitalists centred in Moscow. Although they welcomed and, indeed, had instigated, the high protective tariff barriers which protected home industries, they did not think it right that their country's riches should be enjoyed by outsiders. The Muscovites were aggressive in their self-identity and eager to lay claim on their national heritage. As a group with roots in a merchant tradition stretching back to the eighteenth century, they considered themselves to be the authentic Russian business class. They were eminently conscious of their companies' long pedigrees and of the fact that, unlike most businessmen in St Petersburg, they were the owners and not simply the managers of these companies. The Muscovites were resentful and contemptuous of the close connection between foreign capitalists and the Russian government, and saw the businessmen of St Petersburg not as genuine entrepreneurs but as mere bureaucrats. Local rivalries created strained relations between the business circles of the two capitals.[20]

[19] J. P. McKay, *Pioneers for Profit* (Chicago, 1970), p. 276.
[20] J. D. White, 'Moscow, Petersburg and the Russian Industrialists', *Soviet Studies* xxiv (1973, no. 3)

The Workers

The growth of industry was a mixed blessing for Russia's peasant population. On the one hand it provided employment, in which much needed income could be earned. But in other ways industry brought with it some serious difficulties. Modern factories could produce goods more efficiently and cheaply than the traditional handicraft industries. As a result, many of the latter were put out of business. Thereafter peasants had no choice but to buy what they needed commercially. Observers could note that in the closing years of the nineteenth century common people in Russia no longer wore articles of clothing made of the traditional linen, woven in the villages, but of cotton produced in modern factories by the textile companies. This did not mean that they were becoming wealthier, simply more dependent on large-scale industry. Articles which were bought rather than produced at home, such as salt, sugar, kerosene, tea and matches, had purchase tax levied on them, thus adding to the financial burden on the peasants.[21]

The workforce of Russian industry was formed from peasant recruits, from those peasants who required to supplement their earnings by engaging in non-agricultural occupations. Often they would work in industry only during the winter months, returning to the countryside for the agricultural season. The collectivism of the *mir* was carried over into the factories. The peasants did not go to work in urban industry singly, as individuals. They went as groups of people from the same village or province. A group of this kind was known as a *zemliachestvo*. Entire factories or entire trades within a factory could be worked by people from the same area. In St Petersburg the biggest contingent of peasant workers came from the province of Tver. This was followed, in descending order, by the provinces of Iaroslavl, Novgorod, St Petersburg, Pskov and Riazan.[22]

The existence of *zemliachestvos* served to insulate the workers from the urban environment. It was possible for workers to live and work in the towns without giving up their peasant ways and attitudes. More seasoned and skilled workers, however, were those who had broken their ties with the countryside, brought their families to live with them in town, shaved off their beards and found recreations other than drinking with their *zemliachestvo* cronies. Skilled workers might even give up drinking altogether, learn to read and write, and even wear a collar and tie on Sundays. It was from among the skilled workers who had broken out of the *zemliachestvo* cocoon that workers' study circles recruited their members. Some of these might then go on to join political organizations. For the skilled worker, self-improvement might lead to revolution.[23]

In Russian industry wages, on the whole, were low, paid irregularly and often not in money but in vouchers for company shops. Factories were apt to have a complex system of regulations for workers; and the infringement of

[21] P. Nikolaev, *Revoliutsiia v Rossii* (Geneva, 1905), p. 11. In recent works one encounters the argument that if the peasants could afford to buy such items they could not really be all that impoverished. The argument is an *a priori* one, and does not try to reconstruct how Russian peasants actually lived and which of their economic demands were inelastic.
[22] U. A. Shuster, *Peterburgskie rabochie v 1905–1907 gg.* (Leningrad, 1976), p. 18.
[23] H. W. Williams, *Russia of the Russians* (London, 1920), pp. 420–21.

these brought deductions from the wages. This system of fines was used to reduce the wages bill of the companies which practised it.

Working hours were from 12 to 14 a day. Conditions were dangerous and unhealthy. There had been some factory legislation in the 1880s but this was widely ignored. It was insufficient to protect the workers but enough to irritate industrialists. Living conditions for workers in Moscow, St Petersburg and other industrial centres were cramped and insanitary.[24]

Strikes for better wages and conditions took place from the 1870s onwards. The way the Russian working class was composed had important implications for the labour movement. If more than one *zemliachestvo* worked at a factory a strike would be difficult to organize because of local rivalries. But once a strike had been declared it was likely to be a solid one, even in the absence of trade unions, because the *zemliachestvo* ethic assured solidarity. In case of a prolonged strike the peasant workers could return to their villages and sit it out. Peasant workers, on the other hand, were more conservative and less likely to go on strike. In any case, they had less need to strike because they were not entirely dependent on wages as they continued to derive at least some of their income from agriculture.

It was not only the workers who had *zemliachestvos*; Russian students might belong to them as well, as student societies took the form of associations of people from the same locality. As the students were often poor, the student *zemliachestvos* acted as mutual-aid societies, providing their members with financial and other kinds of help to see them through their studies. Like any other unofficial organization, the *zemliachestvos* were illegal, and membership of one could lead to suspension from university or internal exile. This was the common means by which members of the intelligentsia fell foul of the authorities and joined the revolutionary movement.[25]

The first workers' study circles were formed when some workers from the Vilna province encountered Polish university students from the same region in St Petersburg. Later the Polish students were replaced by Russians and Russian workers came to dominate the workers' circles. At first the circles were concerned mainly with educating the workers – hence the need for members of the intelligentsia to take part. It was from these modest beginnings that the Social Democratic movement in Russia would develop.[26]

The Intelligentsia

The intelligentsia did not constitute a homogeneous social class or estate: it was the category of people from any social group which had acquired an education. Members of the nobility, the clergy, the merchantry or the peasantry could all become *intelligenty* through education. Members of the

[24] A. Monkhouse, *Moscow 1911–1933* (London, 1933), pp. 37–39.

[25] Staryi Student, 'Peterburgskie studencheskie zemliachestva v polovine 80–kh godov i ikh znachenie', *Materialy dlia istorii russkogo Sotsial'no-Revoliutsionnogo dvizheniia* (1895, no. 5), p. 310.

[26] Z. Łukawski, *Polacy w rosijskim ruchu socialdemokratycznym w latach 1883–1893* (Kraków, 1970), p. 36.

liberal professions, such as teachers, doctors, lawyers, accountants and civil servants, could all be considered as belonging to the intelligentsia. Usage, however, latterly tended to exclude civil servants, the *chinovniki*, from the category, as the term 'intelligentsia' acquired the connotation of not only education but also of political radicalism.[27]

The intelligentsia was perceived to have a distinct identity of its own, because education implied acquiring a familiarity with outlooks and attitudes which were alien to traditional Russian society. Education was necessarily Western education, and the intelligentsia was a group that was to some degree Westernized. The intelligentsia's radicalism arose from the impulse to align the reality of Russian life with the concepts of Western civilization.

The intelligentsia was a small and atypical segment of Russian society, but within it took place all the developments of political parties and political thinking. It was the intelligentsia which produced Russian literature and all the Russian commentaries on the life and history of the country. Inevitably, non-Russians are forced to view Russian things through the prism of the intelligentsia. This creates a twofold misapprehension. The first is that we assume that the intelligentsia's preoccupations were those of the Russian people as a whole. The second is that we assume that Russian society and the Russian way of life is capable of being described in familiar, Western terms without loss or distortion. Neither of these assumptions is true, though they have traditionally dominated Western thinking about Russia.

The Autocratic Regime

The form of government in Russia until the turn of the century was autocracy. All political power resided in the tsar. The ministers he appointed were responsible to him alone, and he could dismiss them at will. For that reason a great deal depended on the tsar's personality. The responsibility for ruling the country at a time of great change and social tensions fell on Nicholas II.

Nicholas was a man who was chiefly concerned with family affairs, and his main political ambition was to pass his autocratic power on to his son undiminished. The dominating influence on Nicholas was his wife Alix, the former Princess Alice of Hesse-Darmstadt. Profoundly religious, the Empress was easy prey to mystics who promised relief for her own ailments or help for her son, who suffered from haemophilia. The most notorious of these mystics was Gregory Rasputin, a semi-literate peasant from Siberia, who became part of the imperial entourage in 1905. Encouraged by Rasputin, the Empress urged Nicholas to resist any reforms which might jeopardize the power of the autocracy, a power which she believed to be divinely sanctioned.

The autocratic system of government left little room for civil rights or individual initiative. The tsar's subjects had no right to hold meetings or form organizations without express permission from the government. Not even a Bible society could exist without official permission. People could be arrested

---

[27] V. R. Leikina-Svirskaia, *Intelligentsiia v Rossii vo vtoroi polovine XIX veka* (Moscow, 1971), p. 5.

and imprisoned or sent to Siberia without trial. The press was subject to strict censorship. Additional disadvantages were suffered by various religious groups and nationalities. The Jews in particular were subject to a whole series of restrictions on where they could live, what occupations they might pursue and how many of them might gain access to higher education.

At the turn of the century the Russian government was faced with a severe challenge. The country was ceasing to be mostly agricultural and acquiring to some degree a market-type economy. It now showed features of both an agrarian and a modern industrialized society, in which the elements of both coexisted uneasily. Russia now needed some overall policy to guide it in this extremely complex situation. It also needed to reconcile the powerful competing interests created by the addition of new groups to the traditional social structure: interests of the land-owners, the peasants, the industrialists and the workers all had to be catered for, as well as those of the various and often vying national minorities.

The task was far beyond the resources of the creaking tsarist system. Beyond self-preservation, it had no long-term strategy; it simply reacted to the needs of the moment. The officials who staffed the bureaucracy shunned responsibility, had little technical knowledge, and lacked vision and imagination. They took their cue from whatever opinion seemed to be in favour with their superiors at the time. Their overwhelming concern was personal career advancement. Ministries acted independently of, and sometimes in conflict with, one another. Those civil servants and ministers who did have competence and integrity were appalled by the indifference and venality which surrounded them.[28]

Instead of trying to frame policies of social and economic reform which would have tackled the country's problems at source, the tsarist government concentrated on suppressing expressions of discontent with the existing state of affairs. There existed no legitimate platforms for voicing oppositionist opinion since there were no representative institutions and no freedom of the press. Opposition for the most part had recourse only to illegal means of expression – through clandestine publications and underground organizations. In this way even moderate opposition groups were forced into the position of revolutionaries.

It was in dealing with illegal opposition that the Russian government was best prepared. It had at its disposal an extensive force of secret police, the Okhrana, which had a sophisticated network of agents and informers who specialized in infiltrating subversive organizations. On occasion, even prominent figures in the revolutionary parties would be exposed as police agents. The most notorious cases were those of Evno Azev who had infiltrated the leadership of the Socialist Revolutionaries, and Roman Malinovskii, who became a Social Democrat Duma deputy. However, responding to social tensions with repression and police methods only compounded the problems and in the long term were to prove ineffective.

[28] Iu. B. Solov'ev, *Samoderzhavie i dvorianstvo v kontse XIX veka* (Leningrad, 1973), *passim*.

The Revolutionary Movement

The ideology of the Russian revolutionary movement has its roots in the peasant commune. When Haxthausen was in Moscow in 1843 he met some members of the Slavophile circle: I. V. Kireevskii, A. S. Khomiakov, A. I. Koshelev, and Iu. F. Samarin.[29] This group believed that Russia had a promising future and was superior to the decadent society of the West. The Slavophiles argued that the fabric of Russian society, rooted in the traditional peasant commune, was more integrated and collectivist than that of the West, which was simply an aggregate of individualist, self-seeking interests. Western society, in the Slavophiles' view, was enfeebled and moribund.

Haxthausen would have found in the Slavophiles' views much that was familiar, since their ideas originated in classical German philosophy. In Haxthausen's day several German thinkers deplored what they termed 'civil' or 'bourgeois' society, the fragmented society of individual, competing interests, which they saw as being created by the capitalist system, then developing rapidly in several European countries. Some thinkers, like Fichte and Schelling, believed that civil society would at some time in the future give way to a social order based on fellowship and co-operation; others like Adam Müller and Haxthausen himself argued that the antidote to civil society was the traditional feudal hierarchy of estates: that it was simply a matter of preserving what already existed.

At the time of Haxthausen's visit to Russia, Karl Marx was in the process of elaborating his own views on how the fragmentation of civil society would be overcome. His idea was that civil society was the concomitant of the capitalist system, that it was both the environment which had given rise to capitalism and the social devastation which it created. He thought that it was in the nature of capitalism, through its related processes of circulation and repro-duction, to become eventually the sole economic system in every country of the world. When, however, it had reached this point of culmination, it would collapse under its own weight and give way to the reintegration of society, which Marx termed 'socialism'.

In Russia socialist theory owed a great deal to the ideas of Alexander Herzen, who was one of the people who had met Haxthausen in Russia. In his youth Herzen had been a devotee of German philosophy, though his sympathies leaned towards the Westerners – the group who saw the positive aspects of individualism and personal initiative – rather than to the Slavo-philes. He was a nobleman whose radical sympathies had forced him to flee from Russia. He arrived in the West to witness the failure of the 1848 revolutions, and his subsequent disillusion with Western society led him to advance the theory that the peasant commune in Russia could form the basis for socialism. When Marx published the first volume of *Capital* in 1867 he included a passage ridiculing Herzen's ideas.

But by 1877 Marx himself had come round to believe that the Russian peasant commune offered a convenient basis on which to found a socialist society. In working on the second volume of *Capital*, Marx discovered that,

[29] Haxthausen, *Studien* iii (Berlin, 1852), p. 3.

contrary to what he had previously assumed, the circulation of capital did not of itself expand the capitalist system and erode the existing social structures to create civil society. The dissolution of traditional societies required the application of consciously formulated policies. Consequently it was by no means inevitable that capital would expand throughout the world or reach a point of culmination at which it would give way to socialism. Marx then began to accept that the collectivism of traditional society might serve as the basis for socialism in countries which had retained their precapitalist social institutions.

From 1870 onwards Marx devoted his attention to examining how capital was beginning to circulate in Russia. He was fortunate enough to make contact with Nikolai Danielson, himself an economist, who sent him a wide variety of materials on the Russian economy and Russian society. Marx never succeeded in incorporating this material in later volumes of *Capital*, but he became extremely knowledgeable on the Russian economy.[30]

Marx believed that the key element in the circulation of capital in Russia was the State. It was, in his opinion, State fiscal policy which forced the peasants to sell their grain, and with the proceeds of taxation the government financed the construction of railways. The profits from these went to enrich shareholders in the railway companies and other groups who benefited from resources supplied ultimately by the peasants. If, Marx believed, the peasant commune were to become the foundation of socialism in Russia, this cycle would have to be broken before it succeeded in undermining the traditional peasant society.

Marx's ideas on Russia are significant in a number of respects. First, they show that, contrary to popular belief, Marx did not necessarily expect revolution to occur initially in highly industrialized countries. Secondly, they show that by Marx's criteria Russia before the First World War could not be classed as a capitalist country; traditional social ties were not eroded by capital to produce the kind of individualist society characteristic of the West. Thirdly, Marx's ideas were misrepresented by people in Russia who claimed to be his followers. In fact, Marx's actual opinions would have been condemned by those followers as heresy. Why Marx's thinking should have been misrepresented in this way is explained by the peculiar way Russian radical thought developed in the period after Marx's death.

Because the liberation of 1861 had not helped the peasants as a whole, many people thought that improvement would have to come by other means. In the 1870s many thousands of young people went into the countryside, some to educate the peasants and others to stir them into rebellion. They were given for the most part a hostile reception by the peasants. Many were arrested, imprisoned or exiled to Siberia.

The failure of 'going to the people' led to attempts at more systematic organization. In 1879 the 'Land and Liberty' group was formed, at first for work among the peasants. The group's basic conception was that the function of revolutionaries was to articulate the people's aspirations, as opposed to attributing to the common people the intelligentsia's notions of what the

[30] Marx's correspondence with Danielson was first collected in the volume, *Pis'ma Karla Marksa i Fridrikha Engel'sa k Nikolai-onu*, trans. G. A. Lopatin (St Petersburg, 1908). It has an introduction written by Danielson himself.

people ought to want. The term for this conception was *'Narodnichestvo'*, and it was commonly expressed in the maxim: 'The liberation of the working class is the task of the working class itself.' The words were the opening sentence of the Constitution of the First International, and they had been written by Karl Marx. In the 1870s followers of Marx, like those of M. A. Bakunin and P. L. Lavrov, considered themselves to be 'Narodniks'.[31]

It was an article of faith among the Narodniks that society could be transformed only by a social revolution from below and that it was pointless to engage in political activity. In 1879 Land and Liberty was beset by internal conflict on the question of whether it was legitimate to resort to the political activity of terrorism as opposed to the classic Narodnik tactic of work among the peasants. The organization split on the issue out of which two new parties emerged – 'People's Will' led by Lev Tikhomirov and 'Black Repartition' led by G. V. Plekhanov.

Of the two organizations, People's Will was by far the more successful. In 1881 it managed to assassinate the tsar Alexander II. 'Black Repartition' collapsed, but in 1883 Plekhanov launched a new group in opposition to People's Will called 'The Liberation of Labour', which claimed to be guided by Marxist principles. Plekhanov argued that the class which would bring about the revolution was not the peasantry but the workers (of whom there were then very few), and that the revolution would come after passing through the capitalist phase. All those who held the traditional views on revolution in Russia – especially the followers of People's Will – Plekhanov labelled 'Narodniks', and implied that they were romantics and idealists. The meaning of the term 'Narodnik' thus changed considerably.[32] In Plekhanov's usage, Marxism and Narodism became opposing ideologies. Marxism became synonymous with 'economic materialism' and implied that all countries inevitably passed through the same historical stages. For the sake of his polemic against People's Will, Plekhanov attributed to Marx ideas that Marx had rejected, but these nevertheless became Marxist orthodoxy in Russia.

Plekhanov's version of 'Marxism' was developed by Peter Struve in a polemic against 'Narodniks' in the 1890s, and by Lenin in his work *The Development of Capitalism in Russia*. In this book Lenin maintained that capitalism in Russia was taking root within the peasantry. He based this argument on the fact that inequalities of wealth were beginning to appear in the villages, and that these differentiated the peasants into distinct social groups. This was quite different from the way Marx had approached the question of how capitalism developed. Marx had been well aware of economic inequalities among the peasants, but he had not regarded these as the main sign of developing capitalism. He viewed them in the context of investigating how capital circulated in the country, and the part played by the State in this process. Danielson, who continued to treat the development of

---

[31] 'Narodnik' is commonly translated into English as 'Populist'. This is not a satisfactory rendering since in modern English 'populist' has acquired the connotation of 'demagogue', a sense not implied in the original.

[32] In his article ' "*Narodvichestvo*": a semantic inquiry', *Slavic Review* xxiii (1964), Richard Pipes puts forward the view that it was Struve who gave currency to the altered meaning of *narodnichestvo*. In fact it was Plekhanov who did this in his book *Our Differences*, published in 1884.

capitalism in this way, was classed as a Narodnik by Plekhanov and Lenin. For them the development of capitalism was an inevitable product of the movement of world history; for Marx it had been a cruel and costly outcome of a deliberate government policy. The Leninist idea that capitalism came about with no special effort was to dominate economic thinking for the best part of the twentieth century.

When the Russian Social Democratic Labour Party (RSDLP) was founded in 1898 it was still believed that the intelligentsia played only a subsidiary role in the labour movement, that 'the liberation of the working class was the task of the working class itself'. In a campaign against what Lenin and Plekhanov called 'economism' this doctrine was discredited and abandoned. Lenin's book *What Is To Be Done?*, written in 1902, went on to argue that a socialist conscience had to be brought to the workers' movement from outside, by the intelligentsia, and that a socialist party ought to consist of a small number of dedicated professional revolutionaries. In a split at the Second Congress in 1903, the RSDLP divided into two wings, the Bolsheviks, who agreed with Lenin, and the Mensheviks, who believed with Plekhanov and Julius Martov that the party should have a wider membership. These disputes, however, were largely confined to the intellectuals within the RSDLP, and were limited to the realm of theory. Lenin's ideas had very little influence on how the workers' movement was led. Social Democrat workers continued to organize themselves in small local or factory groups, usually without the participation of *intelligenty*, and were still doing so at the time of the revolution in 1917.

At the beginning of the twentieth century some adherents of People's Will and other proponents of the social revolution came together to form the Socialist Revolutionary Party (SR). The main theoretician of the party was Viktor Chernov, who revived the tradition of People's Will by regarding not only the workers but also the peasants as a force which would carry out the social revolution. There was a great deal of ideological diversity within the SR Party, as it was an amalgam of several revolutionary currents. Although it claimed to represent the interests of the common people, the SR Party was overwhelmingly a party of intellectuals: only 5 per cent of its membership came from the peasantry.[33]

One significant difference between the SRs and the Social Democrats arose from the dispute that had split Land and Liberty into two factions: the question of terror. As heirs of the People's Will tradition, the SRs believed in the permissibility of individual terror. For many in the party this took on moral and almost religious overtones. Boris Savinkov, for example, argued that the assassin was ready to sacrifice his or her life for a higher cause, a sacrifice made even greater because it involved an act of murder, which no moral person could condone.

Russia's more moderate parties, those advocating liberal policies, appeared only during and after the 1905 revolution. It is significant that the revolutionary parties appeared in Russia before the liberal ones. This is to be explained by the nature of the autocratic system. Liberal politics presupposes that some kind of dialogue should take place between the government and

[33] M. Hildermeyer, *Die Sozialrevolutionäre Partei Russlands: Agrarsozialismus und Modernisierung im Zarenreich (1900–1914)*, (Cologne–Vienna, 1978), p. 304.

the political organizations society has produced; that there should be some mechanism by which measures proposed by political parties can be implemented by the government. Before 1905 no such channels were open in Russia. Revolution offered the only solution to the problem of how to bring about changes demanded by the population without the collaboration of the government.

2

The 1905 Revolution and its Aftermath

The Revolution of 1905

On 9 January 1905 government troops in St Petersburg fired on a peaceful demonstration organized to present a petition to the tsar asking that measures be taken to ameliorate the condition of the people. The incident, later known as 'Bloody Sunday', sparked off an upheaval which brought to the surface the many tensions within Russian society which were to have a bearing on the revolution of 1917.

The Character of the 1905 Revolution

The 1905 revolution involved all sections of society and extended to most parts of the Russian Empire. It did not do so in a uniform way but took on different forms in different areas of the country depending on local conditions. The revolution had no overall aim, and the various social and national groups had different and often contradictory grievances and aspirations. The same tensions which brought about the 1905 revolution were to reappear in the revolution of 1917. The most salient of these were the economic condition of the peasants; the conflict between the workers and the industrialists; and the demand for civil rights by the intelligentsia and the more liberal among the nobility and the industrialists. There were also the demands by those in the armed forces for better conditions of service, and by national groups for cultural and political autonomy.

The Peasant Movement

In 1905 the pattern of peasant disturbances was established. The form of peasant action in a given locality depended on the agricultural conditions in that area. Where peasants rented land there were demands for reduced rent; where they were hired labourers they would go on strike for higher wages. In the central Russian provinces where peasants owned the land, the demand was for an increase in land holdings. In these areas the peasants would organize land seizures from the land-owners, sometimes indulging in acts of violence and destruction in the process. There were thefts of hay and grain from the land-owners' estates, and illegal cutting of timber in the forests. In these instances it was often the commune which provided the organizational framework for the peasant disturbances.

The character of the peasant movement depended significantly on the generosity of the land allotment of the liberation settlement. Thus in the provinces of Kurland and Livland, where the peasants had been liberated between 1816 and 1819 without land, the scale and ferocity of the peasants' assault on land-owners' estates was considerable, whereas in the neighbouring provinces of Vitebsk, Minsk, Mogilev, Vilna, Kovno and Grodno, where the peasants had benefited from the 1864 regulations, the destruction of estates occurred in only a few instances.[1] In the central provinces of Russia the peasant movement reached its greatest intensity in the central black-earth region, the middle Volga, and the central industrial provinces.

During 1905 the pattern of peasant unrest reached its height in the early summer, slackened during July, then intensified in the autumn months to culminate in November. As a Soviet historian of the peasant movement has noted, this pattern follows closely the development of the workers' movement during the year.[2]

The Workers' Movement

Among the workers the strike movement was widespread in 1905. A wave of strikes broke out in January as a response to Bloody Sunday. They were especially pronounced in the leading industrial centres – Poland and the Baltic provinces. In February the movement spread to the Caucasus; in the spring it reached the Urals and Siberia. In October the main industrial centres of the country were engulfed in a general political strike. To organize the strike, on 13 October the St Petersburg Soviet of Workers' Deputies was formed, a non-party organization representing some 200 factories. It was chaired first by G. S. Khrustalev-Nosar' and then by Leon Trotsky, both Mensheviks. Soviets swiftly appeared in Moscow and other major towns throughout the country, though none were established in the towns of the Baltic provinces, except in Reval. In the Baltic provinces it was considered that there was no need for such institutions, as a large proportion of the workers was already organized in the Social Democratic Party.[3]

The Bolshevik leadership in St Petersburg in 1905 had a similar approach to the Soviets. Alexander Bogdanov and his associates demanded that the St Petersburg Soviet adopt the RSDLP programme as a condition for Bolshevik participation. As the Soviet would not accept this condition, the Bolsheviks

[1] A. von Transehe-Roseneck, *Die lettische Revolution* ii (Berlin, 1907), pp. 335ff.; B. B. Veselovsky, *Agrarnoe dvizhenie v Rossy v 1905–1906gg.* i (St Petersburg, 1908), pp. 357–60.
[2] S. M. Dubrovskii, *Krest'ianskoe dvizhenie v revoliutsii 1905–1907 gg.* (Moscow, 1956), pp. 51–52.
[3] V. Kapsukas, '1905 Lietuvoje ir Vakaru Baltarusijoje', *Raštai* xii (Vilnius, 1978), p. 556.

abandoned it, leaving it to be dominated by the Mensheviks and Socialist Revolutionaries. The Bolsheviks at this time pursued a similar policy towards the trade and professional unions which appeared in 1905.[4]

Mutinies in the Army and the Fleet

One of the main factors which precipitated the 1905 revolution was the unsuccessful war against Japan. There had been disturbances in the reserve regiments as early as 1904. Naval mutinies took place in Kronstadt, Vladivostok and in Sevastopol. Mutinies among soldiers and sailors reached their peak in June 1905, the most famous incident being the revolt on the *Potemkin*. These incidents were often accompanied by the murder of the regimental or brigade commander. By and large, however, they lacked organization and leadership and were suppressed very quickly. Despite these mutinies, the armed forces as a whole remained loyal to the government in 1905, and for that reason the government was able to quell the revolution and ensure its own survival. This was not to be the case in 1917.

National Movements

The year 1905 was an important landmark in the rise of national consciousness among the peoples of the Russian Empire, and in the campaign against the Russification policies of the tsarist government. The manifesto of 17 October granting civil rights allowed the national movements greater freedom to organize and to publish a variety of newspapers in national languages.

A widespread demand of the national movements was for autonomy within the Russian Empire. This was the aim pursued, among others, by the Finns, the Poles, the Latvians, the Estonians and the Lithuanians. They also demanded freedom to promote their respective national cultures and, in particular, to extend the use of national languages in education.

The most Westernized of the Moslem peoples, the Volga Tatars, took the initiative in forming a political organization to represent the interests of the Russian Empire's Moslem population. The First Congress of the Moslem Union was held in Nizhnii Novgorod during the Fair in August 1905. The congress called for Moslem unity to achieve social and economic reforms, legal equality with the Russian population, a constitutional monarchy and civil liberties. The Moslem peoples also wanted education to be in their own languages.[5]

In some cases national identities manifested themselves in a mutually antagonistic way, as when Armenians and Azeris clashed in Baku in February. In such cases discontent was not directed against the authorities

---

[4] M. N. Pokrovsky, *Brief History of Russia* ii (London, 1933), pp. 168–69; *Izvestiia*, 25 February 1925.

[5] B. Hayit, *Turkestan zwischen Russland und China* (Amsterdam, 1971), pp. 192–93.

but against another national group, so that the main beneficiary was the tsarist government. Indeed, Alexander Khatisian, the liberal Mayor of Tiflis, accused the Russian authorities of complicity in the riots.[6] Pogroms carried out against the Jewish population in the wake of the 1905 revolution also had the effect of deflecting discontent away from the tsarist government and so aroused suspicions of official involvement.

The Government's Reaction

In response to the widespread popular unrest, in February Nicholas II issued a rescript to his Minister of the Interior, A. G. Bulygin, granting the establishment of a consultative assembly. In August, Bulygin announced the regulations governing the proposed elections to this assembly or 'State Duma'. But as the powers of the proposed assembly were so circumscribed and the electorate so narrow, the 'Bulygin Duma' satisfied no one. When the revolutionary upsurge continued unabated, on 17 October the tsar signed a manifesto ordering his government to:

1. grant fundamental civil liberties to the population including freedom of conscience, speech, assembly and association;
2. enfranchise those groups of the population excluded in the earlier regulations as a movement towards universal suffrage;
3. establish the unalterable rule that no legislation could be passed without the approval of the Duma.

The Political Parties

An important consequence of the 1905 revolution and the October Manifesto was the formation of a number of political parties – something which had been hitherto illegal in the Russian Empire. These represented alignments which were to be present in the Duma, and which were to survive into the revolution of 1917. They reflect the attempts by the various groups in Russian society to protect and to further their own interests, and to promote policies which they believed were in the interests of the country and its peoples as a whole.

An organization clearly concerned with self-protection was the Union of Land-owners, which was formed in 1905 in the midst of the peasant disturbances. The land-owners' immediate concern was for action by the government to defend their estates. But for the land-owners peasants who seized land were only one kind of enemy. Another kind were revolutionary or liberal political parties who demanded distribution of land to the peasants in the name of social justice. And because the power and privilege of the land-owning class did not come from its economic performance but from govern-

---

[6] M. Sarkisyanz, *A Modern History of Transcaucasian Armenia* (Nagpur, 1975), p. 154.

ment patronage, the land-owners saw their best chance of survival in the continued existence of the autocracy. Moreover, when land-owners were forced to sell their estates it was the government which could provide them with a new livelihood by giving them posts in the civil service or the armed forces. The land-owning nobility therefore tended to be enthusiastic supporters of the existing system, and the Union of Land-owners reflected this attitude.

The largest political party to emerge in the wake of the 1905 revolution was the Constitutional Democratic Party, commonly called the 'Kadet' Party from the initial letters of its name. The Kadets represented the values of Western liberalism – the rule of law, civil rights and social justice. Its leader was Paul Miliukov, a professor of history at Moscow University. Like Miliukov, the membership of the Kadet Party came largely from the professional classes, the teachers, lawyers, writers, clerks and book-keepers. It was, in essence, a party of the intelligentsia.

The Kadets intended that Russia should be a constitutional and parliamentary monarchy on the Western European model, with the representatives of the people elected by universal, equal and direct ballot, without regard to religion, nationality or sex. They also put forward a rather ambitious programme of social reform, proposing to distribute land to the peasants with compensation to existing owners by the State, introduce an eight-hour working day in industry and to allow a measure of autonomy for the national minorities, particularly the Poles and the Finns.[7]

The Union of 17 October or the Octobrist Party took its name from the manifesto of 17 October 1905. It saw in this document the creation of a new political order, a constitutional monarchy, in which the people were free to organize themselves politically. The Octobrists set out to work within the constitutional framework the manifesto had established. They were a party to the right of the Kadets and were less a party of the professional intelligentsia than of the more liberal land-owners, with a sprinkling of St Petersburg and Moscow industrialists. The chairman of the party was the Moscow industrialist Alexander Guchkov.

Although the Octobrists shared with the Kadets the regard for the rule of law and the provision of civil rights, the Octobrists were emphatic that they intended to preserve continuity with the past and did not wish to see any deep-seated transformations in Russia's political structure. They saw the changes introduced by the October Manifesto as a natural development and improvement of the existing system. For that reason they ruled out the convocation of a Constituent Assembly, which would break the political continuity and create institutions anew. The Octobrists also wished to keep the unity and integrity of the Russian Empire as it had been constituted by history, and rejected any idea of federalism. This made the question of Polish autonomy a serious bone of contention between Guchkov and Miliukov.

As a party representing the interests of the propertied classes, the Octobrists' social and economic programme was much more cautious and vague than that of the Kadets'. They saw the solution to the agrarian problem

---

[7] T. Emmons, *The Formation of Political Parties and the First National Elections in Russia* (Harvard U.P., Cambridge Mass, 1983), pp. 21–69; P. Scheibert, ed., *Die russischen politischen Parteien von 1905 bis 1917* (Darmstadt, 1983), pp. 60–68.

primarily as one which improved productivity of the peasants' land, extended the activities of the Peasants' Land Bank and gave help for resettlement and emigration. Only if all other measures failed were the Octobrists prepared to countenance the distribution of some privately owned land to the peasants.

The Octobrists also recognized the urgency of the labour question and thought that the existing labour legislation ought to be reviewed and improved, though they had no concrete proposals to make. While they believed that the right to strike and to form trade unions ought to be recognized, they also considered that legislation was required to put these rights within a legal framework. The Octobrists' programme was one that, the party hoped, moderate elements among both land-owners and industrialists could agree upon, and that they might make common cause with the more liberal ministers in the tsarist government.[8]

The Labour Group (Trudoviks) was a political grouping brought into being by the First Duma. It originated in April 1906 and was composed of a number of peasant deputies and radical intellectuals who had been elected to the Duma. Its leaders were A. F. Aladin, S. V. Anikin and I. V. Zhilkin. On 28 April 1906 the 'Draft Programme of the Parliamentary Labour Group' was adopted. This demanded a democratic regime, universal suffrage and civil rights. The programme also demanded that all land should be nationalized and given to the peasants.[9]

The First Duma

Shortly after the October Manifesto was published, Count Sergei Witte approached a number of leading political figures including Guchkov, D. N. Shipov and E. N. Trubetskoi to see if they might agree to become ministers in his Cabinet, joining other ministers who were officials in the civil service to form a 'government of public confidence'. By extending this invitation, Witte hoped to gain credibility and popular support for the government. Guchkov and his associates assented to the proposal in principle, but demanded that the government adopt a policy of liberal reform. The negotiations, however, soon foundered when Witte insisted on appointing as Minister of the Interior P. N. Durnovo, a man of right-wing views whom Guchkov and his colleagues considered to be of dubious moral character.[10]

On 23 April 1906 the tsarist government promulgated the Fundamental Laws, which set out the limits of the new constitutional order. The Russian State was declared one and indivisible and the tsar was proclaimed autocrat – his complete control over the executive, the armed forces and foreign policy was confirmed. The State Duma was established as the lower chamber of the legislature; the upper house was the State Council, which had been created by Alexander I. Though legislation had to be approved by the Duma and the State Council before being ratified by the tsar, the government reserved the

[8] Scheibert, *Die russischen*, pp. 69–77; Emmons, *Formation*, pp. 91–113.
[9] P. N. Miliukov, *God bor'by* (St Petersburg, 1907), pp. 396–98.
[10] 'Iz vospominanii A. I. Guchkova', *Poslednie novosti*, 12 August 1936.

right to legislate by decree 'in exceptional circumstances' while the Duma was not in session.

Elections to the Duma took place in March 1906 in accordance with the electoral law promulgated on 11 December 1905, which enfranchised male property-owners and taxpayers over the age of 25. The elections were indirect through four electoral colleges based on social status. The First Duma met on 27 April 1906 and, despite the fact that the elections had been boycotted by the Bolsheviks and Socialist Revolutionaries, the parties of the left dominated the assembly. There were about 170 Kadets, 90 Trudoviks, 100 non-party delegates (principally peasants) and 63 representatives from the various national groups. The Octobrists, on the other hand, had only about 16 delegates.

The deputies elected to the First Duma were deeply divided on what the function of the new institution ought to be, and what kind of action was most appropriate by its members. Many of the deputies from among the peasantry believed that an assembly which represented the people must have considerable authority, and that it could pass any laws it thought necessary, including ones to redistribute the land. The more radical socialist deputies, on the other hand, saw in the Duma a platform from which they might appeal to the country as a whole and agitate the people to mass revolutionary action. This attitude played into the hands of the government and the extreme right, who could argue that the Duma was being used as an instrument of subversion and ought to be dissolved.

Since both the right and the left were prepared to sacrifice the Duma for their own ends, the Kadets found themselves in a particularly difficult situation. They were committed to the principle of parliamentary government, but were acutely aware that the system established by the Fundamental Laws was far short of parliamentary democracy. One possible course of action would have been to co-operate with the government in the hope that the Duma's powers would be gradually extended, and that the tsar's ministers would be made answerable to it. That, however, would have taken time, and was out of keeping with the highly charged atmosphere of the spring of 1906.

Moreover, although the Kadets viewed with dismay the leftist tactic of using the Duma as a means of rousing the masses to action, the undeniable fact remained that it was this very action which had prompted the government to establish the Duma in the first place. The existence of the Duma and the powers which it enjoyed were dependent on the degree to which popular discontent had been mobilized. The Kadets had to reckon with the paradox that given the intransigence of the government, the fate of Russian constitutionalism was decided by the effectiveness of the Russian revolutionary movement.

The attempt made by the First Duma to elicit concessions from the government came in its 'address to the throne'. This contained demands for universal suffrage, direct voting, the right to strike and form unions, equality of citizens before the law, and a land reform based on the expropriation of large estates. In his reply to the address, I. L. Goremykin, the Chairman of the Council of Ministers, refused all of the Duma's demands. He asserted that he saw no reason to change the electoral law, declared that the compulsory alienation of land was unacceptable and stressed that there could be no suggestion of altering the Fundamental Laws in any way. The Duma received the response as a declaration of war, and even the most moderate deputies felt that the government had destroyed any hope of peaceful collaboration. A constant duel between the government and the Duma then ensued.

It was only after considerable hesitation that the government decided to dissolve the Duma. It suspected that such a step might evoke a new revolutionary upsurge in the country. In an attempt to mollify public opinion, the government began negotiations with a view to including in the Cabinet some politically moderate individuals who enjoyed some degree of popular support. The choice first fell on Shipov, a respected figure in the *zemstvo* movement. Shipov, however, suggested that as the leading party in the Duma the Kadets ought to be involved. On the orders of the tsar, negotiations took place between Miliukov and the new Chairman of the Council of Ministers, P. A. Stolypin. As what Stolypin offered was far short of a ministry formed by the majority party in the Duma, the negotiations broke down. Stolypin then grasped the nettle and took the decision to dissolve the Duma, taking elaborate military precautions not only in the capital but also throughout the country as well, in order to forestall any popular disturbances that might erupt. In the event the dissolution on 8 July 1906 took place without any new revolutionary upheaval.[11]

In response to the dissolution some 200 left-wing deputies including 120 Kadets crossed over to Finland and met in Vyborg, where they issued an appeal for passive resistance. They called on the Russian people to refuse to pay taxes or supply recruits for the army. In this way, the Kadets thought they might evoke a popular show of support for the Duma. But they were disappointed; the population remained unresponsive.

The Stolypin Reform

In the days that followed the dissolution of the Duma there were isolated agrarian disturbances in Voronezh, Odessa and Shusha in the Caucasus. There were also military risings at Poltava, Brest-Litovsk, Sveaborg and on the Baltic Sea cruiser *Pamiat Azova*. In these circumstances Stolypin made a further attempt to bring moderate liberals into his Cabinet. He had negotiations with Shipov, Count P. A. Heyden, Prince G. E. Lvov and Alexander Guchkov. The conditions which Shipov and his associates demanded were half of the ministerial portfolios and an undertaking to adhere to the principles of the manifesto of 17 October. Stolypin refused, and the negotiations collapsed.

On 12 August Stolypin was the target of an assassination attempt by terrorists. He escaped the bomb which destroyed part of his villa, killed almost 30 people and left his daughter seriously injured. A week later he issued a decree establishing a system of field courts martial which meted out

[11] P. N. Miliukov, *Tri popytki* (Paris, 1921), pp. 8–27.

summary justice to those found guilty of terrorism or violent political crime. Between their establishment on 19 August 1906 and their abolition in April 1907 the field courts martial imposed over a thousand death sentences. The field courts scandalized liberal opinion in the country and caused the gallows used by the field courts to be referred to as 'Stolypin neckties', an expression coined by the Kadet F. I. Rodichev in 1907 and resented deeply by Stolypin himself.

Stolypin in fact was relatively liberal in outlook and was quite willing to collaborate with the Duma. With the country sufficiently pacified, he intended to embark on an ambitious programme of reform. This included such measures as: freedom of conscience and the removal of restrictions placed on particular religious groups; inviolability of the person; increased opportunity for peasants to acquire land; the establishment of State insurance schemes for workers; reform of local government and the introduction of *zemstvos* into the Baltic and western provinces of Russia; reorganization of local law courts to make them accessible, cheap and efficient; the introduction of universal primary education, and the improvement of secondary and higher education.[12]

The agrarian reform, however, was to be the only one that Stolypin succeeded in introducing. Significantly, this was one measure for which he had support from the conservative groups in Russian society. In 1905 the land-owners had the opportunity to observe that it was the commune which gave peasant disturbances their cohesion and organization. Any measure to undermine the peasant community was therefore likely to meet with their approval.

The reasons Stolypin himself gave in the Duma for the agrarian reform were to improve the state of Russian agriculture by taking measures to overcome the increasing fragmentation of the land among peasant families and to provide material incentives to encourage the industrious and enterprising peasant. Stolypin addressed the problem that any improvements made by a peasant to his allotment would be lost to him at the next repartition, and that consequently he had no incentive to expend his labour or his money on the land. Stolypin's answer to this problem was the privatization of the land. He reasoned that if the industrious peasant owned the land he would be able to retain the fruits of his labour as personal property.[13]

Using clause 87 of the Fundamental Laws to legislate when the Duma was not in session, Stolypin issued his agrarian reform by emergency decree on 9 November 1906. This gave peasants the right to leave the commune freely. Every householder who held allotment lands as a member of a commune was given the right to demand at any time that his share of the land should be accorded to him as private property. It was also envisaged that having received his allotment as private property, the householder might demand in exchange for the scattered strips which composed it a consolidated plot. This consolidated plot was known in Russian by the term *otrub*. If the peasant owner of an *otrub* moved his dwelling house from the village on to his plot of

[12] P. A. Stolypin, *Nam nuzhna velikaia Rossiia* . . . (Moscow, 1991), pp. 50–62.
[13] *Ibid.*, pp. 89–96.

land, the resulting farmstead was then known as a *khutor*. If all the peasants in a given area were to follow this procedure, the end result would be to reconstruct the Russian countryside if not on the model of Western Europe then at least on the model of the Kovno province, where Stolypin had been the Marshal of the Nobility and where such farmsteads were the rule.

The intention of the agrarian legislation was that the consolidation of holdings would be undertaken not simply by individual peasants but by entire villages simultaneously. A whole village could convert its allotments into *otrubs* if the proposal received a two-thirds majority of all those entitled to vote at the communal assembly. In the agrarian law of 14 June 1910, which was designed to facilitate separation from the commune further, this was reduced to a simple majority.

Great pressure was put on the peasants to leave the commune and convert their allotments to private property. Officials were transferred from the capital to the provincial towns to take part in the campaign. Those who were successful in this effort were rewarded and promoted; those who were not were penalized or retired.[14]

Stolypin believed that the agrarian reform he had initiated would require 20 years to complete. In fact it operated for only nine, and did not lead to the radical transformation of Russian agriculture Stolypin had envisaged. In the event, the results were rather modest. It was only very partially successful in stimulating the formation of a class of hard-working, prosperous peasant farmers. Most peasants were reluctant to leave the commune and establish an *otrub* or a *khutor*. This was not through any innate conservatism on the part of the peasants or because they were unaware of the disadvantages of communal land-ownership; it was for sound practical reasons. There was often insufficient land to make individual farms viable, or the land would not be uniformly of a sufficient quality to make profitable farming possible. In that case, householders left with substandard land would face economic ruin.

In circumstances where a peasant community needed all the land at its disposal, it is understandable that friction would be caused by the consolidation of land by individual householders. This portion of the land would be taken out of the common pool and would no longer be available to the community at large, no matter what hardships it had to face and no matter how much need for land was felt. The idea that some might prosper while remaining indifferent to the misery of those around them was a repugnant one to Russian peasants, and caused them to be hostile to those who separated from the commune.

But the peasants who consolidated their allotments were by no means always the wealthier members of the peasant commune. They might well be from among the poorest, whose motive was to raise money by selling their land before moving to the towns to seek employment or leaving to settle in Siberia. Poor peasants who were insolvent might consolidate their land in order to raise money or to pay off debts to wealthier neighbours.

The number of peasants taking advantage of Stolypin's agrarian regulations reached its peak soon after the decree came into operation. Thereafter the number of separations from the commune declined until the onset of the

[14] S. M. Dubrovskii, *Stolypinskaia zemel'naia reforma* (Moscow, 1963), p. 172.

First World War brought the operation of the regulation to an end. By January 1916 a total of 2,478,224 households constituting 22 per cent of all those holding land by communal tenure had availed themselves of the legislation to privatize their allotments. By 1917 land-ownership in the form of *otrubs* and *khutors* constituted only 10 per cent of all peasant land-holdings.[15] The yearly totals of separations for the country as a whole are given in Table 2.1.

Table 2.1   Separations from the communes

Year	Households
1907	48,271
1908	508,344
1909	579,409
1910	342,245
1911	145,567
1912	122,314
1913	134,554
1914	97,877
1915	29,851
Total	2,008,432

It is characteristic that the results of the Stolypin reform varied according to the region of the country. It was most successful in the provinces of the south and west, where the commune was already in decline, and least successful in areas such as central Russia where the commune was well entrenched.

In order to ease the problem of over-population on the land, Stolypin encouraged Russian peasants to migrate to less densely populated areas of the empire – to Siberia and central Asia. From 1909, however, this movement slowed down as new areas for settlement diminished.

The Second Duma

Despite pressure exerted by the government during the elections to the Second Duma, it was unable to obtain the docile majority it desired. This time, however, the extreme right was represented with a contingent of 63 deputies, and the moderate right Octobrist Party had increased its numbers to 34. At the other end of the political spectrum, the Social Democrat and Socialist Revolutionary Parties, who had abandoned their boycott of the elections, had obtained a combined representation of 83. Kadet representation had been reduced compared to the First Duma, but they were still the largest party with 123 deputies. The Trudovik group numbered 97, and there were 22 non-party delegates.

Although the Second Duma, which opened on 20 February 1907, was more

[15] *Ibid.*, p. 305.

radical and more polarized than the First, the latter's dissolution had induced a greater sense of realism about what it was possible to achieve. The government on its part was not anxious to provoke a conflict with the Duma immediately, and Stolypin was initially inclined to be conciliatory. He had, however, to answer calls from the left to abolish the field courts martial. These calls he rejected and justified the continued operation of the courts by referring to the dangerous situation in the country. The Union of the Russian People, an organization of the extreme right, which favoured the preservation of the autocracy, unleashed a campaign demanding the dissolution of the Duma and the modification of the electoral law to ensure a right-wing majority.

Nevertheless, the Duma got down to some serious work. Fifteen commissions were established to examine proposed legislation and budgetary matters. Although this activity was impeded by the government's refusal to supply the commissions with the necessary documentation, by the end of May they had completed their examination of bills on local justice, individual liberty, compulsory education and labour legislation.

The work of the Agrarian Commission was especially significant because it compiled a report on Stolypin's agrarian decree of 9 November 1906. The report was highly critical of the reform and predicted that its operation would cause considerable harm to the poorer peasants. It was believed that the results of the law would not be the intended ones of improving peasant agriculture and increasing peasant land-holdings; on the contrary, the effects would be a decrease in land for the majority of peasants and its concentration in the hands of a comparatively small number of rich proprietors. The Agrarian Commission's report could not be debated on the floor of the Duma, as this was forestalled by the dissolution of the Second Duma on 3 June 1907.[16] The pretext was the discovery of a conspiracy by the Social Democrats to foment mutiny in the armed forces.

Following the dissolution of the Second Duma, Stolypin approached Guchkov and N. N. Lvov to invite them to join his Cabinet. As in the negotiations with Witte, Guchkov and Lvov told Stolypin that their acceptance was conditional on the government's drawing up a definite programme of action and the inclusion of other public figures in the Cabinet. Stolypin was able to accept the second condition but not the first, and the negotiations fell through.[17] Although nothing came of the attempts that were made in this period to supplement the tsar's Council of Ministers with representatives from the political parties, the occurrence did not pass into oblivion. It provided the moderate parties with a vision of how they might legitimately come to power, and how the tsarist regime might be gradually transformed into a constitutional monarchy. It was in accordance with this vision that they were to direct their tactics in later years, especially in the period prior to the February revolution of 1917.

[16] N. Karpov, *Agrarnaia politika Stolypina* (Leningrad, 1925), pp. 54–56.
[17] A. I. Guchkov, 'Vospominaniia', *Poslednie novosti*, 15 August 1936.

The Third Duma

On the same day as the Second Duma was dissolved, a new electoral law came into force. This law was issued in breach of the manifesto of 17 October 1905 and the Fundamental Laws of 1906, which stipulated that no law could be issued without the approval of the State Council and the State Duma. In view of the illegality with which the new electoral law of 3 June was issued, contemporaries referred to the action as a *'coup d'état'*.[18]

The effect of the new regulations was to decrease the number of peasant-worker delegates and to increase the representation of the land-owners and businessmen. It also increased the representation of Russians at the expense of the other nationalities. Contemporary observers who had attended the first two Dumas could note that in the Third the deputies were much better dressed and had an altogether less picturesque appearance.[19]

In the Third Duma the Kadets were reduced to 54, the Trudoviks to 13 and the Social Democrats to 19. The chief beneficiaries of the new electoral law were the Octobrists who had 150 deputies. The representatives of the moderate and the extreme right had also increased to 150. Stolypin had every reason to be pleased with the composition of the Third Duma and, unlike the previous two, it ran its full term of five years.

Guchkov, the Octobrist leader, was one of the few Russian politicians who had defended Stolypin's military courts martial in public, and an alliance was formed between the two men. The Octobrists together with the moderate right or 'Nationalists' ensured a majority in the Duma for Stolypin's legislative measures. This on the one hand made the Duma subservient to the government and limited its function to examing the budget and passing bills of secondary importance but, on the other hand, it established for the representative assembly a certain customary right of existence. The Duma represented a great step forward in a country with absolutist traditions, the greater part of which was still under martial law.

The personal affinity between Stolypin and Guchkov, and the close co-operation between the government and the Duma majority, provided an unprecedented opportunity for the regime in Russia to evolve along moderate-liberal lines. Guchkov willingly gave his support to Stolypin in the Duma because he expected Stolypin to reciprocate by putting into effect a programme of liberal reforms, of which the agrarian legislation was only the first step. Stolypin had told Guchkov that in the future peasants would be allowed to run the local *zemstvo* organizations, be educated in an extended network of schools and credit for improving the land would be made available to them.

However, none of Stolypin's programme of progressive reforms came to fruition. The measures were opposed by the monarchists and land-owning interests in the State Council or rejected by Nicholas II. This was not simply a reversal for Stolypin personally but a severe blow to the future of constitutional government in Russia. It meant that the path of peaceful and orderly

---

[18] A. Ia. Avrekh, *Tsarizm i tret'eiun'skaia sistema* (Moscow, 1966), p. 16.
[19] Sir D. M. Wallace, *Russia on the Eve of War and Revolution* (New York, 1961), p. 60; H. Williams, *Russia of the Russians* (London, 1920), p. 84.

change seemed to be blocked. If reforms were frustrated then revolution became the only alternative.

Stolypin's failure to deliver his promised programme of reform put a strain on the alliance with the Octobrists. Guchkov who, as a result of his pact with Stolypin, had become identified with unpopular government policies, expected that the compromises he had made would eventually pay dividends in the form of liberal reforms. Characteristic of his approach was the speech he made in the Duma on 22 February 1910 pointing out to the government that since the country had been pacified there was no further excuse for delaying reform. He said that he was optimistic about Russia's future, but that this depended on the constitutional order becoming well established. It was, he said, the government's responsibility to take positive action in this direction. Guchkov ended his speech with the words 'We are waiting!'[20]

Despite their success in blocking all the progressive legislation he introduced, the monarchists were also discontented with Stolypin's performance. It seemed to them that Stolypin was unduly influenced by the Octobrists, who were determined to pursue a reforming programme. Moreover, as there was no outpourings of radicalism from the Duma, there was no pretext to demand its dissolution, and consequently there was always a danger that reforms detrimental to the land-owners would be implemented. In the eyes of the monarchists, Stolypin and Guchkov were on the verge of usurping supreme power in the country.

From 1908 onwards the Octobrists showed an increasing tendency to oppose the government. One major area of conflict was military affairs, a subject in which Guchkov, a former combatant in the Boer War, took a particular interest. Guchkov believed that the defeat of the Russian army in the war with Japan had been caused by the poor performance of the military administration, and that reform in this area was necessary. To this end the Duma established a Commission on State Defence and elected Guchkov as chairman. This was to mark the beginning of prolonged involvement by Guchkov in the country's defence policies. These inevitably became politicized as they were a bone of contention between the liberals and the right-wing circles in the tsar's entourage.

In Guchkov's opinion, a major obstacle to reforming the administration of the armed forces was that the key posts were held by grand dukes, who had found their way there by nepotism and patronage. Guchkov created a sensation by making this matter public in the Duma on 27 May 1908. Measures were subsequently taken to move the grand dukes concerned to more prestigeous but less sensitive positions, though not before Guchkov had earned the undying hostility of Nicholas II for has audacity.

At that time, Guchkov and his Commission on Defence enjoyed the co-operation of the War Minister, General A. F. Rediger, who in turn had the support of the Duma in requesting increases in the military budget. This tactic caused annoyance at court where it was felt that the Duma was meddling in matters beyond its competence and attempting to curry favour with the military.

After one of Guchkov's speeches in the Duma criticizing the calibre of the

---

[20] A. I. *Guchkov v tret'ei gosudarstvennoi dume (1907–1912 gg)* (St Petersburg, 1912), pp. 147–52.

high command, Rediger unwarily expressed agreement with what Guchkov had said and was dismissed as a result. General V. A. Sukhomlinov, who was appointed in Rediger's place, pointedly did not collaborate with Guchkov or his commission but delighted Nicholas II by inventing ways to thwart their activities. In this way Sukhomlinov fell foul of Guchkov, who was to prove a dangerous man to cross.

Stolypin became increasingly isolated from both right and left in the Duma. His attempts to introduce a bill to establish *zemstvos* in the western provinces was an episode in which Stolypin found himself at odds with both simultaneously. After the bill was rejected by the State Council in June 1910 Stolypin had Nicholas issue a decree suspending both chambers for three days, and by invoking article 87 of the Fundamental Laws had the law promulgated when the Duma was not in session. This procedure infuriated both the Duma and the State Council, effectively bringing to an end the alliance between Stolypin and Guchkov.

With the loss of Octobrist support Stolypin intended to try to form a pro-government majority in the next Duma with parties and groups to the right of the Octobrists. He did not survive, however, to put the plan into operation. On 5 September 1911 Stolypin was mortally wounded by an assassin's bullet during an opera performance in Kiev. It fell to his successor V. N. Kokovtsev to form the alliance with the right that Stolypin had projected.

The Moscow Merchants in Politics

Stolypin's failure to overcome land-owner resistance to liberal reform was a major setback for the Octobrists, as it demonstrated the limitations of Guchkov's policy of compromise and co-operation with the government. The lesson had a profound effect on the Moscow business circles to which Guchkov himself belonged.

The involvement of the Moscow business circles in politics had undergone its own peculiar evolution. The need for some organization to represent business interests had been felt acutely during the 1905 revolution. There did not emerge, however, at that time any political party which represented the particular interests of Russia's industrialist class. The Octobrists were heavily influenced by the land-owners, and the Kadets saw themselves as independent of any class interest. The industrialists did not find themselves at home in any of these parties, and instead of founding a political party of their own chose to form the purely professional organization, the Council of Congresses of Industry and Trade.

The avoidance of politics was symptomatic of Russian industry's dependence on the government. It received State contracts and was protected by the government's policy of high tariffs against foreign imports. This was especially true of St Petersburg industry, which made its representatives more conservative than their Moscow counterparts. The Moscow industrialists in their turn were highly critical and contemptuous of the dependence of St Petersburg industry on the State and the bureaucracy, but initially they took no initiatives of their own. The antagonisms between the two business communities ensured that even in the Council of Congresses of Industry and Trade there was no united front. When in 1906 the St Petersburg industrialists set up the organization, the Muscovites did not co-operate, leaving the Council of Congresses with a largely St Petersburg membership.[21]

The more conservative among the Moscow industrialists, such as G. A. Krestovnikov and L. Knoop, allied themselves with the Octobrist Party, of which Alexander Guchkov was leader. The younger and more radical among the Muscovites, particularly A. I. Konovalov and P. P. Riabushinskii, envisaged a more far-reaching programme of transforming the country along the lines of a Western democracy, with civilized industrial relations and legalized trade unions. From November 1908 a series of 'economic evenings' were held at the flats of Konovalov and Riabushinskii, at which industrialists met with prominent academics – Peter Struve, Paul Vinogradov, M. M. Kovalevskii, S. N. Bulgakov. This current of opinion gave rise to the group whose mouthpiece was the newspaper *Utro Rossii* (*Morning Russia*) edited by Riabushinskii, S. N. Tretiakov, S. A. Smirnov, and P. A. Buryshkin.[22]

The chief point in *Utro Rossii*'s programme was the emphasis it placed on the role which Russia's commercial and industrial class had to play in the country's future political and economic development. *Utro Rossii* believed that this class ought to replace the land-owners as the leading group in the country. This idea represented a break with the philosophy and tactics of Octobrism. It was now recognized that an alliance with the land-owners could not lead to any far-reaching change because the land-owners were 'the only group which has no cause to be dissatisfied with the present state of affairs'.[23]

Nor did *Utro Rossii* believe that the interests of the industrialists would be represented by the Kadet Party. This, it believed, was essentially a party of the intelligentsia, a group which had little understanding of business and little sympathy for it. The Kadet Party's programme, with its demand for the compulsory alienation of land and the eight-hour working day, was unacceptable to the Moscow industrialists.[24] The latter, therefore, began to act in concert with the Progressist Party in the Duma. The Progressist Party occupied a political position between those of the Octobrists and the Kadets. It had originated in the party of Peaceful Regeneration, which was established in 1906, but had not proved viable. The Progressists had formed a separate fraction in the Third Duma, led by the wealthy land-owner I. N. Efremov.[25] On 6 June 1910 *Utro Rossii* observed dolefully that even if the Progressists were to be successful in the elections to the Fourth Duma there would still be no prospect of putting the industrialists' programme into effect, because in Russia 'an opposition party only becomes a party in power with the help of a revolution'.[26] Although Konovalov and Riabushinskii might

[21] P. Buryshkin, *Moskva kupecheskaia* (New York, 1954), pp. 76–77, 266–67.
[22] V. S. Diakin, *Russkaia burzhuaziia i tsarizm v gody pervoi mirovoi voiny (1914–1917)* (Leningrad, 1967), p. 35; V. S. Diakin, *Samoderzhavie, burzhuaziia i dvorianstvo v 1907–1911 gg.* (Leningrad, 1978), pp. 117–18; Buryshkin, *Moskva*, pp. 284–88.
[23] Diakin, *Samoderzhavie . . .*, p. 184.
[24] Buryshkin, *Moskva*, pp. 76–77.
[25] A. Ia. Avrekh, 'Progressizm i problema sozdaniia partii "nastoiashchei" burzhuazii', *Voprosy istorii* (1980, no. 9), p. 45.
[26] Diakin, *Samoderzhavie . . .*, p. 188.

reject Guchkov's policy of collaboration with the government, they were at a loss to suggest any credible alternative.

The Fourth Duma

Despite the government's attempts to influence the elections to the Fourth Duma in such a way as to produce a majority to the right of the Octobrists, it did not obtain the desired result. Many electors, irritated at the pressure exerted by the authorities, voted for opposition candidates. The composition of the Fourth Duma was consequently very different from that of the Third. The centre of the political spectrum had been weakened by the reduction of the Octobrists to 95, Guchkov himself being defeated. The Progressists, on the other hand, had increased their numbers to 41. Both left and right wings of the political spectrum were well represented.

A prominent Octobrist in the Fourth Duma was its chairman, M. I. Rodzianko, who had presided over the Third Duma during its last year. Among the 10 Trudoviks elected to the Fourth Duma was the young lawyer from Simbirsk, Alexander Kerensky, whose speeches for the defence in political cases had made him a formidable orator. The five-strong Menshevik contingent was led by the Georgian N. S. Chkheidze, who was a veteran of the Third Duma. Among the seven Bolsheviks the most outstanding personality was Roman Malinovskii, who was subsequently exposed as a police agent.

In the spring of 1912 workers in the Lena goldfields in Siberia had gone on strike for better conditions. On 4 April their demonstration had been met with a barrage of gunfire which killed 200 people and wounded many more. The Lena massacre was the signal for a new wave of strikes which swept the country. The period of calm which had followed the suppression of the 1905 revolution was now at an end, and industrial unrest increased steadily in the period immediately before the First World War. Agrarian disturbances also spread as peasants reacted against the imposition of the Stolypin land reform. Applications to conduct general redivisions of the allotments became more common, constituting acts of defiance of government policy and a reassertion of the vitality of the peasant communal system.

It is significant that in his 'We are waiting!' speech in the Duma in February 1910 Guchkov should refer to those who predicted a revolution as pessimists and those who believed in the possibility of a stable and prosperous future for Russia as optimists, since later historians were to adopt the same terminology. But it is also noteworthy that Guchkov's optimism did not consist in the belief that the path Russia was currently following would enable the country to avoid revolution. Revolution, he considered, could only be avoided if the government embarked on a programme of reform.

Guchkov's position, moreover, was consistent with the fact that during Russia's constitutional order the revolution was an ever-present factor in the background. The threat of its occurrence was repeatedly used for party advantage, but it was nevertheless a real possibility and an experience of the recent past. The court and land-owning interests, which frustrated

Stolypin's reform programme, took the view that liberal concessions were only necessary when the regime was being threatened by mass risings. Once this danger had receded there was no longer any need for reform of any kind. This attitude, which gambled with revolution, erected no social or political defences against it, and in that way made revolution the only means of achieving any progressive ends.

3

The First World War

The War and Russian Public Opinion

In February 1914 P. N. Durnovo, who had been Minister of the Interior in Witte's government and who subsequently led the extreme right-wing opposition to Stolypin in the State Council, sent a memorandum to Nicholas II. The memorandum gave a perceptive critique of Russia's recent orientation towards Britain and France, and concluded that Russia's national interests would be best served by a closer alliance with Germany. In Durnovo's view, Russia and Germany represented the monarchist principle in the civilized world, whereas Britain and France embodied the democratic principle. Durnovo argued that a war with Germany would spell disaster for both Russia and Germany because, irrespective of who won, there would inevitably break out in the defeated country a social revolution which would spread to the country of the victor.[1]

Durnovo's memorandum is significant not only for its perspicacity but also for the fact that it voiced the pro-German sentiments of the more conservative sections of Russian society. The aristocratic, land-owning class, as well as the upper ranks of the bureaucracy, to which Durnovo belonged, were unenthusiastic about the war. This caused those of a more liberal frame of mind to suspect that the monarchy, which had close family ties with the Kaiser, would not conduct the war with the necessary resolve.

On the day after Germany's declaration of war, Nicholas II published a manifesto in which he expressed the wish that now all internal disagreements would be forgotten, that the alliance of tsar and people be reaffirmed and that Russia would stand united to repel the aggression of the enemy. Most political groups responded positively to the tsar's appeal, renouncing further opposition to the government for the duration of the war, and pledging support for the war effort. At an extraordinary session of the Duma on 26 July, representatives of the different nationalities it contained – Poles, Latvians, Lithuanians, Jews, Moslems and Baltic Germans – came to the podium to affirm their loyalty to the throne. Despite these protestations, all political and national groups had an eye to the post-war situation, and were conscious that circumstances could arise in which the war might redound to their advantage.

[1] F. A. Golder, ed. *Documents of Russian History 1914–1917* (Gloucester, MA, 1927), p. 19.

Latvians and Estonians entered the war with special enthusiasm because of their antipathy towards the German land-owning class in the Baltic provinces. J. Zālītis, the Duma deputy from Riga, expressed the hope that after the war the privileges of the Baltic Germans would be abolished and the 'Teutonic yoke' removed. Zālītis and his fellow Duma deputy, J. Goldmanis, were instrumental in overcoming the resistance of the Russian High Command to the existence of national troop units within the army and organizing the formation of Latvian Rifle Battalions. The Latvian riflemen proved to be the most effective and disciplined of all the troops at Russia's disposal, though the inefficiency of their Russian commanders was to lead them on occasion into useless sacrifice.[2]

Support for the war in Russia was on the whole an attitude characteristic of liberal opinion, of the commercial and industrial circles, especially those of Moscow. Three main issues were involved: economic competition with Germany in the Russian market; the desire that Russia should acquire Constantinople and the Straits; and Russo-Austrian competition in the Balkans. Moscow newspapers followed the developing conflict between Austria and Serbia, taking decisively the Serbs' side. They called for the boycott of German goods, the sequestration of German companies in Russia and the abolition of German land-ownership. The Petrograd Council of Congresses of Industry and Trade, however, warned that this was likely to damage the interests of Russian industry and undermine the confidence of British and French investors.[3]

The government sanctioned the creation of two unions – the All-Russian Union of Zemstvos, with Prince G. E. Lvov as chairman, and the All-Russian Union of Towns, chaired by M. V. Chelnokov, the Mayor of Moscow. These co-operated to organize hospitals, transport the sick and wounded and provide medical and material help. The unforeseen scale of the war and the vast number of casualties were to extend the functions of these unions and make them more influential than originally envisaged. They were the first organizations to take over what had been State functions and, as such, immediately acquired a political significance in the tug-o'-war between government and opposition. The Union of Zemstvos was mainly an Octobrist organization, whereas the Octobrists competed with the Kadets and Progressists for dominance in the Union of Towns.[4]

Socialism during the War

The outbreak of war created deep divisions within the socialist movement in Europe and not least among the socialist parties and groups of Russia. The parties of the Second International had discussed the eventuality of war at the Congress in Basle in 1912, and resolved to do everything in their power to prevent its occurrence. If war nevertheless broke out, the socialist parties of

[2] Ā. Šilde, *Latvijas vēsture 1914–1940* (Stockholm, 1976), pp. 26–28.
[3] V. S. Diakin, *Russkaia burzhuaziia i tsarizm v gody pervoi mirovoi voiny* (Leningrad, 1967), p. 50.
[4] P. Vinogradoff, *Self-Government in Russia* (London, 1915), pp. 104–105; Diakin, *Russkaia*, pp. 67–71.

the International ought to strive to bring it to a speedy end and exploit the economic and political crisis created by the war to hasten the downfall of the capitalist system. In the event, the German Social Democrats voted in the Reichstag for war credits on 4 August 1914, causing a crisis in the International.

Among the Russian socialist parties none of them voted for war credits, and some socialist deputies in the Duma were exiled to Siberia as a result. Nevertheless, among the various socialist currents there was a considerable range of opinion on what the attitude towards the war ought to be. This was often allied to different conceptions of the economic causes of the war, and how these might lead to a socialist revolution.

At the extreme right of the socialist spectrum was Plekhanov, who considered the war to be a struggle by the *Entente* against Austro-German imperialism, and an entirely just one. He therefore called upon the workers of the Allied powers to support the war in the interests of peace and progress. He believed that the German Social Democrats, like the German bourgeoisie, aspired to exploit other nations, and it was this, he thought, which explained their conduct on 4 August 1914.

The right Socialist Revolutionaries at a socialist conference of *Entente* countries in London in 1915 issued a declaration stating that the participation in the war of the Russian people was to be explained by their wish to defend their territory and to express solidarity with European democracy. The SR declaration incorporated the 'defensist' doctrine, which was common among European socialist parties, that the war was being fought on the part of the given country only for defensive ends, not to make any territorial conquests.

The Mensheviks of the Organizing Committee of the RSDLP headed by the Georgian Irakli Tsereteli, however, in a resolution passed at the Kienthal Conference in 1916, were of the opinion that none of the warring powers represented progress, and that the war was imperialist and reactionary on both sides. But, the resolution continued, Russia was a special case, since the tsarist government was condemned to extinction and was incapable of conducting the war effectively. For that reason, the government would be deposed by the bourgeoisie, which would carry on the war under the slogan of 'war to a victorious conclusion'. In the process, however, the bourgeoisie would introduce democratic reforms, and to that extent it would be in the interests of the Russian working class to co-operate with it.

Further to the left were the groups which formed the left wing at the Zimmerwald Conference including the Menshevik-Internationalists represented by Martov and P. B. Akselrod. This group not only condemned the war and the powers which fought it but also those socialists who lent support to their governments in the war effort. The left wing of the Socialist Revolutionary Party, including such figures as Mariia Spiridonova, B. D. Kamkov and M. A. Natanson, held a similar position.

Lenin occupied the extreme left of the political spectrum with regard to the war. He held that the war was imperialist on both sides and that it was the duty of socialists and working people in general to oppose it. He thought that the Second International was now dead, and that it was necessary to create an new International based on principles which would avoid the kind of opportunism that had led to the collapse of the Second. Lenin considered that in the interests of the common people and the nationalities which composed the Russian Empire the lesser evil would be the defeat of tsarist Russia in the war. The imperialist war, he thought, ought to be turned into a civil war, a transformation which would be made easier by Russia's military defeat.[5]

While sharing many of Lenin's assumptions on the character of the war, Trotsky did not agree with Lenin that for socialists the defeat of one's own country was a lesser evil. A defeat for one country, in his opinion, would only strengthen the opposing powers. And although it would undermine the ruling classes, it would also disorganize the workers and create conditions unfavourable for a socialist revolution.[6]

The Conduct of the War

In the First World War Russia formed part of the coalition against the Central Powers. Its military operations, therefore, were not conducted in isolation but in accordance with the requirements on all the other Allied fronts. When it became evident in the first days of the war that the German forces were being massed in the west, the Russian armies began to be deployed along the western borders of the country. In the north-west they were poised to invade East Prussia, while on the South-West front they faced the Austro-Hungarian forces in the region of Galicia.

British and French appeals for a diversion on the eastern front to retard the swift German advance through Belgium and France obliged the Russian High Command to bring forward their operation in East Prussia. Because of topographical considerations the offensive took the form of a pincer movement involving the I Army under General E. K. Rennenkampf and the II Army commanded by General A. V. Samsonov. Rennenkampf was to launch his attack to the north of the Mazurian lakes in the direction of Königsberg, while Samsonov would skirt the lakes to the west before moving to join up with Rennenkampf's forces. It was a complex manoeuvre requiring a high degree of co-ordination.

On 4 (17) August, Rennenkampf engaged the German formations around Stallupönen, defeating the corps led by General François and forcing it to retreat. Pressing his advantage, Rennenkampf launched a second attack against the German VIII Army in the region of Gumbinnen two days later, winning a decisive victory. As a result of the Russian success, the commander of the VIII Army, Baron von Prittwitz, considered abandoning East Prussia and withdrawing his troops beyond the Vistula. Instead of pursuing the Germans, however, and consolidating his victory, Rennenkampf delayed in resuming the offensive.

Under the impression that the VIII Army was in full flight, Samsonov redirected his forces towards the Vistula to cut off the Germans' retreat. The latter, however, profiting from the respite given them by Rennenkampf, had

[5] H. Zand, 'Partia bolszewików w walce przeciwko wojnie imperialistycznej (1914–1918)', Z pola walki (1977, no.30), pp. 57–60.
[6] J. Riddell, ed., Lenin's Struggle for a Revolutionary International (New York, 1984), pp. 170–71.

begun to regroup. Prittwitz was replaced at the head of the VIII Army by General von Hindenburg and his Chief of Staff, General Ludendorff, and the new command put into operation a manoeuvre that Prittwitz had already planned. Leaving a thin screen of cavalry to occupy Rennenkampf, the remainder of the German forces were directed against Samsonov's forces. These were encircled in the region of Tannenberg and in a battle which raged between 13 and 17 (26 and 30) August, the Russian army was crushingly defeated. Samsonov committed suicide shortly afterwards.[7]

With the arrival of German reinforcements on the eastern front, Hindenburg now turned against Rennenkampf, whose forces continued to occupy East Prussia. His intention was to surround both flanks of the Russian army and inflict a decisive defeat, thereby freeing himself to come to the assistance of the Austro-Hungarians fighting in Galicia. The manoeuvre, however, was unsuccessful and Rennenkampf was able to escape with heavy losses across the Niemen. By the middle of September all Russian troops had withdrawn from East Prussia.

The Russian offensive in the Austrian province of Galicia began simultaneously with that in East Prussia on 5 (18) August on a front 300 miles long. Initially the campaign went well for the Russians. They captured Lwów, Halicz, besieged the fortress of Przemyśl, and took a great many prisoners. The Austro-Hungarian army was not such a formidable opponent as its German ally. It contained a large proportion of Slavs – Ukrainians, Czechs and Slovaks – who were often pro-Russian and surrendered in large numbers. By mid-September the whole of western Galicia was in Russian hands, bringing Hungary and Bukovina within striking distance.

At the end of September Hindenburg transferred the bulk of his forces from East Prussia to Silesia and launched a massive offensive in the south-western provinces of Russian Poland. He advanced to the outskirts of Warsaw but was forced to withdraw to the west. A second German thrust towards Warsaw in November was resisted by the Russians, and the front became stabilized during the winter 35 miles to the west of the city.

At the end of 1914, after four months of war, the balance was reasonably favourable to the Russians. On the one hand they had been defeated in the East Prussian campaign but on the other they had over-run and held Galicia, relieved pressure on the Western front during the battle of the Marne, and had been instrumental in thwarting the Austrian assault on Serbia. Nevertheless the inadequacies of the Russian war effort were making themselves felt. There were shortages of artillery, rifles, munitions and aircraft for reconnaissance. The rate at which artillery shells were used in modern warfare had not been foreseen by the Russian War Ministry. And even the most pessimistic estimates had not predicted the number of casualties which would be suffered.

The Russian offensive in Galicia was resumed in the spring of 1915 with the objective of invading Hungary and forcing Austria out of the war. The Austrians responded by removing their best troops from the Serbian front and directing them to the Carpathians, which now became the theatre for much heavy fighting claiming many casualties on both sides. After a six-

[7] Marshal von Hindenburg, *Out of My Life* (London, 1920), pp. 87–95.

month siege the Austrian fortress of Przemyśl capitulated to the Russians on 9 (22) March.

It now seemed as though Galicia would be a permanent Russian acquisition, and Nicholas II on a State visit to Lwów in April spoke of an indivisible Russia stretching to the Carpathian mountains. But within two weeks the situation had changed completely as a combined Austrian and German offensive was mounted on 19 April (2 May). The offensive breached the Russian front in the sector between the upper Vistula and the foot of the Carpathians at Gorlice. The attackers had a preponderance of troops, machine-guns and artillery. After heavy artillery bombardment, the Germans began their advance. The Russians fell back in confusion and soon were forced into full retreat. By the end of May the Russian armies had withdrawn behind the rivers San and Dniester. Przemyśl was evacuated on 21 May (3 June) and Lwów on 9 (22) June. By the end of June 1915 Galicia was practically cleared of Russian troops.

As the Russian troops fell back, the High Command, to the horror of the government, put into operation a scorched-earth policy to try to deny the enemy any resources in the occupied territory. The populations of the territories were compulsorily evacuated into the interior of Russia, their crops destroyed, their animals slaughtered and their homes set ablaze. The policy created an immense refugee problem for the Russian civilian authorities to tackle.[8]

Simultaneous with the offensive in Galicia, the Germans began operations on the North-West front. Taking advantage of their possession of East Prussia, they launched an offensive at the end of April in the direction of Riga, Dvinsk and Vilna. German pressure on the Russian army in Poland was intensified so that the Russians were forced to abandon Warsaw on 22 July (4 August) and withdraw to the east. It was only at the end of August that the Russians were able to stop the enemy offensive on a line passing through Riga, Dvinsk and the mouth of the river Stryp and descending along the Dniestr to the Rumanian frontier.

As a result of the retreat, the Russian armies were forced to sacrifice a vast expanse of territory comprising 20 provinces of European Russia to the enemy. In this situation Nicholas II decided to take personal command of the army and navy, and travelled on 5 September to General Headquarters (Stavka), which had been moved from Baranovichi to Mogilev, to assume control. The Grand Duke Nikolai Nikolaevich, who had been till then the Supreme Commander-in-Chief, was made Viceroy of the Caucasus and Commander-in-Chief of the Caucasian front. The tsar's decision to assume supreme command was thought inadvisable by most of his ministers, by the Duma and by public opinion. His absence from the capital increased the influence of the tsarina and her adviser G. E. Rasputin over the country's politics.

During the four summer months which the retreat from Galicia had lasted, the Russians had to rely on their own resources. In June an Anglo-French attempt had been made to turn the Germans from the Russian front, but its scope was too limited to have the desired results. In July the Allies decided to

[8] M. T. Florinsky, *The End of the Russian Empire* (New York, 1961), pp. 197–201.

The following labels appear on the map:

Gulf of Finland
Kronstadt • Petrograd
• Tsarskoe Selo

Reval •
ESTLAND

Baltic Sea

Lake Peipus

Gulf of Riga

LIVLAND

• Pskov

NORTHERN FRONT

• Riga

KURLAND

Dvina River

• Smolensk

Danzig •

Vilna •

• Minsk

• Stavka (General Headquarters)

Masurian Lakes

EAST PRUSSIA

WESTERN FRONT

• Warsaw

Brest-Litovsk •

Pripet Marshes

Łódź •

POLAND

Cracow •

Vistula River

GALACIA • Gorlice

Lwów •

• Kiev

Dnieper River

SOUTHWESTERN FRONT

Carpathians

Dniestr River

Danube River

AUSTRIA-

• Budapest

HUNGARY

RUMANIAN FRONT

Odessa •

BOSNIA

Belgrade •

Bucharest •

• Sarajevo

SERBIA

Danube River

Black Sea

MONTENEGRO

RUMANIA

—— The Front in 1917

- - - The Front in 1914

• Sofia

BULGARIA

miles
0   100

0   200
kilometres

Constantinople

GREECE

Salonica •

Sea of Marmara

Aegean Sea

TURKEY

The Eastern Front 1917

launch an offensive to help Russia, but the operation necessitated lengthy preparation and the resulting campaigns in Champagne and Artois began only after the Russian forces had withdrawn from Galicia and Poland.

On 31 December 1915 an inter-Allied conference met again at Chantilly to co-ordinate the Allied efforts for the coming year. It planned for the summer of 1916 a combined Anglo-French offensive on the Somme and allotted the Russians the task of creating a diversion on the eastern front. The Germans, however, forestalled this operation and from February threw all their forces against Verdun. In response to appeals from the Allies, the Russians mounted an offensive on 5 (18) March in the area of Lake Naroch. The attacks were unco-ordinated and were repulsed with heavy loss of life. The offensive was ended on 16 (29) March.

After Turkey entered the war in November 1914 and advanced in the Caucasus, Russia requested a diversion by the Allies. In response an Anglo-French naval expedition was sent to the Dardenelles in March 1915. The failure of this mission was followed by an Allied landing on the Gallipoli peninsula, which met with such firm Turkish resistance that it had to be given up with great loss of men and materials. Subsequently, however, the Turkish attack lost momentum, and the Russians were able to advance into Armenia.

In accordance with decisions taken at the inter-Allied conference at Chantilly, Russia undertook to resume the offensive not later than 15 June 1916. Russian plans had to be brought forward at the request of the Italians following their crushing defeat at Trentino by the Austrians. The improvised Russian offensive under Brusilov along the whole South-West front began on 22 May. The massive attack caught the Austrians off guard, and the Russians were able to occupy a large expanse of territory and to take about half a million prisoners.

As a contribution to the Allied war effort the Brusilov offensive was a considerable success. It dealt a severe blow to Austria's military power and relieved pressure on the Allies at Verdun and at Salonika. It also encouraged Rumania to join the war on the Allied side. But from the Russian point of view the results of the offensive were disappointing. They had a mere tactical significance and did not seem to justify the enormous loss of life they entailed.

Russia proved to be a valuable member of the coalition against the Central Powers. Its contribution prevented the Germans achieving victory on the western front. For Russia itself the war was much less successful but, nevertheless, it had put up a creditable performance and was not actually defeated. The initial stages especially had gone reasonably well for Russia, and might have been better still but for a miscalculation on Rennenkampf's part in the East Prussia campaign. The offensive in Galicia had been a notable if extremely costly success. The subsequent retreat from Galicia and Poland in the summer of 1915 was the most serious reverse for Russia's war effort. It was particularly visible because of the vast number of refugees it generated. The Russian army nevertheless managed to hold the German advance and even to mount subsequent offensives. The assessment of Russia's military performance, however, was soon to become a political issue, a point of contention in the struggle between government and opposition.

Social and Economic Consequences of the War

The Russian contribution to the war effort had been instrumental in preventing the Central Powers from winning the swift and decisive victory they had hoped for. But by doing so it had also ensured that the war would be lengthy and would drain the resources of men and material in all the belligerent countries. None of the military planners had foreseen that this war would be one of attrition, and that it would be fought on such an enormous scale. After its initial stages the war became one less for victory than for survival. It tested the social fabric of all the countries involved, and Russia's especially, as it had committed so much manpower and resources to the war effort.

On the eve of the war Russia's population was 178.4 million people, of whom 17.6 million were liable for military service. During the course of the war 15.123 million men were called up, a figure representing over 8 per cent of the male population. Before the war the Russian General Staff had reckoned that in the event of war 2,533,847 men would be mobilized. In fact in June 1914 the figure was about 4,200,000 – almost twice that estimated. Russian industry, moreover, was only able to produce rifles at the rate of 300–350,000 a month, which was inadequate to meet the requirement. At the beginning of the war there was also a deficit of rifle cartridges to the extent of 300 million, an amount produced by Russian industry in the course of six months. The calculation was that cartridges would be expended at the rate of 50 million a month, i.e., at the same rate as they were produced. In reality, however, the demand was much greater than the supply. The same situation existed with regard to artillery and shells. General Sukhomlinov, the War Minister, admitted in his memoirs that there had been a serious shortage of all kinds of munitions but added in justification that the demands created by such a prolonged war had not been foreseen by anyone.[9]

One method of overcoming the shortfall of military supplies might have been to import them from other countries. But attempts to do this during the war were unsuccessful. Orders were not delivered on time, they were of the wrong type or they were in insufficient quantities. The other avenue open to the Russian government was to mobilize industry at home for the production of munitions. This produced better results but it involved the government in sacrificing some of its responsibility for the defence of the country to the industrialists and professional classes – something it was not very eager to do, initially at least.

Most of the vast number of recruits conscripted into the army were peasants. This had the effect of denuding the villages of young able-bodied agricultural workers. Work on the land fell in this way to the elderly, women, young people and sometimes to prisoners-of-war or refugees from the occupied territories. The shortage of labour in agriculture caused the area under cultivation to diminish year by year, creating scarcities in foodstuffs which affected both the army and the civilian population.[10]

Recruitment fell less heavily on the urban workers. In Petrograd about 17

[9] V. Sukhomlinov, *Vospominaniia* (Berlin, 1924), p. 354; L. H. Siegelbaum, *The Politics of Industrial Mobilisation in Russia, 1914–17* (London, 1983), p. 25.
[10] A. M. Anfimov, *Rossiiskaia derevnia v gody pervoi mirovoi voiny* (Moscow, 1962), pp. 93–106.

per cent of the workers were called up, in the Urals 50 per cent; and in the Donbass 30–40 per cent. But the army's need for munitions caused an increased demand for labour. This was satisfied by attracting new workers from the countryside but, as male labour was already in short supply in the villages, the new industrial workers were often women or youths. The incomers would be put to work in the factories side by side with the skilled and comparatively well paid cadre workers. The cadre workers saw the influx of unskilled female peasant labour as a threat to their own wage-bargaining position and generally resented this 'dilution' of skilled workers. The skilled workers, moreover, prided themselves on their organization and discipline. The peasant workers, by contrast, were new to industrial conditions and were apt to act on impulse. Strikes by peasant workers were unplanned and unprepared.

The war also influenced the national composition of the urban workforce, since the retreat from Galicia, Poland and the Baltic territories in the summer of 1915 brought many refugees from those regions. Industries, along with their workers and their families, were evacuated from the areas under German occupation and relocated in the Russian interior. A million and a half Poles, 500,000 people from Livland, Kurland and Estland and 100,000 from the Lithuanian provinces were resettled in various Russian towns. In December 1915 84,074 refugees were registered in Petrograd. Poles, Latvians, Estonians and Lithuanians constituted 17 per cent of the workers in the Petrograd metal-working and machine-construction industries, the category to which the most skilled, best educated and most industrially experienced workers belonged.[11]

During the war, the war effort claimed 60–70 per cent of all industrial production. There was consequently a marked decline in the quantity of goods available for domestic consumption. The iron, steel and textiles which went to manufacture armaments and uniforms did so at the expense of making agricultural implements and clothing for the peasantry. The peasantry were thereby deprived of an incentive to part with the grain they had produced. This imbalance between town and country was to present serious problems for both the tsarist regime and its successors.[12]

Economic dislocation during the war was exacerbated by the crisis in railway transport. Despite intensive railway building in the 1890s, Russia's rail network was still poorly developed in comparison with those of Germany and Austria. Even before the war began the Russian railways were seriously short of locomotives and wagons. The country also experienced a serious fuel shortage, worsened by the loss of territory to the enemy and the lack of manpower; imports of coal to Russia were impeded by the naval blockade. Lack of fuel caused frequent stoppages in industry and also brought serious hardship to the civilian population which faced the winters without domestic heating.

[11] V. Z. Drobizhev, A. K. Sokolov and V. A. Ustinov, *Rabochii klass sovetskoi Rossy v pervyi god proletarskoi diktatury* (Moscow, 1975), pp. 95–96; J. D. White, 'Latvian and Lithuanian sections in the Bolshevik Party on the eve of the February revolution', *Revolutionary Russia* iii (June 1990), p. 91.

[12] V. P. Miliutin, *Istoriia ekonomicheskogo razvitiia SSSR (1917–1927)* (Moscow–Leningrad, 1929), p. 145.

The Political Impact of the War

The war's progress had a profound effect on Russian politics. In expressing their support for the tsarist government at the beginning of the war, the liberal parties expected some concessions in return. But nothing of the kind took place. So long as the war's conduct went well, the government felt itself in a strong position and saw no need to change its internal policies in any way. It interpreted military success as a vindication of the existing order.

The liberal parties had expected, however, that the reconciliation between the tsar and the rest of society in time of crisis would imply some concessions on the government's part in a liberal direction. When this did not occur they returned to overt criticism of government policies. The retreat from Galicia provided an excellent opportunity for the opposition to point to governmental shortcomings and to demand the transfer of further aspects of conducting the war to voluntary bodies. That particular episode of the war had emphasized the Russian army's inadequacy in artillery and shells, and the 'shell shortage' could be used to agitate for the need to mobilize production and to increase the participation of private industry in supplying the army.

The government responded to this demand by setting up a Special Commission for supplying the army. This, however, did not satisfy the opposition. Not only was the new body a bureaucratic one chaired by the unpopular Sukhomlinov but also the industrialists represented on it were the ones closest to the bureaucracy, overwhelmingly from Petrograd and associated with the Council of Congresses of Industry and Trade. The Moscow and provincial industrialists felt cheated, not least of access to government contracts for munitions. What the Moscow industrialists had in mind by the 'mobilization of production' was the creation of an industrial equivalent of the Union of Towns and Zemstvos. This would be a voluntary organization and would have the right to distribute contracts and supervise their fulfilment. The plan also had political implications: industrialists would not only collaborate with the government in achieving victory but also in the exercise of political power.

The leadership of the Council of Congresses of Industry and Trade was on the whole happy with the Special Conference as it had been constituted, but at its congress in May 1915 the Moscow liberals staged a coup. Riabushinskii, who had just returned from the front, described in colourful terms the retreat of the Russian army and called on Russian industrialists to unite and take the matter of supplying the army into their own hands. For this purpose he proposed the formation of a new organization. This was the Central War Industries Committee (CWIC), which had the function of 'co-ordinating all the activities of various regions and groups, and also for integrating these activities with the functions of the highest governmental institutions'.[13] An extensive article in *Utro Rossii* on the congress's outcome expressed satisfaction that the business circles finally had an instrument with which they could participate in the government of the country.[14]

[13] Diakin, *Russkaia*, pp. 75–76.
[14] M. Wilk, *Moskiewski komitet wojenno-przemysłowy 1915–1918* (Łódź, 1972), p. 49.

Although the Muscovites had succeeded in establishing the CWIC in the form which they had advocated, their victory was incomplete since running the new organization had fallen to the Petrograd Council of Congresses of Industry and Trade. The first chairman of CWIC was N. S. Avdakov, a member of the Petrograd industrial oligarchy. On the other hand, the composition of CWIC's leadership reassured the government and obtained its co-operation in the initial stages of the organization's development. On 10 June Goremykin expressed approval of CWIC to a delegation led by Avdakov. The local war industries committees spread rapidly throughout Russia: within 3 months there were 73, and by 1916, 226.[15]

The Moscow committee, formed on 2 June 1915, was especially important. Its organizers and most active participants were the Moscow Progressists Riabushinskii, Konovalov, Buryshkin and Smirnov. This gave the committee its particular political orientation. The more conservative members of the Moscow business community were less active in it and, although both Prince Lvov, chairman of the Union of Zemstvos, and Chelnokov, the Chairman of the Union of Towns, were vice-presidents of the committee, their role was largely a formal one. A significant element in the committee, on the other hand, was the group of Kadet intellectuals from Moscow University, including its Rector, A. A. Manuilov, reflecting the close links between liberal businessmen and academics in Moscow. There was also a particularly close connection between the Moscow WIC and the Progressist Party.[16]

At the congress of CWIC in July, the Muscovites, supported by the provincial WICs, succeeded in winning control of the CWIC. They reduced the role of the Council of Congresses of Industry and Trade in the organization and elected Guchkov as its chairman and Konovalov as its vice-chairman. The Russian government now began to look on the WICs with some suspicion and tried to impede their activities.[17]

The Union of Towns and Zemstvos had shown the way by which voluntary organizations could acquire political roles; it had been followed by the WICs. The influx of refugees from Poland and the Baltic provinces gave the opportunity for voluntary national refugee organizations to be established which then pursued political aims. This was the case with the Polish Society for Aid to War Victims headed by the Kadet Aleksander Lednicki, which provided the opportunity for the various political groups to operate legally among the Polish refugees.[18] This was also true of the Lithuanian Welfare Committee chaired by the Kadet Duma deputy Martynas Yčas,[19] and of the Latvian Central Welfare Committee headed by Vilis Olavs and Jānis Čakste.[20] The Caucasian counterpart of these organizations was headed by the Armenian Kadet Alexander Khatisian, the Mayor of Tiflis, who was to be a central figure in one of the plots to depose the tsar at the end of 1916.[21]

[15] Wilk, *Moskiewski*, pp. 49, 51.
[16] *Ibid*, p. 53.
[17] Diakin, *Russkaia*, p. 93.
[18] Z. Kormanowa and W. Najdus, eds., *Historia Polski* iii, 3 (Warsaw, 1974), pp. 267–70.
[19] A. Šapoka, ed., *Lietuvos istorija* (Kaunas, 1936, reprinted Vilnius, 1988), pp. 532–34.
[20] Šilde, *Latvijas*, p. 42.
[21] B. B. Grave, ed., *Burzhuaziia nakanune fevral'skoi revoliutsii* (Moscow, 1927), p. 96.

The Progressive Bloc

During the summer of 1915 the government was on the defensive, and felt
obliged to replace some of its ministers with ones more acceptable to the
liberal opposition. On 5 June the conservative N. A. Maklakov resigned as
Minister of Internal Affairs, to be followed a week later by the War Minister
Sukhomlinov, who was widely blamed for the recent reverses suffered by the
Russian army. As Alexander Kerensky observed: 'Przemysl falls and Maklakov goes; Lwów falls and Sukhomlinov goes; Warsaw will fall and Goremykin will go'.[22] Sukhomlinov's position was especially compromised,
because Guchkov had uncovered a personal connection between him and
a Colonel S. N. Miasoedov, executed in March 1915 on a charge of spying for
the Germans. Sukhomlinov was replaced by General A. A. Polivanov, who
had the support of the liberal opposition and was on good terms with
Guchkov.[23]

The acquisition of a power base in the shape of the war industry
committees and the ability to influence the composition of the government
took the liberal opposition within a step of being itself invited to participate in
the government. Its demand was now for a 'ministry of public confidence'.
Accordingly, the liberal parties in the Duma, the Kadets, Progressists and
Octobrists, formed a grouping known as the 'Progressive Bloc', which they
calculated would strengthen their position with regard to the government.
The Progressive Bloc was a coalition of all the fractions in the Duma except
the extreme right and the extreme left. Its programme, published on
8 September, contained two principles of general policy:

1. The formation of a unified government of individuals who had the
   country's confidence and who had agreed a definite programme of
   action.
2. A radical change in the existing methods of administration based on a
   distrust of initiative by the public.

Among the concrete measures agreed to be taken were the implementation of
an amnesty for political and religious crimes; the removal of the restrictions
placed on Jews and various national groups; the legalization of trade unions;
and a strengthening of the institutions of local government.[24]

A sign of how close the liberal parties thought they were to being in
government was the publication on 13 August by *Utro Rossii* of a list of future
members of the War Cabinet. Four portfolios went to the Kadets: Foreign
Affairs – Miliukov; Finance – A. I. Shingarev; Communications – N. V.
Nekrasov; and Justice – V. A. Maklakov. Three posts were assigned to the
Octobrists: Prime Minister – M. V. Rodzianko; Internal Affairs – Guchkov;
Navy – N. V. Savich. Two went to the Progressists: Trade and Industry – A. I.
Konovalov; and State Control – I. N. Efremov. The Centre received one
portfolio: Ober-Procurator of the Holy Synod – V. N. Lvov. Three posts were

[22] Diakin, *Russkaia*, p. 81.
[23] 'A. I. Guchkov rasskazyvaet', *Voprosy istorii* (1991, no. 10–11), pp. 198–200.
[24] P. N. Milioukov, *Histoire de Russie* iii (Paris, 1933), p. 1251.

retained by the most popular ministers of the old State Council: A. V. Krivoshein, A. A. Polivanov and P. N. Ignatiev.[25] Another variant of the list was published in *Utro Rossii* on the following day, reputedly drawn up by the Octobrists. This version weighted rather more heavily in favour of that party. Most of the people mentioned as possible ministers in these lists were actually to hold ministerial office in the Provisional Government during 1917. One document entitled 'Disposition No. 1' circulating in manuscript in the autumn of 1915 prophetically named Alexander Kerensky along with Guchkov and Prince Lvov as the nucleus of a future government.[26]

On 27 August an exploratory meeting took place between members of the Progressive Bloc and some government ministers. There was a fair amount of agreement between the two sides and it appeared at this juncture that, as in 1906, members of the liberal parties might be invited to accept ministerial portfolios. To the Kadets especially it seemed that the tactic of forming the Progressive Bloc had been vindicated. In the event, however, the talks came to nothing, and the Duma went into recess without any ministerial posts being offered to the liberals. Konovalov had the impression that the government had simply played for time until news from the front was better, or until some foreign loans had been secured. The government had succeeded in weathering the crisis and did not feel obliged to make any further concessions. There was acute disappointment and frustration in the liberal camp in the autumn of 1915.[27]

One factor which had been present in 1906 but was less in evidence in the autumn of 1915 was the revolutionary movement. This, however, began to revive from precisely that time onwards. Strikes began to multiply, though their numbers were never to reach pre-war levels. A significant feature was the prominence of political strikes. These took on a peculiar pattern. They commemorated significant dates in the labour movement's calendar: the anniversary of Bloody Sunday on 9 January; International Women's Day on 23 February; the anniversary of the Lena massacre on 4 April; and 1 May.

Simultaneously with the increase in strikes in the autumn of 1915, CWIC's new leadership opened a channel of communication with the labour movement by creating a 'Workers' Group'. The government allowed elections to be held for workers to select representatives to be sent to the WICs. These elections were boycotted by those who opposed the war, so that the Workers' Group was composed of people who were prepared to help the Russian war effort. They were led by the worker at the Petrograd Ericsson factory, K. A. Gvozdev, and his fellow Menshevik defensists, B. O. Bogdanov and G. E. Breido.[28]

---

[25] Grave, *Burzhuaziia*, p. 21; Diakin, *Russkaia*, p. 103.
[26] *Sbornik Sotsial-Demokrata* (December 1916, no. 2), pp. 71–72.
[27] V. I. Startsev, *Russkaia burzhuaziia i samoderzhavie v 1905–1917 gg.* (Leningrad, 1977), pp. 167–68.
[28] *Ibid.*, p. 195.

The Conservative Counter-Offensive

From the beginning of 1916 the liberals lost the initiative and the tsarist court began to recover some of the political ground it had conceded. There was some success in the military sphere. On the Caucasian front the Russian army captured Erzerum on 9 February and Trebizond on 19 April. When the new session of the Duma opened on 9 February, Nicholas II made the unaccustomed gesture of paying a visit to the Tauride Palace where the Duma met and in making a speech mentioning the success of the Russian army in the Caucasus.

On 20 January Goremykin was replaced as premier by the elderly and unpopular B. V. Stürmer, who was well-known for his right-wing views. A few weeks later, the Minister of Internal Affairs, A. A. Khvostov and his deputy, S. P. Beletskii were dismissed. Their removal was at Rasputin's instigation, and testified to the growing influence of the religious mystic in whom the tsarina had so much faith. A bitter blow to liberal opinion was the dismissal on 13 March of the Minister of War, Polivanov, and his replacement by General D. S. Shuvaev, particularly as it was followed by a governmental campaign to restrict the activities of the war industries committees. A further ministerial reshuffle took place in July in which the widely respected Minister of Foreign Affairs, S. D. Sazononov, was removed. His demise was deplored not only by the liberals but also by the representatives of the Allied powers.

These events took place against the background of a groundswell of national unrest in the Moslem areas of the empire, in Transcaucasia and central Asia. In February 1916 the Russian press announced that the government intended to utilize the hitherto exempt Moslem populations for labouring work at the front. In May Moslem nationalist circles meeting in Samarkand decided that in the event of mobilization they would call a mass rebellion in protest and demand freedom from Russian domination.[29]

On 25 June the government issued a decree 'requisitioning' – not 'mobilizing' – the Moslem population for military labour. There were immediate demonstrations denouncing the tsar and Russians in general, and demands for freedom for Moslems and the establishment of an Islamic state. The demonstrations quickly escalated into a full-scale rebellion which embraced the whole of central Asia during July and August 1916. By February 1917 the insurrection had been quelled, but isolated outbreaks continued right till the end of 1917.[30]

In September 1916, A. D. Protopopov, the candidate favoured by Rasputin and the Empress, was nominated for the post of Minister of Internal Affairs. Protopopov's appointment was a further indication to the liberals that the gulf which lay between them and the government was constantly widening. It brought home to them that in the course of the year that had elapsed since the Progressive Bloc was formed little had been achieved. It was even further from power than it had been the previous year, and the government had even managed to strengthen its position. At the beginning of October the bloc

---

[29] L. Bazylow, *Obalenie caratu* (Warsaw, 1977), pp. 117–18, 124–27.
[30] B. Hayit, *Turkestan zwischen Russland und China* (Amsterdam, 1971), pp. 199–204.

decided that its best tactic was to concentrate its fire on Stürmer and discredit him and his government by equating the conservatives' lack of enthusiasm for the war with treason.[31]

Social Movements in 1916

The country's economic situation deteriorated considerably during 1916, bringing with it widespread social unrest. Inflation had gathered momentum and this, together with the disruption of trade, created serious hardship for the population. The price of basic commodities had doubled or trebled since the beginning of the war, but wages had not kept pace. The influx of refugees had created a severe housing shortage, and there were widespread complaints that rents had soared. The short supply of goods created the opportunity for speculation, and much animosity was felt towards traders and shopkeepers as well as landlords.

Inflation gave rise to strikes for higher wages. These became common in the first half of 1916. In January there were 169 strikes throughout the country. The number fell slightly in February but rose again to 154 in May. A large proportion of these strikes were successful, since the management of the firms concerned were reluctant to lose money by prolonged stoppages at a time when considerable profits were to be made.

Another factor in the workers' favour was that skilled labour was in short supply. This fact frustrated attempts to punish strikers by mobilizing them into the army. When this was tried in the strike at the Navale works in Nikolaev in January 1916, it was found that a shortage of skilled labour had been created and the men were sent back to their factory. Following a strike at the Cartridge factory in Tula in January 1916 a different solution was found: the workers were mobilized but returned to the factory to work as soldiers. Although most strikes were economic, there were also a considerable number of political strikes. These often marked important anniversary dates, such as 9 January and 1 May.

In June some Duma members questioned the government on the strike movement. They noted its steady development over the past six months and drew attention to the enigma that it had occurred without the help of any organizations, such as trade unions. The worker's lack of organized leadership was confirmed by the Okhrana's reports of the period. They investigated the activities of the various underground political organizations – the Social Democratic Labour Party – with its subdivisions into Bolshevik, Menshevik and 'United' or Mezhraionka – and the Socialist Revolutionary groups. A report of 28 April noted that the approaching date of 1 May need give no cause for concern. The Social Democrats could be taken care of with the normal police methods, while the Social Revolutionaries were so weak that no special precautions at all need be taken on their account. In fact on 29 May the Petrograd organization of the PSR held a conference at a railway station outside the city attended by 20 people. It was decided to elect a new

---

[31] Bazylow, *Obalenie*, p. 150.

Petrograd committee since the existing one had been extremely inactive, a fact noted by the Okhrana in its report.[32]

Socialist organizations in Russian towns were considerably strengthened after the summer of 1915 by the influx of politically active Polish, Latvian and Lithuanian workers. (There were fewer Estonians since Estland had not been occupied by the Germans.) In Petrograd the Polish workers established the club 'Promień' which published a journal of the same name. At the end of 1916 the legal Promień club gave shelter to the underground socialist organizations, the Social Democracy of the Kingdom of Poland and Lithuania (SDKPiL) and the Polish Socialist Party (PPS), which attempted to organize the workers evacuated from Polish factories. A similar role was played by the Latvian organization in Petrograd, 'Prometejs', which was attached to the Mezhraionka organization before transferring its allegiance to the Bolsheviks. The Bolshevik Vyborg District Committee, which had Latvians in its membership, was also successful in establishing links with Latvian workers.

During the summer of 1916 the strike movement slackened off. In those months the strikes were mostly of short duration and limited to economic demands. The movement intensified again after October in connection with the deteriorating supply situation. Between 17 and 19 October, 10 factories went on strike in the Vyborg district of Petrograd. The 75,000 strikers were joined by soldiers from one of the regiments quartered locally, and with the workers drove back the police.[33]

The Liberal Opposition in 1916

The Progressive Bloc's failure to force the government to make concessions was followed by animated debates on tactics by the liberal oppositionists. While Miliukov held firm to the course of trying to elicit concessions from the government through pressure in the Duma from the Progressive Bloc, many Kadets on the left, like Nekrasov, believed that the government would never make concessions unless compelled to do so by some force in society. They considered that it was insufficient to organize blocs in the Duma, and that it was necessary to mobilize the people and to form alliances with groups on the left, including the Social Democrats and the Trudoviks.[34]

In this view the left Kadets concurred with the Progressists Konovalov and Riabushinskii. As early as 1914 Konovalov and Riabushinskii had made contact with the non-party socialists S. N. Prokopovich and E. D. Kuskova, the Menshevik A. M. Nikitin and the Bolshevik I. I. Skvortsov-Stepanov for the purpose of co-ordinating activities.[35] In the spring of 1916 Konovalov saw the social organization to put pressure on the government as already existing in the form of the Union of Towns and Zemstvos, the WICs and the national refugee committees. All of these had a hierarchical organization of local

[32] *Ibid.*, pp. 176–81.
[33] *Ibid.*, p. 186; R. B. McKean, *St Petersburg Between the Revolutions* (Yale, 1990), p. 395.
[34] Grave, *Burzhuaziia*, pp. 73, 83, 94, 146.
[35] E. D. Chermenskii, *IV Duma i sverzhenie tsarizma v Rossii* (Moscow, 1976), p. 54.

committees subordinate to a central body. Konovalov envisaged the formation of a new labour organization arising from the Workers' Group of the
WICs patterned in the same way: it would be based on local cells culminating
in a supreme body, something like a Soviet of Workers' Deputies. The entire
integrated structure would be a kind of 'Union of Unions' such as had existed
in 1905.[36]

In the summer of 1916, however, the impetus behind the liberal
opposition was weakened. This was as a result of the military successes, which deprived the liberals of their most potent weapon against
the government. It was also due to the revival of the workers' movement,
which affected liberal thinking in two ways. The first was that it made
clear that the workers' interests conflicted with those of the commercial
and industrial community, and could not be accommodated comfortably
within the same all-embracing organization. The liberals were also impressed by the fact that the recent strike movement had been largely
unorganized, and that there was a large discrepancy between the scale of
the movement and the perceptible level of political leadership. The spectre
therefore rose before them of an elemental revolution, terrifying in its
mindless fury, which would be capable of sweeping aside not only the
government but also them as well.[37]

It was this picture that influenced the liberals' tactical considerations in the
latter half of 1916. Their concern was that they should not be left behind by
events and that they ought to introduce some element of organization into the
approaching popular revolt. For this the Workers' Group of the CWIC was a
convenient instrument, and in the latter part of 1916 it began to acquire this
significance.

In September a meeting of liberal politicians took place at the apartments of
M. M. Fedorov, a financier and member of the CWIC. Present were Rodzianko, Miliukov, S. I. Shidlovskii, Shingarev, I. V. Godnev, V. N. Lvov,
Nekrasov, M. I. Tereshchenko and Guchkov. The group discussed what the
role of the liberals ought to be in face of the revolutionary upsurge, which no
one doubted was at hand. It was thought that the government was powerless
to counter the impending revolution. There were only two possibilities, both
of which would bring the liberals to power. The first was that the revolutionary movement would be successful and overthrow the existing order, in
which case after the elemental anarchy had subsided the liberals would be
called upon to take control of the country. The second possibility was that the
government, conscious of its own impotence, would call upon liberal
politicians for assistance, as it had done in 1905–06. But everyone also
agreed that the situation had changed somewhat since that time and that
the new government would only have a chance of success if the tsar were to
abdicate.

None of those present wanted to abolish the monarchy, and believed that
this would only be strengthened by Nicholas II's abdication. They believed,
moreover, that the succession should be determined according to the
Fundamental Laws, and that the tsar should abdicate in favour of his son.

[36] Grave, *Burzhuaziia*, p. 95.
[37] *Ibid.*, p. 101.

As the tsar's son was under age, it would be necessary to institute a regency, an eventuality which was provided for in the Fundamental Laws.[38]

Guchkov, however, did not think things would be so simple. He doubted that the revolutionary forces which would overthrow the tsarist regime would meekly hand over power to the liberals; he believed they were more likely to try to retain it for themselves. This consideration led him, along with Nekrasov and Tereshchenko, to begin organizing a palace coup which would force the tsar to abdicate. Guchkov considered it necessary not only to retain the monarchy but also to include in the government that would be established in the wake of the coup some of the more liberal minded of the tsarist ministers, such as Krivoshein, Ignatiev or Sazonov. Contact was made with high-ranking army officers who were thought likely to sympathize with the plot. Prince D. L. Viazemskii was entrusted with sounding out potential recruits among the officers. But Guchkov's long-standing military connections were also used. General A. I. Krymov, for example, whom Tereshchenko made privy to the conspiracy, had been known to Guchkov from the time of the Russo-Japanese war.

Simultaneously with Guchkov's, independent plans for a palace coup were being elaborated in the Union of Towns and Zemstvos. The intention was to depose the tsar and install in his place the Grand Duke Nikolai Nikolaevich, the former Supreme Commander-in-Chief, then serving as viceroy in the Caucasus. Nikolai Nikolaevich would rule in conjunction with a government which would include Prince Lvov and Guchkov. Prince Lvov asked the Mayor of Tiflis, Alexander Khatisian, to approach the Grand Duke and ask him if he was willing to lead the coup. Nikolai Nikolaevich, however, hesitated and only gave his consent when the revolution had already broken out in Petrograd.[39]

On 1 November, when the new session of the Duma opened, Miliukov made a virulent attack on Stürmer's government, using the fact that conservative circles were unenthusiastic about the war against Germany. Quoting from the German press, Miliukov asserted that the conduct of the Russian government had met with the Germans' full approval. They had welcomed 'the victory of the party at court which is grouped around the young tsarina', a victory which had been at the expense of such able and honest ministers as Polivanov and Sazonov. Were, Miliukov enquired, the actions of the government attributable to folly or to treason? The speech had an immense resonance, especially since it hinted at German sympathies on the part of the Empress.

Stürmer called for Miliukov's arrest and for the dissolution of the Duma but found little support from his ministers, and he was soon forced to resign. His departure occasioned a new round of changes in the Council of Ministers in which A. F. Trepov became premier and N. N. Pokrovskii became Minister of Foreign Affairs. Pokrovskii's appointment was preceded by a notable success in foreign policy. When the Duma met on 19 November the government was able to announce that Britain and France had agreed to Russia's possession of Constantinople and the Straits after the war. In the atmosphere

[38] 'A. I. Guchkov rasskazyvaet', *Voprosy istorii*, (1991, no. 7–8), pp. 203–204.
[39] *Ibid.*, p. 212.

of the times even this achievement did not increase the government's popularity or prestige.

This was demonstrated on 3 November when the extreme right's representative, M. V. Purishkevich, made a speech comparable to Miliukov's, condemning the country's lack of decisive leadership, the 'ministerial leap-frog' and the 'dark forces' which propelled individuals like Protopopov into high positions which they had no capacity to fill. Purishkevich appealed to the government to open the tsar's eyes to the dreadful reality of the situation and beg him to deliver Russia from the baneful influence of Rasputin.[40]

Soon after making his speech, Purishkevich was approached by the young Prince F. F. Iusupov with a plan to assassinate Rasputin in order to save the monarchy from further discredit. Rasputin's murder was carried out at Iusupov's home on 17 December. The results, however, were not those intended. The act of terrorism had served to strengthen the position of the imperial couple and, to carry out the wishes of their deceased spiritual mentor, they embarked on one more round of 'ministerial leapfrog'. In the ministerial changes that were made, Trepov was replaced as premier by Prince N. N. Golitsyn, and Shuvaev, the Minister of War, was replaced by General M. A. Beliaev. The all-important Ministry of the Interior, however, was left in Protopopov's hands. Changes also took place in the composition of State Council, strengthening the right at the expense of supporters of the Progressive Bloc. The reactionary former Minister of Justice, I. G. Shcheglo-vitov, became its chairman.

These developments meant that the liberals' offensive on the government initiated by Miliukov's speech on 1 November had come to nothing. The Progressive Bloc was now without any clear strategy, and it was left to decide on what desperate measures it might take if the government decided to dissolve the Duma. Plots to depose the tsar now were now discussed with some urgency.

Rasputin's assassination had rather unpleasant consequences for Rodzian-ko, the chairman of the Duma. Being a friend of Iusupov's, he found himself under suspicion of complicity in the murder. He, therefore, tried to arrange an audience with the tsar. It was at this inconvenient moment that General Krymov appeared in Rodzianko's flat along with several members of the Progressive Bloc to report that the army would welcome a *coup d'état*. Shingarev, Shidlovskii and Tereshchenko all agreed that such a measure was necessary, but Rodzianko declared that he had taken the oath of loyalty to the tsar and would never use force against him.[41]

On 7 January Rodzianko had his audience with the tsar at which, in emotional tones, he warned Nicholas of the dangers of the present situation and advised him to change course. Rodzianko's coolness towards the plans for a *coup d'état*, however, and his subservience to Nicholas II had alienated him from the members of the Progressive Bloc. Whereas they had formerly viewed him in his capacity of the chairman of the Duma as the natural premier of a liberal cabinet, they were now determined to look elsewhere. The choice now fell on Prince Lvov, the chairman of the Union of Zemstvos.

[40] Golder, *Documents*, pp. 166–75.
[41] *Ibid.*, pp. 116–17.

The Workers' Group

On 9 January 1917 about 142,000 workers from 132 factories in Petrograd went on strike to commemorate Bloody Sunday. Meetings were organized at several factories and, following these, some workers went on to hold demonstrations in the streets. They tried to reach the centre of the city but were prevented from doing so by the police. On the following day there was an orderly return to work. A similar strike took place in Moscow, though the example was followed in few provincial towns. Prior to 9 January the police authorities throughout the country had taken measures to prevent workers' demonstrations. Their efforts had been successful except in the two capitals.

The 9 January political strikes had been organized by several political groups: Bolsheviks, Menshevik-Internationalists, Mezhraiontsy, Socialist Revolutionaries and Anarchists. Though previously the Workers' Group of the CWIC had opposed industrial action, it too supported the strikes on 9 January in both capitals, as well as in those provincial towns where the attempt to stage a strike was made.[42]

The Workers' Group intended to follow up its efforts on 9 January with a political strike and a demonstration outside the Duma on 14 February, the day on which the new session of the Duma began. The intention was to encourage the Duma to form a 'government of national salvation'. The Workers' Group's activities had begun to worry the authorities, especially since its meetings were attended by members of underground revolutionary groups. On 3 January the commander of the Petrograd military district, General S. S. Khabalov, had written to Guchkov complaining that in the past months the group had organized meetings which had discussed the immediate conclusion of peace, the overthrow of the government and the implementation of the Social Democratic programme. Khabalov's protests were ignored, and on the night of 26–27 January nine members of the Workers' Group were arrested in their homes.[43]

The action caused considerable consternation in the ranks of the liberal opposition. On 29 January a meeting took place attended by members of the WICs, the Union of Towns and Zemstvos and the Duma. There were 40 people in all, including Guchkov, Konovalov, Miliukov, Kerensky and Chkheidze. Miliukov was highly critical of the Workers' Group, accusing it of usurping the Duma's role as the body that dictated how the campaign against the government ought to be conducted. Most of the others present, however, defended the group. After the meeting Guchkov campaigned assiduously for the release of the imprisoned members of the Workers' Group. Gvozdev and others left at liberty continued to organize the demonstration on 14 February.[44]

Not only Khabalov had noted the leftward turn of the Workers' Group in January 1917: so too had the leadership of the revolutionary political groups in Petrograd. They had surmised that the group was adjusting its tactics to suit the prevailing anti-war mood of the workers, and that the aim was to

[42] Bazylow, *Obalenie*, p. 283–85.
[43] Grave, *Burzhuaziia*, p. 179.
[44] *Ibid.*, pp. 181–82.

exploit the workers' movement for the benefit of the liberal opposition. The revolutionary parties had no quarrel with new-found radicalism of the Workers' Group but they objected to its attempts to subordinate the workers' actions to the interests of the Duma Progressive Bloc – as was the clear intention of the proposed demonstration on 14 February.[45]

The revolutionary groups – the Bolsheviks, the SRs, the Mezhraionka and the Menshevik Initiative Group – did not support the demonstration. The Bolsheviks even resolved to stage a rival demonstration of their own on Nevsky Prospekt to mark the second anniversary of the arrest of the Bolshevik Duma fraction. These manoeuvres testified to the intense competition between the Workers' Group and the revolutionary parties for leadership of the revolutionary movement. As it happened, however, neither demonstration had any great success. No appreciable numbers appeared on the Nevsky Prospekt, and though about 500 people gathered round the Duma building, they were soon dispersed by the police.[46]

Theories of Imperialism

The political rivalries and alignments formed during the war were carried over into the revolution and helped shape its development. The same is true of the theoretical debates which took place among Russian socialists in exile during the war years. These discussions determined many of the assumptions held during the revolution about what socialism was and how it would come about. It is significant that debates did not deal with the question of socialism directly or examine the concrete social and economic conditions in Russia. Instead they were centred on 'finance capital' or 'imperialism', but in fact these topics had an important bearing on how it was believed that socialism in Russia would emerge.

The stimulus for the wartime discussion on imperialism was the publication in 1910 by the Austrian economist, Rudolf Hilferding, of the book Das Finanzkapital (*Finance Capital*). Hilferding thought of himself as continuing Marx's work, and he examined what he believed to be the most recent trends within the capitalist system. Two of his findings were to have great influence: that the economies of individual countries were becoming increasingly interdependent so that the world economy as a whole was becoming more integrated, and that in the most advanced countries companies were merging with one another to form monopolies and trusts, and that these were becoming controlled by the banks. The conclusions Hilferding drew from these observations was that the capitalist system was laying the economic foundations for socialism by creating a single world economy, and that by integrating the various sectors of the economy in such a way it made possible a system of centralized regulation.[47] It was at this time that socialism came to be equated with centralized economic planning. This assumption, together with the belief that the coming socialist revolution would be on an interna-

[45] A. G. Shliapnikov, *Semnadtsatyi god* i (Moscow–Petrograd, 1923), pp. 31–33.
[46] Shliapnikov, *Semnadtsatyi*, pp. 56–57; Bazylow, *Obalenie*, p. 344.
[47] R. Hilferding, *Das Finanzkapital* (Vienna, 1923), pp. 218, 241.

tional scale and that socialism was maturing within the capitalist system, were shared by most German and Russian socialists. There were, however, differences of emphasis and interpretation which divided political groups and which were connected, at least indirectly, with attitudes towards the war.

After Hilferding the other important influence on perceptions of socialism during the war was the German socialist Karl Kautsky. Kautsky believed that the present war was caused by competition between industrial nations as they tried to acquire additional agrarian territory for their economic needs. This was the driving force behind 'imperialism'. But Kautsky thought that after the war an 'ultra-imperialist' age would dawn when relations between powers would be regulated by voluntary agreements. As economies became more international, unions of states would be established and in Europe this would take the form of a United States of Europe.[48]

Trotsky was attracted by the idea of a United States of Europe but believed that the capitalist system prevented its coming into being. He thought that the present war was breaking down the boundaries of nation states and creating an international base for socialist revolution. The conquest of State power by the proletariats of different countries would bring about the democratic unification of Europe by the creation of a United States of Europe. In this way the 'dictatorship of the proletariat' would be organized on an all-European scale.[49]

Nikolai Bukharin also thought that the recent growth of the world market had brought even isolated regions into the orbit of capitalism and created an ever broader base for the world socialist economy. He took this to signify that the conditions for socialism had now matured and that the proletariat should now seize power and turn the imperialist war between 'nations' into a civil war between classes. Bukharin believed that Kautsky had over-estimated the vitality of capitalism and the likelihood of an ultra-imperialist stage. In Bukharin's view this would require the parties in the agreement to hold equal positions in the world market. But the chances of 'national' capitalist groupings ever achieving the necessary degree of economic and political parity Bukharin considered to be negligible.[50]

During 1916 Lenin wrote his pamphlet *Imperialism, the Highest Stage of Capitalism*. The examination of recent economic trends it presented was designed to show that capitalism had now reached the end of its development, and that nothing lay beyond except socialism. He conceived his essay as a rebuttal of Kautsky's conception of 'ultra-imperialism'. Like Bukharin, Lenin could not envisage the kind of co-operation between states that would make 'ultra-imperialism' or a United States of Europe possible. National economies, Lenin pointed out, developed at different rates. This consideration also meant that a multilateral peace accord would be unlikely to come about.[51]

The arguments Lenin deployed against Kautsky also applied to Trotsky, and it was in regard to Trotsky's conception of a United States of Europe that Lenin wrote 'Unequal economic and political development is a necessary law

[48] K. Kautsky, *Nationalstaat, Imperialistischer Staat und Staatenbund* (Nurnberg, 1915), p. 75.
[49] L. Trotsky, 'Nash politicheskii lozung', *Nashe slovo*, 24 February 1915.
[50] N. Bukharin, 'Mirovaia ekonomika i imperializm', *Kommunist* (1915, no. 1–2), pp. 44–45.
[51] V. I. Lenin, *Polnoe sobranie sochinenii*, 55 vols. (Moscow, 1958–65) vol xxvii, p. 98.

of capitalism. It follows that the victory of socialism is, at the beginning, possible in a few capitalist countries, even in one taken separately'. There is no indication, however, that at this stage Lenin thought that Russia could be a country in which socialism would initially triumph.

In 1916 Bukharin added some refinements to his conception of what the coming revolution would involve. He drew attention to the fact that Marx and Engels had considered the State to be an instrument of class oppression, a means of maintaining the domination of the bourgeoisie over the proletariat and that, consequently, after the socialist revolution in a classless society the State would wither away. Bukharin argued that in recent times the institutions of finance capital – the monopolies and trusts – had come to merge increasingly with the State apparatus. In this way an all-embracing Leviathan State had been created in the most advanced countries, and it was this Leviathan State that the concerted forces of the workers would be compelled to destroy in their struggle for socialism.[52]

When Bukharin's article on the State was published in December 1916 it prompted Lenin to investigate the question for himself. He agreed with Bukharin that the existing State ought to be destroyed but believed that during the transition to socialism a temporary form of State was necessary to ensure the supremacy of the proletariat over the bourgeoisie. This would be the 'dictatorship of the proletariat' and would take the form of a government of Soviets.

In his Swiss exile Lenin followed closely the political developments in Russia. In January 1917 he gave a lecture to young workers on the 1905 revolution, which he concluded by saying that people of his own generation 'might not live to see the decisive battles of this coming revolution' but that the youth would be 'fortunate enough not only to fight, but also to win in the coming proletarian revolution'. This has been interpreted to mean that Lenin was taken by surprise by the revolution in February 1917. But Lenin's words are not unambiguous. They could also imply that Lenin assumed that a revolution was in the offing, but that there was likely to be a considerable interval of time between the onset of the world socialist revolution and its final culmination – which Lenin at 46 might not survive to witness. This would accord with Lenin's conceptions at the time of uneven development and the staged progress of the world revolution.

In fact in an article dated 31 January 1917 Lenin mentioned the possibility of there soon being in Russia 'a government of Miliukov and Guchkov, if not of Miliukov and Kerensky'.[53] When Lenin learnt of the overthrow of tsarism and the establishment of the Provisional Government he wrote to Aleksandra Kollontai: 'In the last number of *Sotsial-Demokrat* we spoke of the possibility of a government of Miliukov and Guchkov if not of Miliukov and Kerensky. It turns out that it is *both – and* all three together'. Lenin obviously thought he had predicted the composition of the new government pretty accurately.[54]

One piece of evidence Lenin had to base his prediction on was the document entitled 'Disposition No. 1' dated September 1915 and emanating from the liberal opposition. The document spoke of a government with a

[52] *Ibid.*, xxxiii, pp. 331–38.
[53] *Ibid.*, xxx, p. 341.
[54] *Ibid.*, xlix, pp. 339–40.

nucleus of Prince Lvov, Guchkov and Kerensky. It had been supplied to
Lenin by the German General Staff. Both the Germans and Lenin would have
been dismayed by the prospect of such a government – the Germans because
it was one dedicated to pursuing the war more effectively and Lenin because
it could delay the socialist revolution by many years. With the Germans'
encouragement, Lenin published the document in one of his journals in the
hope that the Russian authorities might take steps to forestall the liberals'
accession to power.[55] But Lenin and the Germans were too late. By the time
Lenin's journal reached Russia the government of Lvov, Miliukov, Guchkov
and Kerensky had already become a reality.

[55] J. D. White, 'Lenin, the Germans and the February revolution', *Revolutionary Russia* v (June
1992), pp. 1–21.

4

The February Revolution

The Six Days of the February Revolution

It is usually stated as an indisputable fact that the February revolution was spontaneous and leaderless. To this it is habitually added that the underground political parties had been weakened by arrests, that the party leadership was in prison or abroad and that the people on the ground in Russia were inexperienced in political organization.

It is less well recognized that this interpretation was the official Soviet one until 1930 and that it gained currency not because it was true but because it served the purpose of safeguarding the prestige of the Communist Party and the party leaders during the 1920s. Since there was no Bolshevik Party in evidence in February 1917, the argument ran, the proletariat was unable to take power; but in October, when the workers were led by the Bolshevik Party, a successful proletarian revolution ensued.

The absent experienced leaders would include Stalin, Kamenev, Zinoviev, Bukharin and, of course, Lenin. But what exactly was this group of people experienced in? It was certainly not in organizing strikes, demonstrations or insurrections. For the most part, its experience was in writing pamphlets and newspaper articles, usually directed against other socialist parties. These people only acquired the reputation of being revolutionary leaders after the event. The corollary was that since they were not present in Petrograd in February 1917 there could have been no leadership in those events. It also followed that since there was no credit to be derived for them from the February revolution, there would be no credit for anyone.

Most of our information about the underground political parties in the February revolution comes from the reminiscences of some members of a *zemliachestvo* organization consisting of former workers at the Sormovo factory near Nizhnyi Novgorod. They included V. N. Kaiurov, I. D. Chugurin, A. S. Kuklin, N. F. Sveshnikov, I. M. Gordienko and A. K. Skorokhodov. The group belonged to the Vyborg District Committee of the Bolshevik Party, and Skorokhodov and K. I. Shutko were the Vyborg committee's representatives on the St Petersburg committee, which co-ordinated Bolshevik activities on a city-wide basis. The Bolshevik leadership for Russia as a whole was also located in Petrograd. This 'Russian Bureau' consisted of A. G. Shliapnikov, V. M. Molotov and P. A. Zalutskii. Shliapnikov, who was a former worker, was closely associated with the Sormovo *zemliachestvo*, and was himself the author of memoirs on the February revolution.

Shliapnikov recalls the situation in the working-class districts of Petrograd in 1916. The rising cost of living and difficulties in obtaining foodstuffs had created considerable hardship. In the factories the working day had been extended to 12 hours and above. Compulsory labour had been introduced, and it was impossible to change workplace at will. There was the constant threat of being conscripted and sent to the most forward positions at the front for the slightest expression of insubordination.[1]

As the strength of the workers' movement grew, the competition for its leadership increased. At the beginning of 1917 the anti-war underground parties in Petrograd – the Bolsheviks, the Mezhraiontsy and the Socialist Revolutionaries – were feeling their influence on the workers slipping away to an increasingly militant Workers' Group, which had temporarily abandoned its pro-war stance for tactical advantage. It had the backing of Guchkov and other members of the CWIC, who saw the Workers' Group as a means of influencing the labour movement. Shliapnikov was much relieved when the demonstration organized by the Workers' Group on 14 February failed to draw a large crowd.

Towards the end of February the Bolshevik Vyborg District Committee decided to call the workers out on strike on 23 February, when International Women's Day was to be celebrated. (International Women's Day was on 8 March, but the Russian calendar was 13 days behind that in the West.) No member of the committee foresaw that the strike which began on 23 February would be the beginning of a revolution. The demonstration, however, struck a chord with ordinary people in Petrograd and the women in particular, who experienced the increasing hardship of inflation and the shortage of supplies. Demonstrators marched from the Vyborg district across the Leteinyi and Troitskii bridges, filling Liteinyi Street and Nevsky Prospekt. The slogan they uttered was 'Bread, bread . . .', which seemed to the police chief to sound like a continuous moan. A lockout at the Putilov factory served to add emphasis to the workers' grievances. This demonstration of popular discontent, moreover, showed no readiness to subside, but gave every indication that it could be a preliminary to a revolutionary upsurge.[2]

This was a possibility that the members of the Vyborg District Committee had contemplated for some time, but they had in mind the next big date on the labour movement's calendar – 1 May (18 April according to the Russian calendar). Accordingly, the members of the committee had advised the workers to maintain discipline and conserve their forces for the decisive day. But now the success of 23 February prompted them to consider whether it might not be better to bring forward their plans.[3]

On the evening of 23 February the Vyborg committee called a meeting of all the Bolshevik organizations in the city. There the crucial decision was made to

[1] A. G. Shliapnikov, 'Fevral'skie dni v Peterburge', *Proletarskaia revoliutsiia*, (1923, i, 13), p. 70.
[2] A. P. Balk, 'Poslednie piat' dnei tsarskogo Petrograda (23–28 fevralia 1917 g.)', *Russkoe proshloe* i (1991), p. 26.
[3] V. N. Kaiurov, 'Shest' dnei fevral'skoi revoliutsii', *Proletarskaia revoliutsiia* (1923, i, 13), p. 158; E. N. Burdzhalov, *Vtoraia russkaia revoliutsiia* (Moscow, 1967), p. 120. Burdzhalov quotes from Chugurin's unpublished memoirs that he and other members of the Vyborg committee were trying to 'keep the workers' mood on the boil until 1 May'.

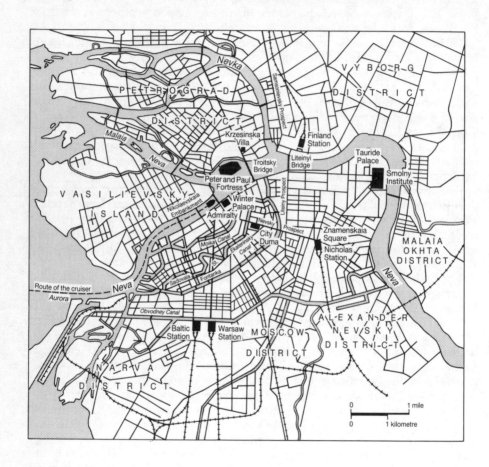

Petrograd 1917

continue the strike, organize a demonstration on the following day on Petrograd's main street, Nevsky Prospekt, strengthen contacts among the soldiers, and try to obtain weapons.[4]

On the 24th the movement gained strength. Strikes, meetings and demonstrations began to multiply throughout the various city districts, especially as news of the Putilov lockout spread. In the course of the day many skirmishes between workers and police took place. But despite the efforts of the police and Cossacks, by evening the whole of Nevsky Prospekt was full of workers. At midday the authorities decided that it would be necessary to deploy troops to contain the movement.[5]

Now that it was clear that the demonstrations had extended into a second day, the need for some kind of leadership and direction for the movement was felt. It was necessary to have information about what was happening in the various city districts and some kind of co-ordinating activity had to be embarked upon. It was at this stage that the members of the Vyborg District Committee began to suggest to the Bolshevik leadership that it should issue a manifesto setting out the anti-war aims of the movement. Shliapnikov, however, still thought the moment premature.[6]

By Saturday 25th the strike movement in Petrograd had become general and had spread to even small enterprises. As the working men and women negotiated their way round the police cordons, clearing new paths across the ice on the Neva, to converge in thousands on the city centre, troops were being deployed on the streets. During the day unarmed demonstrators were fired upon.[7]

At this juncture relations between Shliapnikov and the members of the Vyborg District Committee became rather strained. This was not only on account of Shliapnikov's delay in issuing a manifesto but also because the Vyborg workers wanted Shliapnikov to supply them with weapons to fight against the tsarist police force. Kaiurov, Chugurin and other workers from Sormovo had experience of this kind of fighting, since they had mounted similar operations in 1905. Shliapnikov, however, would not agree to supply them with the few dozen revolvers he had. He was anxious lest armed workers came into conflict with the army, and that instead of joining the revolution the soldiers would help crush it. Shliapnikov argued that any arms that were needed should be obtained by winning over the troops. He was acutely conscious that the success of the revolution hinged on the mood of the soldiers.[8]

At 11 p.m. on the 25th the Council of Ministers held an emergency session at the home of the chairman Prince Golitsyn, at which the Police Chief A. P. Balk and the commander of the Petrograd garrison, Khabalov, were in attendance to report on events in the capital. Having appraised themselves of the situation, the ministers decided that energetic measures ought to be taken to suppress the revolt. Only Pokrovskii, the Foreign Minister, thought that the government ought to offer its resignation so that one more acceptable

[4] N. F. Sveshnikov, 'Otryvki iz vospominanii', *Petrogradskaia pravda*, 14 March 1924.
[5] Balk, 'Poslednic', p. 32.
[6] Sveshnikov, 'Otryvki,'.
[7] Shliapnikov, 'Fevral'skie', pp. 87–88.
[8] *Ibid.*, p. 88.

to public opinion could be appointed. Pokrovskii's isolation on this matter was a sign that the moment for an orderly transfer of power had passed. The outcome would now be decided by armed force.[9]

During the meeting Guchkov repeatedly tried to contact Balk by telephone to try to secure the release of Gvozdev and other members of the Workers' Group of the WIC who had been arrested some hours before. During the day a congress of WIC's had opened in Petrograd, despite the misgivings of the police and the Okhrana. The proceedings had been every bit as inflammatory as the authorities had suspected, and in the small hours of the 26th Gvozdev and his associates had been arrested and the congress closed.[10]

In their swoop that night the police arrested about 100 people in all belonging to various revolutionary organizations, among them five members of the Bolshevik St Petersburg Committee, including Kuklin, Skorokhodov and E. Eizenšmits from the Latvian section. On discovering this, Shliapnikov asked the Vyborg District Committee to take over the functions of the St Petersburg Committee in directing the workers' movement.[11]

On Sunday 26th government posters appeared threatening that disorders would be put down with armed force. Despite this, demonstrations again took place in the centre of the city. At midday soldiers of the Volhynian Regiment on Znamenskaia Square opened fire on the crowds, and in other parts of the city troops also fired on demonstrators. In the course of the day at least 50 people were killed and 100 wounded. Ominously for the government there were several instances of fraternization between soldiers and demonstrators. The Mensheviks, however, began to urge an end to the demonstrations and a return to work, as the government demanded.

On the evening of the 26th the combined Vyborg and St Petersburg Committee met twice, once with Shliapnikov, where the argument about issuing weapons was repeated, and once out of Shliapnikov's earshot at the Udelnaia station. At this later meeting the members of the Vyborg committee worked out a detailed plan for the following day, involving the seizure of weapons from the Cartridge factory, the assault on the police stations and the freeing from prison of their comrades who had been arrested that morning. It was also decided to extend fraternization with the soldiers and to speed up the publication of a party manifesto.[12]

Monday 27 February was the critical day of the revolution. It was then that the tide turned decisively in its favour, as the troops began to desert to the insurgents' side. Early in the morning the Volhynian Regiment at its barracks declared that it would not fire on the demonstrators during the coming day. One officer, who tried to impose discipline, was shot. The Volhynians then went to enlist the Lithuanian and Preobrazhenskii regiments, which were quartered in adjoining streets. Soldiers from the three regiments then set off up Liteinyi Prospekt towards the Vyborg district, where the barracks of the Moscow Regiment were situated.[13]

[9] Balk, 'Poslednie', pp. 39–41.
[10] *Ibid.*, pp. 41–42.
[11] Sveshnikov, 'Otryvki'.
[12] I. Gavrilov, *Ocherki po istorii vyborgskoi partorganizatsii gor. Leningrada* (Leningrad, 1933), p. 86; Shliapnikov, 'Fevral'skie', p. 96; Sveshnikov, 'Otryvki'.
[13] E. P. Semenov, 'Fevral'skie i martovskie dni 1917 g.', *Istoricheskii vestnik* (March 1917, no. 2), p. 15.

That same morning, as planned, the Bolshevik Vyborg Committee had gathered a large contingent of workers and soldiers and headed towards the city centre. By midday they had captured the Cartridge factory and distributed weapons among themselves. They then took the Remand Prison, whose guards gave in without any resistance, and whose prisoners were freed. The prison and the District Court were set on fire.[14]

The way across the Liteinyi bridge to the Petrograd side was blocked by a police cordon armed with machine-guns. This cordon was now caught between the armed contingent from the Vyborg side and the regiments advancing from the opposite direction. Fierce fighting took place on Liteinyi Prospekt near the bridge, and there were severe casualties from the machine-gun fire. Police resistance, however, was broken, allowing the insurgents to pass in both directions.

The insurgents now divided their forces. Some turned back towards the Vyborg district and went to the barracks of the Moscow Regiment. There they were fired on by the officers and training units, but the barracks were nevertheless taken. Some of the combined forces now went back towards the city centre while others remained on the Vyborg side, breaking into the Kresty and other prisons, setting free many activists from a range of political groups, among them the recently imprisoned members of the Workers' Group of the WIC. The Okhrana building was captured and set ablaze, its records also being destroyed. After opening the prisons, the attack on police stations and the hunting down of individual policemen began.[15]

The Formation of the Petrograd Soviet

The newly released members of the Workers' Group immediately set off for the Tauride Palace, where along with representatives of the trade-union and co-operative movements they established themselves as the 'Provisional Executive Committee of the Soviet of Workers' Deputies'. The Provisional Executive Committee consisted of K. A. Gvozdev, B. O. Bogdanov, N. Iu. Kapelinskii, K. S. Grinevich, Noa Chkheidze, M. I. Skobelev and Frankorusskii. In order to convoke the Soviet, the committee issued a leaflet calling for representatives of workers and soldiers to meet at seven o'clock in the Duma building. Those troops who had come over to the side of the people were enjoined to elect one representative for each company. Factory workers were to elect one deputy for each thousand; factories with less than a thousand workers could elect one deputy each.[16]

The Petrograd garrison consisted of about 466,000 men, while the number of workers employed in Petrograd and its outlying districts in factories with a workforce of over 50 people was 380,000. Since a military company could consist of as few as 100 soldiers, this system of representation was to give pre-

[14] Gavrilov, *Ocherki*, p. 86.

[15] *Ibid.*, p. 86; S. N. Valk, R. Sh. Ganelin *et al.*, *Oktiabr'skoe vooruzhennoe vosstanie: Semnadtsatyi god v Petrograde* i (Leningrad, 1967), pp. 64–66.

[16] *Kak sovershilas' velikaia russkaia revoliutsiia: Podrobnoe opisanie istoricheskikh sobytii za period vremeni s 23 fevralia po 4 marta 1917 g.* (Petrograd, 1917), p. 11.

eminence in the Petrograd Soviet to the soldiers. This was an understandable enticement on the part of the Provisional Executive Committee, since when the leaflet was composed the revolution had still to be consolidated and everything depended on winning over the troops.

At the same time as the Provisional Executive Committee of the Soviet was distributing its leaflet, the Bolshevik Vyborg Committee was distributing one of its own, urging the population to form a Provisional Revolutionary Government by electing deputies to a Soviet which would meet at the Finland station in the Vyborg district.[17] In the event, the vast majority of people sent their representatives to the Soviet in the Tauride Palace, though the Soviet in the Vyborg district was indeed established, and survived as the local Soviet of the Vyborg district.[18]

The revolution's success was causing some alarm to the combined Vyborg and St Petersburg Committee. It had been involved in what it had considered to be a workers' anti-war movement, and considerable blood had been spilt on that account. Now, however, when the movement was about to triumph, defensists and the intelligentsia, who had until now stood aloof, were trying to usurp the leadership. This prompted the committee to conclude that there could be no further delay in issuing a party manifesto to emphasize the anti-war character of the revolution. And since Shliapnikov had been so tardy about the matter, Kaiurov and his associates decided to compose the manifesto themselves. Only then did they take it to the Russian Bureau for the official party stamp to be put on it. It began to be distributed late on the 27th.[19]

The manifesto was addressed 'To All Citizens of Russia' and stated that the task of the working class and the revolutionary army was to establish a 'Provisional Revolutionary Government' which would head a new republican order. The manifesto called upon the workers and soldiers to elect their representatives to this government, the immediate tasks of which would be the convocation of a Constituent Assembly, the institution of land reform and an eight-hour working day, and the establishment of ties with the proletariats of the belligerent powers with a view to ending the imperialist war.[20]

At 9 p.m. with 250 people present, the first plenary session of the Soviet opened at the Tauride Palace. Following speeches by representatives of the Volhynian, Pavlovskii, Lithuanian and other regiments, it was decided that the Soviet should be called the 'Soviet of Workers' and Soldiers' Deputies'. It was reported that Kronstadt had joined the revolution. The Soviet went on the discuss food supply in the capital, defence and policing.[21]

A Provisional Executive Committee was elected consisting of Chkheidze (President), Kerenskii, M. I. Skobelev (Vice-Presidents), Iu. M. Steklov, Sukhanov, Shliapnikov, P. A. Aleksandrovich and Kapelinsky. It was

[17] Gavrilov, *Ocherki*, p. 88; Semenov, 'Fevral'skie', p. 19. Semenov states that the leaflet was distributed to the crowds from aeroplanes.

[18] S. Skalov in his memoirs describes making the choice to go to the Tauride Palace rather than to the Finland station. See S. Skalov, '27 fevralia 1917 g. v Peterburge', *Krasnaia nov'*, (1931, no. 3), p. 118.

[19] Kaiurov, 'Shest'dnei', p. 167.

[20] N. N. Sukhanov, *Zapiski o revoliutsii* i (Moscow, 1991), p. 125; reproduced in Shliapnikov, 'Fevral'skie', p. 124.

[21] N. Avdeev, *Revoliutsiia 1917 goda (Khronika sobytii)* i (Moscow–Petrograd, 1923), p. 41.

decided to add two representatives each from the various socialist parties, and these began to attend from the 28th. To extend the Soviet's control throughout the city, it was resolved to appoint members of the Executive Committee and other people recommended by it as 'commissars for the establishment of people's power in the districts of Petrograd'.[22]

A most important matter to occupy the Executive Committee in its first days was what its relationship with the Provisional Committee of the Duma, formed that day, should be. Chkheidze and Kerensky were delegated to this committee. Both of them were members of the committee, but in giving them a mandate the Executive Committee wanted to ensure that the Duma members did nothing without the knowledge of the Soviet. There was a fear that they might still make some kind of agreement with the tsarist government.

The Formation of the Duma Provisional Committee

The Duma deputies who had gathered at the Tauride Palace on the morning of the 27th learnt from Rodzianko that the Duma and the State Council had been prorogued. To observe legality, the deputies adjourned to another room and reconvened as a private gathering. They then discussed the situation and set about electing a Provisional Committee from the members of the Duma. The Provisional Committee consisted of Rodzianko (Octobrist), V. V. Shulgin (Nationalist), V. N. Lvov (Centre), I. I. Dmitriukov (Octobrist), Shidlovskii (Progressive Bloc), M. A. Karaulov (non-party), Konovalov (Progressist), Kerensky (Socialist Revolutionary), V. A. Rzhevskii (Progressist), Miliukov (Kadet), Nekrasov (Kadet) and Chkheidze (Menshevik). The Provisional Committee's immediate task was to try to establish order in the city, and to make contact with other organizations and institutions. These organizations included the Council of Congresses of Industry and Trade and the Moscow War Industries Committee.[23]

While the Soviet was in its first session, the Duma Provisional Committee met and decided that it should take power into its own hands, a decision which was immediately communicated to the Soviet. To the committee was added Colonel B. A. Engelhardt, who was given command of the Petrograd garrison, becoming head of the Duma's Military Commission.

By this time the tsarist government's position had deteriorated to such an extent that the Council of Ministers telegraphed to the tsar that it could no longer cope with the situation. In fact, during the day the tsarist ministers, Shcheglovitov and Sukhomlinov, were arrested by the insurgents and brought to the Tauride Palace.

In the evening a meeting was held in Petrograd of various public bodies,

[22] Shliapnikov, 'Fevral'skie', p. 112; N. N. Sukhanov, *The Russian Revolution 1917*, ed., abridged and trans. by J. Carmichael (Oxford 1955), p. 60.
[23] *Kak sovershilas'* . . ., pp. 7–9; P. N. Miliukov, *The Russian Revolution, Vol. 1: The Revolution Divided: Spring 1917*, ed. R. Stites, trans. T. Stites and R. Stites, (Gulf Breeze, FL, 1978), p. 27; P. V. Volobuev, 'Monopolisticheskaia burzhuaziia i vremennoe pravitel'stvo', *Monopolii i inostrannyi kapital v Rossii* (Moscow–Leningrad, 1962), p. 247.

including the War Industries Committee, the Union of Towns and Zemstvos, the town Duma and various voluntary and charitable organizations. After a short discussion they passed a resolution approving the Duma Provisional Committee's decisions not to disperse and to take power into its hands; it expressed the belief that Russia would 'finally achieve complete victory over the external and internal enemy'.[24]

On the morning of 28 February elections took place to the Petrograd Soviet and also to the Vyborg Soviet. The members of the Bolshevik Vyborg Committee, Shliapnikov's Russian Bureau, the Mezhraionka and some of the left-wing Socialist Revolutionaries thought of the soviets as forms of a 'provisional revolutionary government' which would consist entirely of socialist parties and which would be the sole power in the country.[25] This, however, was to be a minority view.

The plenary session of the Petrograd Soviet was opened by Chkheidze at 1 p.m. He gave a report on the proceedings of the previous day to a crowded meeting, which approved the composition of the Executive Committee. But, according to Shliapnikov, the atmosphere of the meeting was one of muddle and confusion. The festive spirit of the revolution distracted everyone from getting to grips with the events unfolding in the country. The day-to-day business gravitated from the Soviet to the Executive Committee.[26]

Troops continued to come to the Duma building. There they were addressed by Rodzianko, who urged them to keep order, to obey their officers and to return to their barracks. Miliukov made a speech in which he too emphasized the need for military discipline and, with the tsarist authorities in mind, asserted that the soldiers should submit to no other authority than to the Provisional Committee of the Duma.[27]

At the session of the Soviet Executive Committee on that day the membership was extended by representatives from the various socialist groups. The new members included K. I. Shutko from the Bolsheviks, G. M. Erlikh from the Jewish Socialist Party, the Bund, V. N. Zenzinov from the SRs, A. V. Peshekhonov from the Popular Socialists, L. M. Bramson from the Trudoviks, B. O. Bogdanov and B. S. Baturskii from the Mensheviks. Mieczysław Kozłowski from the SDKPiL and Pēteris Stučka from the Latvian Social Democratic Party. Other left-wing representatives included Steklov and Sukhanov, who later wrote extensive memoirs of the Russian revolution.[28]

Groups of soldier delegates to the Soviet reported the disquiet of the garrison troops occasioned by Rodzianko's speech in the morning and appeals by the Duma Provisional Committee for the soldiers to return to their barracks and obey their officers. On their return, the officers had taken up where they had left off – with the tsarist military regulations – something quite unacceptable to the soldiers. The drafting of new regulations governing the soldiers' daily lives, both on and off duty, was delegated to a group of representatives from the garrison. It was decided that the regulations would be discussed at meeting of the Soviet on the following day.

[24] Semenov, 'Fevral'skie', pp. 22–23.
[25] A. G. Shliapnikov, Semnadtsatyi god, i (Moscow–Leningrad, 1923), p. 185.
[26] Shliapnikov, 'Fevral'skie', p. 120.
[27] Kak sovershilas' . . ., pp. 16–23.
[28] Shliapnikov, 'Fevral'skie', p. 122.

In the evening telegrams were sent to all the towns of the Russian Empire containing formal notification of the formation of the Duma Provisional Committee. Copies of the telegram, signed by Rodzianko as President of the Duma, were also sent to commanders of the fronts and commanders of the Baltic and Black Sea Fleets.[29]

On the following day a telegram from the Central War Industries Committee to all regional and local WICs announced that State power had passed into the hands of the Executive Committee of the State Duma under the chairmanship of Rodzianko. The members of the committee were listed, and it was stated that its instructions were being carried out without question. The telegram also contained the information that Guchkov had been appointed chairman of the Committee's Military Commission. (Engelhardt had resigned from the position late on the 28th.) From this telegram, as well as from those sent by Rodzianko, it is clear that Rodzianko at least thought of the Duma Provisional Committee, now often referred to as the 'Duma Executive Committee', as the new government of Russia.[30]

Order No. I

On 1 March the meeting of the Soviet turned immediately to the question of the soldiers. After a lengthy and heated discussion a number of resolutions were carried establishing the principles of soldiers' conduct in the new political situation. These were that:

1. soldiers will not give up their weapons to anyone;
2. soldiers will elect their representatives to the Soviet;
3. in their political actions the soldiers will be subordinate only to the Soviet;
4. the subordination of troops to the officers should take place only at the front; and
5. military units should carry out the orders of the Duma Military Commission only so long as these orders do not conflict with the resolutions of the Soviet.[31]

The Soviet Executive Committee decided to combine these resolutions and publish them in the form of an order. The drafting was done by a commission composed of delegates to the Soviet from the Petrograd Garrison and headed by N.D. Sokolov. The document which resulted was to be known as Order No.1, and it contained the following points:

1. All military and naval units were to form committees from the elected representatives of the lower ranks.
2. Those companies which had not already done so had to send a representative to the Petrograd Soviet.

[29] Semenov, 'Fevral'skie', pp. 40–41.
[30] *Ibid.*, pp. 56–57.
[31] V. I. Miller, *Soldatskie komitety russkoi armii v 1917 g.* (Moscow, 1974), pp. 25–30.

3. In political matters the actions of the military were subordinated to the Soviet and to the army and navy committees.
4. The orders of the Military Commission of the Duma were to be carried out only where they did not conflict with those of the Soviet.
5. Weapons should be kept in the custody of the military committees and should on no account be turned over to the officers.

Point 6 embodied the general principle that 'during the performance of their military duties the soldiers must observe the strictest military discipline, but outside the service and the ranks, in their political, general civic and private life, soldiers cannot be deprived of those rights which are enjoyed by all citizens'. Point 7 abolished the special forms of address used by soldiers and sailors towards their superiors, and the condescending expressions used by the officers towards subordinates.[32]

Order No. 1 was quickly telegraphed to the fronts and was to contribute to undermining discipline there. In retrospect, blame was laid on the document for the disintegration of the army in 1917. But this was a symptom rather than a cause. It grew out of the authoritarian conditions in the Russian army and embodied the benefits the soldiers expected from the new revolutionary order. Order No. 1 reflected the dynamic that had led the soldiers to join the revolution during the February days. Their continued loyalty to the revolution, and therefore the security of the revolution itself, could be ensured only if the troops saw their interests being served. This fact was appreciated well enough at the time, and helps account for the generous representation of the soldiers on the Soviet. Significantly, the Provisional Government in its programme (composed on the same day as Order No. 1) also included the principle that, off duty, soldiers should enjoy the same rights as civilians.

The Formation of the Provisional Government

At the same time as the question of the soldiers was being discussed, the Duma Provisional Committee was deliberating the formation of a new government. This was despite the fact that for almost three days the Provisional Committee headed by Rodzianko had been the body which ran the country. The formation of a different government, therefore, represented a considerable change in direction, though in retrospect its magnitude has been lost in the general speed of events. It nevertheless had far-reaching implications for the stability of the new regime.

The main motive for by-passing the Provisional Committee was to remove Rodzianko. In discussions which had taken place in the Progressive Bloc at the end of 1916 it had been decided that Rodzianko was an unsuitable person to head the future government of Russia. He was considered to be too stubborn and domineering. This was a view held by Miliukov, who was the person in charge of drawing up the list of ministers for the new government.[33]

[32] R. P. Browder and A. F. Kerensky, eds., *The Russian Provisional Government 1917* ii (Stanford, 1961), pp. 848–49.
[33] Miliukov, *Russia Revolution*, p. 30; A. Ia. Avrekh, *Masony i revoliutsiia* (Moscow, 1990), pp. 163–64.

Miliukov achieved his purpose by making the government a non-Duma organization. It would have been possible to form a government by allocating ministerial portfolios to certain members of the Provisional Committee. But this was not done. Instead, Miliukov included people who were not members of the committee or even members of the Duma. Among these were Prince Lvov, Guchkov and Professor Manuilov, thus bringing the list of ministers into greater conformity with those lists which had been drawn up from 1915 onwards.[34]

By making the new Provisional Government independent of the Duma, Miliukov was able to exclude Rodzianko and include other people who were more acceptable. But the disadvantage was that he had deprived the Provisional Government of the legitimacy and authority of the Duma. For, although elected on a limited franchise, it was nevertheless a representative institution. The new government, on the other hand, was a group of self-appointed individuals, and this was to be one of its serious weakness in the coming months. At first sight it seems odd that Miliukov, an experienced student of politics, should make such a grave mistake in the way he set about forming a government. However, at the time Miliukov was drawing up his list of ministers he was still under the impression that this would be a cabinet in a constitutional monarchy and that there would continue to be a sovereign from whom the government's authority would derive. This did not turn out to be the case.

The post of prime minister in the new government was given to Prince Lvov, a former member of the First Duma and chairman of the All-Russian Union of Zemstvos. The Ministry of Foreign Affairs went to Miliukov, and the Ministry of War and Navy to Guchkov. Nekrasov was given the Ministry of Transport, and Manuilov the Ministry of Education. Shingarev was given the Ministry of Agriculture. Of the two economic ministries, the Ministry of Trade and Industry went to Konovalov, the vice-chairman of the Central War Industries Committee, and the Ministry of Finance to Tereshchenko. It was proposed to offer the Ministry of Justice to Kerensky and the Ministry of Labour to Chkheidze. Chkheidze however, refused to accept the post.

Tereshchenko, a financier and sugar magnate from the Ukraine who chaired the Kiev WIC, was not a prominent figure in politics and had not figured in any previous lists of Cabinet members. This gave rise later to speculation that he had appeared in the government as a result of some conspiracy. The explanation, however, was that Miliukov and his colleagues had difficulty in filling the post of Minister of Finance. The most suitable candidate was Shingarev but he was more urgently needed in the Ministry of Agriculture. Tereshchenko was therefore a last-minute suggestion by one of his friends – Konovalov or Nekrasov. Tereshchenko's appointment and the circumstances surrounding it illustrate the fact that in the Provisional Government serious economic expertise was a rather a scarce commodity.[35]

[34] Avrekh, *Masony*, p. 161.
[35] *Ibid.*, pp. 171–72.

The Provisional Government and the Soviet

At the meeting of the Soviet Executive Committee on 1 March the question of the formation of a government was also discussed. The majority opinion was that since a liberal bourgeois government would be a considerable improvement on the tsarist regime, the Duma Provisional Committee should be encouraged to take power in the country. The general opinion also was that the intervention of the Soviet in this matter should be limited to presenting the new government with a set of demands, monitoring their implementation and exercising a right of veto over ministerial candidates. It would, however, refuse any participation in the government.

The Executive Committee drew up a list of nine demands to put to the Duma Committee:

1. An amnesty for all political prisoners, including those convicted of terrorist acts.
2. Freedom of the press, and assembly, and the right to form unions and go on strike.
3. No steps must be taken to predetermine the future form of government.
4. The abolition of all restrictions based on class, religion or nationality.
5. Preparations for the convocation of a Constituent Assembly on the basis of universal, equal, direct suffrage and secret ballot, which would determine the form of government and the constitution of the country.
6. The substitution of a people's militia with elected leadership for the police.
7. Elections to institutions of local administration.
8. The reorganization of the army on the basis of self-government, including the election of officers.
9. The troops which had taken part in the revolution should not be removed from the city and should not be disarmed.[36]

On the evening of 1 March, Chkheidze, Sokolov, Steklov and Sukhanov of the Executive Committee of the Soviet met with the Duma Provisional Committee to discuss the question of the future form of government. The members of the Executive Committee were prepared to allow the Provisional Committee to form the government, on condition that their demands were met. Sukhanov found that the Duma Committee, and Miliukov in particular, was surprisingly receptive to the proposals the Soviet made.

There were two conditions the Duma Committee would not agree to. These were that the Provisional Committee would take no steps that would determine the future form of government of the country. This was unacceptable because the Committee still envisaged a regency. Miliukov, as might be expected, was particularly insistent on this point. He did not, however, appear to notice the contradiction between his insistence on retaining the monarchy and the principle that the future form of government would be decided by the Constituent Assembly.[37]

[36] Avdeev, *Revoliutsiia*, pp. 50–51; Sukhanov, *Zapiski* i, pp. 141–43.
[37] Miliukov, *Russia Revolution*, pp. 31–32; Sukhanov, *Zapiski*, p. 121.

The other rejected condition was that officers should be elected. Nevertheless, the Provisional Committee did agree that while on duty soldiers should be subject to strict military discipline, but that when off duty they should be entitled to the same rights as other Russian citizens. In view of the denunciations later heaped on Order No.1 it is ironic that the Provisional Committee had accepted its main premiss – that political freedom was extended to persons serving in the armed forces as far as military circumstances allowed. And, while the outcome of the revolution had still seemed in doubt, the new government had agreed that those military units which had taken part in the revolutionary movement would neither be disarmed nor withdrawn from Petrograd. This agreement had been made when Guchkov was in Pskov negotiating the tsar's abdication. He returned to find his position as War Minister significantly undermined by it. The same difficulty was to be faced by General L. G. Kornilov who replaced Khabalov as commander of the Petrograd Military District on 2 March.[38]

Sukhanov expected that Miliukov would put forward a list of demands by the Provisional Committee, but none were made. In fact the Soviet's demands were published with the list of the Provisional Government's ministers as the programme of that government. Miliukov and his ministerial colleagues had contributed nothing of their own.[39]

At the plenary session of the Soviet on 2 March, Steklov reported on the negotiations with the Duma Provisional Committee the night before. The Executive Committee then proposed that the Soviet call upon the population to support the new Provisional Government in so far as it adhered to the principles set out in the programme. The formula of 'in so far as' became a characteristic one for the conditional support of socialists for the Provisional Government during the early part of 1917.

A complication for Kerensky was that the socialist parties in the Soviet were opposed to any of their members entering the Provisional Government. Kerensky faced the dilemma of either entering the government and resigning from the Soviet or of remaining in the Soviet and turning down his ministerial portfolio. He was able to retain both positions, however, by making an emotional speech in the Soviet plenum of 2 March. In this he offered to lay down his life for the revolution, and said that if the Soviet asked him to do so, he would resume the post of vice-chairman which he had just resigned. Kerensky's oratory had the desired effect, and his audience entreated him to resume the office of vice-chairman of the Soviet.[40]

In the discussion which followed Steklov's report on the negotiations of the night before, three currents of opinion emerged on what the Soviet's attitude towards the new government ought to be. Some Bolshevik delegates deplored the fact that there was no mention in the Soviet's demands of ending the war, the agrarian question or the eight-hour working day. They thought that there should be no dealings at all with the Duma committee and that the Soviet should constitute itself as a provisional revolutionary government. But the readiness of the Duma committee to agree to the Soviet's conditions had cut the ground from under the feet of those who argued in this fashion. Since

[38] 'A. I. Guchkov rasskazyvaet', *Voprosy istorii* (1991, no. 9–10), p. 207; Avdeev, *Revoliutsiia*, p. 54.
[39] Sukhanov, *The Russian Revolution 1917*, *Zapiski*, p. 124.
[40] *Ibid.*, p. 127; *Kak sovershilas'* . . ., p. 56.

the new government was pledged to implement so many of the Soviet's demands there seemed to be little point in replacing it. This current of opinion, that of the left wing, was in a minority. Also in a minority was the right's viewpoint, represented by the Bundist member M. G. Rafes and the SR Zenzinov, which wanted representatives of the Soviet to enter the government. Most delegates in the Soviet favoured the Executive Committee's formulation of support for the Provisional Government 'in so far as' it carried out the programme agreed with the Soviet. This position was carried by a massive majority of something like 400 to 15. Since there were around 30 Bolshevik delegates in the Soviet, it follows that many of them voted against the call for a provisional revolutionary government.[41]

The End of the Monarchy

In the meantime the question of the monarchy was being settled. On 1 March the Duma committee had decided to ask Nicholas II to abdicate in favour of his son Aleksei, with the Grand Duke Mikhail as regent. It resolved that Guchkov and Shulgin should be sent to the tsar immediately to obtain his consent. When they arrived at Pskov the next day Shulgin and Guchkov discovered that Nicholas, having learnt of the failure of a punitive expedition by General N. I. Ivanov to put down the rising in Petrograd, had already decided to abdicate. His abdication, however, would not be in favour of his son but of his brother, the Grand Duke Mikhail.[42]

Shulgin and Guchkov came away satisfied with their mission, bearing a manifesto announcing the tsar's abdication and nominating Mikhail as successor. In point of fact, the document was of dubious legality, for although Nicholas could legitimately abdicate on his own behalf he had no right to do so for his son. By this time, however, who the successor to Nicholas might be was becoming increasingly irrelevant as in Petrograd the tide had turned decisively against the monarchy. On 2 March Miliukov had made a speech in the Duma building listing the members of the new government. When the question of the monarchy was raised, Miliukov's audience made it plain that tsarism was unpopular. The meeting nevertheless ended amicably.

When Rodzianko contacted General N. V. Alekseev at Stavka the following day, he asserted that since the abdication of the tsar had been in favour of the Grand Duke, not of his son, the matter of the succession would have to be decided by the Constituent Assembly. He later informed General N. V. Ruzskii that the prospect of the monarchy's continuation had given rise to new mutinies of the soldiers and outbreaks of rioting in Petrograd.[43]

On the morning of 3 March the Grand Duke Mikhail received a delegation of all the members of the Provisional Government and Rodzianko, Shulgin and Karaulov from the Duma Provisional Committee. After hearing arguments from Miliukov and Guchkov, who favoured the continuation of the

[41] Avdeev, *Revoliutsiia*, pp. 54–55; Gavrilov, *Ocherki*, p. 96.
[42] Browder and Kerensky, *Russian Provisional* i, pp. 99–102.
[43] T. Hasegawa, *The February Revolution* (Seattle and London, 1981), pp. 548–99.

monarchy, and Kerensky, who passionately opposed it, Mikhail decided to forgo the opportunity of becoming tsar – at least until the matter was decided by the Constituent Assembly. Until such times as the Constituent Assembly met, Mikhail recognized full State power as being vested in the Provisional Government.[44]

On that day Miliukov on behalf of the Provisional Government sent a radio telegram for general distribution throughout the country, outlining the events that had taken place in the capital, listing the members of the new government and summarizing its programme.[45] He stressed this programme had been arrived at through discussions with the 'working population of Petrograd' and that the new government enjoyed the workers' support. It was on this basis, clearly, that Miliukov intended to claim legitimacy for the Provisional Government.[46]

The Spread of the Revolution

News of the revolution in Petrograd and reactions to it spread throughout the country in an uneven manner. This was in part due to the suddenness of the movement so that the new government had neither the time nor the opportunity to inform the population systematically or fully about the changes that had taken place. The areas which first received the news were the large industrial centres, because of their railway and telegraph links with the capital. But an important factor was that in the localities the tsarist authorities were still in charge, and in a position to withhold information about the February revolution from the rest of the population. Nevertheless, the events in Petrograd were soon felt throughout the rest of the country.

The Baltic Fleet

The revolution spread quickly to the Baltic Fleet, where events took a particularly extreme form as sailors took their revenge for the harsh discipline and poor conditions under which they had served. A mutiny among the sailors began at the naval base in Kronstadt on the night of 28 February. By the following day the entire base was in their hands, a number of officers including the Governor General of Kronstadt, Admiral R. N. Viren, being killed. Two days later the Commander of the Fleet, Vice-Admiral A. I. Nepenin, was shot by a sailor in Sveaborg port. In the first days of March the movement spread to the naval bases at Helsingfors and Reval.[47]

Moscow

In Moscow during Saturday 25 and Sunday 26 February there had only been rumours of disturbances in the streets of Petrograd. On the 27th newspapers

---

[44] *Kak sovershilas' . . .*, pp. 71–78.
[45] *Ibid.*, pp. 79–81.
[46] *Ibid.*
[47] E. Mawdsley, *The Russian Revolution and the Baltic Fleet* (London, 1978), pp. 1–21.

had received telephone reports of the revolution and the formation of a government from members of the Duma. On the evening of that day there was a meeting at the city Duma of representatives of Moscow public organizations and of workers. It was decided to form a Provisional Committee and appeal to the population for organization and order.[48]

On 28 February the newspapers ceased to appear, tramcars stopped running and meetings were held throughout the city. Crowds gathered round the building of the city Duma, where representatives of various local institutions met at 5 o'clock p.m., including the Union of Towns and Zemstvos, the War Industries Committee, the Stock Exchange Committee and the Merchants' Society. A Provisional Committee was formed, the elections for which had taken place during the day. As in Petrograd, a socialist organization, the Provisional Revolutionary Committee, assembled in the same building. Some military units also came to the Duma to declare their solidarity with the people.

On the morning of 1 March the demonstrations were renewed but now with the participation of many military units. During the course of the day, those units remaining loyal to the old regime were won over to the side of the revolution, only one incident of armed conflict taking place between the two sides. This was on Kamennyi bridge, where two soldiers were killed and four wounded. Throughout the day crowds of people, often aided by soldiers, disarmed policemen. The same day also saw the release of all political prisoners held in Moscow.

During the day elections took place in local factories to the Soviet of Workers' Deputies. This assembled in the Duma building at 7 p.m. and began to concern itself with questions of provisioning and the maintenance of public order. It received a delegation from the Vtorov factory, with the request that it order the resumption of work on the making of shells and other military supplies. The request was rejected on the grounds that ending the strike might lead to the restoration of tsarist rule.[49]

Late in the evening the orders of the Duma committee for the arrest of the military commander of Moscow, General I. I. Mrozovskii, were carried out. The city governor, General V. N. Shebeko, and his deputies as well as the police chief and his local superintendents were also arrested. In place of the city authorities a 'commissariat' was established by the Provisional Committee of the Duma. This consisted of a governor, Leontiev and his deputies. To replace the police chief and his superintendents five attorneys were appointed. Whereas the police force as a whole was replaced by a militia, most of city governor's staff remained in place to serve under the new commissariat.[50]

Kiev

In Kiev news of the events in Petrograd was received through the bulletin of the Petrograd Stock Exchange even before a telegram from the Duma Provisional Committee arrived on the 28th. Power in Kiev became centred

[48] Semenov, 'Fevral'skie', pp. 50–51.
[49] *Kak sovershilas'* . . ., pp. 90, 93.
[50] *Ibid.*, pp. 90–91.

in the building of the city Duma. Here on 1 March was created a body called the Council of Public Organizations. As this body was large and unwieldy, an Executive Committee was created, consisting of representatives of the city Duma, the Union of Zemstvos, the Union of Towns, the War Industries Committee, Ukrainian organizations, Jewish organizations, workers' organizations and the army.[51]

The chairman of the council was Starodomskii, a Kadet. He had three vice-chairmen – Barskii, Dorotov and Karum. Barskii was a Kadet and Dorotov, who was also vice-chairman of the Kiev Soviet, was a Menshevik. The chairman of the Kiev Soviet was Nezlobin, an SR, who had been the leader of the workers' group in the Kiev War Industries Committee, whose chairman was Tereshchenko.

As Kiev was close to the South-West front, the new regime was introduced with the consent of the commander of the military district, General Khodorevich. When the Executive Committee elected a commissar it was not to replace but to monitor the actions of the town governor. When the committee raised the matter of control of the police, Khodorevich contacted Prince Lvov and then consented to the closing of the local Okhrana and the uniformed police force. Khodorevich also consented to the establishment of a militia, and allowed members of the Kiev garrison to take part in the Executive Committee's activities.

The commander of the South-West front, General A. A. Brusilov, addressed a telegram to Dr Starodomskii, the Kadet chairman of the Executive Committee, appealing for calm and promising that General Khodorevich and his staff would subordinate themselves to the new government. He asked that the military authorities be regarded as appointees of the new government and not as enemies.[52]

The Baltic Provinces

In the Baltic territories information about events in the Russian capital came relatively late, because of their proximity to the front. It was only on 3–4 March that the population of Riga discovered what had taken place. By that time, however, they knew of the abdication of the tsar and the formation and composition of the Provisional Government. The news caused crowds to gather in the streets and meetings to be held to discuss the situation. It was learnt that a Soviet had been established as a counterweight to the Provisional Government and a means of control over it. The soldiers in Riga discovered from the Soviet's bulletin the contents of Order No. 1 and began to put these into effect.[53]

The Provisional Government in Petrograd recalled the governor of Livland and appointed in his place Andrejs Krastkalns, the mayor of Riga. In accordance with the instructions of the Provisional Government Krastkalns abolished the police force and replaced it with a militia.[54]

[51] A. A. Gol'denveizer, 'Iz Kievskikh vospominanii (1917–1921)', *Arkhiv russkoi revoliutsii*, 1922, vi pp. 161–70.
[52] *Kak sovershilas'* . . ., pp. 93–94.
[53] W. Lieven, *Das rote Russland* (Berlin, 1918), pp. 11–14.
[54] Ā. Šilde, *Latvijas vēsture 1914–1940* (Stockholm, 1976), p. 80.

From 26 February to 1 March railway and postal communications between Reval and Petrograd were broken. This fact alone caused rumours to circulate in Reval about what was taking place in the capital. On the 28th the commander of the Naval fortress, Admiral A. M. Gerasimov, issued a decree stating that events in Petrograd were insignificant disturbances and warning the workers of Reval not to repeat them. As a precaution against such disturbances spreading to the Fleet, Gerasimov issued an order to Rear-Admiral V. K. Pilkin not to allow his sailors on shore.

News of the events in Petrograd, however, reached the working population of Reval and, on 1 March, a number of strikes broke out involving some 17,700 people. On the following day the strikes continued and meetings and demonstrations took place. A demonstration by shipyard workers was joined by a training squadron of sailors who were quartered in the town. The demonstrators then made their way to the docks to join forces with the sailors. Despite the threats of their officers, many from the warships *Bogatyr*, *Oleg*, *Rurik*, etc., came ashore and joined the demonstration.

From the docks the demonstrators returned to the town. They opened the prisons and released the prisoners, attacked police stations and law courts, and the most hated of the prisons were set ablaze. Guards were disarmed and the weapons distributed among the demonstrators. There were several casualties in these incidents, one of them being Admiral Gerasimov who was wounded by a bayonet.

The destruction of tsarist authority in Reval and the release of criminal elements from prison had encouraged robbery and looting. At 4 p.m. on 2 March an extraordinary session of the town Duma was held. To maintain order in the town and protect private property it formed a Residents' Committee of nine members. The Duma also expressed its support for the new government in Petrograd. In the evening of the same day a meeting of Bolshevik and other political activists in the 'Valvaja' temperance society decided to form a people's militia. It was to be organized by the Bolshevik I. V. Rabchinskii, then working in the Reval War Industries Committee.

On 3 March a mutiny broke out in one of the Reval fortress's artillery regiments in the course of which six of the most unpopular officers were shot. Rear-Admiral P. N. Leskov, who had replaced Gerasimov, sought assistance from the newly formed people's militia. Rabchinskii addressed the soldiers and was able to restore order in the fortress.

Elections to the Reval Soviet took place on the morning of 3 March and its first meeting was opened at 3 p.m. on the same day in the 'Grand Marina' cinema. The Menshevik representative from the Fleet, M. Luchin, was elected chairman. The session was attended by two State Duma deputies, who reported on developments in the capital. Although some speakers registered scepticism about the Provisional Government, most representatives of the Fleet who were present gave it their support. The authority of the Provisional Government was extended to Reval and the rest of Estland on 5 March, when in place of the existing governor the Mayor of Reval, Jaan Poska, was appointed commissar of the province.[55]

---

[55] J. Saat and K. Siilivask, *Velikaia Oktiabr'skaia sotsialisticheskaia revoliutsiia v Estonii* (Tallinn, 1977), pp. 39–47.

Siberia

The first news of the revolution in Petrograd reached Siberia as early as 27–28 February through telegrams sent to political exiles. By 1 March telegraph information was received in Tiumen, Omsk, Tomsk, Irkutsk, Vladivostok and other major towns. Between 2 and 5 March news had reached all the towns in Siberia and the far-eastern region. By this time knowledge of the revolution had spread as far as Sakhalin and even Kamchatka.

The tsarist authorities in Siberia at first tried to suppress the information and made appeals to the population for calm. In the first days of March, however, meetings and demonstrations took place on the streets of Siberian towns. The police were disarmed, tsarist officials were arrested, and the many political prisoners held in Siberian captivity were freed. These then helped consolidate the new regime in the region. They co-operated with local WICs and other 'public organizations' to form such institutions as the Coalition Committee in Omsk, the Committee of Public Organizations in Irkutsk and the Committee of Social Security in Krasnoiarsk. It was often the chairmen of these committees who were appointed commissars of the Provisional Government.

Simultaneously with these committees, Soviets appeared in Siberia. On 2 March a Soviet was formed in Tiumen, on 3 March in Irkutsk and Omsk, on 4 March in Chita, Khabarovsk and Vladivostok. In all, between 1 and 5 March 20 Soviets were established in Siberia, and by the end of March there were 67.[56]

The Return of the Political Exiles

The amnesty which the Provisional Government granted brought back to Petrograd and other Russian towns many of the political leaders who had been in exile in Siberia. Among them were Stalin, M. K. Muranov and Kamenev, who arrived in Petrograd on 12 March, taking over the leadership of the Bolshevik Party from Shliapnikov and his associates. The newcomers were extremely critical of the policies which had been adopted hitherto by the party newspaper *Pravda* on the question of the war and the Provisional Government. Stalin, Muranov and Kamenev favoured a policy of monitoring the Provisional Government rather than of opposition to it. They advocated the formula of supporting the Provisional Government 'in so far as' its actions were in the interests of the working class. With regard to the war, the attitude of the returned Bolshevik leaders was one indistinguishable from defensism: they believed agitation against the war disorganized the army. In the issue of *Pravda* for 15 March Kamenev published an article condemning the slogan 'Down with the war!' and declaring that the Russian people would 'hold firmly to its posts and answer a bullet with a bullet and a shell with a shell'.

The new direction of *Pravda* caused an outcry by Shliapnikov and the

[56] *Istoriia Sibiri* iii (Leningrad, 1968), pp. 471–78

Petrograd Bolsheviks. Meetings were held with the returnees at which this dissatisfaction was expressed, and Muranov and Stalin felt compelled to dissociate themselves from Kamenev's views on the question of the war. Following these discussions the former editorial board of *Pravda* was reconstituted with the addition of the newcomers, and the newspaper's policy returned to its former anti-war stance.[57]

Shliapnikov in retrospect presents this episode as one in which Kamenev, Muranov and Stalin represented a current of opinion which was alien to the rest of the Bolshevik Party. This point of view has been perpetuated by later historians, Trotsky especially, who used it for political ends. But on a broader perspective it was the returnees' opinions which were the mainstream of socialist thought in Russia after the February revolution. The views of Shliapnikov and other Petrograd Bolsheviks, on the other hand, were exceptional, and maintained a precarious existence in the face of the overwhelming consensus of opinion throughout the country.

With the help of the German General Staff, Lenin was able to make his way back to Russia at the end of March. He travelled in a sealed train with a number of political émigrés whom the Germans thought might be useful in undermining the Russian war effort. Lenin returned to Petrograd on 3 April. Among those who came to the Finland station to welcome him and the other exiles were not only members of the Bolshevik Party such as Shliapnikov and Chugurin but also a delegation from the Petrograd Soviet led by the Menshevik, Chkheidze. Chkheidze did not miss the opportunity to urge Lenin to co-operate with the other socialist parties. Lenin, however, did not reply to Chkheidze directly, but made a short speech, predicting the dawn of the world socialist revolution. Lenin was then driven to the Bolshevik Party headquarters in an armoured car from the top of which he made speeches at various places on the way.

The St Petersburg Committee of the Bolshevik Party had its headquarters in the villa of Matylda Krzesińska, a former prima ballerina at the Mariinskii theatre, who complained bitterly and without avail about the use to which her home was being put. There Lenin began to outline his views on what policies the Bolsheviks ought to pursue in the coming weeks and months. These ideas were soon to be incorporated into a series of notes to be known as the *April Theses*. These constitute one of the most important documents of the Russian revolution because the course of action they urged on the Bolshevik Party was to help it come to power six months later.

The *April Theses* set out to determine the Bolshevik attitude to the two most important questions of the day: the war and the Provisional Government. On the question of the war, Lenin insisted that the Bolshevik Party must on no account give any support to defensism. He was of course aware that defensism was extremely widespread among Russian socialists, and even extended into his own party in the person of Kamenev, if not of Muranov and Stalin. Lenin recommended, therefore, that this mistaken view should be overcome by patient and persistent explanation that as long as political power remained in the hands of the present capitalist government, a truly

---

[57] A. G. Shliapnikov, *Semnadtsatyi god* ii (Moscow–Leningrad, 1925), pp. 183–85.

defensive war was impossible. A war conducted by the capitalists would continue to be an aggressive and predatory one. A genuinely defensive war would be possible only when power had passed into the hands of the workers and the poorer peasants.

In Lenin's view, the questions of the war and political power were intimately connected. As far as political power was concerned, Lenin argued that no support should be given to the Provisional Government. In his view this was a government of capitalists and it would inevitably act like a capitalist government. In particular it would conduct the war in an imperialist fashion, trying to make territorial conquests.

The kind of government Lenin advocated was a system of Soviets which would extend throughout the country at all levels. This idea was the peculiar contribution Lenin made to the political thought of 1917. Lenin did not advocate in his *April Theses* that the Provisional Government be overthrown. That was unnecessary, since all that was needed was for the Soviets to withdraw their support from the Provisional Government and declare themselves to be the sole authority in the country. In that way all power would pass to the Soviets. But the socialist parties who held the majority on the Petrograd Soviet had no intention of taking power. It was therefore the socialist parties, the Mensheviks and the Socialist Revolutionaries not the Provisional Government itself, that stood in the way of putting into effect Lenin's slogan of 'All power to the soviets!'

Lenin's conception of a government of Soviets was connected with the even more radical idea of destroying the existing State machinery, abolishing the police, the army and the bureaucracy. He advocated that public officials should be elected and, if found wanting, replaced at any time. He thought that the salaries they received should not exceed that of a skilled worker. In this way, he thought, the bureaucracy would be made answerable to the people and not become an independent and oppressive force. This was an idea Lenin was to expand in his pamphlet, *The State and Revolution* which was published in 1918.

Lenin was also to explain in *The State and Revolution* that since the State's function was to maintain the exploitation of one class by another, in a socialist system there would be no need for any State. Hence the State would 'wither away'. Before this happened, however, a temporary form of State would be necessary to enforce the rule of the proletariat over the bourgeoisie. This would be the 'dictatorship of the proletariat'. In Russia, Lenin asserted, this would take the form of Soviets.

But if there were to be a 'dictatorship of the proletariat' in Russia, did that imply that Lenin thought the country ripe for socialism? Before returning to Petrograd Lenin had still thought Russia too backward economically for this. But the *April Theses* seemed to imply that socialism might indeed be possible, and certainly spoke of the proletariat and poorer peasants taking power.

The *April Theses* themselves said very little about socialism, and that mention was ambiguous. Lenin simply stated that the immediate task was not to introduce socialism but to bring production and distribution under the Soviets' control. Sukhanov, who heard Lenin speak at this time, was left rather puzzled by the omission of any economic arguments to justify the policies Lenin advocated. The signs are that Lenin himself did not have any arguments of this kind.

Lenin and Trotsky

Lenin's *April Theses* came as a surprise to most members of the Bolshevik Party, but to different degrees and in different ways. To those such as Kamenev and Stalin, who had taken a defensist stance on the war and had advocated giving conditional support to the Provisional Government, the whole document contradicted their current political thinking. But for the more radical sections of the Bolsheviks – Shliapnikov, Kaiurov, Chugurin and other members of the Vyborg District Committee – Lenin's attitude towards the war and the Provisional Government broadly coincided with their own. It reminded them of their leaflet, *To All Citizens of Russia*.[58] The only element in Lenin's theses that was novel to them was the idea that all political power in the country should be transferred to the Soviets. It was an idea, moreover, that was not unwelcome.

In his autobiography and later in his *History of the Russian Revolution*, Trotsky was to claim that in his *April Theses* Lenin adopted the Trotskyist theory of 'permanent revolution'. In the latter work it is asserted that the ideas contained in the *April Theses* are identical to those Trotsky was putting forward in a series of articles for the émigré newspaper *Novyi mir*. One has only to compare these two documents, however, to confirm that no such identity of views exists. On the important issue of what the future form of State power will be, Trotsky and Lenin diverge radically. Whereas Lenin favours destroying the existing State, Trotsky advocates utilizing it to transform the country.

The contemporary significance of the *April Theses* was that they represented a break with the consensus of opinion within which Russian socialist parties operated in the spring of 1917. By doing so they seemed to condemn the Bolsheviks to perpetual isolation and insignificance. But in fact they contained the essential ingredients for eventual success. They dissociated the Bolsheviks from the failures of the Provisional Government, and they contained in embryo the programme of peace, bread and land which would be the things most desired by the people at large, and those which the Provisional Government had most patently failed to provide.

[58] *Sed'maia (aprel'skaia) konferentsiia RSDRP (bol'shevikov)* (Moscow, 1958), pp. 18–19.

5

The Provisional Government

The Predicament of the Provisional Government

From its inception the Provisional Government was undermined by the ambiguity of its status. On the positive side, it could claim to be the legitimate successor of the tsarist regime, since on his abdication it was to the Provisional Government that the Grand Duke Mikhail transferred his power. On the other hand, the Provisional Government was 'provisional' because it acted as the government of the country only until such time as the Constituent Assembly met and decided what form of government and constitution Russia would have. The Provisional Committee of the Duma had not ceased to exist, as the Duma had not been formally abolished; that was only to happen in June 1917.

Its caretaker status implied that the Provisional Government should not embark on any legislation that would predetermine matters which were the proper province of the Constituent Assembly. This limitation severely circumscribed the Provisional Government's scope for action and condemned it to inactivity on many key areas of concern to the population. The impatience and frustration which resulted contributed significantly to the Provisional Government's eventual downfall in October 1917.

But despite its commitment to deferring substantive reforms until the Constituent Assembly, the Provisional Government did nevertheless legislate on a number of important matters, which changed significantly the existing political conditions. In fact, it came to power with a programme of reform that had been put forward by the Soviet. The government justified these measures, however, by arguing that they were necessary to dismantle the existing unjust and oppressive structures of autocracy, that they were necessary as preparatory measures for the convocation of the Constituent Assembly or that they were necessary in the critical economic situation in which the country found itself. The Provisional Government, therefore, saw fit to legislate on some matters but not on others, and seemed to favour some social groups or nationalities rather than others. Naturally those who were not favoured became disillusioned in the Provisional Government and its good faith.

Apart from the ambiguities of its constitutional position, the Provisional Government's power was limited by its relationship with the Petrograd Soviet. While the Provisional Government had claims to authority, it was the Soviet that wielded actual power over the population. In a letter written on 9 March, Guchkov complained of the situation to General Alekseev. According to Guchkov the Provisional Government possessed no real power and its orders were only carried out in so far as this was permitted by the Soviet, which held in its hands the most important levers of actual power, such as the troops, the railways and the postal and telegraph service. It was, Guchkov stated, possible to say directly that the Provisional Government only existed by the grace of the Soviet of Workers' and Soldiers' Deputies.[1]

The state of affairs Guchkov described was widely referred to at the time as 'dual power', and usually in terms of disapproval, those on the right believing that the Provisional Government ought to be the sole authority while those on the left advocated that all power should go to the Soviet. The Menshevik and Socialist Revolutionary leaders of the Soviet Executive Committee, however, did not regard themselves as in competition with the Provisional Government for political power. Nor did they regard the Soviets as potential institutions of government. They saw their role simply as monitoring the activities of the Provisional Government and ensuring that its policies were in the interests of the ordinary working people. They did not think that this monitoring undermined the Provisional Government's prestige; on the contrary, they maintained that the control they exercised improved the process of governing the country.[2]

A special 'Liaison Commission' of the Soviet, consisting of the Mensheviks Chkheidze, Skobelev, Steklov and Sukhanov, and the SR V. N. Filippovskii, was formed on 7 March to exchange information and maintain close relations with the Provisional Government. Tsereteli joined the commission 10 days later when he returned to Petrograd along with a group of other exiles from Siberia. Most members of the Provisional Government were willing to accept collaboration with the Soviet in this way; but Guchkov and Miliukov found it irksome and degrading.[3]

Civil Rights

In its first few weeks, the Provisional Government issued a large volume of legislation embodying the measures proposed by the Soviet. These included an amnesty for all political prisoners, the abolition of the death penalty, the abolition of restrictions based on religion and nationality, the abolition of the gendarme corps and its replacement by a militia force. Women were given the same political and civil rights as men. In the provinces the governors and vice-governors were removed from office and replaced by the chairmen of the zemstvo administrations as commissars of the Provisional Government.

As the Provisional Government believed that zemstvo organizations would play a big part in the new system of local government, on 21 May regulations

[1] Revoliutsionnoe dvizhenie posle sverzheniia samoderzhaviia (Moscow, 1957), pp. 429–30.
[2] R. P. Browder and A. F. Kerensky, eds., The Russian Provisional Government 1917 (Stanford, 1961), 3 vols., iii, pp. 1216–19.
[3] V. D. Nabokov, V.D. Nabokov and the Russian Provisional Government (New Haven, CT, and London, 1976), p. 88.

were issued for elections to provincial, regional and *volost zemstvos*. *Volost zemstvos*, those at the lowest level, were to be established for the first time, having always been opposed by the tsarist regime. *Zemstvo* organizations were to be extended to Siberia, central Asia and other parts of the empire where formerly they had not existed. *Volost zemstvo* organizations, however, where established did not have a great longevity as they quickly gave way to the *volost* Soviets, with which they had to compete.

A law was passed in April giving freedom of association, making it possible to hold meetings or form societies and unions without special permission being required. This was followed by a law establishing freedom of the press, including a provision for a right of reply for those who considered they had been misrepresented. Various organizations and groups took advantage of the press freedom to publish their newspapers. The Petrograd Soviet published *Izvestiia*, the Bolsheviks *Pravda*, the Mensheviks *Rabochaia gazeta*, the SRs *Delo naroda*, the Menshevik Internationalists (the group to which Maxim Gorky and Sukhanov belonged) *Novaia zhizn'*, the Kadets *Rech'*, and the Provisional Government's own newspaper was *Vestnik Vremennogo Pravitel'stva*.

This legislation gave Russians a civic freedom that was quite unprecedented in their history. Nor were there many countries at the time which could vie with Russia for the liberality of its laws. Lenin could remark when he returned to Petrograd in April that now Russia was the freest of all the belligerent countries. It was to be in the environment created by the Provisional Government's legislation that the events of 1917 were to unfold. In fact, the dismantling of the autocratic structures of government was the prelude to the outbreak of a great deal of lawlessness throughout the country. The breakdown of authority in the localities meant that it was difficult for central government to have its decisions carried out.

One of the most important tasks confronted by the Provisional Government was to arrange for the convocation of the Constituent Assembly, and on 8 March a Special Commission was established for drafting the Statute on Elections for the Constituent Assembly. The Commission's work could not be done quickly, as there was no precedent for holding elections with universal suffrage. The Provisional Government had undertaken, moreover, that 'universal suffrage' implied the participation of women in the elections. The main questions to be decided were what kind of electoral system to employ, what the constituencies were to be and how the armed forces would take part.

It was eventually decided to employ a system of proportional representation for the elections. This seemed appropriate for a country like Russia, with a vast territory inhabited by different nationalities. The method had the additional advantage that the existing administrative division of Russia into provinces and regions could be used as electoral districts; if the first-past-the-post system had been chosen, then the whole country would have required to be divided anew into more or less equal constituencies.

It was intended that in the army the various fronts would serve as electoral districts, and as the elections could only take place during a lull in the fighting it was decided that the elections would be held in the autumn. The original date set for the elections was 17 September. But as the compilation of electoral registers turned out to be a lengthy process the elections were postponed until 12 November. In fact they were forestalled by the Bolshevik seizure of power in October.

Nationalities

In order to counter German moves to restore Polish independence, and in this way encourage the Poles to fight for the Central Powers, the Provisional Government hastened to issue a declaration to the Polish people promising unification and independence, subject to the decision of the Constituent Assembly. On 28 March a 'Liquidation Commission' chaired by Aleksander Lednicki was set up to deal with the practical implications of Poland becoming an independent state.

One of the Provisional Government's first acts was to issue a manifesto on 7 March confirming the constitution of the Grand Duchy of Finland granted by Alexander I, and promising its full implementation. Although many Finns hoped they would be granted independence, the Provisional Government took the position that it could do no more than confirm Finland's constitution, since it had no right to take action before the Constituent Assembly. The Finns, however, felt aggrieved, because soon after coming to power the Provisional Government had recognized Poland's independence. On 5 July the Finnish *sejm* resolved to take upon itself supreme power in the country. In reply the Provisional Government dissolved the *sejm*, sparking off a wave of strikes and demonstrations in Finland.

The Provisional Government regarded Poland and Finland as exceptional cases. It thought that to offer similar rights to other nationalities would have meant predetermining Russia's future. For that reason decisions on the constitutional status of other nationalities had to be postponed until the Constituent Assembly. Nevertheless, these nationalities did make their ambitions known to the Provisional Government at this time. On 18 March, a Lithuanian delegation composed of M. Yčas, P. Januškevičius and V. Belskii visited Prince Lvov.[4] Representatives of the Latvians and Estonians approached the Provisional Government to consider ethnic Latvian and Estonian territories distinct administrative units to be called 'Latvia' and 'Estonia' respectively. Only the Estonians were successful in this endeavour, the Provisional Government issuing a decree on 30 March uniting Estland with the northern part of Livland and the island of Saaremaa to form the territory of Estonia. Jaan Poska, the Mayor of Reval, was appointed commissar for Estonia, and a provincial assembly or 'Maapäev' was established.[5]

The Ukrainian question was to prove an especially troublesome one for the Provisional Government. On 17 March in addition to the other organizations already established in Kiev, a Central Council or Rada was set up by a group of Ukrainian intellectuals led by the historian, M. Hrushevskyi, with claims to represent the Ukrainian population of the region. This organization quickly

[4] *Pirmasis nepriklausomos Lietuvos dešimtmetis* (London, 1955), p. 44.
[5] H. Kruus, *Grundriss der Geschichte des estnischen Volkes* (Tartu, 1932), p. 208.

overshadowed the others, which had a mainly Russian, Polish or Jewish membership. To give itself some kind of legitimacy, the Rada convened an All-Ukrainian National Congress on 6 April, to which various professional, military and cultural societies sent delegates. The congress duly recognized the Rada as the supreme national authority. The Rada also received the recognition of the First Ukrainian Military Congress held on 5–8 May. That congress put forward the demand that there should be separate Ukrainian military units, and that a fleet should be recruited from both the existing Baltic and the Black Sea Fleets.

The Rada drew up a list of national demands which it presented to the Provisional Government by a delegation led by Volodymyr Vynnychenko. These included recognition in principle of autonomy for the Ukraine; participation of Ukrainian representatives at any future international conference involving Ukrainian territories in Galicia; the appointment of a special commissar assisted by a regional council to administer all provinces with a Ukrainian population; the formation of separate Ukrainian military units in the Russian army; Ukrainian to be the language of instruction in secondary and higher education; and the appointment in Ukrainian provinces of Ukrainian-speaking officials.[6]

As the response from the Provisional Government was unfavourable – not least for fear of creating a precedent which other nationalities would follow – on 10 June the Rada issued a defiant manifesto, its 'First Universal'. In stirring language the universal, without breaking links with central government, took a step towards proclaiming Ukrainian autonomy, asserting that the Ukrainian people on their own territory should have the right to manage their own lives. Shortly afterwards the Rada took a further step towards independent action by establishing a General Secretariat, headed by Vynnychenko, which assumed to some degree the functions of a Ukrainian Cabinet.[7]

The source of the Rada's popularity was that it appealed to the peasants. The Rada, they were told, would protect them from a redivision of the land with landless peasants from the north. And since it was not the Ukraine that had become involved in the war, Ukrainians were under no obligation to fight. This message was to assure the Rada of peasant support and give the appearance of a large following for Ukrainian nationalism.[8]

On 28 June a delegation from the Provisional Government composed of Kerensky, Tereshchenko and Tsereteli went to Kiev. After several days of negotiation with the Rada leaders, the delegates returned to Petrograd with an agreement that was approved by the majority of the Provisional Government. The government consented to recognize the General Secretariat and work through it. It also agreed that, although the land question remained a matter for the Constituent Assembly, the Provisional Government would respond favourably to the elaboration of bills by the Ukrainian Rada for the purpose of submitting these to the Constituent Assembly. The extent to which the Provisional Government had capitu-

[6] Browder and Kerensky, *Russian Provisional* i, pp. 375–76.
[7] *Ibid.*, pp. 383–85.
[8] A. A. Goldenveizer, 'Iz kievskikh vospominanii (1917–1921)', *Arkhiv russkoi revoliutsii* vi (1922), p. 177.

lated to the Rada's pretensions caused its Kadet members to resign and created one of the most serious crises to be faced by the Provisional Government.[9]

Foreign Relations

Among the conditions submitted by the Soviet to the Provisional Government on 1 March none had concerned foreign policy. In fact, to obviate possible conflict, the subject had been studiously avoided by both parties. Consequently, in that area it appeared that the Provisional Government had its hands free. Miliukov, the new Foreign Minister, was eager to emphasize that in the sphere of foreign policy at least the revolution had made no change; that there was complete continuity between the war aims of the tsarist government and that of his own. He also wished there to be the same continuity on the part of the Allies, and he stressed that he expected all the agreements made with them to remain in force, particularly the agreement on the Dardenelles concluded in 1915. He stated that the Provisional Government was just as determined to acquire Constantinople and the Straits as its predecessor had been.

The Allies, for their part, were favourably disposed towards the new regime. Recognition of the new government came quickly, the first country to recognize the Provisional Government being the USA, which did so on 9 March; France, Britain and Italy followed suit on the 11th. They hoped that Russia, under its new, democratic government would pursue the war more effectively.

The Allies, however, and especially the British, were much less enthusiastic about Miliukov's insistence on the continuity of Russia's war aims. It was the British, after all, who had tried for so long to prevent Russia's gaining access to the Straits. They considered that it would threaten their route to India. British interests required that, ideally, the Russians should help them defeat the Central Powers but should ask for no territorial concessions in return.

The Petrograd Soviet's leaders found themselves increasingly at odds with the policies being pursued by the Provisional Government's Foreign Minister. They were overwhelmingly defensist, and propounded the doctrine of 'a peace without annexations or indemnities'. Their views on what Russia's war aims ought to be were set forth in the Soviet 'Appeal to the Peoples of All the World' on 14 March. This appeal stressed the transformation in Russian politics that had taken place as a result of the downfall of tsarism, and suggested that this had profound implications for Russia's foreign relations since the chief pillar of reaction in the world was no more. The document equated the coming of democracy to Russia with the desire for peace, and with the renunciation of the acquisitive ambitions of governments. The new democratic Russia, the appeal promised, would oppose the policy of conquest of its ruling classes by every means, and summoned the peoples of Europe to

[9]   Browder and Kerensky, *Russian Provisional* i, pp. 389–92.

do likewise. Russia's objectives in the present war were only to defend the liberty that had been gained against all attempts to crush it, whether from within or from without. The appeal, in fact, was a classic statement of the defensist position.[10]

It soon became obvious that Miliukov did not have the support of his colleagues in the Provisional Government. On 9 (22) March the British newspaper the *Daily Chronicle* published an interview Kerensky had given to its Petrograd correspondent Harold Williams in which he advocated 'internationalizing' Constantinople. This caused considerable interest in British parliamentary circles, and when the Russian ambassador K. D. Nabokov was approached on the matter, he replied that Kerensky had merely expressed his personal opinion and scarcely spoke in this instance on behalf of the new government. Miliukov tried to counteract the impression Kerensky had given by stressing in the instructions to his ambassador the reciprocity of the agreements, and making it plain that the Provisional Government 'would on no account refrain from pursuing Russia's vital interests, set out in the corresponding treaty agreements'.[11]

But Miliukov's approach to foreign policy was not only opposed by the socialist Kerensky, but also by most other members of the Provisional Government as well. This became evident to the Soviet when the Liaison Commission met with the Provisional Government to discuss foreign policy matters on 24 March. The representatives of the Soviet put forward their arguments in favour of a defensist position, maintaining it was essential for the Provisional Government to make an official statement renouncing all war aims but defensive ones. They found an especially sympathetic audience in Nekrasov and Tereshchenko, who favoured issuing a joint declaration on war aims with the Soviet. Miliukov, however, defended the existing policy on war aims, but Prince Lvov, Tereshchenko and Nekrasov all made it plain they did not share his views.

After further negotiations with the Soviet, the Provisional Government's *Declaration on War Aims*, drafted by Miliukov, was published on 28 March. As a concession to the Soviet, it contained the statement that Russia did not intend the 'domination of other nations, the seizure of their national possessions, or the forcible occupation of foreign territories'. On the other hand, the declaration went on to say that the Russian people would not allow their country to emerge from the war humiliated or deprived of its vital forces. Tsereteli and the other members of the Liaison Commission were satisfied with the content of the declaration, but deplored the fact that it was published as a domestic statement for internal consumption rather than as a diplomatic note addressed to the Allies.[12]

Miliukov did not receive much support for his attitude towards Russia's war aims from the diplomatic representatives of the Allied powers. The

---

[10] *Ibid.*, ii, pp. 1077–78.
[11] N. Rubinshtein, 'Vneshniaia politika kerenshchiny', *Ocherki istorii oktiabr'skoi revoliutsii* i (Moscow-Leningrad, 1927), p. 360.
[12] Browder and Kerensky, *Russian Provisional* ii, pp. 1045–46; P. N. Miliukov, *The Russian Revolution, Vol. 1: The Revolution Divided: Spring 1917*, ed. R. Stites, trans. T. Stites and R. Stites (Gulf Breeze, FL, 1978), p. 65; I. G. Tsereteli, *Vospominaniia o fevral'skoi revoliutsii* i (Paris–The Hague, 1963), pp. 62–73.

British ambassador, Sir George Buchanan, favoured the internationalizing of Constantinople rather than its outright acquisition by Russia as Miliukov proposed.[13] The French ambassador Maurice Paléologue took a different view. He was less interested in keeping Russia out of the Straits than keeping the country in the war. He was much more supportive of Miliukov, and believed the Foreign Minister ought to take a firm line with the Soviet.

The defensist view was given added impetus by groups of French and British socialists who arrived in Russia on 5 April. They included Albert Thomas, Marius Moutet, Marcel Cachin and Ernest Lafont from France and Will Thorne, James O'Grady and William Sanders from Britain. Their respective governments saw the delegations' role as bolstering the Soviet's determination to continue the war and strengthen it against more extreme socialists who called for the immediate conclusion of peace. This latter current of socialist opinion had recently been much reinforced by the arrival of Lenin and other political émigrés back in Russia.

Besides the delegation of socialists, the British and French governments sent special envoys to Russia to encourage the war effort. The French sent Albert Thomas and the British sent Arthur Henderson. Thomas replaced Paléologue as ambassador but, although given leave to do so by the British government, Henderson declined to take over from Buchanan. Thomas was less sympathetic to Miliukov than Paléologue had been. The French socialist minister took the view that Miliukov's utterances served only to alienate Russian public opinion from the war effort. In this respect Thomas and Buchanan were in agreement.

Kerensky had formed the opinion that Miliukov's continuance as Minister of Foreign Affairs was having a divisive effect, and he thought it necessary to bring matters to a head. Consequently, on 12 April he made a statement to the press saying that the government was about to consider the question of dispatching a note to the Allies, informing them of Russia's revised war aims.[14]

Miliukov said he was prepared to deliver the declaration of 28 March to the Allies as a statement of the Provisional Government's position on war aims, but that he would accompany this with a note he himself would compose. Miliukov intended the note to eliminate the possibility that the Allies would interpret the declaration to mean that Russia was now willing to renounce Constantinople and the Straits. This was accepted by the other members of the Provisional Government, and Miliukov duly issued the note on 18 April.[15]

Miliukov's note stated that in the new democratic conditions which obtained in Russia, the pronouncements of the Provisional Government could not give any reason to think that the revolution which had taken place would lead to the weakening of Russia's role in the common struggle of the Allies. On the contrary, Miliukov maintained, the new concord experienced in the country had reinforced the determination to fight the war to a victorious conclusion. And while Russia would fully observe its obligations towards its Allies, the Provisional Government expected the Allies in their

[13] Sir G. Buchanan, *My Mission to Russia and Other Diplomatic Memories* ii (London, 1923), pp. 117–18.
[14] A. Kerensky, *Russia and History's Turning Point* (New York, 1965), p. 246.
[15] Browder and Kerensky, *Russian Provisional* ii, p. 1097.

turn to 'establish those guarantees and sanctions' which were required to prevent the outbreak of wars in the future.[16]

The April Crisis

Miliukov's note was published in Petrograd on 20 April. It presented the Bolsheviks with a marvellous opportunity to discredit the Provisional government and the moderate socialists at the same time by showing that the government continued to pursue imperialist aims. On 23–24 April, crowds of workers and soldiers took to the Petrograd streets shouting 'Down with the bourgeois government', 'Down with Miliukov and Guchkov'. The movement soon acquired a considerable scale. At that point Guchkov, the War Minister, and Kornilov, the Commander of the Petrograd Garrison, discussed what resources they had at their disposal in the event of an armed conflict. They came to the conclusion that they could count on 3,500 men in all against some 100,000 demonstrators. The difficulty Guchkov and Kornilov faced was that the Provisional Government was tied by an obligation not to withdraw the units of the garrison from Petrograd; nor were any new units allowed to enter the city.

At the height of the demonstration, a session of the Provisional Government took place at which Guchkov gave a report on the state of affairs. He stated that the existence of the government itself was not at stake, since 3,500 men could be deployed to defend it. It was not intended that government troops should take the offensive because the movement would possibly subside, and the shedding of blood might cause disturbances. But should there be an armed attack by the demonstrators there would be an armed response. This report was followed by a stunned silence, after which first Konovalov and then Tereshchenko warned Guchkov that at the first shedding of blood they would resign. It was made clear to Guchkov that he would receive no support from his colleagues for any use of force against the demonstrators. The incident convinced Guchkov that the Provisional Government as it was then constituted was incapable of dealing with the problems that confronted it. He was to resign shortly afterwards, and he and Kornilov, who also resigned from his post, began to devise ways to establish the kind of government which would free itself from the constraints of dual power.[17]

Within the Provisional Government the group consisting of Kerensky, Nekrasov and Tereshchenko, supported by Prince Lvov, had come to favour the idea of forming a coalition in which representatives of the Soviet would take part. Both Miliukov and Guchkov, however, believed that the Soviet's interference had enfeebled the government, and were firmly opposed to any coalition. On 27 April, Prince Lvov sent a letter to Chkheidze asking him to bring the idea of a coalition government before the Executive Committee of the Soviet. The SR leadership readily agreed, but the Mensheviks were much

---

[16] *Ibid.*, p. 1098.
[17] 'A. I. Guchkov rasskazyvaet', *Voprosy istorii* (1991, no. 9–10), pp. 205–208.

less enthusiastic. They were very conscious of the risks involved: they would be held responsible for the Provisional Government's performance, and by leaving the Soviet, Menshevik leaders would weaken their influence in it and leave the field more open to their rivals, the Bolsheviks. Guchkov's resignation on 29 April, however, added urgency to the situation, and at a session of the Soviet Executive Committee on 1 May, it was decided to participate in a coalition government, the resolution being most resolutely opposed by the Bolsheviks and the Menshevik-Internationalists.

As conditions for its representatives entering the coalition, the Executive Committee demanded that

1. the Government should in its foreign policy strive to bring about peace as quickly as possible without annexations or indemnities, on the basis of self-determination of peoples in conformity with the Provisional Government's declaration of 28 March;
2. the army should be democratized;
3. measures should be taken to combat the economic crisis by imposing State control over the economy;
4. an agrarian policy be implemented which would prepare for the transfer of the land to the peasants;
5. the fiscal system be restructured in order to transfer the tax burden on to the propertied classes.

The Executive Committee also demanded protection for labour, the strengthening of democratic self-government and the earliest possible convocation of the Constituent Assembly.

The first of these points would have made it impossible for Miliukov to continue in the post of Foreign Minister. But in any case Kerensky and his supporters had decided on a reshuffle of ministerial posts, and offered Miliukov the Ministry of Education. Miliukov refused and resigned from the government. After intense negotiations between representatives of the Soviet and the Provisional Government, the members of the new coalition were agreed. Of the 15 portfolios, five went to socialists: Minister of War and Navy, Kerensky (SR); Minister of Justice, P. N. Perevertsev (SR); Minister of Supply, A. V. Peshekhonov (Popular Socialist); Minister of Agriculture, Chernov (SR); Minister of Labour, Skobelev (Menshevik); and Minister of Post and Telegraph, Tsereteli (Menshevik). There were four Kadet ministers: Minister of Finance, Shingarev; Minister of Education, Manuilov; Minister of Welfare, Prince D. I. Shakhovskoi; and Minister of Transport, Nekrasov. There were also five non-socialist ministers without any party affiliation: Minister-President and Minister of the Interior, Prince Lvov; Minister of Foreign Affairs, Tereshchenko; Minister of Trade and Industry, Konovalov; Ober-Procurator of the Holy Synod, V. N. Lvov; and State Controller, I. V. Godnev.

The new coalition government stood to the left of the first Provisional Government in terms of personnel, having lost Miliukov and Guchkov, and reinforced the left wing which had been represented by Kerensky, Nekrasov and Tereshchenko. It also brought together the Soviet and the Provisional Government, ending the policy of 'control' and 'monitoring' of the Provisional Government by the Soviet. The coalition initially enjoyed wide popularity but, as the Menshevik leaders had foreseen, when the government failed to live up to its promises the moderate socialists were held responsible by the more radical groups for the unsuccessful policies.[18]

The Army

By the time Guchkov assumed his post as War Minister, he had already lost the initiative in exerting control over the army. He was tied by the agreement not to withdraw the garrison from Petrograd that had been made with the Soviet while he had been absent in Pskov negotiating the tsar's abdication. When Miliukov had told him of the agreement on his return to Petrograd, Guchkov had been horrified. Moreover, as telegraph communications with the fronts were controlled by the Soviet, Order No. 1 was quickly transmitted to all the armies before Guchkov had learnt of its existence. These were setbacks from which Guchkov was not able to recover.

Guchkov was instrumental in having Kornilov appointed as Commander of the Petrograd Garrison. This was a sensitive post, and clearly Guchkov wanted someone he could trust to occupy it. His first preference had been Krymov, but Krymov refused the post, being reluctant to renounce command of his Cossack division. In any case, by that time Krymov had acquired the reputation of being a representative of the counter-revolution, whereas Kornilov was believed to accept genuinely the new revolutionary order. This, to Guchkov's mind, made him suitable for the post. Once appointed, Guchkov explained that his main task was to create a reliable basis of support for the Provisional Government, and if not win over the entire garrison then at least to create in it some reliable units which could be trusted even in the event of an armed conflict. Kornilov, however, was able to make very little headway in this direction, and in retrospect Guchkov confessed that from the very first days of its existence he felt the fragility of the Provisional Government.[19]

With regard to Order No. 1, Guchkov at once telegraphed to Stavka, requesting that measures be taken to stop the dissemination of the document. He also had a meeting with Steklov and other members of the Soviet Liaison Committee attached to the War Ministry to explain to them the deleterious consequences that the order would have on military discipline. Most members of the committee were in favour of rescinding the order, but Steklov adamantly defended it.

Finally, a compromise was reached by which the order would be annulled with regard to units engaged in combat at the front, but would remain in force for units in the rear. Guchkov was reluctant to accept this compromise and, to gain time, set up a special Commission of Officers of the General Staff, chaired by the Deputy War Minister, General Polivanov, to examine the Soviet's proposal.

[18] H. Zand, *Z dziejów wojny domowej w Rosji* (Warsaw, 1973), pp. 13–14.
[19] 'A. I. Guchkov', pp. 200, 206.

The Polivanov Commission recommended that the compromise be accepted as the lesser evil. The Soviet subsequently promulgated Order No. 2 on 6 March, which stated that Order No. 1 was applicable only to the Petrograd garrison and that the soldiers' committees mentioned in the order should not elect officers. It also alluded to the fact that the implications of having elected officers was being studied by a special commission. In fact, following his clash with the Soviet on Order No. 1, Guchkov made the Polivanov Commission permanent. He foresaw that the Soviet would make further demands on the War Ministry to democratize the army, and he hoped that such a commission, consisting of military specialists, would provide him with telling arguments for rejecting the Soviet's proposals. Guchkov also made use of the commission in putting through the military reforms which he thought necessary.

It had always been Guchkov's conviction that the efficiency of the Russian army was undermined by the favouritism and nepotism which influenced the promotion of officers. On becoming War Minister he took measures to try to remedy this situation. On 2 April he issued an order stating that only outstanding ability, tested by service, should be the criterion by which senior officers were appointed.[20]

Guchkov began a campaign of military reform by dismissing a large number of senior officers whom he considered to be incompetent or unsuitable. In the course of this 'slaughter', 150 senior officers, including 70 commanders of infantry and cavalry divisions, were placed on the retired list. Apart from officers who were dismissed, some resigned of their own accord as they could not be reconciled to the new regime. Others were ejected through pressure exerted by the soldiers' committees, a procedure which Guchkov deplored and sought to discourage.[21]

While working in the War Ministry, Guchkov made the unwelcome discovery that the new revolutionary climate had infected not only the army rank and file but also the officers and generals as well. They were less willing to carry out orders and more inclined to safeguard their own personal interests, resisting service at the front and working only a set number of hours a day. Some commanders displayed a populist urge to parade their democratic sympathies before their men. Guchkov found himself in complete agreement with Kornilov's generalization that in units where disintegration was most pronounced, the lack of discipline was invariably due to commanders who pandered to the soldiers' anarchistic impulses.

As part of the democratization of the army, on 19 March the Soviet, in agreement with the War Minister, decided to appoint commissars to the Ministry of War, Stavka, the Commanders-in-Chief of the various fronts and to the Fleets at Helsingfors, Kronstadt and Reval. Their functions would be to try to remove causes of conflict between officers and men, and seek to ensure a smooth transition to a the new democratic regime in the armed forces.

At the end of April the Soviet sent Guchkov 'The Declaration of Soldiers' Rights' with the suggestion that he should distribute it to the armies in the

[20] Browder and Kerensky, *Russian Provisional* ii, p. 875.
[21] A. I. Denikin, *The Russian Turmoil* (London, 1922), pp. 146–49; Browder and Kerensky, *Russian Provisional* ii, p. 875.

form of an order from the War Minister. The Declaration stated, among other things, that except when on duty soldiers need not subordinate themselves to their officers, need not salute them, etc. In Guchkov's opinion, in some respects, the declaration went further than Order No. 1, and he found it completely unacceptable. To strengthen his hand, Guchkov gave the declaration to the Polivanov Commission which, consisting of military people, he assumed would be of the same opinion as himself. The Polivanov Commission, however, to Guchkov's dismay approved the declaration without any amendments. Guchkov steadfastly refused to sign the declaration right up to his resignation. On becoming War Minister, one of Kerensky's first acts was to sign the Declaration of Soldiers' Rights, though with some modifications to strengthen the commanders' powers.

During May, in his capacity as War Minister, Kerensky made a tour of the fronts, making impassioned appeals to the troops in an attempt to revive their morale and fighting spirit in preparation for a new offensive by the Russian armies. In April the Germans had recommenced military operations on the Russian front, which had been halted since the revolution. Taking advantage of the spring thaw, which isolated the Russian beach-head on the western bank of the Stokhod river, they launched a successful local attack, seizing the bridgehead and taking some 10,000 prisoners. The attack added urgency to the Russian plans to begin an offensive.

Kerensky gave the order on 16 June to begin the offensive. This was launched two days later on the South-Western front in the direction of Lwów. Initially the Russian forces had considerable success, especially the VIII Army commanded by General Kornilov, which was fighting against Austro-Hungarian units. This broke through the enemy lines along a 20-mile front and, occupying the towns of Halicz and Kalusz, captured more than 10,000 prisoners and 100 guns. But as the Russian troops advanced their resolve weakened, and minor attacks by the enemy caused them to fall back in confusion. By 2 July the offensive had come to an end.

When the Germans came to the aid of the Austro-Hungarians and counter-attacked on 6 July, the whole Russian army began to retreat in panic. Resistance to the enemy was put up only by infantry and cavalry officers; everywhere the roads were blocked by deserters. Discipline broke down completely as the soldiers killed their officers and robbed and pillaged the local population. The worst incident was at Tarnopol, where the fleeing Russian soldiers sacked the town.

The Agrarian Question

The land question was one of the most crucial for the Provisional Government, and one in which it was under considerable pressure to institute immediate reform. The government, however, considered that in such a important matter it was essential to wait for the decision of the Constituent Assembly. Nevertheless, pending the decision of the Constituent Assembly it decided on 16–17 March to take the preliminary step of nationalizing the Imperial Appanages and the Cabinet lands and properties. This was not a measure of great practical importance because the land belonging to the Imperial Appanages and the Cabinet had been largely used for leasing or sale to peasants.

However insistent the peasants' demands might be, no comprehensive legislation on the land question could be produced quickly. The country's vast size and the wide disparity in agrarian conditions made the enterprise a very complex and lengthy one. The 1861 reform had taken three years to prepare. The Provisional Government was determined, moreover, that in agrarian relations the rule of law must prevail; the land must not be redistributed by arbitrary seizures but by legislation passed by legitimate and democratic procedures. In recognition of the urgency of the land question, and in order to expedite future legislation on it, on 19 March the Provisional Government resolved to entrust the task of collecting all the necessary materials and information to the Ministry of Agriculture. A special Land Committee within the ministry would be formed to carry out this assignment.

Already by the spring of 1917 peasants were beginning to take matters into their own hands. The government received reports from various provinces of seizure by the peasants of the land-owners' lands and implements, failure to pay rents, illegal cutting of timber and disputes between members of peasant communes and individual farmers. Due to the breakdown in local authority, the government was powerless to take any effective steps to prevent incidents of this kind.

On 21 April the Minister of Agriculture announced that pending the settlement of the land question by the Constituent Assembly, a system of land committees would be established to prepare for the land reform and undertake urgent provisional measures. The committee attached to the Ministry of Agriculture, the Main Committee – its title reminiscent of the institution which supervised the 1861 reform – would provide general direction and draw up an overall plan of land reform on the basis of the information and views submitted by the local land committees. It was also empowered to restrict or suspend existing laws if these were likely to impede the systematic solution of the land question by the Constituent Assembly, and to abolish existing offices or institutions if these were found to be superfluous in the new conditions. This was a provision directed at the machinery created to carry out the Stolypin agrarian reform, of which the chairman of the Main Committee, A. S. Posnikov, heartily disapproved. The regulation also gave instructions for the formation of local land committees in each province, region and *volost*, the latter to include in its membership some representatives of the new *volost zemstvo* assemblies.[22]

The Main Committee proved slow and ineffective in drawing up a scheme of land reform. The provincial and regional committees tended to be dominated by the liberal *zemstvo* gentry. The *volost* committees, however, although voluntary, were established with alacrity by the peasants, who saw in them the prospect of land reform.

When Chernov became Minister of Agriculture in the coalition govern-

[22] *Ibid.* ii, pp. 528–36; A. N. Antsiferov *et al.*, *Russian Agriculture during the War* (New Haven, CT, 1930), pp. 57–62.

ment, he tried to have restrictions put on commercial transactions in landed property which might obstruct the Constituent Assembly in elaborating a future land reform. This was a measure which had been demanded by peasant organizations. Chernov was not able to issue any such regulation, however, because of the opposition from the Kadet members of the government, the land-owners and the land banks.[23] Prince Lvov in particular objected to the policies pursued by Chernov, and this was one of the factors which led to his resignation in July. Only on 12 July was the prohibition on land transactions issued. The buying and selling of land continued nevertheless.

Closely associated with the land question for the Provisional Government was that of food supply. This was a problem inherited from the tsarist regime, which found it increasingly difficult to procure grain and other agricultural produce to supply the army and feed the towns. This indeed had been a contributory factor to the revolutionary upsurge in February.

In attempting to alleviate shortages, the Provisional Government introduced bread rationing on 24 March. On the following day regulations were issued establishing a State monopoly on the grain trade so that all grain crops had to be surrendered to the State to be distributed through State supply organizations. Peasants were allowed to retain sufficient grain for sowing the next crop, and feeding themselves and their families. In return for the grain it received, the State paid the peasants a fixed price.

These measures did not succeed in eliminating the private trade in grain, where high prices were paid for agricultural produce. Inflation, however, made it increasingly less worth while for the peasants to part with their grain for money. As a result the market mechanisms became less effective in supplying the towns with food.

The peasants found the grain monopoly and fixed prices burdensome and often concealed their grain from the State collection agencies. They were prepared to reconcile themselves to the system, however, if they were able to buy at reasonable prices the manufactured goods they needed, including agricultural implements. But as the crisis in industry deepened, manufactured goods were increasingly scarce and expensive. The peasants were consequently unable to spend the money they received from the government in return for the grain on industrial goods. The money was left to accumulate in peasant hands, further fuelling inflation, and exacerbating the rift in market relations – never very deeply rooted – between town and country.

In order to improve the supply of manufactured goods to the countryside, the government announced in March that it intended to establish fixed prices on articles of prime necessity and make these available to the population at the lowest possible prices. In April a commission was established to examine the situation with respect to supplying the population with such products as metal goods, leather and leather goods, sugar, tea, kerosene, soap, textiles and paper. On 7 June, Peshekhonov, the Minister of Supply, undertook responsibility for the procurement and distribution of a number of manufactured articles of prime necessity. This measure, however, made little

---

[23] A. L. Sidorov, ed., *Ekonomicheskoe polozhenie Rossii nakanune Velikoi Oktiabr'skoi sotsialisticheskoi revoliutsii: Dokumenty i materialy* iii (Moscow–Leningrad, 1957), p. 225.

impact on the supply problem, and in May Peshekhonov expressed the opinion that its real solution would be State control of all branches of the economy: industry, transport, exchange and distribution.[24] This solution was not applied because of resistance from both inside and outside the Provisional Government, and the problem of exchange between town and countryside continued to worsen. By October the then Minister of Supply, Prokopovich, was contemplating the necessity of taking the grain from the peasants by force. He was spared this unpalatable expedient by the Bolshevik seizure of power.

Industry and Labour

One of the conditions the Mensheviks had imposed when consenting to join the coalition government was that the economic disruption in the country should be combated by the establishment of the 'planned organization of the economy and labour'. They had in mind the kind of all-embracing State control of industry which had been introduced in Germany during the war. The State monopoly of grain and the imposition of fixed grain prices had already gone some way in this direction.

The Mensheviks were especially enthusiastic advocates of State regulation of the economy. Their programme of measures had been elaborated by V. G. Groman, N. E. Cherevanin and other Menshevik leaders of the economic department of the Executive Committee. On 9 May the economic section adopted a resolution which demanded 'State participation in all branches of industry, State control of all enterprises and institutions'. On 13 May, Skobelev put this programme to the Soviet, only to be censured strongly by his ministerial colleagues in the Provisional Government.[25]

The socialist members' insistence of the coalition on measures to regulate the economy caused considerable friction within the Provisional Government. The minister responsible for Trade and Industry, Konovalov, reflecting the views of the Moscow business community to which he belonged, confessed to a 'sceptical attitude' towards the 'public and State control and that method of regulating industry' which was being proposed, and felt compelled to resign only two weeks into the life of the new government, on 18 May.[26]

The formation of the coalition government had profound implications for Russian business circles. Whereas under the tsarist regime it was the Petrograd industrialists who had close connections with the government, now the positions were reversed; it was the Moscow industrialists who had a special relationship with the Provisional Government, which they had helped create, and in which some of their representatives served. The Muscovites hoped to consolidate their victory by merging the Petrograd-dominated Council of Congresses of Industry and Trade into an all-Russian organization which Moscow would dominate. Nothing came of this project for,

[24] Browder and Kerensky, *Russian Provisional* ii, pp. 662, 633–35.
[25] B. M. Freidlin, *Ocherki istorii rabochego dvizheniia v Rossii v 1917 g.* (Moscow, 1967), p. 102.
[26] Browder and Kerensky, *Russian Provisional* ii, p. 670.

although an All-Russian Union of Trade and Industry was formed on Riabushinskii's initiative at the First Commercial-Industrial Congress held in Moscow from 19 to 22 March, the proposed merger never took place. The Petrograd industrialists refused to accept the Muscovites' leadership, and rivalries between the two business communities continued unabated.[27]

Spring 1917 saw a realignment of alliances between the Moscow industrialists and the political parties. The Progressist Party, to which the more liberal Muscovites had belonged, split into the Republican-Democratic Party – a right-wing group similar to the Octobrists – and the Radical-Democratic Party, a non-socialist party to the left of the Kadets. Rather than join either of these parties, which had limited appeal and were to prove ephemeral, Konovalov, Riabushikskii, Buryshkin and their circle formed a new alliance with the Kadets, Konovalov becoming one of its leading members. The Muscovites had long resisted association with the Kadet Party, but as the elections to the Constituent Assembly approached they needed to attach themselves to a political party with wide support to ensure that their interests, as a small minority in the country, would be given expression. The Muscovites were not alone, however, in aligning themselves with the Kadets. The collapse of the rightist parties following the February revolution had made the Kadet Party the only viable locus for right-wing currents. The attachment of this kind of support soon made the party the chief representative of right-wing opinion. This was eventually to discredit the Kadet Party and frustrate the purpose for which the Muscovites had allied with it.[28]

Although there was agreement between Petrograd and Moscow that there was a need to join forces to protect industrial and commercial interests in the difficult situation created by the revolution, there was divergence of opinion about what the main dangers were. The Petrograd industrialists, whose enterprises were located in the city where the labour movement was most active, were anxious about the growing industrial unrest, the activity of the factory committees and the inflated wage demands. They believed that the main task confronting industrialists was combating the workers' movement.[29]

The Muscovites saw the main danger to themselves coming from a rather different quarter. This was from the disruption of trade caused by government measures to regulate the economy. They thought that the grain monopoly and the imposition of fixed prices were wasteful and damaging to the running of the economy as a whole. In their opinion the government should allow the free play of market forces and not introduce regulatory measures, which in the opinion of the Muscovites were tantamount to the socialism advocated by Lenin and the Bolsheviks. The demands by the socialists in the coalition government for the planned organization of the economy were consequently most unwelcome.

[27] R. Sh. Ganelin and L. E. Shepelev, 'Predprinimatel'skie organizatsii v Petrograde v 1917 g.', *Oktiabr'skoe vooruzhennoe vosstanie v Petrograde* (Moscow–Leningrad, 1957), pp. 281, 297.

[28] *Torgovo-promyshlennaia gazeta*, 9 August 1917; V. V. Komin, *Bankrotstvo burzhuaznykh i melkoburzhuaznykh partii Rossii v period podgotovki i pobedy Velikoi Oktiabr'skoi Sotsialisticheskoi revoliutsii* (Moscow, 1965), pp. 69, 140, 366–73; V. Ia. Laverychev, 'Vserossiiskii soiuz torgovli i promyshlennosti', *Istoricheskie zapiski* (1961, no. 70), p. 42.

[29] Ganelin and Shepelev, 'Predprinimatel'skie', p. 283.

The advocates of State regulation in the Provisional Government, however, found a rather unexpected ally. Arthur Henderson arrived on the scene at the moment when the conflict had arisen between the socialist ministers and Konovalov. Henderson took it upon himself to acquaint the coalition government and the Soviet with the British experience of State regulation of industry. His intervention had the effect of dispelling the idea that State regulation of the economy should be equated with socialism.[30] In June, Henderson (on behalf of a number of British firms operating in Russia) requested that the Provisional Government institute a system of State control on the lines established in Britain.[31]

An indication that the Provisional Government was moving in the direction of State regulation was provided by the memorandum dated 8 June presented by the acting Minister of Trade and Industry, V. A. Stepanov. The document was at great pains to stress that the introduction of 'socialism' in Russia was not being contemplated. On the other hand, the government could not recommend the return to a free market, which had been demanded chiefly by representatives of the Moscow business community. The parlous state of the economy – the crisis in transport, the extreme disruption of the monetary system, the exhaustion of industrial raw materials, the strained food situation and the acute struggle between labour and capital – ruled out leaving matters to 'the free play of private interests'. Stepanov referred to the fact that both Germany and Britain had adopted State regulation of the economy, and even tsarist Russia, in a faltering way, had taken some steps in that direction.

The further measures Stepanov suggested that Russia might take were: the extension of the control presently exercised over products such as textiles, leather, paper, metals and fuels; the syndication of the various branches of industry in order to establish effective control over them; the imposition of wage limits; and the elaboration of a plan to make optimum use of labour.[32]

The measures aimed at regulating the economy were strenuously opposed by the industrialists' organizations. When, for example, proposals were made at the end of June for compulsory syndication of industry for State regulation, the industrialists objected and the Provisional Government did not pursue the matter.[33]

For their full implementation the measures outlined in Stepanov's memorandum had to wait until the Bolsheviks came to power. Then, however, they were interpreted in a socialist light.

In the establishment of planning institutions the first coalition government also anticipated the Soviet regime by setting up the Economic Council and the Central Economic Committee. The Economic Council was conceived by Skobelev, the Minister of Labour, with the aim of drawing up a general plan for the organization of the national economy and the regulation of economic matters. The Central Economic Committee was designed to coordinate and implement the measures decided on by the Council, and consisted of representatives of the various government departments. The

[30] Tsereteli i, pp. 197–99.
[31] *The Times*, 30 June 1917.
[32] Sidorov, *Ekonomicheskoe* i, pp. 220–25.
[33] Ganelin and Shepelev, 'Predprinimatel'skie', pp. 289–92.

Council, whose first meeting was on 21 July, did not achieve much during its short existence, except to serve as a precedent for Vesenkha, the corresponding Soviet body.[34]

The economic disruption of the country as a whole, which inclined the Provisional Government towards regulation, also determined its attitude towards labour problems. On taking up office, Konovalov at once announced his intention to implement the reforms he had long envisaged to liberalize labour relations. He promised that criminal penalties for organizing meetings and strikes would be abolished; that draft laws would be prepared on the length of the working day; that there would be comprehensive protection of labour, improvement of workers' insurance, arbitration chambers, labour exchanges, and other measures designed to promote the workers' welfare.

A serious obstacle to putting these reforms into effect, however, was the dramatic fall in industrial output in the war years. Labour productivity fell steadily throughout the revolutionary period. The reasons for this were well understood by the more perceptive of the industrialists themselves. The decline in labour's productivity was the outcome of the sum total of economic conditions in the country – the lack of raw materials, the shortage of fuel, the breakdown of the transport system and the disruption of trade. In this situation, a shortening of the working day or an increase in wages could only mean that fewer goods would be produced at greater expense, so exacerbating the problem. There was, therefore a reluctance by the government to legislate on labour matters and to compel employers to improve the condition of the workers, who suffered most from the economic crisis.

An obvious course of action for the government would have been to tackle the underlying causes of the economic decline. But the most effective way it believed this could be done – State regulation of the economy – was the method most resisted by the employers. The option which was left to the employers, in the attempt to prevent further decline, was to refuse the demands of the workers for better pay and shorter hours. This was to be one of the engines which powered the revolution.

The July Days

The popularity of the coalition government throughout the country in the spring of 1917 was reflected in the composition of the First All-Russian Congress of Soviets which opened in Petrograd on 3 June. Of the delegates whose party affiliations were established there were 284 Socialist Revolutionaries, 248 Mensheviks, 105 Bolsheviks, 32 Menshevik-Internationalists, 10 Jewish Bundists, 5 Popular Socialists, 1 Anarchist and 73 non-aligned socialists. The congress's first debate was on the coalition government, and the vote of confidence in it was passed by a majority of 543 to 126. The chief opponents of the coalition were the Bolsheviks. Tsereteli had defended the principle of coalition on the grounds that there was not in Russia a single party which was prepared to take power by itself. Lenin,

[34] Browder and Kerensky, *Russian Provisional* ii, pp. 677–78.

however, replied that the Bolsheviks were just such a party. Their small numbers at the congress made such an eventuality seem unlikely.

Before the congress closed on 24 June it created a new institution to replace the Petrograd Executive Committee. This was the Central Executive Committee – CEC. It was to consist of 300 members, of whom half were to be elected by the congress, 100 were to be local provincial representatives, while the remaining 50 were to be taken from the Petrograd Executive Committee. The new institution, however, continued to be dominated by the Menshevik and SR leadership.[35]

On 9 June posters signed by the Bolshevik Central Committee were pasted up in the working-class districts of Petrograd summoning workers and soldiers to a peaceful demonstration on the following day. The slogans would be: 'Down with the ten capitalist ministers!', 'All power to the soviets!', 'Control and organization of industry!', 'Down with the war!' and 'Bread, peace and freedom!'.[36] The Soviet, however, issued an appeal to the population, saying that it had not sanctioned this demonstration and that workers and soldiers should not heed the Bolshevik summons. The Bolsheviks duly cancelled the demonstration. The Soviet itself decided to hold a demonstration on 18 June. This event was a triumph for the Bolsheviks, as processions filled the Petrograd streets carrying banners demanding 'All Power to the Soviets!' and 'Down with the Ten Capitalist Ministers!'

On the day after this show of strength by the Bolsheviks and other leftist groups, the Provisional Government made a show of force of its own by sending troops to storm the Durnovo villa in the Vyborg district. Following the February revolution the former residence of the tsarist statesman was occupied by a number of left-wing organizations, including the Anarchist-Communists – many of whom had returned to Russia from emigration in the USA – the Social Revolutionary Maximalists, the People's Militia of the Vyborg District and the Bakers' Union. In order to recapture prisoners freed by the Anarchists the previous day, the villa was seized by government troops in the early hours of the 19th, and some 60 of its occupants were arrested. It seemed to the leftist groups and their supporters that the raid had been mounted as a reprisal for the anti-government demonstration of the previous day, and there was both anger and apprehension about this – at least apparent – onset of counter-revolution.[37]

There was also considerable resentment against the Provisional Government among the troops of the Petrograd garrison at the end of June. The failure of the offensive had led to the disbanding and dispersal of some mutinous and unreliable regiments. On the same day as the raid on the Durnovo villa, Kerensky ordered 500 machine-guns from the 1st Machine-Gun Regiment to be sent to the front. On the 21st, moreover, the commander of the regiment had spoken of 'reorganizing' the regiment and reducing it to only a third or a quarter of its present size. The machine-gunners suspected that the intention was to disband the regiment. The prospect of being disbanded and disarmed also faced the Grenadier, Moscow and Pavlov Regiments, and other units of the Petrograd garrison. There were indications

---

[35] N. N. Sukhanov, *The Russian Revolution 1917* (Oxford 1955), p. 384.
[36] Browder and Kerensky, *Russian Provisional* ii, p. 1311; *The Times*, 25 June 1917.
[37] *The Times*, 25–27 June 1917.

too that the newly created CEC did not intend to honour the agreement arrived at between the Soviet and the Duma Provisional Committee in March that troops from the garrison should not be removed from the capital. The CEC's military section had pronounced that 'reserve units should complement the combat forces on a general basis'. On 21 June, Chkheidze had accompanied General P. A. Polovtsev, the Commander of the Petrograd Military District, to persuade the 1st Machine-Gun Regiment to send their machine-guns to the front.

The technical expertise involved in operating machine-guns determined that the 1st Machine-Gun Regiment contained more ex-industrial workers than infantry units. Many of them had been metal workers in St Petersburg before the war. They were thereby more politically conscious than most garrison troops and had connections with the Petrograd workers.[38]

At the end of June among the Petrograd workers there was increasing discontent. This was due to rapidly rising prices and the employers' refusal to allow wage increases. In the second half of June, moreover, there was a supply crisis, as only a fraction of the food needed reached the towns. There were long queues to buy what food there was. Towards the end of the month a number of factories went on strike in several industrial centres.

The event which precipitated the political crisis at the beginning of July was the collapse of the coalition government. In the early hours of 3 July the Kadet Ministers Manuilov, Shakhovskoi, Shingarev and the acting Minister of Trade and Industry, Stepanov, announced their resignations from the Provisional Government. The remaining Kadet, Nekrasov, resigned from the Kadet Party rather than leave the government. The reason given by the Kadet ministers for their action was the agreement that had just been concluded between the Provisional Government and the Ukrainian Rada. But it was clear that the Ukrainian question was not the only factor which had led the Kadets to withdraw their support from the coalition.

One important consideration for the Kadets was the failure of the offensive, of which they had been the most persistent advocates. Hopes that the military situation would improve had been disappointed. And so too had the expectations that military success would bring with it a strengthening of order and discipline in the country. It must have seemed to the Kadets that the policies of the Provisional Government were encouraging the downward spiral into anarchy. On every issue the right wing of the government had been forced to capitulate to the left, sometimes with encouragement of the Allied representatives, Albert Thomas and Arthur Henderson. In this way Russia had been deprived of territorial acquisitions; the army had been 'democratized' until it was no longer capable of fighting; and the peasants were being encouraged to take agrarian matters into their own hands. By their resignation, the Kadets hoped to force the government to change course. The immediate consequence, however, was to provide the occasion for armed demonstrations against the Provisional Government.

On the morning of 3 July representatives of the 1st Machine-Gun Regiment prepared to go to the Tauride Palace to discuss with the military section of the CEC the plans to 'reorganize' the regiment. They were addressed by I. S.

[38] O. N. Znamenskii, *Iul'skii krizis 1917 goda* (Moscow–Leningrad, 1964), pp. 16–17.

Bleichman and other Anarchists, who called on them to overthrow the Provisional Government. The Bolsheviks at the meeting argued, on the other hand, that the projected street demonstrations were premature. It was nevertheless decided to proceed with anti-government demonstrations later in the day.

Delegates were chosen to go to the Petrograd garrison, the factories and also to Kronstadt to summon the workers, soldiers and sailors to take part in the demonstration. As the machine-gunners' regimental committee had not shown much enthusiasm for the demonstration, it was decided to disband the committee and form a 'Provisional Revolutionary Committee' to lead the regiment in the demonstration. Several Bolsheviks among the machine-gunners were elected to this committee, and took part in the work of organization, irrespective of the attitude of the party leadership towards the event.

In the evening the machine-gunners held their demonstration and were joined by contingents from almost all the factories and military units of the Vyborg side. The support of the Moscow and Grenadier Regiments was also enlisted, and while the main procession went to the Tauride Palace, others, led by the Grenadiers, headed for the Krzesińska villa, the Bolshevik headquarters. They were addressed by Ia. M. Sverdlov, M. I. Kalinin, N. I. Podvoiskii, and the Bolshevik machine-gunner I. N. Ilinskii and other speakers. (Lenin, being unwell, had left Petrograd on 29 June to return only on the morning of 4 July.) The Bolshevik speakers counselled restraint, a message which took on especial urgency when it was learnt that a column of demonstrators on Nevsky Prospekt had been fired on causing some casualties.[39]

It was clear that the demonstrations would continue on the following day and, in view of this fact, the Bolsheviks decided to maintain a presence in the movement's organization. A midnight meeting of the Bolshevik Central Committee, the St Petersburg Committee, the military organization, the Commission of the Workers' Section of the Petrograd Soviet and the Committee of Trotsky's Mezhraiontsy, who were at that time in the process of merging with the Bolshevik Party, resolved to organize a peaceful demonstration under the slogan 'All power to the soviets'.[40]

On the morning of 4 July the demonstration began in the Vyborg district, with the slogans suggested by the Bolsheviks on 9 June.[41] Delegates were then sent to the CEC to present their demands. Meanwhile a large contingent of Kronstadt sailors landed at the Nikolaevskaia embankment from boats and barges.[42] They made their way to the Krzesińska villa to hear Lenin, who had now returned to Petrograd, give a speech. Lenin appeared on the balcony and, apologizing for the fact that his illness allowed him to say only a few words, greeted the revolutionary Kronstadters on behalf of the Petrograd workers. He expressed confidence that the slogan of 'All power to the soviets!' would eventually triumph, and concluded by calling for 're-straint, steadfastness and vigilance'.[43]

[39] Znamenskii, *Iul'skii*, p. 74.
[40] *Ibid.*, p. 64.
[41] N. N. Sukhanov, *Zapiski o revoliutsii* ii (Moscow, 1991), p. 333.
[42] Znamenskii, *Iul'skii*, p. 95.
[43] V. I. Lenin, *Polnoe sobranie sochinenii* xxxiv, pp. 23–24; Znamenskii, *Iul'skii*, p. 96.

As Lenin later argued, this was hardly the speech of someone advocating a seizure of power, an allegation which was subsequently to be made against the Bolsheviks by the Provisional Government. He is most probably to be believed. For there could have been no Bolshevik seizure of power without Lenin's approval and encouragement. His absence from the meeting on the night of the 3rd had precluded this, so that any decision to stage a coup could only have been taken on the morning of 4 July. At that time, however, the future course of events was as unpredictable as the onset of the crisis had been the previous day. It was impossible to know what the alignment of forces on both sides would be. In these circumstances, the Bolshevik leadership was most unlikely to contemplate seizing power seriously, particularly when the party organization was so unprepared, being preoccupied with its merger with Trotsky's Mezhraiontsy.

Near Nevsky Prospekt at 2 p.m. the demonstrators came under fire from the roofs and attics of the surrounding buildings. Having advantage of cover, the attackers could not be reached by the return fire of the Kronstadters and they suffered heavy casualties. In the course of the day there were further such attacks on the demonstrators in different parts of the city. This incensed the Kronstadt sailors even further against the Provisional Government, and when Chernov was cornered by some of them he was rescued only by the courageous intervention of Trotsky.[44]

By the evening, the Provisional Government and the staff of the military district had brought into Petrograd troops from the Northern front, principally officer cadets from the training schools at Oranienbaum and Peterhof. Throughout the day there had been an intensive campaign by the representatives of the Provisional Government and the CEC to win over uncommitted units of the Petrograd garrison to its side. They eventually succeeded in enlisting the help of the armoured-car division. But most garrison units were unwilling to take the side of the government against the demonstrators.

As a measure to discredit the Bolsheviks and win over the neutral military units, the Minister of Justice, Perevertsev, leaked documents to the newspapers from military intelligence linking Lenin with the German General Staff. The information published consisted of the testimony by the Ensign Ermolenko, who had been sent through the lines to agitate in favour of an immediate separate peace with Germany. Ermolenko vouched for the link between Lenin and the German General Staff, and provided the names of secret agents in Stockholm who handled the financial transactions between the Germans and the Bolsheviks. Later, Lenin and Trotsky had no trouble in challenging the evidence on which the allegations were based, but at the time the supposed revelations helped to shift the sympathies of the garrison troops in the government's favour.

On the evening of 4 July there was another meeting of the Bolshevik Central Committee, the St Petersburg Committee, the military organization and the Mezhraionka. In view of the fact that troops were coming from the front it was essential not to allow another street demonstration. An appeal to the workers and soldiers in this spirit was duly composed and distributed.

On 5 July the CEC opened negotiations with the Bolsheviks to work out

[44] Sukhanov, *Zapiski* ii, p. 334.

terms on which the armed forces would stand down from confrontation. But after the Provisional Government learnt of the approach of the V Army from the Northern front, all agreements were ignored and early on the 6th a massive contingent of heavily armed troops was sent to the Krzesińska villa and the Peter and Paul fortress, where the Kronstadt sailors were quartered. On the morning of 6 July the sailors surrendered and left the fortress. The Krzesińska and the Durnovo villas were captured by government troops on the same day.

The Provisional Government ordered the arrest and trial of all those involved in 'the organization and leadership of the armed insurrection against the State power, and also those who incited and instigated it'. A small meeting of leading Bolsheviks on 7 July decided that Lenin should not stay to stand trial but should go underground. On 22 July, however, Trotsky and A. V. Lunacharskii were arrested and imprisoned. Soon after the July days, on Kerensky's orders, the 1st Machine-Gun Regiment was disarmed and disgraced on Senate Square as an example to other troops. Lenin's wife, who watched the scene, was struck by the resentment which the men conveyed. She was not surprised when in October the machine-gunners took the side of the Bolsheviks.[45]

The elements of continuity between the July and the October days provide an insight into the significance of both events for the way in which the Bolsheviks came to power. For them the experience of July, though traumatic, was highly instructive. It showed them what a seizure of power would involve, what kind of opposition could be expected and what kind of problems they would have to deal with. It showed in particular that in order to take power they would have to be assured of at least the neutrality of the Petrograd garrison and that some way would have to be found of ensuring that troops loyal to the government would not stream into the city and overwhelm the revolutionaries, as they had done in July.

[45] N. K. Krupskaia, 'Vospominaniia o Lenine', *Vospominaniia o Vladimire Il'iche Lenine* i (Moscow, 1968), pp. 471–73.

6

The Social Movements in 1917

The Peasants

The conflict between landlord and peasant was endemic in Russia, and outbreaks of peasant disturbances persisted even in the nominally peaceful years between the revolutions. The peasant movement in 1917 was a period of renewed intensity of the long-standing struggle in Russia for control of the land.

There were, however, some specific features of the peasant movement during 1917 that had been created by the downfall of the tsarist regime and the establishment of the Provisional Government. In the localities the tsarist authorities were removed and replaced by peasant committees in the villages and the *volosts*. The Provisional Government intended that these committees should be replaced by the organizations of *zemstvo* local government. The elections to these were to take place at the end of the summer and in the autumn of 1917. By that time, however, the peasants had found that their needs were adequately met by the existing institutions, and showed little enthusiasm for the *volost zemstvos*.

Even before the creation of the peasant *volost* committees, the Provisional Committee of the Duma, in an effort to overcome the catastrophic food shortage, had called into being *volost* and village food committees. They had been charged with maximizing the amount of grain taken to the collection points. Then, on 25 March, when the State monopoly on grain was established, the *volost* and village food committees were given the task of putting the monopoly into effect. They also had the important function of ensuring that all available land was under cultivation so that, if a land-owner failed to sow any of his land, the unsown area would be placed at the disposal of the food committees, which could then rent it out to local peasants at a fair price to be determined by the committee.[1]

By the Provisional Government's agrarian legislation of 21 April, land committees were established at the *volost* level. Between May and August over 4,000 such committees had been set up, comprising 88 per cent of the *volosts*. By the spring of 1917, therefore, there was quite a proliferation of

---

[1] R. P. Browder and A. F. Kerensky, eds., *The Russian Provisional Government 1917* ii (Stanford, 1961), pp. 618–22.

committees in the countryside, which created the likelihood of great confusion. The government's intention had been that the various committees would be brought together under the wing of the *volost zemstvo* organization. But this did not in fact take place.

The co-ordinating institution behind all the committees, whatever their function, was the peasant commune. It was the commune at its village and *volost* assemblies that elected peasant committees, food committees, land committees and other new institutions. The commune also decided on the legal status and sphere of competence of the various committees. In this way the commune acquired the various functions which had been given to the committees established by the Provisional Government. It had now acquired unprecedented powers, and it tried to increase these even further by arrogating to itself functions which had not been envisaged by the Provisional Government. Peasant committees tried not only to extend their competence but also to extend their influence upwards, using their representation on regional and provincial committees to pressure these higher institutions into swifter action on the land question. If historians of the peasant movement in 1917 have found that it is marked by relatively few outbreaks of violence and criminality, that is because, at least in part, there were so many opportunities for legal or semi-legal peasant action.[2]

Commune assemblies now became more democratic. They were attended not just by family heads but by women, landless peasants, labourers, teachers and refugees. Peasants who had gone to work in the towns increasingly returned to take part in village life, bringing to the countryside the political doctrines they had learnt in the urban environment.[3]

Peasant committees were not slow to use their powers to acquire private land which lay unused, perhaps through shortage of labour. The committees also took it upon themselves to regulate rents, not only for the confiscated land but also for land already rented by peasants from land-owners. They would fix a rent which, in their opinion, gave the land-owner a fair return on his investment.

One of the earliest and most widespread forms of peasant action in 1917 was the removal of the prisoners-of-war or refugees who worked on land-owners' estates. The peasants considered that it would be more just if the prisoners worked for the poorer members of the community. But since conscription had created a shortage of labour in the countryside, the loss of the prisoners and refugees was a serious one for estate owners. They might have to leave some of their land uncultivated and, in that case, it was liable to be confiscated by the *volost* committees and leased to the peasants.[4] There was a strong incentive for peasants to obstruct the efforts of land-owners to sow their land and generally make it difficult for agricultural work to take place. This was a common form of peasant action in 1917.[5]

Having in mind that the promised land reform was likely to deliver the

[2] V. I. Kostrikin, *Zemel'nye komitety v 1917 godu* (Moscow, 1975), p. 140.
[3] V. V. Kabanov, 'Oktiabr'skaia revoliutsiia i krest'ianskaia obshchina', *Istoricheskie zapiski* (1984, no. 11), p. 109.
[4] Kostrikin, *Zemel'nye*, p. 50.
[5] M. N. Pokrovskii and Ia. A. Iakovlev, eds., *Krest'ianskoe dvizhenie v 1917 godu* (Moscow–Leningrad, 1927), p. iv.

landlords' estates into their hands, the peasants were anxious that the value of these should in no way be diminished. They accordingly tried to prevent the removal or sale of any of the estate's equipment or livestock. Naturally they were eager to prevent the sale of the estates themselves, perhaps to foreign nationals, which would put them out of their reach.[6] As the peasants also coveted the timber in private and State forests, there were many instances of peasants preventing the cutting of timber. There were even more instances of the peasants themselves engaging in the illegal timber cutting.

In May a police report from Voronezh listed the kinds of illegal activities perpetrated by the peasants in the province: they obstructed the carrying on of private agriculture; they seized estates in whole or part; they grazed their cattle on private meadows; they damaged crops; they removed labourers and prisoners-of-war; they prevented the use of implements and livestock; and they set extremely low rates for rent, often insufficient to meet the bank's interest charges, and which they insisted be paid not to the land-owner but to the *volost* committee. They set inordinately high rates for labouring and prohibited the hiring of labourers from other *volosts*. They imposed levies on behalf of the commune, and they prohibited the cutting of timber, even for use in defence work. The report adds that these activities took place with the connivance and encouragement not only of the *volost* but also of the regional committees.[7]

Outright seizures of estates took place from the spring of 1917, and such incidents showed a general increase over the period from March to July. A special trouble spot was the Ranenburg region of the Riazan province, whose Executive Committee encouraged the local peasants to take over the estates and requisition seed, implements and livestock.[8] As a rule, the estates were taken over in an orderly way, with the land and its appurtenances being inventoried, and a portion of the property set aside for the land-owner. Violence towards estate owners was rare and only in the case of especially hated individuals. Even when the estate was sacked and the buildings destroyed, this was mostly done in an organized fashion. The sacking would be decided upon at a meeting of the village or even of the *volost* committee *skhod* before being carried out. Any goods obtained would be distributed equally according to communal tradition. Since the whole commune was involved in the sacking, no single person was considered to be responsible for the action; responsibility was placed by its members on the commune as a whole. As one might expect, the geographical pattern of peasant disturbances shows most incidents in those provinces where the communal tradition was most entrenched: in the central black-earth region where the land was most congested and agriculture was the main source of peasant income.[9]

In the northern industrial provinces a common form of peasant disturbance was the illegal cutting of timber in private forests. In the black-earth centre and Volga region, peasants would also graze their cattle on private pastures and cut hay on the land-owners' meadows. Agricultural strikes took place in

6. Pokrovskii and Iakovlev, *Krest'ianskoe*, p. 49.
7. *Ibid.*, p. 47.
8. *Ibid.*, pp. 12–13.
9. Kabanov, 'Oktiabr'skaia', pp. 113–14.

Livland and in the Ukraine, where peasant households were comparatively large and made wide use of hired labour.

Characteristic of the commune's renewed vitality in 1917 was the compulsion of those who had separated from the commune under the Stolypin legislation to return to it. Communal peasants had never reconciled themselves to the formation of *otrub* and *khutor* holdings, and in 1917 demanded that the laws encouraging it be revoked. Separated and consolidated land was reclaimed by the commune. Sometimes this led to violent clashes between separators and the peasants belonging to the commune, but in many instances the separators returned their holdings to the commune voluntarily. The consolidated land was redivided, and the separators were allotted one of the communal holdings.[10]

The communal practice of repartitioning the land was revived. The commune decided who was entitled to receive a share and in the more democratic village assembly land was rather generously distributed. Workers, who had returned from the towns to their native villages, were given a share in the land, reversing the pre-war tendency to regard migrant workers as being no longer commune members. About half of the refugees settled in Russian villages were given a share in the land. This practice, was, however, not conducive to productive agriculture. Arable land had to be divided up into an even larger number of ever narrower strips, thus exacerbating a problem which had existed before the revolution. The extra land obtained by confiscating the landlord estates did not compensate for the extra demand for land. In any case, much of the estate land was too far from the village for the peasants to cultivate.[11]

Agrarian disturbances reached a peak in July, then fell off during August to rise again in September. S. M. Dubrovskii, the Soviet historian of the peasantry, pointed out that this pattern of peasant action repeats that of 1905. He concluded from this that the fluctuation is in part at least to be explained by seasonal work in the fields.[12] The slackening of peasant disturbances after July also corresponds to the hardening of government attitudes after the July days, and attempts to put down the the peasant movement by force. During this period the government took measures against the peasant committees, carrying out arrests of their members and returning to the land-owners the land the peasants had appropriated during the previous months.

The government's inaction in instituting land reform prompted the peasants to take more extreme forms of action in the autumn of 1917. The supply crisis also caused serious unrest in the countryside. The renewed offensive by the peasants began in early September in Tambov province, where in the course of three days, 24 estates were destroyed. The Provisional Government responded with martial law in the province and military punitive brigades. Almost simultaneously violent seizure and destruction of estates began in Saratov. Besides the Saratov and Tambov provinces, individual cases of land seizure occurred in almost all of the black-earth and Volga provinces.[13]

[10] Pokrovskii and Iakovlev, *Krest'ianskoe*, p. 274.
[11] Kabanov, 'Oktiabr'skaia', pp. 118–20.
[12] S. M. Dubrovskii, *Krest'ianstvo v 1917 godu* (Moscow–Leningrad, 1927), p. 25.
[13] Pokrovskii and Iakovlev, *Krest'ianskoe*, pp. 269–73.

Despite the dispatch of punitive detachments, the seizures did not abate. In the middle of October a new wave of land seizures began which this time engulfed almost the whole of central Russia. It began in the Riazan province, where in the Ranenburg region (*uezd*) as many as 40 estates were sacked. Along with the mass plundering of estates in Riazan there was a massive felling of timber.

At the beginning of October widespread seizures of estates began in Nizhnii Novgorod province. The stimulus here was the shortage of grain, but often grain removal was accompanied by destruction of the estates. Thefts of timber and foodstuffs were common during the autumn of 1917 in the non-black-earth provinces, where provisioning difficulties were especially acute. Land-owners increasingly began to abandon their estates and to flee to the towns, leaving their properties to the peasants.

Because Russian workers were largely recruited from the peasantry and maintained links with the countryside, the workers' and the peasants' movements in 1917 had close links. Almost every factory in Petrograd had several *zemliachestvos* of workers from Smolensk, Kostroma, Riazan, etc. Through these organizations during 1917 the urban workers were able to exert some influence on what took place in the villages. According to a prominent member of the Smolensk *zemliachestvo*, their main aim in 1917 was to help the peasants of their particular province make sense of the revolutionary events and to make sense of the Provisional Government's policies. They did this by corresponding with the villages, sending representatives to peasant congresses and the dispatch of political literature to the countryside. Within the *zemliachestvos* there was a contest for influence between the Bolshevik and Socialist Revolutionary Parties. Their membership grew throughout the year, there being 21 *zemliachestvos* with 30,000 members on the eve of the October revolution.[14]

The Workers

The Democratic Regime in the Factories

When the workers returned to the factories after the February revolution, they were determined that things should not continue as before. They wanted improved pay and conditions and shorter working hours. They wanted in particular the introduction of an eight-hour working day. The Petrograd workers were supported in these expectations by the Petrograd Soviet. On 10 March, delegated by the Executive Committee, Gvozdev, who had collaborated with Guchkov and Konovalov on the Central War Industries Committee, negotiated with the Petrograd Society of Factory Owners. He assured them that if they agreed to the introduction of an eight-hour working day and higher wages, this would pacify the workers, and they would go back to normal working. The Society of Factory Owners assented, and signed an agreement introducing an eight-hour working day in factories belonging to members of the society, consenting to the establishment of conciliation

[14] I. G. Gavrilov, 'Na vyborgskoi storone v 1914–1917 gg.', *Krasnaia letopis'* (1927, no. 2), p. 56.

chambers and recognizing the workers' factory committees. The society added that these arrangements would be temporary until a decision for the whole country was reached.[15]

In Moscow the Soviet tried to repeat the success of its Petrograd counterpart, but to no avail. When its representatives met the Moscow Trade-Industry Committee on 14 March they were told by Tretiakov, Riabushinskii and S. I. Chetverikov that the question of the eight-hour working day was not a matter for an agreement between employers and workers but one which had a significance for the whole nation. On those grounds they refused to agree to an eight-hour working day in Moscow. The workers, however, instituted unilaterally an eight-hour day in many of the factories.

In other parts of the country the eight-hour working day was introduced unevenly. In Kiev the Soviet urged caution in establishing an eight-hour day as it did not want to over-estimate its strength. In the Donbass the coal-owners refused to introduce it. The miners for their part agreed to work beyond eight hours a day but declared that they would consider work performed after eight hours as overtime. The Baku oil producers consented to introduce the eight-hour working day in principle, but encouraged their employees to work overtime.

The question of higher wages was a cardinal one for all workers following the February revolution. In some cases during March they managed to obtain wage increases of 35–50 per cent. During the war large differentials had appeared between skilled and unskilled workers, and between men and women. At the beginning of 1917 an unskilled worker earned around 2–3 rubles a day, while a fitter or a turner received 15–18 rubles. Women in the metal-working industry got between 1.50 and 1.75 rubles a day. Even doing the same job women were paid considerably less than men.

Immediately following the revolution a campaign was launched to establish a minimum wage. This was achieved on 22 April, when minimum daily rates were established of 5 rubles for a man and 4 rubles for a woman. Many industrialists interpreted this as a maximum beyond which wages need not rise. But in many cases employers, especially those in small concerns, simply ignored the regulation.

Although between February and October workers might achieve wage increases of 50–100 per cent, price rises for food and other articles of prime necessity were running on average at about 110 per cent. Rents had risen by over 300 per cent compared with the pre-war level. Real wages for most workers fell in the period.

Even if they had the money to buy them, in 1917 supplies of food and other necessities were difficult to obtain. There was a chronic shortage of bread caused by the shortfall in grain deliveries to the towns. The situation was made worse by the closure of many bakeries, which had refused to implement the eight-hour working day and concede wage increases. In Petrograd only 60 per cent of the bread required was produced. There were shortages of items such as kerosene, clothing and shoes. Long queues formed when these items were on sale. Never having enough to eat, because of the inordinate rise in prices and the constant shortages, led to an increase in morbidity in the

---

[15] Browder and Kerensky, *Russian Provisional* ii, pp. 712–13.

population, especially among the children of workers.[16]

As a means of preventing strikes, the Provisional Government established conciliation chambers to settle disputes between workers and employers. The idea of conciliation had been a favourite one of Konovalov and Gvozdev, dating from their collaboration on the WICs. The conciliation chambers were concerned immediately after the February revolution not only with wage claims but also with requests for reinstatement by managers and supervisory staff of the factories, who had been expelled by the workers. These were people who had in the past acted unfairly, cruelly or rudely towards the workers, or had even betrayed the more political active workers to the police or the Okhrana. The cases for reinstatement were heard in the conciliation chambers, the workers presenting their evidence for past grievances. The procedure became in effect a trial of the tsarist regime in industry, and in fact very few of the cases heard ended in conciliation. In most instances the workers' allegations were upheld.

The Factory Committees

The factory committees were institutions that emerged during the February revolution and they were to play an important part in the workers' movement during 1917. Like the Soviets, they provided a form of organization for the workers and a means of representing worker interests. They were elected at open meetings of the factory and often each shop or section of the works was represented on the committee. The committees usually had a membership of 40–50, but there might be as few as five or as many as 100. In the State-owned factories in Petrograd working on defence production, the formation of factory committees was encouraged by the flight of the management, which feared – not without grounds – reprisals from the workers for their behaviour in the past. Such factories gained early a taste of what it was like to keep the factories running by themselves, an experience that would become more widespread with the passage of time.

Factory committees were recognized by the agreement made between the Provisional Government and the Petrograd Society of Factory Owners on 12 March. In the document the functions of factory committees had been defined as being to:

1. represent workers of a given enterprise in their relations with the government or public institutions;
2. formulate opinions on questions pertaining to the workers' socio-economic life in a given enterprise;
3. settle problems arising from workers' interpersonal relations in a given enterprise; and
4. represent workers before management in matters concerning labour–management relations.

On 23 April the Provisional Government issued a law recognizing factory

---

[16] I. A. Baklanova, *Rabochie Petrograda v period mirnogo razvitiia revoliutsii (mart–iiun' 1917 g.)* (Leningrad, 1978), pp. 40–53.

committees and defining their functions based on the principles agreed between the Petrograd Soviet and the Petrograd employers on 12 March. In practice, however, the factory committees paid little attention to the written law, and acted according to constitutions which they themselves drew up.

One of the factory committees' chief concerns was a matter which did not appear among the functions they were allowed in law: hiring and firing. They were anxious that none of the management staff they had excluded should be re-employed at the factory; and they were eager that no disruptive elements would be hired which would impair the factory's efficiency. Naturally, the workers were vitally concerned about layoffs, and they were anxious to satisfy themselves that these were absolutely necessary when they occurred.

Factory committees engaged in a wide range of activities arising from the needs of factory workers. Often the factory committees would give rise to a number of commissions specializing in particular spheres. A common concern of the committees was provisioning and the supply of workers at the factory with food and other necessities. Some factories devoted part of their production to goods, such as agricultural implements, which could be given to the peasants in exchange for grain. Factory committees sometimes looked after health provision and the maintenance of safety and hygiene at the factory. They were also involved in providing cultural and educational facilities for the workers. At the Baltic factory in Petrograd, for example, the cultural-educational commission ran primary education courses for the women workers with the help of the young ladies from the Bestuzhev Courses.

In the provinces the factory committees played less of a part than in Petrograd and Moscow. Outside the capital, however, the Soviets were more subject to pressure from below, and these carried out the functions performed by the factory committees in the capital: they looked after provisioning problems, took measures to prevent lockouts and factory closures and they tried to obtain necessary supplies of raw materials and fuel for the enterprises in their area. At many factories in the Urals, in fact, Soviets were constructed in the same way as factory committees elsewhere, with representatives being elected from each shop or section. In the Donbass many local Soviets were centred on the mines, and their activities were concentrated on keeping them in production.[17]

In Kronstadt the dockyard factory committees and foundries worked in concert with the local Soviet. The two organizations had divided their activities into two branches: one political and the other industrial. The Kronstadt factory committees, according to a contemporary observer, claimed and exercised the right to inspect the management's books and accounts, saw to it that no materials left the premises without good reason and in general ways looked after the welfare of the industry and its members.[18]

[17] B. M. Freidlin, *Ocherki istorii rabochego dvizheniia v Rossii v 1917 g.* (Moscow, 1967), pp. 111–17.
[18] M. Philips Price, *My Reminiscences of the Russian Revolution* (London, 1921), p. 89.

'Workers' Control'

During 1917 factory committees became increasingly involved in workers' control of production and distribution. This arose out of the worsening economic situation. Wage increases were refused because of falling labour productivity. This in turn was caused by the lack of fuel, raw materials and transport to convey the supplies to the factory. By the summer of 1917 lack of raw materials and fuel in the Petersburg region caused 40 per cent of the workers' time to be spent idle, when the workers would not be paid. In the worst cases the factory had to close down completely through lack of supplies, orders or finance.

The workers felt that the management was not doing enough to tackle the problems they could observe at first hand. They were insufficiently energetic in securing orders, looking for fuel and chasing up supplies of raw materials. They believed that management ought to eliminate the inefficiencies and waste in the use of existing resources.

Factory committees increasingly took upon themselves the functions they thought management was failing to perform. Factory committees sent out delegations to look for supplies of fuel and to track down missing raw materials. They contacted other factories in an effort to gain the articles they needed. They kept discipline within the factory and penalized fellow workers for lateness, absenteeism and drunkenness. In this way the factory committees tried to keep their enterprises running and thus provide a livelihood for the workers.[19]

Despite the efforts of the factory committees to preserve their factories in the difficult economic climate, the factory owners did not view the factory committees as allies. The employers tended to view the workers' interference as part of the problem rather than the solution. They saw the factory committees as manifestations of anarchy and, leaving out of account the rising rate of inflation, accused them of making unreasonable wage demands. Employers tended to see the main economic problem as falling labour productivity, and tried to find means of tackling this rather than the supply difficulties which undermined the productivity of labour. In this respect the workers were right in thinking that employers did not try hard enough to obtain raw materials and fuel.

When, for example, the factory committee of the Petrograd Admiralty Shipbuilding Works met at the beginning of August in the presence of the management, the factory owners' perspective dominated. The discussion centred round the causes for the decline in labour productivity, the reasons suggested giving a concrete insight into the conditions of the time. One engineer proposed that labour productivity was low because the workers tired themselves out with politics. He also thought, however, that an important factor was the lack of bread: besides not having enough to eat (thus impairing their strength), people tended to conserve their energy to queue for necessities. They were also afraid of unemployment and tried to prolong the work they had. The consensus of the meeting was that the reintroduction of piece rates should be explored.[20]

[19] P. N. Amosov *et al.*, eds., *Oktiabr'skaia revoliutsiia i fabzavkomy* i (Moscow, 1927), p. 81.
[20] I. I. Mints *et al.*, eds., *Fabrichno-zavodskie komitety Petrograda v 1917 godu. Protokoly* (Moscow, 1979), pp. 81–82.

Employers also thought that the economic situation would be remedied if discipline could be restored in the factories, perhaps by giving the workers an object lesson in a taste of unemployment. This was the course of action suggested by N. N. Kutler, the chairman of the Council of Congresses of Industry and Trade, when he addressed the Provisional Government on 10 May. Many workers suspected that these political motives were behind factory closures rather than objective economic causes. These suspicions created the need for another aspect of workers' control: to monitor how the factory was being run and to forestall any attempt at sabotage by management.

The factory committees' functions were discussed at the First Conference of Petrograd Factory Committees, which opened in the Tauride Palace on 30 May. There were 600 delegates from 367 factory committees of Petrograd and its environs. The dislocation of the economy, which was causing such hardship to the workers, had led many delegates to the conclusion that the only means of remedying the situation was to intensify the movement for workers' control, uniting the factory committees into an organization that would embrace the whole of the country.

In his address to the conference, the Minister of Labour, Skobelev, maintained that regulation of the economy was not the affair of a separate class but of the State as a whole. The working class's obligation was to assist the State in an organized way, through their trade unions. Lenin in his brief contribution disagreed with these views, arguing that because the State was a capitalist organization State control of industry could only be capitalist control, and hence no improvement on what already existed. Real control of the economy, Lenin asserted, was workers' control. The implication that Lenin favoured a decentralized method of regulating the economy was quite misleading; his own preferred policy, and the one which would be introduced when the Bolsheviks came to power, was State control. On this occasion Lenin was simply playing to the galleries.

At the First Conference of Factory Committees, however, the Bolshevik resolution was carried overwhelmingly. The conference elected a central institution – the Central Council of Factory Committees – of whose 25 members 19 were Bolsheviks. The factory committees were to be a strong base of Bolshevik support in 1917. And the Bolshevik Party for its part was quick to try to capitalize on this support. The abortive Bolshevik demonstration of 10 June proposed slogans which emerged from the Conference of Factory Committees: 'Down with the anarchy in industry and the lockouts of the capitalists!', 'Hail the control and organization of industry!'[21]

The Trade Unions

Immediately after the February revolution trade unions began to be established rapidly in Petrograd and in other towns throughout the country, especially during March and April. In this period about 30 unions were formed in Petrograd with a total membership of around 200,000 people. One of the first to be formed was the Bakers' Union on 5 March, with its headquarters in the Durnovo villa. The textile workers, who were over-

---

[21] Browder and Kerensky, *Russian Provisional* iii, p. 1313.

whelmingly women, held the inaugural meeting of their union on 11 March. In April it had 10,000 members; in June, 25,000 and by July, 28,000. One of the biggest was the Union of Metalworkers, which had its inaugural meeting on 12 March with 2,000 people in attendance. By the middle of April it had 50,000 members (25 per cent of all the metalworkers in Petrograd), and by June it had 126,000. Shliapnikov was elected to the Union's Executive Commission in May.[22]

Initially many small craft unions were formed, but mergers took place throughout 1917 in attempts to form unions uniting entire branches of production. By June, when the Third All-Russian Conference of Trade Unions met, there were in the country as a whole 967 unions uniting 1,475,429 people. The conference decided in principle to encourage the formation of production unions. It elected an All-Russian Central Council of Trade Unions (ARCCTU) consisting of 16 Bolsheviks, 16 Mensheviks and 3 SRs.[23]

The relationship between the trade unions and the factory committees was a constant subject for debate within the labour movement during 1917. It was discussed extensively at the First Conference of Factory Committees, where D. B. Riazanov argued that the factory committees' role was ephemeral, that they should constitute the primary cell of the trade unions. This was in general the opinion of the Mensheviks, represented at the conference by B. V. Avilov and Cherevanin, who advocated the policy of State regulation of the economy. The majority of the conference delegates, however, took the view that the factory committees had a special role in keeping the factories running, and exercising control over production and distribution – something the trade unions were still unable to do. It was resolved that the factory committees should have friendly relations and working contacts with the trade unions.

By the time the Second Congress of Factory Committees met between 7 and 12 August, the economic situation had deteriorated considerably. A large number of firms had closed down and many workers had become unemployed. The figures, while incomplete, present eloquently the picture of the decline of Russian industry (Table 6.1).

Table 6.1   The decline of Russian industry, 1917

Month	Works closed	Discharged	Workforce (average)
March	74	6,644	90
April	55	2,816	51
May	108	8,701	81
June	125	38,755	310
July	206	47,754	232
Total	568	104,670	184

[22] Baklanova, *Rabochie*, pp. 154–58; Freidlin, *Ocherki*, pp. 165–83.
[23] Baklanova, *Rabochie*, pp. 170–71.

The figures suggest that there was an escalation not only in the numbers of enterprises closing but also in the scale of the enterprises which closed, smaller firms falling victim first, to be followed by the larger ones in later months. In the majority of cases the reason cited for closure was the lack of raw materials and fuel; this was followed by lack of orders, and only 57 firms cited 'unreasonable wage demands' as reasons for closure. Nevertheless, in the period after the July days the employers had gone over to the offensive, and increasingly demanded that the activity of the factory committees be restricted. On 28 August Skobelev issued a circular prohibiting factory committees from interfering in the hiring and firing of workers.[24]

Rising unemployment caused divisions to appear among the workers' ranks. Some workers felt that if there had to be layoffs, married women should be discharged first. There was animosity towards Chinese labourers, whose low wages caused them to displace local workers.

The prospect of unemployment prompted demands to be made at the Second Conference of Factory Committees for State aid to unemployed workers. Since it was unlikely this would be provided, the implications were discussed of how the unemployed would actually find a means of subsistence: by returning to the villages, as many were to do at that time, particularly those who had close connections with the countryside. The influx of unemployed workers, of course, increased the peasants' need for more land and encouraged them to seize land from the land-owners and the peasant separators. Unemployment, or the threat of unemployment, made all urban workers vitally interested in the speedy transfer of all land to the peasantry. It is significant that the same economic pressures which intensified the movement for workers' control were also the ones which added urgency to the peasants' seizures of the land-owners' estates.[25]

The Strike Movement

With the deterioration of the economy and the spread of unemployment, the workers tended to intervene more in the enterprises in which they were employed. They not only tried to facilitate the running of the factory and keep a close watch on management but also involved themselves in the actual running of the factories. In some cases they took over the enterprises completely and ran them themselves. In the wake of the attempted coup by Kornilov, the workers became more active in guarding their factories, often forming armed Red Guard organizations for the purpose. Tensions between workers and employers increased, now taking on more overtly political overtones. An observer in the Odessa shipyards noted that the period was characterized by numerous processions by workers and revolutionary organizations. One of these was by Russian citizens who had been deported from Britain in the summer of 1917 as a result of a convention signed between Britain and Russia.[26]

In the late summer and autumn 1917 a wave of strikes swept Russia. One

[24] N. N. Golovin, *The Russian Army in the World War* (New Haven, CT, 1931), p. 159; A. Pankratova, *Fabzavkomy Rossii v bor'be za sotsialisticheskuiu fabriku* (Moscow, 1923), p. 218.
[25] Amosov *et al. Oktiab'skaia* i, pp. 221–22.
[26] *The Times*, 4 September 1918.

of the first of these began on 16 August when 30,000 Moscow leather-workers came out on a strike, which soon engulfed the whole industry throughout Russia. The strikers demanded higher wages and a say in hiring and firing. In September the workers on the oil fields at Baku went on strike in support of collective bargaining agreements. In the Donbass a prolonged conflict between miners and coal-owners culminated in a miners' strike in October. Textile workers from 115 mills, driven by the threat of starvation, went on strike on 21 October, having failed to come to a settlement with the employers.[27]

In view of the fact that enterprises were being forced to close or were being closed for tactical reasons by employers, the strikes were an act of desperation by the workers in all branches of industry. They were unlikely to be successful, and they would certainly impair the economy as a whole. In these conditions the workers turned increasingly to the Bolsheviks, who promised some solution to the 'impending catastrophe'.

The Army

Army Committees

The revolution's development in the army followed the same pattern as that among the peasantry and the workers. It intensified and subsided in concert with the other social movements during 1917, and showed many parallels with them. The multitude of ties between peasants, workers and soldiers suggests that these were not three separate movements but different aspects of a single popular movement.

The developments of 1917 must be viewed against the background of three years of fighting, which had strained the country's resources and undermined an army that had held a formidable enemy at bay and had taken enormous casualties in the process. The army suffered from the same shortages and bottlenecks as the population in general, and by the end of 1916 soldiers' letters showed increasing disaffection and a growing desire for peace.[28] The February revolution was to provide an opportunity for the simmering discontent in the army to come to the surface. The occasion was also one on which the workers' and the soldiers' move-ments coalesced.

Like the peasants and the workers, the soldiers formed committees. These emerged during the February revolution among the Petrograd garrison troops. They were either soldiers' committees formed in the regiments while the struggle for power was still going on or soldiers' committees which had taken command of the regiments after the officers had fled, fearing the wrath of their men.

The publication of Order No. 1 encouraged the formation of soldiers' committees by urging the creation of a hierarchy of committees in companies,

[27] Freidlin, *Ocherki*, pp. 216–36; D. P. Koenker and W. G. Rosenberg, *Strikes and Revolution in Russia, 1917* (Princeton, NJ, 1989), pp. 247–68.
[28] M. Frenkin, *Russkaia armiia i revoliutsiia 1917–1918* (Munich, 1978), p. 28.

battalions, regiments, etc. At the same time, since Order No. 1 was concerned with what the soldiers' attitude should be to the returning officers, it set the tone of the initial relationship between the soldiers' committees and the command structure. The order's premiss was that military discipline in the field should be maintained but that the old regime in the army with its petty humiliations should be ended, and that off duty, soldiers should be able to enjoy the same civic rights as the rest of the population. The officers, who might be sympathizers with the old regime, could not be trusted with access to weapons and therefore these should be under the control of the company and the battalion committees.

Although Order No. 1 made no specific mention of it, many army units deposed unpopular officers or those suspected of harbouring monarchist sympathies, and elected new ones. Those officers who were retained might now find themselves under the supervision of soldiers' committees. Even though Order No. 1 advocated the maintenance of military discipline, the source of this discipline was no longer the command structure but the Petrograd Soviet or the revolution itself. The officers' power, in consequence, was considerably diminished.

The attitude of the new government and the Soviet was ambiguous towards the devolution of power in the army. It was, after all, to this very process that they owed their existence. They could not afford, even if they had so desired, to reverse the movement completely. In any case, the new government would have been obliged, through mere prudence, to initiate a purge of the officer caste. And since both the government and the Soviet espoused liberal or socialist values, both would have felt impelled to set about democratizing the army. Their motives would not simply have been humanitarian but also practical, since they believed that a democratized army would fight the war more effectively.[29]

The officers were by no means all opposed to a new democratic regime in the army. Although traditionally, officers were recruited from the nobility and the soldiers from the peasants, thus reproducing the social antagonisms of the Russian countryside, the war had considerably modified this pattern. The enormous mobilization of the Russian population into the army quickly outstripped the supply of officers from traditional sources, and officers had to be recruited from the intelligentsia and even from among workers and peasants who had shown an aptitude for warfare. Officers of this type tended to be more democratically inclined, and might even be followers of the SR or Menshevik Parties.[30]

Order No. 1 spread rapidly from the Petrograd garrison to the army in the field, affecting different fronts to varying degrees. On the Northern and Western fronts, proximity to Petrograd and other urban centres ensured that the soldiers knew of the revolution before they were informed of it by their officers. The soldiers interpreted this withholding of information as an indication that the officers' sympathies were with the old regime, and that they hoped for its restoration. This engendered mistrust between officers and men. On the Northern and Western fronts the formation of soldiers' com-

[29] I. G. Tsereteli, *Vospominaniia o fevral'skoi revoliutsii* i (Paris–The Hague, 1963), p. 398
[30] V. I. Miller, *Soldatskie komitety russkoi armii v 1917 g.* (Moscow, 1974), p. 37.

mittees took place rapidly, and from their inception these committees had an anti-officer orientation.

On the South-West, Rumanian and Caucasian fronts, by contrast, where the soldiers had no independent access to information about the revolution, they first learnt of it from the officers and in the way the officers wished the information to be presented. On these fronts the formation of committees took place more slowly and often on the officers' initiative, who saw their participation as a 'revolutionary' means of keeping order among the troops.[31]

Although the impact of the February revolution was uneven on the different fronts, it nevertheless had some common characteristics. These were:

1. the purge of commanding officers;
2. the attempt to institute the election of officers;
3. the creation of soldiers' organizations – committees;
4. distrust towards officers.[32]

Stavka initially tried to prevent the formation of soldiers' committees. At the beginning of March, Alekseev, the Supreme Commander-in-Chief, inundated the Provisional Government with requests that it take measures to restore the authority of the military command structure. In reply on 9 March, Guchkov sent Alekseev a confidential letter to the effect that the Provisional Government possessed no real power, that its orders were only carried out in so far as this was permitted by the Soviet and that in fact the Provisional Government only existed by the grace of the Soviet.[33] The implication was that the Provisional Government had no choice but to acquiesce in the formation of the soldiers' committees.

What could be done, however, was to tame the committees by setting out regulations governing their functioning. This was the tactic adopted by Alekseev as early as 11 March. On that day he dispatched telegram no. 2137 in which he advocated that where army committees were formed the officers should enter them in order that they might influence the course of events.[34] These recommendations were quickly taken up by front commanders, who issued various regulations on the setting up of army committees. To institute some kind of order into the multiplicity of regulations which resulted, on 30 March Stavka issued its Order No. 51, incorporating a 'Provisional Ordinance' setting out the rights and duties of company, regimental, divisional and army committees. It was envisaged, for example, that a company committee would 'act as an intermediary between the company command and the soldiers in all questions of the internal running of the company'; it would assist in maintaining discipline in the company; and military affairs would lie outside its competence. The 'Provisional Ordinance', however, reflected Stavka's hopes rather than the actual state of

[31] *Ibid*, p. 56.
[32] Frenkin, *Russkaia*, p. 87.
[33] *Revoliutsionnoe dvizhenie posle sverzheniia samoderzhaviia* (Moscow, 1957), pp. 429–30; Miller, *Soldatskie*, p. 71; A. K. Wildman, *The End of the Russian Imperial Army* i (Princeton, NJ, 1980), p. 260.
[34] Miller, *Soldatskie*, pp. 72–73.

affairs. According to one observer, the regulations it contained were 'simply disregarded'.[35]

The Provisional Government also issued regulations on the constitution of army committees. These were incorporated into the War Ministry's Orders No. 213 and 271 promulgated on 16 April and 8 May respectively. These regulations entrusted to the committees the functions of upholding the integrity of the army, the maintenance of military discipline, the control of provisioning, settling disputes between officers and men, fostering education and sport among soldiers and sailors, and preparing for the Constituent Assembly elections.[36]

In contrast to the Stavka's Provisional Ordinance, the War Ministry's regulations allowed company committees to make contact with public and political organizations of their choice, including the Petrograd and local Soviets. Moreover, in preparation for the Constituent Assembly elections, the company committees were allowed to have dealings with political parties and to receive their newspapers and other printed material. They could also invite speakers from the various political parties to explain their party programmes. Consequently there were ample opportunities for the soldiers to be exposed to a variety of political currents.[37]

The publication of the Provisional Government's regulations did not succeed in creating any homogeneity in the structure and functions of the army committees; it only provided one more model on which committees might be constituted. Thus, committees might be based on the Petrograd Soviet's Order No. 1, the Stavka's Order No. 51, or the Provisional Government's Orders No. 213 and 271. Many committees, however, were run according to constitutions drawn up by the soldiers themselves, and they often acted independently, refusing to recognize the authority of higher committees. Such conflicts would usually result in deputations being sent to the War Ministry or the Petrograd Soviet.[38]

Some committees consisted of soldiers alone while some had a mixed composition of soldiers and officers. There was also a great variety in the competence of the committees. Some dealt mainly with economic questions; some with sanitation and hygiene; some with the struggle against desertion; and some organized duty rosters, etc. They might even try to interfere in questions of strategy. The committees which had been formed earliest concerned themselves more with political questions; those formed later, with the participation of officers, tended to confine themselves to economic matters.

The Northern front, which was situated close to both Petrograd and Riga, developed the most extensive system of committees. In the XII Army delegates from the regimental committees sent representatives to the army's Soviet of Soldier's Deputies, which formed an Executive Committee – Iskosol. The officers in the XII Army initially had their own Soviet, whose Executive Committee – Iskomof – was headed by Lieutenant G. D. Kuchin, a prominent Menshevik close to Tsereteli. The solders' and the officers' organizations,

[35] Sir A. Knox, *With the Russian Army, 1914–1917* ii (London, 1921), p. 603.
[36] L. M. Gavrilov, *Soldatskie komitety v Oktiabr'skoi revoliutsii* (Moscow, 1983), p. 32.
[37] *Ibid.*, p. 33.
[38] *Ibid.*, p. 36.

however, later merged. Until November 1917 Iskosol was a bastion of support for the Provisional Government, not only in the Army but also through the unoccupied Latvian territories. It promoted continuation of the war and combated Bolshevik influence. The Soviet of the Latvian regiments – Iskolastrel – from its inception embraced both officers and men. Its leadership was in the hands of Mensheviks and non-party soldiers; the Bolsheviks were represented by Kārlis Pētersons, who had been a participant in the 1905 revolution in Libau, and imprisoned and exiled repeatedly for revolutionary activities. In 1916 he had joined the Latvian Riflemen's Reserve Regiment. When the Riflemen's newspaper, *Brīvais Strēlnieks* (*The Free Rifleman*), began to appear in April, it was under Menshevik control. Later it fell under Bolshevik influence, as Pētersons joined its editorial board in August.[39]

Though the creation of committees inevitably reduced the command structure's power, it did not of itself undermine army discipline. In many ways the committees helped maintain it. They acted as a restraining influence on the soldiers, and were instrumental in preventing serious excesses against the officers and major outbreaks of violence. The committees resolved conflicts between officers and men and, on a wider scale, prevented the army being divided along officer–soldier lines. Many officers adapted themselves readily to the new conditions and participated in the commit- tees. Because such officers were likely to have Menshevik or SR sympathies, it was these parties which had the greatest influence in the army committees in the early period of the revolution.[40]

Desertions and the Dissolution of the Army

A worrying phenomenon for Stavka and the Provisional Government was the rapid increase in the number of desertions from the army following the February revolution. Desertions were prompted by war-weariness, the decline in discipline and by the desire of the peasant soldiers to return to the villages and take part in the division of the land.

On the one hand, the soldiers would have been keen enough to wait for the land question to be decided by the Constituent Assembly, as this was likely to delay the division of the land until such times as they returned home. On the other hand, however, rumours reached them from the villages that the division of the land had already begun, and this prompted the soldiers to leave for home so that they would be there when the division took place, and so be entitled to a share.[41]

On 16 April General Alekseev reported to Guchkov that in the armies of the Northern and Western fronts between 1 and 7 April, 7,688 soldiers were reported to have deserted, a figure he feared grossly under-estimated. As Alekseev suggested, there are no reliable figures for army desertions during the revolutionary period. Since there was every reason to do so, the numbers of deserters were systematically played down. What statistics there are, however, are sufficient to show what the patterns of desertion were.

---

[39] Ā. Šilde, *Latvijas vēsture 1914–1940* (Stockholm, 1976), pp. 104–107; *Latvijas PSR mazā enciklopēdija* iii (Riga, 1968), pp. 771–72; Miller, *Soldatskie*, p. 65; Wildman, *End* i, p. 277.
[40] Frenkin, *Russkaia*, p. 86.
[41] *Ibid.*, pp. 188–89.

The total number of reported desertions from the beginning of the war to the February revolution was 195,130. From 1 March to 15 May, 85,921; from 15 May to 1 June, 16,342; from 1 to 15 June, 11,213; from 15 June to 1 July, 19,294; from 1 to 15 July, 23,422; and from 15 July to 1 August, 13,805. This gave a total number of desertions from 1 March to 1 August of 365,137. Clearly, the February revolution triggered a wave of desertions which lasted until the middle of May. After May the number of desertions tailed off until the autumn, when the failed Kornilov coup stimulated what General N. N. Golovin called a 'spontaneous self-demobilization' of the army. The pattern of desertions follows in this way that of peasant disturbances and industrial unrest.

Individual fronts show the same trend. On the Northern front from the beginning of the war until the February revolution, 49,055 deserters were reported; and from February to the first half of May, 25,724. On the Western front the corresponding figures are 13,648 and 24,700. The Rumanian front reported 67,845 deserters before February and 16,576 between February and May. A significant feature of the phenomenon was that the largest proportion of desertions were not from the front-line troops but from those in the rear, in reserve units. A contemporary observer on the Western front in the spring of 1917 could note that, whereas the troops at the front line maintained discipline, those in the towns had ceased to do so.[42]

Fraternization between Russian and German troops took place on all fronts except the Rumanian and Caucasian fronts. This was intensified in April during the Easter religious festival. Although fraternization had taken place sporadically before the revolution, it had been discouraged by both sides. After February, however, it was supported by the German General Staff, and provided an opportunity to distribute German propaganda literature among the Russian troops. Fraternization was also advocated by the Bolsheviks, both as a means of bringing the war to an end and as a means of spreading the revolution to Germany.

There were instances where troops refused to obey their commanders' orders. On 28 March the commander of the VIII Army on the South-West front reported that the 45th Azov and the 47th Ukrainian Infantry Regiments had refused go into the attack. On the Caucasian front the 6th Rifle Regiment disobeyed the order to commence an offensive. In the period after the February revolution such incidents multiplied and involved ever larger troop formations.

The Influence of the Bolsheviks

While the pacifism which spread throughout the Russian army in 1917 was overwhelmingly of a spontaneous kind, the Bolshevik influence did make itself felt in a few, politically important, areas. The chief of these was the Northern front, which was close both to the revolutionary centres of Petrograd and Riga as well as to Finland and the bases of the Baltic Fleet. It was the front which covered the approaches to Petrograd and, as the July

[42] E. N. Giatsintov, 'Tragediia russkoi armii v 1917 goda', *Russkoe proshloe* (1991, no. 1), p. 82; Frenkin, *Russkaia*, pp. 194–95; Wildman, *End* i, p. 364; Golovin, *Russian Army*, pp. 123, 260.

days demonstrated, the Provisional Government's survival could depend on troops being sent from that front.

Bolshevik organizations were formed comparatively quickly in military units stationed in Finland, where there were less subject to official prohibitions than in Russia proper. They were, moreover, situated in coastal towns where the Baltic Fleet was based, which had its own Bolshevik organizations. In March 1917 a group of Bolsheviks from Petrograd and Kronstadt moved to Helsingfors to found a party organization there.

The main part of the Northern front passed through Latvian territory where several Bolshevik groups existed that conducted agitation among the troops. The Latvian Social Democratic group, the SDLK, moreover, had its headquarters in Riga. This group was able to extend its influence in the XII Army, and in particular to the two Latvian rifle brigades, which formed part of that army.

This was a paradoxical phenomenon in view of the fact that it was precisely the Latvian regiments out of the whole Russian army that were among the best disciplined and the strongest motivated. From this it might be assumed that the Latvians would be the least likely to show Bolshevik sympathies. In many respects, however, the Latvian riflemen belonged to categories from which the Bolsheviks drew their main support. They were workers, farm labourers or poor peasants. Their antipathy to the Germans was first and foremost to the Baltic Germans, who formed the land-owning élite and the merchantry in Livland and Kurland. Moreover, among the Latvian riflemen were a large number of SDLK members. In the spring of 1917, company and regimental committees began to fall into Bolshevik hands. As a result, when the Second United Congress of the Latvian rifle regiments met in Riga between 12 and 17 May, there were many Bolshevik supporters among the delegates.

Despite the speeches of General R. D. Radko-Dmitriev, Commander of the XII Army and, Kuchin, the chairman of Iskosol, urging continuation of the war, the congress by an overwhelming majority adopted a resolution proposed by the Bolshevik Jūlijs Daniševskis calling for all power to the Soviets and an end to the war. The congress elected a new Iskolastrel in which the SDLK had a majority. By the 'May Resolution' the Latvian riflemen had gone over to the Bolsheviks' side, giving them their most loyal and valuable allies.[43]

The Russian parts of the XII Army also became subject to Bolshevik influence. On 30 April the Bolshevik group of the XII Army published the first issue of *Okopnaia pravda* (*Trench Truth*). As one member of the editorial board, F. P. Khaustov, was an SR Maximalist, the newspaper advocated SR as well as Bolshevik policies. It called for socialization of the land, an end to the war and no separate officers' committees but common committees for officers, soldiers, workers and peasants. Fraternization with the Germans at the front was held to be desirable in order to revolutionize the enemy's army.[44]

The military organization of the Bolshevik Party in Petrograd published a

---

[43] Šilde, *Latvijas*, p. 104; Miller, *Soldatskie*, p. 181.
[44] W. Lieven, *Das rote Russland* (Berlin, 1918), p. 55; Miller, *Soldatskie*, pp. 190–91.

newspaper for soldiers, primarily of the Petrograd garrison, entitled *Soldats-kaia pravda*. Its editors were N. I. Podvoiskii, V. I. Nevskii and A. F. Ilin-Zhenevsky. Ilin-Zhenevsky, somewhat ironically, worked as personal secretary to the War Minister, Aleksander Guchkov. The newspaper took into account the fact that the soldiers were overwhelmingly peasants and, accordingly, concentrated on the question of the land.[45]

The June Offensive

It was a constant feature of Russian politics that success or failure in battle should have repercussions in the political arena. The June offensive of 1917 was no exception in this respect. It was to be an acid test for the newly democratized Russian army. Success in the offensive would have vindicated the committee system and the freer military regulations. By the same token, the collapse of the offensive was taken as an indictment of the committees, and those, like General A. I. Denikin, who had always been hostile to them, felt their criticisms to have been justified.

Although there were a number of reasons for the offensive's failure (shortcomings in the strategy pursued by General A. E. Gutor, the Commander-in-Chief of the South-West front; the difficult terrain; and the weather), the only cause which was given currency was the damage done to the army's fighting capacity by the committees and the new military regulations.

The atrocities committed by the retreating Russian army on the civilian population at Tarnopol was the factor which compelled even those who favoured army democratization to condemn what had taken place. It made the case for the restoration of the death penalty at the front unanswerable. It was in this context that Kornilov replaced Gutor as Commander-in-Chief of the VIII Army and began his dizzying rise to prominence.[46]

Signs of a new confidence by right-wing officers were not long in making their appearance. On 16 July a large group of deserters from the Ostrolenka Regiment in the region of Tarnopol was subjected to a barrage of artillery fire. The survivors were rounded up and put on trial, though some of the death sentences imposed were commuted by Kerensky to imprisonment.

In the new atmosphere following the failure of the offensive and the July days, the Bolshevik newspapers *Okopnaia pravda* and *Soldatskaia pravda* were closed down. Arrests of known Bolsheviks were carried out on the various fronts. The Northern front was subjected to a particularly thorough purge. There the arrested soldiers were sent to Dvinsk, where their cases were heard. In at least one case an entire Bolshevik-oriented company was taken into custody and sent to Dvinsk. Some of these 'Dvintsy' were later taken to Moscow, where they became involved in the October revolution.

For the moment the counter-revolutionary forces had the upper hand. The committees' power was curbed, and the officers regained some of their authority. This situation, however, was an uneasy and an unstable one.

[45] A. F. Ilyin-Genevsky, *From the February Revolution to the October Revolution 1917* (London, 1932), pp. 49–51.

[46] L. E. Heenan, *Russian Democracy's Fatal Blunder: The Summer Offensive of 1917* (New York, 1987), p. 116.

The importance of the Kornilov Affair for the army was that it finally discredited the officers and restored the political advantage to the committees. Then the floodgates of desertion opened, and the old imperial army set about in earnest the process of 'self-demobilization'.

The Inter-Relationship of the Social Movements

A survey of the peasants', the workers' and the soldiers' movements during 1917 reveals some striking features they have in common. The most obvious of these is that all three social groups organized themselves in committees. The peasants had village or *volost* committees, the workers had factory committees and the soldiers had company, regimental and army committees. The formation of all types of committee, moreover, occurred with remarkable rapidity immediately after or even during the February revolution. In most cases too, the committees arose without any formal preparation or a precise definition of their respective spheres of competence.

Frequently, committees of all kinds were reluctant to accept any restrictions on their powers or to recognize any higher authority than themselves. There was a distinct tendency for the committees to extend the area into which they were prepared to intervene. In the countryside the peasant committees took responsibility for an increasing range of functions – the renting of land, the removal of labourers from estates, the prohibition of land and timber sales, etc. In the towns, factory committees progressed from a general supervision of the enterprise to participation in its actual running. Army committees displayed the same pattern, but instead of taking over increasing responsibility for carrying on the war – which would have been a more exact parallel with the factory committees – they took a more active part in bringing it to an end.

Between peasants', workers' and soldiers' committees there were not simply similarities but also contact and interchange. Workers kept a channel of communication with the villages open through the *zemliachestvo* organizations, bringing together the workers' and the peasants' movements. Soldiers were mostly peasant conscripts whose main focus was life on the land. Significantly, soldiers were drawn into the peasants' struggle against the land-owners on the territory where they were stationed. In other words, the network of committees formed by the various groups in society overlapped and complemented one another.

The relationship of committees to one another contrasts markedly with their attitude to other kinds of institution. To governmental structures, industrial management or to landed property, the collectivist institutions reacted with hostility and suspicion. All kinds of committee showed an impulse to establish 'control' or 'supervision' over capitalists, land-owners and officers – over forces which, for the moment at least, remained beyond the power of the collective.

The archetype of the committee, or the Soviet, is the peasant commune, the *mir*. In the case of the peasant committees the relationship is a direct one; in the case of factory committees and soldiers' committees it is more indirect.

But it is nevertheless the *mir* which provides the underlying model for the committees. In this way, the driving force behind the social aspects of the 1917 revolution was not socialist ideology – though it might take that guise – but the inherent collectivism of Russian society, threatened by incipient economic liberalism and given a new lease of life by the privations of a debilitating war.

7

The Kornilov Affair

The Roots of the Conspiracy

On 7 July, Prince Lvov resigned as Prime Minister of the Provisional Government, objecting to the proposal of the government's socialist ministers to declare a republic and to institute a radical land reform, as pre-empting the decision of the Constituent Assembly. He was replaced as premier by Kerensky, who continued to hold the post of War Minister.

The group of ministers which remained from the first coalition government, calling itself the 'Government to Save the Revolution', then took a series of measures designed to establish order in the country and army, reversing the erosion of authority which the July crisis had highlighted. Warrants were issued for the arrest of Lenin, Zinoviev and Kamenev. Regiments which had participated in the July disturbances were disbanded and the men sent to the front. The circulation of Bolshevik newspapers at the front was banned and several of these papers were closed. Other severe laws were passed as a consequence of the German counter-offensive and the Russian collapse, which were taking place at that time.[1]

An important measure designed to re-establish discipline in the army was the restoration of the death penalty at the front. The initiative for this had been taken by General Kornilov, whom Kerensky had appointed as Commander-in-Chief of the South-West front on 7 July, just as the German counter-offensive began and the Russian army was retreating in disarray. Kornilov at once ordered that the commanding officers take decisive action and shoot deserters and looters. On 8 July Kornilov sent telegrams to General Brusilov, the Supreme Commander, to the War Minister and the commissars of the various fronts in which he drew attention to the need to employ extraordinary measures, including the death penalty, in the theatre of military operations. On the 12th the law restoring the death penalty for military personnel in wartime and the establishment of military revolutionary courts was duly approved.[2]

The stern measures promulgated by Kerensky were designed not only to restore order but also to send reassuring signals to the Kadets in the hope of persuading them to revive the coalition. On 15 July Kerensky had a meeting

[1] R. P. Browder and A. F. Kerensky, eds., *The Russian Provisional Government 1917* ii & iii (Stanford, 1961), p. 979.
[2] *Ibid.*, pp. 982–83.

with the two Kadets, N. M. Kishkin and V. D. Nabokov, and two representatives from the business community, N. N. Kutler from Petrograd and
Tretiakov from Moscow. In connection with their negotiations with Kerensky, the Kadet Party and the Moscow All-Russian Union of Trade and
Industry each set out its terms for participating in the coalition in a
memorandum presented to Kerensky before he left for Stavka the following
day. The Petrograd Union of Trade and Industry confined itself to commu-
nicating the general principle that the new coalition ought to take account of
the needs of the business community, something the government in its
present form was signally failing to do.

The memoranda of the Kadet Party and the Moscow merchants were
similar in content and contained the following main points:

1. Implementation of all basic social reforms and decisions on questions
   relating to the form of State power should be postponed until the
   Constituent Assembly.
2. That on questions of war and peace the principle of complete solidarity
   with the Allies should be maintained.
3. That measures should be taken to restore the army's fighting capacity by
   instituting strict military discipline and eliminating interference by army
   committees in questions of military strategy and tactics.

In addition, it was demanded that Chernov should be removed from his post
of Minister of Agriculture. In the Cabinet which the Kadets and the Muscovites proposed, Kornilov's name appeared opposite the post of Minister of
War. When Kerensky appointed Kornilov Supreme Commander a few days
later he could have been in no doubt that his choice would be welcomed by
the groups whose support he was striving to secure.[3]

As the SRs would only consent to remain in the coalition if Chernov
retained his post, Kerensky faced deadlock in forming a new coalition, and on
21 July he resigned in real or feigned despair. In view of Kerensky's key
position in Russian politics, the Kadets, along with the socialist parties,
agreed that Kerensky should resume his post as premier and form a Cabinet
of his own choosing, including Chernov in it if he thought fit.[4]

On 25 July the new coalition government was announced. It had the
following membership: Prime Minister and Minister of War and Navy,
Kerensky; Deputy Prime Minister and Minister of Finance, Nekrasov
(Kadet); Minister of Foreign Affairs, Tereshchenko (non-party); Minister of
Justice, A. S. Zarudnyi (Popular Socialist); Minister of Supply, Peshekhonov
(Popular Socialist); Minister of Agriculture, Chernov (SR); Minister of Labour,
Skobelev (Menshevik); Minister of Post and Telegraph, A. M. Nikitin
(Menshevik); Minister of Education, S. F. Oldenburg (Kadet); Minister of
Welfare, I. N. Efremov (Radical-Democrat); Minister of Transport, P. P.
Iurenev (Kadet); Minister of Trade and Industry, Prokopovich (non-party);
State Controller, F. F. Kokoshkin (Kadet); Ober-Procurator of the Holy Synod,

[3] *Bulletins de presse* (15 July 1917), p. 668.
[4] P. N. Miliukov, *The Russian Revolution, Vol. 2: Kornilov or Lenin? – Summer 1917*, ed., trans. and
     with an introduction by G. M. Hamburg (Gulf Breeze, FL, 1984), pp. 27–28; R. Abraham,
     Alexander Kerensky: The First Love of the Revolution (London, 1987), p. 239.

A. V. Kartashev (Kadet); and Minister of the Interior, N. D. Avksentiev (SR).

Kerensky, who had retained his post as Minister of War and Navy, had appointed Savinkov, an ex-SR terrorist, as Assistant Minister of War and V. I. Lebedev (SR) as Assistant Navy Minister. Although more Cabinet posts went to socialists, the second coalition was to be less radical in its policies than the first. Much of its effort was devoted to attempts to strengthen governmental power and to restore order in the country.

But even before the Provisional Government had embarked on its new course, various groups of people were already engaged in efforts to establish an authoritarian form of government in Russia. They looked to General Kornilov as the man who might provide the necessary kind of strong leadership.

Guchkov's resignation as War Minister and the circumstances surrounding it provided the impetus for him to become involved in a conspiratorial organization which attempted to establish a dictatorship headed by Kornilov. Both Guchkov and Kornilov had undergone the experience of the April crisis when the Petrograd Soviet had refused to allow troops to be used to dispel street demonstrations. The incident had prompted both men to resign their posts, and for Guchkov to conclude that the Soviet would have to be liquidated. The event had been especially traumatic for Guchkov because he had not been supported by his Cabinet colleagues, not even by Konovalov who, like himself, belonged to the Moscow business community. The indications were that the Muscovites would not countenance the use of force to assert the government's authority.

This circumstance caused Guchkov to ally with his former rivals, the Petrograd industrialists, who had never been as liberal as the Muscovites. In Petrograd a counter-revolutionary organization was already in existence. In March the industrialists, A. I. Putilov and A. I. Vyshnegradskii, along with V. S. Zavoiko, whom Putilov had placed on the board of the Lianozov Bank in 1916, the journalist E. P. Semenov and others, had come together 'to save Russia from anarchy and revolution' On 9 April a meeting of Zavoiko, Semenov, B. A. Suvorin, Professor V. D. Pletnev (Kornilov's adjutant), V. N. Troitskii-Seniutovich and others had agreed to approach General Kornilov to ask for his co-operation.[5] By 9 April Putilov and Zavoiko were able to report that Kornilov had agreed with their programme of action and was willing to co-operate with them. Zavoiko voluntarily joined the army and served as Kornilov's orderly. When at the end of April Kornilov was given the command of the VIII Army, Zavoiko went with him. Kornilov was much impressed by Zavoiko's literary talents, and accordingly he entrusted his orderly with the drafting of orders and documents.

To justify its existence officially, the secret committee called itself the Society for the Economic Rehabilitation of Russia. The society's membership was largely drawn from the Union of Congresses of Industry and Trade, and its central committee consisted of Putilov, N. N. Kutler (who was to negotiate with Kerensky on 15 July on the formation of a new coalition government), N. A. Belosvetov, V. A. Kamenka and A. P. Meshcherskii. Initially the society's function was to prepare for the elections to the Constituent

---

[5] *Poslednie novosti*, 20 February 1937.

Assembly, an important task for the Petrograd industrialists because even with proportional representation their representatives were in danger of being swamped by the great mass of peasant delegates. It collected money with which to conduct propaganda to secure seats for moderate bourgeois candidates in the Constituent Assembly. But as the Constituent Assembly elections were still some way off, it carried on propaganda on behalf of the war effort. After his resignation as War Minister, Guchkov took over the leadership of the society and collaborated with Kornilov in conducting an anti-socialist propaganda campaign at the front. For this purpose, large sums of money were collected and put at Kornilov's disposal.[6]

The Society for the Economic Rehabilitation of Russia, however, was not the only such organization in Petrograd. The Republican Centre was founded in May 1917 under the auspices of the Siberian Bank. Its founding members were F. A Lipskii, K. V. Nikolaevskii, P. N. Finisov, the former Duma member A. F. Aladin, Colonel Shuvaev and Kornilov himself. The centre concerned itself with propaganda work, but its chief attention was paid to organizing a military section. Initially this was headed by Colonel Romanovskii, later by Admiral A. V. Kolchak, and latterly by Colonel L. P. Desimeter. This section included representatives from societies such as the Military League (General I. I. Federov), the Army and Fleet Officers' Union (Colonels Novosiltsev and Pronin), the Union of Cossack Troops (Colonel A. I. Dutov), the Union of St George Cavaliers, the Union of Military Duty (Colonel F. Vinberg), the Union of War Wounded and several others.[7]

The Republican Centre and the Society for the Economic Rehabilitation of Russia carried on their activities in complete ignorance of each other's existence until the middle of July 1917, when a meeting took place between Finisov and Putilov in the Crimea. Here plans were made for future co-operation between the two organizations, and from that time the Republican Centre gave access to its wide military contacts to the wealthier Society for the Economic Rehabilitation of Russia.

Kornilov's Programme

On 16 July Kerensky called a conference of military commanders at Stavka 'to form a circumstantial and impartial view' of the real situation at the front and of the strategic consequences of the German breakthrough. He also hoped to sketch out a plan for future military policy. General Denikin, the Commander-in-Chief of the Western front, made a lengthy speech describing the breakdown in discipline which, in his opinion, had resulted from the establishment of soldiers' committees, the appointment of military commissars and the promulgation of the Declaration of Soldiers' Rights. As a means of restoring discipline he recommended that the declaration be revoked, commissars and committees should be abolished and that the death penalty be extended to non-combat areas.[8] Kornilov was not present at the conference

[6] 'A. I. Guchkov rasskazyvaet', *Voprosy istorii* (1991, no. 9–10), p. 209.
[7] Browder and Kerensky, *Russian Provisional* iii, pp. 1534–35.
[8] *Ibid.*, ii, pp. 991–96.

as he was required on the South-West front. But he sent a telegram with his comments on the military situation.

In contrast to Denikin's speech, Kornilov's telegram impressed Kerensky as being the work of a man with a deeper and wider insight into the situation than his compeers. Kornilov's opinion was that the present disasters were not only due to the soldiers' demoralization but also to the long-standing deficiency of the commanding staff. He thought that simultaneous with the punitive measures, immediate steps should be taken for the improvement of the officer corps. Unlike Denikin, Kornilov did not deny the beneficial activities of the army committees, and the dedication and heroism of their individual members. Ironically, the telegram which had impressed Kerensky so much was, as he discovered later, not written by Kornilov himself but by Zavoiko. Moreover, soon after the conference Kornilov wrote to Denikin saying that he had read the report Denikin had made at Stavka on 16 July with great satisfaction and that he, Kornilov, 'would sign such a report with both hands'.[9]

It was directly after this conference at Stavka that Kerensky decided to dismiss Brusilov and appoint Kornilov in his place. Savinkov, who had made the suggestion, was given the post of Assistant War Minister on the spot.

On receiving notice of his appointment as Supreme Commander-in-Chief on the morning of 19 July, Kornilov sent back a list of conditions under which he would accept the post. These were responsibility only before his conscience and before the whole people; absolute non-interference with his military orders, including appointments to the High Command; extension of all measures lately adopted at the front to all districts in the rear where there were army reserves; and acceptance of the proposals set out in his telegram to the Supreme Commander at the conference of 16 July at Stavka.[10]

Almost simultaneously with the sending of this telegram there arose the first conflict between Kerensky and Kornilov. As the appointment of members of the High Command had been claimed by the new Supreme Commander, Kornilov appointed as his successor on the South-West front General Valuev. General Valuev had already arrived at Stavka when a telegram was received which appointed to the command of the South-West front General A. V. Cheremisov, one of the favourites of the new 'revolutionary democracy'. On learning of General Cheremisov's appointment, Kornilov at once telegraphed to the Minister of War, asking him to cancel it and warning him that otherwise he would find it impossible to accept the Supreme Command. On 20 July Kornilov wired Savinkov telling him that before receiving a definite answer to his telegram he would not start out for Stavka. Kerensky explained the state of affairs by pointing out that the appointments of Kornilov and Cheremisov were made at the same time. To both his telegrams, Kornilov received on 20 July a compliant reply from the Provisional Government. All measures were to be accepted 'in principle' and to decide the matter of Cheremisov's appointment the military commissar, M. M. Filonenko, was to be sent to Kornilov.[11]

On 22 July Filonenko arrived at the headquarters of the South-West front.

[9] A. I. Denikin, *The Russian Turmoil* (London, 1922), p. 296.
[10] Miliukov, *Russian Revolution*, p. 54.
[11] *Ibid.*, p. 55.

He wanted to discuss not only the question of Cheremisov but also points in the list of conditions Kornilov had submitted, which required clarification with the Provisional Government. One of these points was what Kornilov meant by the phrase, 'responsibility before his conscience and the people'. Kornilov said that by this he understood responsibility before the Provisional Government which, he believed, had the trust of the people. After these discussions, at midnight on 24 July, Kornilov finally entered on his duties as Supreme Commander.[12] Self-esteem was satisfied, but mutual suspicion between Kornilov and the Provisional Government remained.

On 3 August Kornilov arrived in Petrograd to report on the strategic situation, bringing with him a memorandum to be read before the Provisional Government. It contained the following demands: that the death penalty should be instituted immediately in the rear for civilian as well as for military personnel; that the former authority of officers should be restored while the competence of civilian commissars should be curtailed; that any member of a soldiers' committee indulging in activities unlawful or detrimental to the strengthening of discipline in the army should be dismissed and court-martialled; that soldiers' meetings at the front should be prohibited; that only those newspapers which had been approved by the military authorities were to be allowed to circulate; all politically harmful elements were to be excluded from the reserve units; and all revolutionary-minded regiments were to be disbanded and held in concentration camps.[13]

Kerensky, who does not reveal the contents of Kornilov's memorandum, says that it contained a number of proposals, 'most of which were acceptable in principle', but formulated in a way that would be found objectionable.[14] It was decided, therefore, that the memorandum should be revised by Filonenko and Savinkov. Kornilov then left for Stavka with the distinct impression that there was a reluctance in the Provisional Government to implement his proposals. His impression is understandable: Kerensky must have realized that the measures Kornilov advocated would be anathema to a considerable section of public opinion, and it is doubtful if he seriously supposed that it was possible to dress them up in a way that would be acceptable. On the other hand, Kerensky did not want to antagonize Kornilov by rejecting them out of hand.

On 6 August Kornilov's Chief of Staff, General A. S. Lukomskii discovered that Kornilov had given an order for the Caucasian Native Division, consisting of Kabardians, Daghestanis, Tatars, Ingush and Ossetians, as well as Cossack units (colloquially known as the 'Wild Division'), to be moved from the South-West front to the area of Nevel-Novosokolniki-Velikie Luki, a location equidistant from Petrograd and Moscow. The troop formations in the area were put under the command of General Krymov. In Lukomskii's judgement the troop concentrations were more consistent with an attack on Petrograd or Moscow than with strengthening the Northern front – the explanation Kornilov initially gave him. Subsequently Kornilov informed him that he had deployed these forces to put down an anticipated Bolshevik uprising at the end of August. He said he was placing Krymov in charge

[12] *Ibid.*, p. 56.

[13] N. Ia. Ivanov, *Kornilovshchina i ee razgrom* (Leningrad, 1965), p. 53.

[14] A. F. Kerensky, *The Prelude to Bolshevism: The Kornilov Rebellion* (London, 1919), p. 72.

because, if the need arose, Krymov would not hesitate to hang all the members of the Soviet.[15]

There is no firm evidence that Kornilov intended any violent action against the Provisional Government or the Soviet at this stage. But the choice of both the troops and the commander is significant. The Caucasian tribesmen of the 'Wild Division' did not understand Russian and were therefore insulated from the contagion of revolution. General Krymov was a long-standing friend of Guchkov's and could be relied upon to help Guchkov in his objective of liquidating the Soviet.

Between 4 and 10 August, Savinkov and Filonenko had been working on the revised memorandum to be presented by Kornilov to the Provisional Government. The first part of the new document contained all the demands made by Kornilov in his first note of 3 August. There followed two new sections with provisions of greater significance since they concerned matters which were not purely military but encroached on the field of politics. The first of the additional sections demanded that the railways be placed under military control, and that any failure to carry out a order connected with the working of the railways should be regarded in the same way as a refusal to obey an order at the front and be subject to the same penalty. To enforce this principle, military revolutionary courts should be set up at the main railway centres. The second section proposed to declare all factories working on defence under martial law; to prohibit all meetings on factory premises; to demand from workers a certain minimum production quota; to dismiss immediately and send to the front those workers who failed to meet the quotas; to prohibit workers from interfering in economic matters; and to ban strikes for the duration of the war under penalty of capital punishment. Kerensky's attitude towards the report was ambiguous. On 8 August he declared to Savinkov that under no circumstances would he sign such a document. Nor did he actually do so when Kornilov came to Petrograd two days later for the presentation of his memorandum to the Provisional Government. On the other hand, at no time does Kerensky seem to have opposed Kornilov's programme on principle, and Kornilov went away with the understandable impression that the memorandum's substance was quite acceptable to Kerensky.[16]

In a conversation between Kornilov and Kerensky the Supreme Commander remarked that there had come to his notice rumours of his proposed dismissal. He did not believe them, but if it so happened that they had some foundation, he warned Kerensky not to carry out this measure.

At any rate Kerensky, realizing the document's inflammatory capabilities, refused to present it to the Provisional Government but, on the following day, Kornilov's first report of 3 August was accepted as the official statement on military policy. At this session the Provisional Government also adopted a resolution specifically limiting Kornilov's address at the Moscow conference. The content of his speech was to be purely military, and no mention was to be made of those clauses in his report which related to railways and factories.[17]

The Moscow conference did not go well for Kornilov. To begin with,

[15] Browder and Kerensky, *Russian Provisional* iii, p. 1548.
[16] Ivanov, *Kornilovshchina*, pp. 57–58.
[17] Kerensky, *Prelude*, p. 72.

Kerensky's opening speech contained an oblique threat against him and his associates: '. . . let those plotters beware who think the time has come to overthrow the government relying on bayonets.'[18] A further irritation to Kornilov came at 11 p.m. on 13 August when Kerensky telephoned to remind him of the Provisional Government's decision concerning the avoidance in his speech of any reference to his plans for the new regime on the railways and in the factories. Kornilov replied that he would say what he liked. However, at that very moment Kornilov's speech, dictated by Filonenko and taken down by Savinkov, had already been prepared.[19] Kornilov was extremely irritated by Kerensky's behaviour, and at Stavka on 23 August he told Savinkov: 'Kerensky insulted me undeservedly at the Moscow Conference.'[20] By the time the conference ended on 14 August, Kornilov despaired of trying to work any longer with Kerensky to implement by peaceful means his programme of military reform.

Kornilov had already taken steps in a different direction. At the end of the Moscow conference he sent for Putilov, Vyshnegradskii and Meshcherskii from the Society for the Economic Rehabilitation of Russia and told them he intended to dispatch an army corps to Petrograd to disperse the Bolsheviks and, in order to avoid street fighting, a movement would have to be organized within the capital to give assistance to General Krymov. Kornilov inquired whether the society would be willing to finance the enterprise and, on receiving the assent of its three representatives, named contacts at Stavka – V. I. Sidorin, Desimeter and Pronin. Before his visitors departed, Kornilov told them: 'I see you have done your part. But there might be a need for quite a lot of money. Couldn't you also induce the Muscovites . . .?' Accordingly, on the following day, Putilov contacted Tretiakov and communicated to him Kornilov's request for funds from the Moscow merchantry. To this Tretiakov made the reply: 'I take no part in such adventures.'[21]

Tretiakov's reply is highly significant as it provides an insight into what kind of support Kornilov did and did not have. Much as Tretiakov might have sympathized with Kornilov's programme, he was not prepared to envisage the use of violence to implement it. After all, Guchkov had joined forces with Putilov, presumably because he was unable to mobilize the Moscow merchantry behind the use of force to restore military and industrial order. He had resigned from the Provisional Government in great part because the Muscovite Konovalov had refused to countenance the use of force to restore order in the capital. Guchkov was an exception in this respect, as his stance on Stolypin's military field courts had shown. Konovalov's attitude was more typical, not only of the Provisional Government but also of the Moscow merchants. It is not surprising, therefore, that Tretiakov should withhold his support from Kornilov's 'adventure'. From the very outset Kornilov lacked the backing of a powerful and influential section of Russian society.

On 21 August Riga fell to the Germans and, as the front was drawing near to Petrograd, the Provisional Government decided to take some measures to

[18] Miliukov, *Russian Revolution*, p. 104.
[19] *Ibid.*, pp. 107–108.
[20] Browder and Kerensky, *Russian Provisional* iii, p. 1555.
[21] *Poslednie novosti*, 29 January 1937; Browder and Kerensky, *Russian Provisional* iii, p. 1530.

improve the capital's security. It was resolved to make Petrograd an independent military and administrative unit, and to subordinate the garrison troops to a single person directly responsible to the government. It was also decided to change the composition of the troops in the capital by sending all the units that had taken part in the July days to the front and replace them with more reliable ones, with cavalry units in particular. This involved asking the Commander-in-Chief for troops to be placed at the disposal of the Provisional Government. However, bearing in mind the danger of a right-wing coup, the Provisional Government specified that the troops sent to Petrograd should not include the Third Cavalry Corps and should not be commanded by General Krymov.

On 23 August Savinkov arrived at Stavka, where he found Kornilov in a state of depression and highly critical of Kerensky's irresolution. He was mollified, however, when Savinkov told him that the Supreme Commander's plans had been approved by Kerensky and would be implemented within a few days.[22]

Savinkov also communicated to Kornilov the Provisional Government's request that a cavalry corps should be placed at its disposal in case of emergency. This request was a very convenient one for Kornilov, because it legitimized the orders he had already given to send troops to Petrograd. Moreover, by merging two items on Savinkov's agenda – the ratification of the army reforms and the Provisional Government's request for troops – Kornilov also had a very convenient way of legitimizing the mission of Krymov's forces. This was to maintain that Savinkov had said that when the army reforms were announced a Bolshevik uprising could be expected, and troops would be required to quell it. Put in this way, it would be possible for Kornilov's forces to enter Petrograd, carry out whatever repressive measures they thought fit and still be able to claim that it had all been done at the request of the Provisional Government. This was the justification Kornilov was subsequently to advance for his actions.

There were, however, two flaws in this argument: the first was that Savinkov did not admit to putting matters as Kornilov and his supporters said he did. The other was that Savinkov had emphasized to Kornilov that the forces sent to Petrograd should not include the 'Wild Division' and that they should not be commanded by General Krymov. These specifications made a significant distinction between what Kornilov had done and what he had been requested to do. In the event the specific instructions were ignored.

At around midnight on the 23rd, General Kornilov received Lipskii and Finisov from the Republican Centre. Their discussions were on a subject that went somewhat beyond what one would normally expect to be a military commander's sphere of competence. They concerned the list of ministers for a reconstituted Cabinet. Among those mentioned for potential office were Kerensky, Plekhanov, General Alekseev, Admiral Kolchak, N. N. Pokrovskii, P. N. Ignatiev and Prince Lvov. Finisov and Lipskii pointed out that in view of the extreme bitterness among the officers, Kerensky should be brought to the Stavka in the interests of his own safety.

While this meeting was taking place, V. N. Lvov, the former Procurator of

[22] *Ibid.*, iii, p. 1555.

the Holy Synod, was waiting to see Kornilov, ostensibly on an important mission from Kerensky. On 22 August, at the instigation of Aladin and I. A. Dobrynskii, a leading figure in the St George Cavaliers, Lvov had called on Kerensky to tell him of disturbing rumours emanating from Stavka that a plot was afoot to establish by force of arms Kornilov as a dictator. According to Lvov, Kerensky was dangerously lacking in support, and some formidable elements were opposed to him. Lvov's advice was to reorganize the government to widen its base to include members of the Kadet Party and industrialists. Lvov offered to negotiate with unspecified parties on Kerensky's behalf, and Kerensky raised no objection to his doing so.[23]

A few hours after Savinkov's departure Lvov was admitted to Kornilov's study. He announced that he had come on an important mission from Kerensky, and proceeded to discuss with the Supreme Commander ways in which the government might be reorganized. Lvov informed Kornilov that Kerensky was prepared to leave office if in Kornilov's judgement this was necessary. He asked Kornilov to state what his preference was on how the government ought to be reconstituted. Kornilov declared that the only solution was a dictatorship and the proclamation of a state of martial law throughout the country. He added that he himself was willing to take on the role of dictator if it was offered to him. But he was convinced that however the government was constituted, he as Supreme Commander should be a member of it.

Kornilov instructed Lvov to tell Kerensky that extremist disturbances were in the offing, and that he should expect an attempt on his life. He also asked that Kerensky should come to Stavka to decide finally on how the government was to be reconstituted, and that he would guarantee Kerensky's safety on his word of honour.[24]

Meanwhile Savinkov had returned to Petrograd and given Kerensky a brief report on his talks with Kornilov. Kerensky was informed that the Third Cavalry Corps was on the way, and that Savinkov had succeeded in dissuading Kornilov from including the 'Wild Division' and appointing Krymov.

Rumours of a Bolshevik coup were circulating in Petrograd, but the Bolshevik newspaper *Rabochii* denied that any such action was contemplated, and warned its readers against persons unknown who were putting about rumours and conducting provocative agitation.

On 26 August Lvov returned to Kerensky to report on the outcome of the meeting with Kornilov. He said that the situation had completely changed since they had last met. A Bolshevik rising was imminent and Kornilov would not answer for Kerensky's life anywhere but at Stavka. A number of measures laid down by Kornilov would have to be undertaken urgently. When Kerensky asked him to write these down, Lvov produced the following list of Kornilov's proposals:

1. That martial law should be proclaimed in Petrograd.
2. That all military and civil authority should be placed in the hands of the Supreme Commander.

[23] C. Anet, *La révolution russe* ii (Paris, 1918), p. 175.
[24] *Ibid.*, pp. 174–76.

3. That all ministers, including the Prime Minister, should resign, and that temporary executive power should be transferred to assistant ministers until the formation of a cabinet by the Supreme Commander.[25]

Kerensky interpreted this as an ultimatum from Kornilov, and from then on tried to gather proof that the Supreme Commander was engaged in a rebellion against the legitimate government. To this end he attempted to get Kornilov to incriminate himself in the course of a conversation Kerensky conducted with him by direct wire on the evening of the 26th. In fact the results of this ploy were necessarily inconclusive, because Kerensky simply asked Kornilov to confirm the message he had instructed Lvov to pass on. Kornilov duly confirmed this without asking precisely what message it was that Lvov had given Kerensky.

The Failure of the Coup

Kerensky was entirely satisfied with the results of his conversation with Kornilov. He now had, he considered, ample proof of Kornilov's guilt. Back in his study the conversation with Lvov was repeated in the presence of a witness, and Lvov placed under arrest. Savinkov was horrified at the turn of events, believing that there must have been some misunderstanding, and urged Kerensky to get in touch with Kornilov immediately to clarify matters. Kerensky replied that it was already too late to come to terms. He had sent a telegram to Stavka saying that General Kornilov had been relieved of his duties and that Lukomskii was to take over temporarily. The telegram was simply signed 'Kerensky' and did not bear an official number. Kerensky called a meeting of military specialists to discuss the possibility of putting up armed resistance to Kornilov, and only then did he consult the ministers of the Provisional Government. At this meeting, at which 14 ministers offered their resignations, Kerensky was given special powers to deal with the situation. Kerensky read the government a declaration he had drawn up accusing Kornilov of mutiny and placing Petrograd under martial law. He agreed to delay its publication, however, while talks took place with Stavka.

The telegram dismissing Kornilov was received at Stavka on the morning of the 27th, and was greeted with general amazement. Kornilov could only conclude that the Provisional Government had fallen under the influence of the Soviets. Kornilov asked Lukomskii if he would take over as Supreme Commander-in-Chief as Kerensky ordered. Lukomskii said that he would not. Kornilov agreed that it was his duty to remain at his post, and wired to Krymov to speed up his progress towards Petrograd.

During the 27th, Savinkov attempted to resolve what he still believed to be a misunderstanding, and spoke to Kornilov on the direct wire. Savinkov pointed out that when he had been at Stavka he had not made any proposals on behalf of Kerensky for a reconstituted government. He protested that even the government's unwillingness to implement Kornilov's reform programme

[25] Browder and Kerensky, *Russian Provisional* iii, pp. 1563–64.

did not justify the action Kornilov was taking. Savinkov accordingly requested Kornilov to submit to the Provisional Government and surrender his post. Kornilov for his part reminded Savinkov that a government reorganization had been discussed when Savinkov had been at the Stavka on 24 and 25 August in connection with the Provisional Government's hesitation in carrying out the necessary reforms. He said that the Third Cavalry Corps was being sent at the request of the Provisional Government itself. (To this Savinkov replied that as a matter of historical accuracy, on Kerensky's instructions he had asked Kornilov for a cavalry corps 'to establish martial law in Petrograd and to crush any insurrection against the Provisional Government from whatever quarter it might come'.)[26]

Kornilov stated that Lvov had presented for his choice three variations of governmental reorganization drawn up by Kerensky himself:

1. The withdrawal of Kerensky from all parts of the government.
2. The participation of Kerensky in the government.
3. A proposal to Kornilov to assume the dictatorship which was to be proclaimed by the existing Provisional Government.

He added that he had wanted Kerensky and Savinkov to come to Stavka to make a final choice and that, as he had definite information about a Bolshevik insurrection, he considered their presence in Petrograd dangerous for both of them.[27] In these explanations there did not seem to Savinkov to be anything which could not be resolved by negotiation. Kerensky, however, had already sent out an order to halt the movement of Kornilov's troops on the railways.

At 8 p.m. on the 27th, Savinkov reported to the ex-ministers of the Provisional Government on his conversation with Kornilov during the day. He now thought that confusion had been caused because Kornilov had assumed that Lvov was sent as an official envoy of the government. It was decided to entrust Kerensky with negotiating with Stavka. At this session a 'Directory' of five ministers was set up to deal with the situation, consisting of Kerensky, Nekrasov, Tereshchenko, Savinkov and Skobelev.

The 28th was an anxious day for the governmental committee, as the possibility of reconciliation between the sides receded and Krymov's forces advanced on Petrograd. It was expected that they would occupy the city. Kornilov published appeals to the population, the army and to the Cossacks disputing Kerensky's presentation of events and justifying his own course of action. An especially significant document of this kind was Order No. 897, as it contains some unique admissions by Kornilov about his actions. The order was composed at the time when Kornilov's troops were heading towards Petrograd, but Savinkov had refused to confirm that they had been requested by the Provisional Government. In other words, Kornilov was in open revolt, without any political cover. In the order, Kornilov admitted that he had taken it upon himself to dispatch the troops to Petrograd, and that Savinkov's request for troops had only 'corresponded with the decision already taken'. Kornilov also acknowledged that he was acting in conjunction with a number

---

[26] N. I. Golovin, *Rossiiskaia kontr-revoliutsiia v 1917–1918 gg.* i (Tallinn, 1937), p. 50.
[27] *Ibid.*, p. 49.

of 'public organizations which were endeavouring to save Russia', and that
with their help he intended to provide the country with a strong government.
The disruption of Kornilov's communications ensured that Order No. 897
never reached its intended audience.[28]

During the afternoon of the 28th, a meeting of members of the Republican
Centre took place in Petrograd. As railway traffic had been stopped, contact
with Krymov had been lost, and without Krymov's instructions the group
was reluctant to assume responsibility for operations inside the city. Finisov
and Desimeter were therefore dispatched to find Krymov. It was also decided
that, as the Bolsheviks had not obliged by staging any disturbance, such
demonstrations would have to be manufactured.

On the night of the 28th it became apparent that the directive to stop
movement on the railways was having the desired effect, and Krymov's
advance was being halted. Only some of the units dispatched to Petrograd actually got through, and many of those had become separated from
their commanders. Sections of track along which the Caucasian Native
Division was travelling were torn up by railwaymen. Kornilov, moreover,
had not come personally to lead his troops; he had remained behind at
Stavka.

There were some powerful forces which even in the early period of the
Kornilov movement made their opposition to it known. The commander of
the Moscow Military District, Colonel A. I. Verkhovskii, for example,
dissociated himself from Kornilov and expressed support for the Provisional
Government. He was summoned to Petrograd by the Executive Committee of
the Soviet and was appointed War Minister in succession to Savinkov. And,
in keeping with Tretiakov's refusal to take any part in Kornilov's 'adventure',
on 29 August the Moscow press published the resolution of the Moscow
Duma which declared: '. . . Moscow calls on all the towns of Russia, on
everyone who loves his country, not to allow the freedom we have won to be
drowned in a blood-bath.'[29]

There was also a decided lack of confidence at Stavka in the success of the
advance on Petrograd. Only some of the officers were fully behind Kornilov,
mainly those who were professional soldiers. Those who had had become
officers during the war, and were drawn from the student intelligentsia, had
often been inclined to co-operate with the soldiers' committees and stood
aloof from the Kornilov movement. Apart from Denikin, V. N. Klembovskii
and a few others, there were not many dedicated supporters of Kornilov and,
in the event, even they did not act with any great resolve. Kerensky's swift
and unexpected denunciation of Kornilov as a traitor had deprived the
advance of the troops on Petrograd of legitimacy, and placed a stark choice
before the officer corps. Support for Kornilov had now become an offence,
and only the very committed were prepared to face the consequences in the
event of failure.

Neither was the mood of the troops in Kornilov's favour. They regarded
Kornilov as the man who had restored the death penalty and who was
attempting to destroy the liberties gained by the revolution. The soldiers'

[28] *The Times*, 10 October 1917.
[29] *Russkoe slovo*, 29 August 1917, quoted by M. Wilk, *Z pola walki* (1977, no. 3), p. 254.

committees especially had no reason to help Kornilov. As soon as they picked up Kerensky's telegram declaring Kornilov a traitor, they ceased to send out Kornilov's radio communications, impeded troop movements and began to arrest officers they suspected of being Kornilov sympathizers.[30]

Kornilov's troops, even the Cossacks and the soldiers from the Caucasus, were not impervious to revolutionary propaganda, as Kornilov had reckoned. The Soviet Executive Committee and other Petrograd organizations sent out delegations to meet the troops and explain to them the real state of affairs. Delegates from the All-Russian Moslem Union conferred with their co-religionists in the Native Division in languages its troops understood. As a consequence, the division dissolved in the same way as many Russian units had done previously.

On the evening of the 30th, Krymov was arrested by Cossacks and brought to Petrograd. He was questioned by Kerensky, who did not miss the opportunity to make a theatrical speech. Thoroughly disillusioned by the failure of his mission, Krymov committed suicide shortly after his encounter with Kerensky. According to Guchkov, he felt let down by Kornilov's inaction and declared that if he had the chance he would shoot Kornilov himself.[31]

The Consequences of the Attempted Coup for the Provisional Government

Kerensky set up a Commission of Enquiry on the 31st chaired by I. S. Shablovskii, the Chief Naval Prosecutor, and including Colonel R. R. Raupakh, N. Ukraintsev and N. L. Kolokolov. They were later to be joined by two representatives of the Soviet – M. I. Lieber and V. N. Krokhmal. They set out at once for Stavka.[32]

Kerensky had taken upon himself the position of Supreme Commander-in-Chief, and sent Alekseev, his Chief-of-Staff, to Stavka on 31 August to place Kornilov under arrest. Kornilov, in characteristic fashion, began to dictate terms for his own capitulation but, nevertheless, surrendered peacefully to Alekseev.[33] The Commission of Enquiry arrived at midnight and set about its task.

The Commission's work was to have unfortunate results for Kerensky. Raupakh, who had been appointed a member on Shablovskii's recommendation, was a committed supporter of Kornilov, and influenced his associates so that they interpreted the evidence in a way favourable to Kornilov. In particular, the commission accepted Kornilov's case that the Third Cavalry Corps led by General Krymov had been requested by the Provisional Government itself to quell disturbances emanating from the Soviet, and that consequently Kornilov was innocent of any rebellion. These findings

[30] A. Wildman, 'Officers of the general staff and the Kornilov movement', in E. R. Frankel *et al.*, eds., *Revolution in Russia: Reassessments of 1917* (Cambridge, 1992), pp. 95–99.
[31] 'A. I. Guchkov rasskazyvaet', *Voprosy istorii* (1991, no. 12), p. 174.
[32] N. Ukraintsev, 'The Kornilov affair', *Soviet Studies* xxv (October 1973, no. 2), pp. 287–88.
[33] Miliukov, *Russian Revolution*, pp. 224, 228.

8

The October Revolution

Politics after Kornilov

When Kerensky accepted the resignations of the ministers of the Provisional Government on the night of 26 August he brought the second coalition to an end. The question of how to reconstitute the government then became a matter of some urgency. Kerensky's immediate solution was to form a 'Directory', an inner Cabinet of five members headed by himself and vested with plenary powers.[1] But this was at best a temporary expedient; Kerensky hoped to form another coalition to replace the one which had collapsed. In this, however, he encountered the opposition of the Soviet Executive Committee, which considered that the involvement of the Kadets and the propertied classes in general in the Kornilov mutiny had made them unacceptable as coalition partners.

Immediately after the collapse of the Kornilov movement, however, Kerensky opened negotiations with that section of the propertied elements which had distanced itself from involvement with Kornilov, namely the Moscow industrialists. He endeavoured to persuade representatives of this group to join the new coalition. After protracted discussions, a third coalition government was formed on 25 September.[2] It was to remain in office until the Bolshevik accession to power in October.

Muscovites were well represented in the new Cabinet. From the Moscow business community were Tretiakov (Chairman of the Economic Council), Konovalov (Minister of Trade and Industry) and S. A. Smirnov (State Controller). The Kadet Minister of Welfare, N. N. Kishkin, and the Menshevik Minister of Justice, P. N. Maliantovich, were also from Moscow. The former commander of the Moscow Military District, General Verkhovskii, became War Minister.

Other members of the Cabinet were: M. V. Bernatskii, Minister of Finance; Tereshchenko, Minister of Foreign Affairs; Admiral N. D. Verderevskii, Minister for the Navy; S. L. Maslov (SR), Minister of Agriculture; Gvozdev, Minister of Labour; A. V. Liverovskii, Minister of Transport; Nikitin,

---

[1] The members of the Directory were: Kerensky, Tereshchenko (Minister of Foreign Affairs), A. M. Nikitin (Minister of Post and Telegraph (Menshevik)), A. I. Verkhovskii (War Minister) and D. N. Verderevskii (Navy Minister).

[2] P. N. Miliukov, *The Russian Revolution, Vol. 3: The Agony of the Provisional Government*, ed., trans. and with an introduction by G. M. Hamburg (Gulf Breeze, FL, 1987), p. 45.

Minister of Post and Telegraph (Menshevik); Kartashev, Minister of Religious Affairs; S. S. Skazkin, Minister of Education (Kadet); and Prokopovich, Minister of Supply.

The process of forming the new coalition had taken place independently of the Democratic Conference and the Pre-Parliament – institutions that had been created in the wake of the Kornilov affair on the insistence of the Soviet Executive Committee to decide the question of political power. The Democratic Conference, which met in the Alexandrinskii theatre in Petrograd, was convoked on 14 September. It was conceived as the body which would decide on the appropriate form of government for Russia until such time as the Constituent Assembly met. Much of the discussion at the conference centred round the question of whether a new coalition government ought to be formed, that is, a government in which not only the socialist parties but also the Kadets would be represented. Many on the left believed that their involvement in the Kornilov affair had made the Kadets' participation in the government unacceptable. On 19 September a vote was taken on the issue, in which 766 delegates accepted a coalition on principle and 688 opposed it. An amendment was then adopted by 739 votes to 139 excluding those members of the Kadet and other parties who had been implicated in the Kornilov conspiracy from the coalition. A second amendment to exclude the Kadet Party as a whole from the coalition was also adopted by 594 votes to 495. This latter amendment conflicted with the initial vote in favour of coalition, so that the conference was left in some confusion about what exactly it had voted for. The confusion was only increased when the self-contradictory motion to have a coalition without the Kadets was voted on, and left and right combined to reject it by 813 votes to 183. After a great many speeches and discussions it had emerged that the conference had decided nothing whatsoever. But by the time this outcome had been reached the new coalition government was already in existence.[3]

In the immediate aftermath of the Kornilov Affair, Kerensky took a number of measures designed to appease his left-wing supporters. On 1 September, without waiting for the decision of the Constituent Assembly, he declared Russia a republic. He shelved the Kornilov programme for the restoration of discipline in the army. He also released some of the Bolsheviks who had been arrested after the July days. On 4 September Trotsky, Lunacharskii, V. A. Antonov-Ovseenko and P. E. Dybenko all walked free from the Kresty prison, Trotsky becoming immediately the chairman of the Petrograd Soviet.

Trotsky was at liberty in time to lead the Bolshevik delegation to the Democratic Conference on 18 September; Lenin was threatened with arrest should he dare show his face. At the conference Trotsky read a declaration on behalf of the Bolshevik Party opposing any idea of a new coalition and calling for the transfer of all power to the Soviets. He said that, as the present conference did not reflect the change of opinions in the working masses, a new Congress of Soviets should be called.[4]

Having read the declaration, Trotsky led the Bolshevik delegation out of

[3] C. Anet, *La révolution russe* ii (Paris, 1918), pp. 199–200.
[4] *The Bolsheviks and the October Revolution: Minutes of the Central Committee of the Russian RSDLP (bolsheviks). August 1917–February 1918*, trans. A. Bone (London, 1974), pp. 52–57; *Bol'sheviki Petrograda v 1917 godu: Khronika sobytii* (Leningrad, 1957), p. 536.

the conference. This was a serious blow to the conference's prestige, because the Bolsheviks were now an influential party, which had been gaining control of Soviets up and down the country. That was why, if a new Congress of Soviets were to be called, as Trotsky suggested, it was likely to be Bolshevik in complexion.

Two days after Trotsky made his declaration, the Democratic Conference decided to convoke a Council of the Republic, or 'Pre-Parliament', to sit permanently until the convocation of the Constituent Assembly, and to which the new coalition would in theory be responsible. Given their support in the local Soviets, the Bolsheviks were only interested in such a body if it were to contain a strong element of workers', soldiers' and peasants' deputies, and for this reason they proposed to delay its formation by two weeks, until the new Congress of Soviets met. When the Pre-Parliament held its first session on 23 September, the Bolshevik delegation read out a declaration condemning attempts to form a coalition and demanding that a truly revolutionary government be formed. But instead of staging a walk-out of the Pre-Parliament, as they had done of the Democratic Conference, a compromise was reached between the left and right wings of the party whereby it was decided to withdraw Bolshevik representation from the presidium but, nevertheless, to continue participation in the Pre-Parliament.

The Decision to Seize Power

This compromise reflected the search for direction which confronted the Bolshevik Party in September 1917. The aftermath of the Kornilov Affair had made it a credible political force, but its new-found authority created serious dilemmas for its leadership. From the perspective of the beginning of September there were a number of courses open to the Bolshevik Party by which it might acquire, or at least partake in, State power.

The first of these was the elections to the Constituent Assembly. This represented the most legitimate way for the Bolsheviks to come to power, but it was also the most hopeless. For although the Bolshevik Party had increased its following among urban workers, there was no prospect of it ever gaining appreciable support from the peasants. The peasants would cast their votes for the SRs, the party which they thought most likely to give them the land. The best the Bolsheviks could hope for was to form an alliance with the left SRs and constitute with them a bloc in the Constituent Assembly.

The second possibility was to await the opening of the Second Congress of Soviets. Since many of the local Soviet organizations had fallen to the Bolsheviks, most delegates to the Second Congress were likely to be Bolshevik and the new CEC that would be elected would have a Bolshevik majority. It would then be open to the congress to declare that it was taking State power into its hands, and by this means the slogan 'all power to the Soviets' would have become a reality. This route to power, which is associated with the name of Trotsky, had the advantage that it would forestall the Constituent Assembly and yet retain a measure of democratic legitimacy. It was also a peaceful means of coming to power, and it did not require any special preparation.

This method, however, had some potential shortcomings. It was by no means certain that when all the delegates to the congress met they would deliver the Bolshevik Party the majority it needed. There was also some doubt whether the congress would be allowed to meet, as there were strong indications that the Provisional Government and the Soviet CEC would try to postpone it, if not dispense with it altogether. If left too late, the elections to the congress would clash with those for the Constituent Assembly, and the opportunity offered by the congress would be lost.

If the Congress of Soviets did declare itself the sovereign body in the country, any Bolshevik government would be answerable to it for its actions. The third possibility was to seize power by armed insurrection. This method would forestall both the Constituent Assembly and the Congress of Soviets and deliver power squarely into the hands of the Bolshevik Party. This was the option canvassed by Lenin from the beginning of September. This option got round the uncertainties associated with the Congress of Soviets, but there were two serious objections which could be raised to it. The first was that it lacked legitimacy: the Bolsheviks were open to the charge that they were usurping power. The second was that it was a high-risk enterprise. It was likely to result in casualties, perhaps in severe casualties. And if the attempt to seize power should fail, then the reprisals that would follow would eliminate the Bolshevik Party as a serious contender for political power for the foreseeable future.

The problem of legitimacy, however, was not insuperable. After all, it only existed for the educated élite in the country; and in any case the rule of law had been violated repeatedly during the past few months, most notably during the Kornilov Affair. Moreover, Lenin envisaged that a Bolshevik uprising would generate its own legitimacy; it would be an uprising whose purpose would be to satisfy the demands of the common people for peace, bread and land, which the existing regime had refused to give them. And as Lenin pointed out, no one would be able to dislodge a Bolshevik government which promised the immediate implementation of such a programme. In this way the Bolshevik programme was to serve as an instrument of insurrection.

As for the element of risk involved in an armed conflict, this was considerably diminished by the disintegration of the army that had steadily been taking place, encouraged by Bolshevik propaganda. The failure of the Kornilov movement had also demonstrated graphically how counter-revolutionary forces could be halted without firing a shot. Besides which, the revolution now had armed forces of its own in the form of the Red Guards and sympathetic regiments of the Petrograd garrison.

The dangers inherent in Lenin's strategy, however, gave added weight to the fourth possibility open to the Bolshevik Party in September 1917. This was to take advantage of the party's growing support and influence to join the mainstream of Russian democratic politics. The Bolshevik Party might then collaborate in a government composed entirely of socialist parties, and in this way exert an increasing influence on government policy. This was the option favoured by Zinoviev and Kamenev. It was a matter of considerable regret to them when the Bolshevik Party decided to withdraw from the Pre-Parliament on 5 October, as this seemed to them to deprive the party of its most promising course of action.[5]

[5] *Bolsheviks and October Revolution*, p. 78.

Not all the possible courses of action were mutually exclusive, and circumstances at times favoured now one, now the other. Lenin canvassed his views in a series of letters sent from Vyborg in Finland from mid-September. In his absence the prevailing point of view was Trotsky's, which saw the Congress of Soviets as the event which determined Bolshevik strategy. Lenin protested violently against this policy, and to make sure his views became known, began to address his letters to local Bolshevik organizations. In the Petersburg District Committee, V. I. Volodarskii and Lashevich opposed Lenin's call for an immediate insurrection, arguing that the party should await the Congress of Soviets, and Lenin felt constrained to reply to them in a letter written on 1 October.[6]

On 23 September, the same day as the Pre-Parliament met, the Soviet CEC decided to call the Second Congress of Soviets on 20 October. This now became a pivotal date for all Bolshevik activities. On the following day, the Bolshevik Central Committee resolved to campaign for the Congress of Soviets. It was also thought desirable in this respect to call district and regional congresses of Soviets in advance to prepare the ground for the Second Congress. On the 26th, however, came the first indication that the convocation of the Congress was likely to be resisted, for at the session of the Soviet CEC Bureau on that day, F. I. Dan suggested postponing the Second Congress of Soviets, as it would impede the elections to the Constituent Assembly. Trotsky replied that if the Congress was not called in a constitutional manner, it would be called in a revolutionary way.[7] The episode, however, served to reinforce Lenin's conviction that it was mistaken to rely on the Congress of Soviets bringing the Bolsheviks to power.

German successes in the Gulf of Riga at the beginning of October forced the Provisional Government to contemplate moving to Moscow along with the Pre-Parliament. The news of this intention caused the left wing in Petrograd to accuse the Kerensky government of planning to surrender Petrograd to the Germans. Rumours of this kind stopped the government pursuing the matter further, and it was left to the Pre-Parliament to decide on whether any action should be taken.[8] On 6 October a meeting of the Soldiers' section of the Petrograd Soviet condemned the Provisional Government's plans to transfer to Moscow, saying that if the government was incapable of defending Petrograd it should either conclude peace or make way for another government which would have that capability.[9]

At the Bolshevik Central Committee meeting on 3 October, plans were made for holding a Congress of Soviets of the Northern Region in Petrograd on 8 October. The decision was also taken to withdraw the Bolshevik delegation from the Pre-Parliament, a decision with which Kamenev registered his profound disagreement, as it seemed to commit the party to a highly dangerous course of action. Two days later, Trotsky carried out the decision by reading a declaration to the Pre-Parliament criticizing the Kerensky government for having reduced the Pre-Parliament to a consultative body

[6] *Bol'sheviki Petrograda* . . ., p. 581; V. I. Lenin, *Polnoe sobranie sochinenii* xxxiv, pp. 340–41.
[7] O. A. Polivanov, 'TsIK Sovetov nakanune Petrogradskogo vooruzhennogo vosstaniia', *Voprosy istorii* (1992, no. 2–3), p. 168.
[8] Miliukov, *Russian Revolution*, pp. 107–108.
[9] *Bol'sheviki Petrograda* . . ., p. 585.

and increased the representation in it of the propertied classes. He then demonstratively walked out of the Mariinskii Palace with the Bolshevik delegation. As Kamenev had pointed out, the step was a decisive one, because it served to eliminate the possibility of co-operation with other socialist parties, and to point the party in the direction of either taking power through the Congress of Soviets or staging an armed insurrection, as Lenin constantly urged.

On 9 October the Petrograd Soviet created the embryo of the Military Revolutionary Committee (MRC), the organization which would capture political power two weeks later. Initially its purpose was somewhat different; at first it was concerned with the movement of troops in and out of the capital. After the Kornilov Affair it was widely believed that the military authorities' demands for soldiers to be sent to the front were motivated by the political aim of removing revolutionary troops from the capital and replacing them with 'reliable' units. The government was widely distrusted in this matter, and it was thought desirable to establish a special committee which would monitor troop movements and organize the defence of the capital independently of the Petrograd military district.[10]

The proposal to create such a Committee of Revolutionary Defence was raised by the Bolsheviks at the meeting of Soviet Executive Committee on 9 October. The Mensheviks and SRs rejected the idea on the grounds that the creation of a military headquarters in competition with the official one would lead to dual power. The plenary meeting of the Petrograd Soviet which followed, however, adopted the Bolshevik proposal on the grounds that Kerensky was preparing to surrender Petrograd to the Germans, and that the Soviet placed no credence in Kerensky's strategic reasons for withdrawing troops from Petrograd.

The Soviet instructed the Executive Committee, together with the soldiers' section and representatives of the Petrograd garrison, to organize a Committee of Revolutionary Defence. The committee – soon to become known as the Military Revolutionary Committee – was empowered to collect all information relating to the defence of Petrograd and its approaches, take measures to arm the workers and, in this way, to undertake the defence of the capital and protect its inhabitants from the Kornilovites. The same meeting of the Soviet elected the delegates which would represent it at the Congress of Northern Soviets.[11]

On the following day, 10 October, an important meeting of the Bolshevik Central Committee took place. Lenin, who had moved from Vyborg to Petrograd shortly before, attended it in heavy disguise. The meeting took place in Sukhanov's flat, unbeknown to the assiduous chronicler of the revolution, as he had been encouraged to stay away that evening by a ruse of his wife, G. K. Flakserman, who was a member of the Bolshevik Party.

Twelve members of the Bolshevik Central Committee were present: A. S. Bubnov, F. Dzierżyński, Kamenev, Kollontai, Lenin, A. Lomov, G. Ia. Sokolnikov, Stalin, Sverdlov, Trotsky, M. S. Uritskii and Zinoviev. At the meeting, which lasted the whole night, Lenin put his arguments in favour of

[10] Iu. S. Tokarev, 'K voprosu o sozdanii Petrogradskogo voenno-revoliutsionnogo komiteta', in
    I. I. Mints, ed., *Lenin i Oktiabr'skoe vooruzhennoe vosstanie v Petrograde* (Moscow, 1964), p. 173.
[11] *Bol'sheviki Petrograda . . .*, pp. 598–99.

an immediate armed uprising. He thought that the international situation was propitious; there were signs that the proletarian revolution was maturing in Germany. The government's intention to abandon Petrograd also demanded immediate action. Support for the Bolshevik Party had grown enormously compared with the beginning of July. The agrarian movement was now gaining in scale and intensity. All these considerations pointed to the fact that the moment for an insurrection was ripe.

The preamble to the resolution which was eventually passed bears a close resemblance to Lenin's address to the meeting. It would therefore appear at first sight that Lenin's point of view triumphed. But the resolution does not recommend the immediate armed uprising that Lenin urged, but the more vague statement that: 'Recognising that an armed rising is inevitable and that the time for it has come, the Central Committee suggests that all party organisations be guided by this, and approach the discussion and solution of all practical questions from this point of view (the Congress of Soviets of the Northern Region, the withdrawal of troops from Petrograd, the action of our people in Moscow and Minsk, etc.).'[12] Even this resolution to 'be guided' by the recognition that an armed uprising was inevitable was not accepted unanimously. Zinoviev and Kamenev voted against it, and presumably argued against it at some length during the meeting.

Zinoviev and Kamenev both believed that leaving the Pre-Parliament had been a mistake by the Bolshevik Party, since this had deprived it of the chance of co-operation with other socialist parties. It was they who put up the most determined opposition to Lenin at the meeting. They argued that even if an armed uprising were successful, socio-economic conditions would cause the regime's downfall. They said that problems of supply would bring down a Bolshevik government within two weeks.[13]

Those, like Trotsky, who favoured waiting for the Second Congress of Soviets, proved less of an obstacle to Lenin because they at least accepted that power must pass to the Soviets, and did finally vote for the resolution. In 1920, Trotsky recalled that he and his fellow members of the Petrograd Soviet at the meeting associated the insurrection's fate with the course of the conflict arising from the withdrawal of garrison troops from Petrograd. He contrasted this position with Lenin's, which did not make the connection.[14]

This information is important because it helps elucidate a number of matters surrounding the meeting of the 10th. It establishes that the exploitation of the conflict over the withdrawal of troops from the capital was a further development in the tactic of awaiting the Second Congress of Soviets, and of the desire to maintain 'Soviet legality'. Lenin's specific reference to the withdrawal of troops from Petrograd in the resolution can therefore be interpreted as a concession to Trotsky's camp and an inducement to him to vote for the resolution.

[12] *Bolsheviks and October Revolution*, p. 88.
[13] A. Lunacharskii, K. Radek and L. Trotsky, *Siluety: Politicheskie portrety* (Moscow, 1991), p. 68; L. Trotsky, 'Vospominaniia ob Oktiabr'skom perevorote', *Proletarskaia revoliutsiia* (1922, no. 10), p. 58.
[14] *Ibid.*

The Military Revolutionary Committee

The conflict over the withdrawal of troops from the capital had already given rise to what would be the Military Revolutionary Committee and, although this body was not mentioned in the minutes of the meeting, its character and future tactics were destined to be elaborated at the Congress of Soviets of the Northern Region, which was to open on the following day. Significantly, this congress was mentioned in the resolution along with the withdrawal of troops from Petrograd. This points to the existence if not of a predetermined plan by Trotsky and his supporters, then at least of an awareness of the possibilities which the formation of the MRC offered.

The only occasion when an organization was mentioned in the minutes of the meeting was when Dzierżyński suggested forming a 'political bureau' to provide political leadership in the days ahead. It was to consist of seven people: Lenin, Zinoviev, Kamenev, Trotsky, Stalin, Sokolnikov and Bubnov. Every current of opinion in the Central Committee was represented in the bureau, so that the political leadership it was capable of providing could have been only of the most general kind. Significantly, however, its membership included the editors of *Pravda* (or *Rabochii put*, as it was then known); it was probably envisaged that the newspaper would prepare the ground politically for the Bolsheviks' accession to power, as indeed occurred.[15]

Being convinced that the Bolshevik Party had embarked on a ruinous course of action, Zinoviev and Kamenev did not let the matter rest. On the day after the Central Committee meeting they circulated a document containing a detailed refutation of Lenin's arguments to various Bolshevik organizations, in much the same manner as Lenin had previously done with letters urging an immediate insurrection. A copy of the document also went to the Congress of Northern Soviets, which opened in Petrograd that day. Lenin took the precaution of sending a special letter to its delegates.

The Congress of Soviets of the Northern Region, which met from 11 to 13 October, brought together representatives of 23 Soviets, including Petrograd, Moscow, Kronstadt, Reval, Helsingfors, the Northern, Western and South-Western fronts, the Baltic Fleet, etc. In his opening address, Antonov-Ovseenko explained that the idea of convoking the present congress had originated in the regional committee in Finland, and that initially it had been intended to hold it in Helsingfors. The aim of the congress, he said, was to link the whole of the Northern Region into a single powerful organization.[16]

The congress then heard reports from the various local Soviets, Trotsky speaking as the representative of the Petrograd Soviet, and M. N. Pokrovskii as that of the Moscow organization. Dybenko pledged the support of the Baltic Fleet, and Kārlis Pētersons of Iskolastrel declared that 40,000 Latvian riflemen would be ready to help Petrograd in the struggle for Soviet power.[17]

Antonov-Ovseenko then spoke on behalf of the Finnish regional committee. This committee, he said, had been formed in the wake of the Kornilov

[15] Lunacharskii, Radek and Trotsky, *Siluety*, p. 70.
[16] *Rabochii put*', 13 October 1917.
[17] G. F. Sivolapova, 'S"ezd sovetov severnoi oblasti v 1917 g.', *Istoricheskie zapiski*, 105 (1980), p. 57.

mutiny, and had become an organization of revolutionary power. No order of the Provisional Government was carried out in Finland unless it was countersigned by the commissar of the regional committee. Antonov-Ovseenko's report was followed by that of A. L. Sheiman, a delegate from Helsingfors, who greeted the congress in the name of a Soviet which had taken power some time ago. The speech by the Kronstadt delegate was of a similar character. In Kronstadt, he said, power already belonged to the Soviet; no instruction in Kronstadt was carried out unless it was approved by the military technical commission attached to the Soviet.[18]

The report from the Reval Soviet is not recorded in the summary of the conference sessions in *Rabochii put*, but it is clear from other sources that the situation in Reval mirrored those in Helsingfors and Kronstadt. From the time of the Kornilov mutiny the Reval Soviet had virtually controlled the town and the whole area of the naval fortress. Prompted by the Germans' capture of the Moon Sound islands, the Reval Soviet, the Executive Committee of the Soviets of the Estland territory and committees of military personnel had established on 2 October a committee to defend the region of the naval fortress. This committee was able to exert its authority over all the military forces in the fortress's region.[19]

These developments had alarmed both the Provisional Government and the staff of the Northern front, and on 8 October General Cheremisov had ordered General P. N. Krasnov to place immediately at the disposal of the Reval authorities two regiments of the Third Cavalry Corps to restore order. Cheremisov also proposed to replace the commander of the fortress, Rear-Admiral Leskov, with a more resolute appointee. On 11 October the Executive Committee of the Reval Soviet began negotiations with Cheremisov to persuade him to retain Leskov. These developments would be reported to the Congress of Soviets of the Northern Region by the Reval delegation.[20]

On the 12th the congress took up the theme of the military political situation. Antonov-Ovseenko in his introductory speech stated that the Provisional Government did not answer the needs of the revolution and should now be 'removed'. In his speech Lashevich recalled the government's efforts to transfer some units of the garrison from Petrograd, and said that there had now been created a special soldiers' revolutionary committee, which in effect would have the capital's military forces at its disposal. Lashevich called on other Soviets to follow this example and set up similar committees in their areas. Lashevich was followed by an SR who spoke in the same vein. Rabchinskii, the Reval delegate, also advocated the establishment of local MRCs.[21]

Lashevich's speech indicates that already on 12 October the MRC was seen as a potential instrument of insurrection. At that time, moreover, the MRC had not been officially constituted and Lashevich was not able even to refer to it by the name it would be given. Its constitution was due to be approved that

[18] *Rabochii put'*, 13 October 1917.
[19] J. Saat and K. Siilivask, *Velikaia Oktiabr'skaia sotsialisticheskaia revoliutsiia v Estonii* (Tallinn, 1977), p. 230.
[20] Saat and Siilivask, *Velikaia*, pp. 230–31.
[21] *Rabochii put'*, 14 October 1917; Sivolapova, 'S"ezd sovetov severnoi oblasti v 1917 g.', pp. 59–60.

same day, and several of the delegates attending the congress would become its leading members. Inevitably the MRC's character would be influenced by the experience of similar bodies already in existence in Helsingfors, Reval and Kronstadt. And in fact the later tactics of the Petrograd MRC mirrored closely the methods of the committees described by delegates to the Congress of Soviets of the Northern Region.

After the proposal for the creation of a Committee of Revolutionary Defence had been approved on 9 October, its organizational plan was drawn up by the young Estonian left SR, Lazimir. Trotsky later asserted that the Bolsheviks deliberately used Lazimir as camouflage for their own conspiratorial purposes.[22] But that is highly improbable because the positions Lazimir held made him the obvious choice for the task. He was a member of the Soviet Executive Committee, vice-chairman of its military section and chairman of the soldiers' section of the Petrograd Soviet.[23]

The MRC's organizational plan was approved at a closed session of the Executive Committee of the Petrograd Soviet on 12 October, and by the plenary session of the Soviet on the 16th, at which the Menshevik Broido pointed out that such an organization could be transformed into something altogether more threatening and dangerous.[24]

Although the statutes of the MRC provided for the representation of several organizations connected with the Petrograd Soviet, all its activities were directed by a small bureau consisting of the SRs Lazimir and G. N. Sukharkov, and the Bolsheviks N. I. Podvoiskii, Antonov-Ovseenko and Sadovskii. The bureau worked closely with the military section of the Bolshevik Party, the Northern Regional Committee and the military section of the Finnish Regional Committee.[25]

The Accession to Power

On 15 October, Antonov-Ovseenko travelled to Wenden to attend the First Conference of Bolshevik Army Organizations of the Northern front. His mission was to enlist the backing of the Northern front for the insurrection in the capital. He was promised the help of the Latvian riflemen, and was encouraged by the fact that one of their commanders, Jukums Vācietis, was pro-Bolshevik.

On the following day, Antonov-Ovseenko took part in an extraordinary conference of the Latvian Social Democratic Party in Walk. He outlined the plans for an insurrection in Petrograd and requested that the Latvian riflemen take measures in the XII Army to prevent the movement of counter-revolutionary troops to Petrograd. In accordance with the decision of the Congress of Soviets of the Northern Region the conference resolved to create a network of military revolutionary committees from representatives of the Latvian

[22] K. Siilivask et al., eds., Revolutsioon, kodusõda ja välisriikide interventsioon Eestis (Tallinn, 1977), p. 256; Trotsky, 'Vospominaniia', p. 53.
[23] E. D. Orekhova, 'Vystuplenie', in Mints, Lenin, p. 496.
[24] S. Oldenbourg, Le coup d'état bolchéviste (Paris, 1929), pp. 64–65.
[25] Sivolapova, 'S"ezd sovetov severnoi oblasti v 1917 g.', p. 65.

Social Democratic Party, the military organization of the XII Army, the Latvian regiments and the local Soviets in the Baltic region.[26]

On 18 October an MRC of the XII Army was set up in Wenden. It included representatives of the Soviets of Wenden, Wolmar, Walk and Iuriev. Local MRCs were also attached to the Soviets of Walk and Pernau. On 22 October at a joint session of the Executive Committee of the Estonian region and the Reval Soviet there was formed into the MRC of Estonia, with Rabchinskii as its chairman and Viktor Kingissepp as its vice-chairman.[27]

On 16 October the Bolshevik Central Committee met again, this time along with the party members from a number of organizations: the Petrograd committee, the Military Organization, the Petrograd Soviet, trade unions and factory committees. Lenin reported on the Central Committee meeting of the 10th, and read the resolution taken there, explaining the reasons he believed that the time for insurrection was ripe. The representatives of the various bodies gave reports on the mood in their respective organizations. Few showed signs of optimism. Several speakers reported that their localities or organizations would follow the Soviet, but not the Bolshevik Party. Lenin, for his part, defended the resolution adopted on the 10th against the objections of Zinoviev and Kamenev. Zinoviev observed that the resolution could not be considered mandatory, otherwise they would not now be discussing it. He proposed that if the Second Congress of Soviets met on the 20th, it should not disperse until the convocation of the Constituent Assembly. The meeting approved the resolution of the 10th, and a closed session of the Central Committee set up a Military Revolutionary Centre consisting of Sverdlov, Stalin, Bubnov, Uritskii and Dzierżyński to enter the MRC. This was the first sign that the Bolshevik Party regarded the MRC as the body which might lead the insurrection. In the light of the discussion that had just taken place, it had the distinct advantage of being a Soviet and not a party organization, and thus might command wider support.

On the following day, prompted by the Provisional Government, the CEC postponed the Second Congress of Soviets from 20 to 25 October. The significance of this move was noted by the American journalist, John Reed: 'By prodigious efforts, the government and the moderate Socialists have succeeded in side-tracking the All-Russian Convention of Soviets . . . which was to have been called for October twentieth – or at least they think they have side-tracked it. We wait. If it meets, things will happen, for almost all the Soviets have gone Bolshevik in the past two months – since the Kornilov affair.'[28]

On 17 October an editorial in the newspaper *Novaia zhizn* written by V. A. Bazarov noted that it was common knowledge that there were serious disagreements among the Bolsheviks on the advisability of an armed uprising. Bazarov himself believed that such an action would be doomed to failure, and would have disastrous consequences. He was thus somewhat dismayed

---

[26] A. V. Rakitin, *V.A. Antonov-Ovseenko* (Leningrad, 1989), pp. 125–28.

[27] Saat and Siilivask, *Velikaia*, pp. 232–33; *Bor'ba za sovetskuiu vlast' v Pribaltike* (Moscow, 1967), pp. 302–303; A. Ezergailis, *The Latvian Impact on the Bolshevik Revolution* (New York, 1983), p. 229.

[28] Polivanov, 'TsIK Sovetov', p. 169; E. Homberger and J. Biggart, eds., *John Reed and the Russian Revolution: Uncollected Articles, Letters and Speeches on Russia, 1917–1920* (London, 1992), p. 60.

that the Bolshevik opponents of the uprising had only distributed a hand-written leaflet stating their case. In the next issue of the paper Kamenev contributed an article agreeing that an insurrection would be misguided. He added, however, that he knew of no such decision by the Bolshevik Party.[29]

These items in *Novaia zhizn* prompted Lenin to begin an energetic campaign in public to refute the substance of Zinoviev and Kamenev's arguments, and in private to have them expelled from the party on the grounds that they had opposed a Central Committee decision in the non-party press. In the latter attempt Lenin was unsuccessful, and Zinoviev and Kamenev remained in the party to give expression to a more moderate current of opinion. In the capital, rumours of a Bolshevik uprising circulated widely, including governmental circles. These were fuelled by the open polemic Lenin conducted against Zinoviev and Kamenev. On the other hand, however, the controversy made it more difficult to predict what action the Bolsheviks would actually undertake. The government nevertheless took steps to strengthen its defences but, by the 21st, only 37 officers, 696 cadets and 75 soldiers were available to defend the Winter Palace where the Provisional Government met.

Whereas the Bolsheviks' own Military Section was dubious about the chances of organizing sufficient forces to carry out an insurrection in the way Lenin would have liked, the MRC made swift progress in establishing its authority over the units which composed the Petrograd garrison. A meeting of the garrison conference on the 21st welcomed the formation of the MRC and promised it support in all its undertakings.[30] The MRC permitted the Cartridge factory to allow ammunition to leave its premises only by an order signed by three of its members. It began to send its commissars to military units and other points of strategic importance such as telephone exchanges, railway stations and printing works. It became increasingly difficult to move troops or articles of strategic significance without the permission of the MRC.

The next stage would be for the MRC to gain control of communications and possible centres of resistance: the Peter and Paul fortress, the bridges over the Neva, the headquarters of the military district, the Admiralty and the banks. Antonov-Ovseenko and his colleagues in the MRC had at their disposal the soldiers of the Petrograd garrison, the armed workers of the Red Guard and the sailors of the Baltic Fleet. This combined force would be able to overwhelm any that the Provisional Government could call upon, provided that no fresh troops were to arrive in the capital.

Securing the approaches to Petrograd had been a major objective of the Congress of Soviets of the Northern Region, and the MRC's links with local soviets and soldiers' committees made this possible. Moreover, when asked by Kerensky to dispatch troops to Petrograd, the commander of the Northern front, General Cheremisov, was not to display any undue haste in doing so.[31]

On the night of 21–22 October, Lazimir, Sadovskii, and K. A. Mekhonoshin from the MRC appeared before Colonel G. P. Polkovnikov, the commander of the Petrograd military district, and demanded that all orders issued by the military authorities should be countersigned by a commissar of the MRC or

[29] *Novaia zhizn'*, 17, 18 October 1917.
[30] *Petrogradskii voenno-revoliutsionnyi komitet* i (Moscow, 1966), p. 60.
[31] S. N. Valk and R. Sh. Ganelin *et al.*, *Oktiabr'skoe vooruzhennoe vosstanie: Semnadtsatyi god v Petrograde* ii (Leningrad, 1967), p. 323.

remain invalid. Polkovnikov replied that he did not recognize any commissars, did not require any such guardianship and that the decisions of the Petrograd Soviet were not binding on him. The MRC delegation then withdrew and, after a new garrison conference had met in the Petrograd Soviet's premises in the Smolny Institute, a message was sent out to all military units of the garrison, saying that despite the confidence the soldiers of the garrison had shown in the MRC on the 21st, the military district's command had refused to recognize the MRC. This, the declaration said, had shown the command to be an instrument of counter-revolution, and none of its orders should be carried out unless countersigned by the MRC.[32]

This turn of events alarmed the Provisional Government considerably, and it contacted the commissar of the Northern front, V. S. Woytinsky, asking him to send troops to Petrograd. But neither on the 22nd nor the 23rd was any order actually given to dispatch military units to Petrograd.

On 23 October the chances of the Provisional Government receiving any troops from the Northern front diminished considerably when Soviet power was established in Reval. Organized by the MRC of the Estonian region headed by Rabchinskii, who was in direct telephone contact with Sverdlov in Smolny, workers, sailors and soldiers took under their control the most important strategic points in Reval. The rapidity and efficiency of the operation left the military authorities helpless. On the following day the MRC's control extended, as the garrison expressed its readiness to subordinate itself to the Soviet. Of primary concern to the Soviet leadership in Reval was preventing the movement of troops from the Northern front to help Kerensky. By taking power at this opportune time, the Estonian Bolsheviks had secured Petrograd from the west.[33]

At this juncture it might have been possible for the Bolsheviks to have launched a successful armed uprising, Antonov-Ovseenko being among those who urged such a course of action. But the majority of the Bolshevik leadership in Petrograd, including both Trotsky and Stalin, favoured delaying till the Congress of Soviets met. Negotiations with the staff of the Petrograd military district were reopened, and the demand to countersign orders was dropped, though more commissars continued to be sent out to military units and points of strategic importance.[34]

One of the most crucial points of strategic importance was the Peter and Paul fortress. At an extraordinary meeting of the MRC on the 23rd, Antonov-Ovseenko suggested sending in a few reliable companies of the Pavlovsk regiment and making an attempt to secure the fortress. The committee, however, by a majority, decided to hold meetings in the fortress and try to win over the garrison. Trotsky and Lashevich addressed the garrison troops, who eventually resolved to take orders only from the MRC.

At the insistence of Konovalov, Kerensky summoned the ministers to the Winter Palace for a discussion of the current situation. They decided that the unauthorized formation of the MRC was a criminal act, and that its members ought to be arrested.

[32] *Proletarskaia revoliutsiia* (1922, no. 10), p. 87; *Petrogradskii* p. 63.
[33] Saat and Siilivask, *Velikaia*, p. 240; K. Siilivask *et al.*, eds., *Revoliutsiia, grazhdanskaia voina i innostrannaia interventsiia v Estonii (1917–1920)* (Tallinn, 1988), pp. 260–61.
[34] Trotsky, 'Vospominaniia', p. 56. ·

At a meeting of the Petrograd Soviet at 8 p.m., Antonov-Ovseenko reported on the activities of the MRC. Almost all units of the garrison had recognized its authority. The MRC was aware of the measures the government was taking in the event of an uprising, such as summoning troops from the front and from various cities, but it had also taken its own measures. Thus an infantry division and two regiments in Wenden had refused to go to Petrograd. Antonov-Ovseenko noted that, despite threats, the MRC's commissars had not been arrested, and he believed no one would dare to do so.[35]

In the small hours of 24 October, the Provisional Government began to take measures against the Bolsheviks. The printing works of *Rabochii put* was surrounded by armoured cars and the order was given to close the printshop and break up *Rabochii put* and *Soldat*. The workers managed to save most of the matrix. A meeting of the Bolshevik Central Committee was held at which Kamenev proposed that no one should leave Smolny without the permission of the Central Committee. At 11 a.m., protected by Red Guards, *Rabochii put* was printed.

During the day the MRC put out a number of proclamations exploiting the government's aggressive action, claiming that the counter-revolution had begun to mobilize its forces. It was stated that this was a threat by the counter-revolution to the Congress of Soviets and the Constituent Assembly.[36]

Meanwhile, the MRC continued to deploy its forces. The cruiser *Avrora* positioned on the river Neva opposite the Winter Palace was given the task of backing up the forces deployed against the Provisional Government, including troops from Kronstadt and the Keksholm regiment from the Petrograd garrison. Early in the evening the MRC established control over the central telegraph office and the food-supplies depot. Throughout the night and into the morning of the following day the MRC continued to establish its control over one institution after another.

The MRC sent a message to Reval instructing local garrisons to guard the approaches to Petrograd, strengthen guards at railway stations and not to allow the passage of counter-revolutionary troops to the capital. From Reval the message was relayed on to Narva and other soviets in Estonia. Kerensky in fact gave orders to send several military units from Reval, but by the time Kerensky's request reached its destination, it fell into the hands of the new authorities in the town, who naturally took no action other than to instruct the commander of the naval fortress that no troops should leave the area. Seeing the hopelessness of Kerensky's position, the commander of the Northern front, Cheremisov, abandoned his attempts to send troops to Petrograd and ceased co-operation with the Provisional Government.[37]

Lenin, in hiding in the Vyborg district, was becoming impatient at the tardiness, as he saw it, with which the insurrection was moving. He once more tried to appeal to the local committees of the party. In the letter he wrote at that time he even displayed at this late stage some doubt in the entire strategy of taking power through the MRC. 'Let the MRC take power', he wrote, 'or some other institution.'[38] Around 6 p.m., against the orders of the

[35] Miliukov, *Russian Revolution*, p. 179; Rakitin, *V. A. Antonov-Ovseenko*, p. 148.
[36] *Petrogradskii*, pp. 83–85.
[37] Saat and Siilivask, *Velikaia*, p. 242.
[38] V. I. Lenin, *Polnoe sobranie sochinenii* xxxiv, p. 435.

Central Committee, Lenin emerged from hiding and went to Smolny. Trotsky and Kamenev were there manning telephones, following excitedly the course of events in the city.

At 10 a.m. on the 25th, Lenin drafted a declaration saying that the Provisional Government had been overthrown and that power had passed to the MRC. The text of the document satisfied Lenin's wish that the insurrection should take place before the Congress of Soviets. The intention was that the Winter Palace be captured and the Provisional Government be arrested soon afterwards. But because not all of the forces the MRC intended to deploy were in place, the attack on the palace had to be postponed until late in the evening. The palace meanwhile was being defended by army cadets and members of the Women's Shock Battalion, positioned with machine-guns behind barricades constructed from piles of firewood.

A meeting of the Petrograd Soviet opened in Smolny at 2 p.m. Trotsky began the proceedings by announcing that the Provisional Government no longer existed; some ministers had been arrested, and the remainder would soon follow. The insurrection, he stated, had taken place so far without bloodshed. Lenin then took the floor and outlined the policy of the future Soviet government. This would be the conclusion of peace, publishing the secret treaties and giving land to the peasants. 'In Russia', Lenin concluded, 'we must now set about building a proletarian socialist state.'[39]

During the evening the operation to capture the Winter Palace went ahead. The MRC threw a ring of troops from the Pavlovsk and Keksholm regiments round the Winter Palace and Palace Square and gradually drew it tighter. The occupation of the palace itself began at 9:40 p.m. with a blank shot fired by the cruiser *Avrora*. After some clashes in the rooms and corridors of the palace, punctuated by negotiations between the two sides, the cadets and members, the women's battalion finally surrendered. It was around 2 a.m. on the 26th when the ministers of the Provisional Government were arrested by Antonov-Ovseenko and led to the Peter and Paul fortress.[40] Kerensky was not among them; he had borrowed the American ambassador's car and escaped from Petrograd.

Lenin was unwilling that the Second Congress of Soviets should be opened until the Winter Palace was captured and the Provisional Government placed in custody. At 10:40 p.m., however, it proved impossible to wait any longer, and chaired by F. I. Dan, the first session commenced, still with the sounds of gunfire reaching the assembly. At that moment 670 delegates had registered for the congress with the following party affiliations: Bolsheviks, 300; Mensheviks, 68; SRs, 193; Ukrainian Socialists, 7; Anarchists, 3; Bund and Poalei Zion, 10; PPS and PSD, 10; Menshevik-Internationalists, 14; National-Socialists, 3; Lithuanian Liaudininkai, 4; non-party, 36; and those whose party affiliation was unknown, 22. This made the Bolsheviks the largest party in the congress, but it did not give them an overall majority. This majority could only be obtained in conjunction with the Left SRs and the Menshevik-Internationalists who, as it was to emerge, wished to form a government

---

[39] S. A. Piontkovskii, *Oktiabr'skaia revoliutsiia v Rossii* (Moscow, 1924), pp. 64–66.

[40] N. I. Podvoiskii, 'Vospominaniia ob Oktiabr'skom perevorote', *Proletarskaia revoliutsiia* (1922, no. 10), p. 78; *Oktiabr'skoe vooruzhennoe vosstanie*, p. 358.

of 'all socialist parties'.[41] Lenin's fears about the Second Congress of Soviets had been confirmed.

In his opening address, Dan deplored the fact that, as he was speaking, his fellow Mensheviks in the Provisional Government were under fire in the Winter Palace. He proceeded straight away to the election of the Presidium. This was on the basis of proportional representation, so that the Bolsheviks got 14 seats, the SRs 7, the Mensheviks 3 and the Menshevik-Internationalists 1. Martov proposed putting on the agenda the question of resolving the conflict taking place in the city by peaceful means. On behalf of the Bolsheviks, Lunacharskii supported this proposal, but at that juncture the politics of the Northern front intervened. E. D. Kuchin and Ia. A. Kharash, representatives of the Iskosol organization of the XII Army, made speeches condemning the Bolsheviks. They were answered by Kārlis Pētersons of Iskolastrel.[42] This exchange was followed by a walk-out of a large number of Menshevik and Right SR delegates. This made the Bolsheviks' task of obtaining a majority in the congress somewhat easier.

After the interval called at 2 a.m., the fall of the Provisional Government was announced, and Lunacharskii read a declaration written by Lenin giving in broad outline the policy of the Soviet government. This government had still to be created and, during the 26th, the Bolsheviks conducted negotiations with the Left SRs with a view to forming a coalition government, the Left SRs at this stage refusing to enter such a government until the possibility of a government of all socialist parties had been explored.

When the congress session opened at 9 p.m. on 26 October, 625 delegates were registered, of whom 390 were Bolsheviks or had now declared Bolshevik sympathies. At this session Lenin put forward the measures he had promised in the previous day's declaration. He read a decree proposing that peace be concluded by all the belligerent nations. He then introduced a land decree, based on the SR land programme, abolishing landed estates and putting the land at the disposal of peasant committees.

These decrees were an integral element in the Bolshevik strategy for taking power. By promulgating them the Bolsheviks were on the one hand showing that they had an answer to the most severe problems that had dogged the Provisional Government during its eight months of existence; and, on the other, they were putting into effect the two measures most desired by the people at large – the provision of peace and land. By implementing the people's will in this way, the Bolshevik revolution would acquire the legitimacy it clearly lacked if judged by normal democratic standards. These decrees were so important for the Bolsheviks that they were issued even before any legislative mechanism existed.

It was only after the decrees had been adopted that the congress discussed the matter of constituting a Soviet government. The decision was then taken 'to form a workers' and peasants' government to be called the Council of People's Commissars to rule the country until the convocation of the Constituent Assembly'. The new council would be considered to be a government responsible to the Congress of Soviets and its Executive Com-

[41] *Ibid.*, pp. 353–54.
[42] Ezergailis, *Latvian Impact*, p. 237.

mittee. The commissars of the new government were: Chairman of the Council, Lenin; People's Commissar of the Interior, A. I. Rykov; Agriculture, V. P. Miliutin; Labour, Shliapnikov; Army and Navy Affairs, a committee consisting of Antonov-Ovseenko, N. V. Krylenko and Dybenko; Trade and Industry, V. P. Nogin; Education, Lunacharskii; Finance, Skvortsov-Stepanov; Foreign Affairs, Trotsky; Justice, G. I. Oppokov; Food Supply, I. A. Teodorovich; Posts and Telegraph, N. P. Avilov; and Nationalities, Stalin.

The last item of business for the congress was the formation on the principle of proportional party representation of a new CEC of 102 members: 62 Bolsheviks, 30 Left SRs, 6 Menshevik-Internationalists, 3 Ukrainian Socialists and 1 SR Maximalist.[43]

Traditionally the Bolsheviks' acquisition of power is presented by historians, both sympathetic and hostile, as a well organized and planned *coup d'état*. But a closer examination shows that the Bolsheviks had different and conflicting plans about how they would acquire political power. In general, Trotsky's vision of a gradual and cautious route dominated, with Lenin's conception of an armed uprising being implemented only belatedly and inefficiently. The Bolsheviks' conquest of power was not a single event which took place on 25 October but a process which began with the defeat of the Kornilov movement, and was consolidated only well after the formation of the Bolshevik government. In the initial period of its existence there were many who assumed that this government would last only a few weeks at most, and there were not a few people's commissars who shared that opinion.

---

[43] A. I. Razgon, *VTsIK Sovetov v pervye mesiatsy diktatury proletariata* (Moscow, 1977), p. 30.

9

First Steps of the Soviet Regime

Kerensky and Krasnov

The formation of the Bolshevik government might have remained an ephemeral episode had Kerensky succeeded in his intention of raising an army to march on Petrograd and crush the Bolshevik uprising. On leaving the capital on 25 October, Kerensky made his way to the Northern front's headquarters in Pskov. There he tried to enlist the help of the front commander, General Cheremisov but Cheremisov claimed that he had no troops to spare to place at Kerensky's disposal.

Kerensky then sought out General Krasnov, who had replaced General Krymov as commander of the Third Cavalry Corps. After its unsuccessful advance on Petrograd in August, corps units had been dispersed to various locations on the Northern front so that Krasnov had squadrons available totalling only some 700 men.[1] When representatives of the two Cossack regiments, which had been sent to Reval at the beginning of October to keep order, approached the Reval MRC for permission to rejoin the main body of the Third Cavalry Corps, Viktor Kingissepp refused to let them leave the area.[2] In the aftermath of the Kornilov affair, moreover, the Cossack troops which made up these regiments were distrustful of their officers, and the officers, for their part, were resentful of the Provisional Government for its treatment of Kornilov and felt particular animosity towards Kerensky.[3]

Despite Krasnov's warnings that the troops he commanded were insufficient for the kind of operation Kerensky had in mind, the Cossack units were nevertheless transported by train to Gatchina, 24 miles to the south of Petrograd, where they prepared their advance on the capital. From Gatchina, Kerensky sent out telegrams to various military commanders requesting that they send reinforcements immediately. He received a considerable number of telegrams in reply promising the immediate dispatch of troops but, in the event, only a single regiment of infantry arrived. This was not only through the obstruction of commanders like Cheremisov, who had no desire to help Kerensky, but also because Vikzhel, the Executive Committee of the railwaymen's union, had decided to remain neutral in the conflict between

---

[1] S. P. Melgunov, *The Bolshevik Seizure of Power* (Santa Barbara, CA, and Oxford, 1972), p. 106.

[2] J. Saat and K. Siilivask, *Velikaia Oktiabr'skaia sotsialisticheskaia revoliutsiia v Estonii* (Tallinn, 1977), p. 251.

[3] A. Kerensky, *The Catastrophe* (New York, 1927), p. 343.

Kerensky and the Bolsheviks and not to facilitate troop movements. Vikzhel wanted a government established that contained representatives of all the socialist parties and urged Kerensky to negotiate with the Bolsheviks.

With limited forces at their disposal, Kerensky and Krasnov captured Tsarskoe Selo on the night of 28 October. On the following day, however, they encountered numerically superior Bolshevik forces, which included a well trained contingent of sailors from Kronstadt. In the battle which took place on the Pulkovo heights, Krasnov's advance was checked, and he was forced to withdraw to Gatchina. A premature cadet uprising in support of Kerensky, which took place in Petrograd that day, was quickly suppressed by pro-Bolshevik Red Guards and sailors. Such was the last, and somewhat inglorious, act of the Provisional Government, and with it the Bolshevik acquisition of power became considerably more secure.

The Bolshevik victory at Pulkovo heights was important in two respects. Not only did it destroy the chances of a swift restoration of rule by a new Provisional Government but it also allowed the Council of People's Commissars to escape the pressure applied by Vikzhel to form a government of all the socialist parties. Before Pulkovo, the Bolsheviks had responded positively to Vikzhel's call to broaden the base of the government, but once the threat posed by Krasnov's Cossacks had receded, negotiations of this kind were dropped rather rapidly.

While the Bolsheviks were still under pressure by Vikzhel, they skilfully deployed the weapon Lenin had designed in September. This was to identify themselves with the decrees on peace and land issued by the Second Congress of Soviets. Bolshevik spokesmen presented matters as if whoever was against their party was against the two decrees. Arguments of the same kind were later deployed to discredit critics of the spate of edicts that were promulgated by the Council of People's Commissars and that were designed to strengthen the Bolsheviks' hold on power.

The first of these was the Decree on the Press issued on 27 October. This was designed as an emergency measure to close down all publications that encouraged resistance or insubordination to the new government, spread sedition through the distortion of facts or instigated actions of a punishable nature. The decree contained a reassuring clause that the measures would be repealed and a free press established as soon as the situation returned to normal.[4] When by the beginning of November the Soviet government was out of any immediate danger and the decree remained in force, the CEC raised objections to it. It was pointed out in particular that the measure might have been appropriate during the actual struggle for power, but not subsequently. To this Trotsky and Lenin replied that the conditions of civil war still existed, and until final victory had been assured no opportunities would be given to the bourgeoisie to slander the Soviet government.[5]

[4] Iu. Akhapkin, ed., *First Decrees of Soviet Power* (London, 1970), pp. 29–30.
[5] J. Keep, trans. and ed., *The Debate on Soviet Power: Minutes of the All-Russian Central Executive Committee Second Convocation, October 1917–January 1918* (Oxford, 1979), pp. 69–74.

The Spread of the Revolution

In Moscow the conquest of power took much longer and was much more costly in lives than it had been in Petrograd. Once the insurrection had been begun in Petrograd, it became vital for the Bolsheviks that the revolution spread throughout the country and not be left isolated in the capital. On the 25th the Bolshevik leadership in Moscow began to try to follow their comrades in Petrograd and take power by the same method. In the Moscow Soviet they proposed that a Military Revolutionary Committee be elected to transfer power to the Soviets. The SRs declined to take part in the elections so that the Moscow MRC originally consisted of four Bolsheviks and three Mensheviks. Following the example of the Petrograd organization, the Moscow MRC issued an appeal stating that orders and instructions not issued or signed by it should be disregarded.[6] That same day the MRC sent Kremlin garrison soldiers to occupy the post and telegraph offices. The print shops of right-wing newspapers were occupied and sealed.[7]

These actions by the Moscow Bolsheviks suggest a belief that the Petrograd pattern of revolution had a universal application. But conditions in Moscow differed considerably from those in the capital. In Petrograd the powerful engine of revolution had been the distrust in the authorities caused by the Kornilov affair, and the consequent need to monitor their every action through the MRC. In Moscow this engine was absent because the civil and military authorities in Moscow had distanced themselves from the Kornilov movement. And behind that lack of involvement in the Kornilov affair were deeper, long-standing differences between the respective social structures of Petrograd and Moscow. In Petrograd, social groups were more differentiated than in Moscow, where a common sense of identity was strong and had been reinforced by decades of being the city which provided the most determined opposition to the St Petersburg establishment. But in the last days of October 1917, a crucial difference between the two cities was that the Moscow authorities had the advantage of having witnessed how power had been transferred in the capital, and were unlikely to be caught out in the same way.

At the meeting of the Moscow City Duma on the 25th the SR chairman, V. V. Rudnev, gave a report on events in the capital to date – the seizure of strategic points, the dispersal of the Pre-Parliament and the siege of the Winter Palace. He also referred to the occupation of the post and telegraph offices in Moscow. Rudnev proposed creating a Duma organization to oppose the Bolsheviks. As a result, the Committee of Public Security was formed, which included representatives of the *zemstvos*, the SR and Menshevik fractions in the Soviet, the headquarters of the military district, the trade unions of the post and telegraph workers, and Vikzhel. The Committee began to muster the armed forces it could rely on in the city. These included the cadets of the Alekseev and Aleksandrovskii military academies, who took up position in the city centre.

By the morning of the 26th, the outlying districts of Moscow were

[6] *Moskovskii Voenno-Revoliutsionnyi Komitet Oktiabr'-noiabr' 1917 goda* (Moscow, 1968), p. 23.
[7] J. Sobczak, *Pierwsze dni rewolucji: kronika 6 XI–3 XII 1917 r.* (Warsaw, 1977), p. 127.

controlled by the workers, while the city centre, with the exception of the Kremlin, was in the hands of forces loyal to the Committee of Public Security. New contingents of Red Guards were formed, but there was a serious shortage of arms. To gain access to the weapons in the Kremlin arsenal, E. M. Iaroslavskii was appointed commissar of the Kremlin and O. Berzins commissar in charge of distributing arms.

Encouraged by Vikzhel, who wanted to see the establishment of a government of all socialist parties, the MRC entered into negotiations with Colonel K. I. Riabtsev, the SR commander of the Moscow military district. Riabtsev was eager to gain time to allow military reinforcements to arrive in the city. In the event these for the most part were intercepted by pro-Bolshevik forces and were persuaded not to interfere. By bargaining with the MRC, Riabtsev also hoped to remove the garrison troops from the post and telegraph offices, and especially from the Kremlin. He promised to recall the forces that had encircled the Kremlin if the MRC withdrew one of the regiments guarding it from within. The MRC agreed to these conditions.

At 6 p.m. on the 27th, Riabtsev broke the cease-fire conditions and again surrounded the Kremlin with detachments of cadets. He demanded that the rest of the MRC's forces be withdrawn from the Kremlin, and that the arms which had been removed be returned. The MRC rejected these conditions, upon which its Menshevik members resigned. Late in the evening came the first casualties of the revolution in Moscow as an armed clash took place between the cadets stationed there and a group of 'Dvintsy', soldiers who had been arrested for spreading Bolshevik propaganda and imprisoned in Dvinsk before being transferred to the Butyrki prison in Moscow. They had been released in September on the insistence of the Moscow Bolsheviks.

Taking advantage of the poor communications between the MRC and the Kremlin, Riabtsev telephoned Berzins on the morning of the 28th, and told him that during the night units loyal to the MRC had been disarmed, the members of the MRC had been arrested and that the entire city was now in his hands. Riabtsev told Berzins that if he did not surrender the Kremlin within 25 minutes he would begin an artillery bombardment.[8] Berzins was deceived by this ruse and opened the Troitskii gate of the Kremlin.[9]

The loss of the Kremlin and the heavy casualties it had entailed served to polarize the sides in the conflict. A meeting of the Moscow garrison, which had hitherto remained neutral, resolved that it would not subordinate itself to the staff or the Committee of Public Security, but would henceforth only obey orders from the MRC. The Moscow Bolsheviks, the trade unions and the Moscow group of the SDKPiL called on the workers to come out on general strike. They also tried to mobilize the outlying workers' districts against the forces occupying the city centre and the Kremlin, surrounding Riabtsev's cadets and gradually dislodging them from the positions they held.

The workers, however, were slow to respond; they did not move to help in the fighting. In any case there were too few weapons. The Red Guard in the city districts numbered tens rather than hundreds. At first the main opposition to the cadets occupying the city centre came from the Kremlin garrison

---

[8]   *Ibid.*, p. 207.
[9]   *Ibid.*, p. 209.

soldiers, who gradually began to retake the streets and buildings. They were helped by the arrival of reinforcements from nearby towns – Tula, Podolsk, Orekhovo-Zuevo and Vladimir.[10]

The MRC agreed to a 24-hour cease-fire commencing at midnight on the 29th. Riabtsev hoped that while negotiations took place the troops he had been promised would arrive from the front. In the event the expected reinforcements failed to appear and the truce was quickly broken, the MRC's forces occupying the city telephone exchange and the Alekseev military academy. Attempts to bring about a cease-fire were abandoned and fighting broke out with new intensity on 31 October. By 1 November most of the city was under the MRC's control, though fierce fighting continued in the city centre. By the morning of 3 November, the MRC was again in possession of the centre of Moscow, including the Kremlin, where Riabtsev's cadets had made their last stand.

The cadets were disarmed and allowed to return to their units. Subsequently many of them applied to the Moscow Soviet for passes to leave the city. These were granted, though the destination of most cadets was the Kuban where they joined the Volunteer Army to fight against Soviet power.

As at the beginning of November it appeared as though there would be a coalition government in Petrograd, it was initially proposed to form a local organ of power on the same basis. In practice, however, it was the MRC which increasingly took on the function of the government in Moscow, running both the city and the surrounding Moscow region as Soviet power extended into the localities.[11]

Power was established practically simultaneously in the whole of the region surrounding Petrograd, an area embracing Finland, Estonia and the unoccupied part of Livland. This pattern was essential to the revolution's success and had been assiduously cultivated by the MRC. It ensured that the approaches to the capital had been covered before the conquest of power in Petrograd began. The territory between the Northern front, from where counter-revolutionary troops might have been dispatched, and Petrograd was defended by a string of towns that were already, or soon to be, in Soviet hands. As soon as the news came through of events in Petrograd, the MRC of the XII Army ordered Latvian infantry regiments to occupy the towns of Wenden, Wolmar, Walk and Iuriev, all strategic points on the route between the front and the capital. In Narva the Soviet took power on 26 October, and on the following day the Iuriev MRC took power in the town and the surrounding district. On 27 October the whole of Estonia passed into Soviet control, as the agents of the Provisional Government were removed from their posts and their functions handed over to the local Soviets. The governor of Estonia, Jaan Poska, surrendered his authority to Viktor Kingissepp, the chairman of the Estonian MRC.[12]

The main centre of resistance in the Baltic region was in the town of Walk where the XII Army had its headquarters. There on 28 October Iskosol had formed a 'Committee for the Salvation of the Revolution' which tried to send

[10] *Ibid*, pp. 212, 235.
[11] M. N. Pokrovskii, 'Kak voznikla sovetskaia vlast' v Moskve', *Oktiabr'skaia revoliutsiia* (Moscow, 1929), p. 215.
[12] Saat and Siilivask, *Velikaia*, pp. 243–49.

troops to help Kerensky. The troops were prevented from leaving by Latvian riflemen and Estonian railwaymen, the railwaymen recognizing the authority of the Estonian MRC rather than Vikzhel. On 7 November the Latvian 6th Rifle Regiment under Vācietis entered Walk and established Soviet power in the town. On 16–18 November, the Second Congress of Soviets of Latvia sitting in Wolmar declared Soviet power in Latvia.[13]

In the brief period between November 1917 and February 1918, when the German armies invaded, the Bolshevik governments in Estonia and the unoccupied part of Latvia carried out the same kind of reforms that were being effected in Petrograd. Factories, where they existed, were given over to workers' control. Red Guards were formed, and oppositionist newspapers were closed down. The land was nationalized, but in keeping with the long-standing policy of Latvian and Estonian socialists, the large estates were not divided up but were retained as the basis for collective farms.[14] These experiments were of short duration, however, being brought to an end by the breakdown of Soviet–German peace negotiations at Brest-Litovsk and the advance of the German armies as far as Narva.

In most towns in central Russia, news of revolution in Petrograd caused the local soviets to remove the agents of the Provisional Government and assume power themselves. This took place most quickly and easily in the central industrial Russian heartland. There the industrial workers were numerous and the land problem was acute. The central provinces were also relatively homogeneous in their national composition.

The army from the Estonian coast to Mogilev, comprising the Northern and Western fronts, was quickly won over to the new Soviet government's side. The revolution spread swiftly through the Baltic Fleet, the troops stationed in Finland and through the Reval army group.

Kerensky's flight left the country without a premier and a commander-in-chief of the army. This caused considerable confusion at Stavka. The Chief of Military Staff, General N. N. Dukhonin, therefore took over the responsibility himself and on 1 November declared himself acting Supreme Commander-in-Chief. Since the Decree on Peace had received no response in any quarter, on 8 November Lenin requested Dukhonin to begin immediate armistice negotiations with the Germans. He refused, and the following day the Soviet government removed Dukhonin from his post and appointed Lieutenant Nikolai Krylenko in his place. On 20 November revolutionary armies occupied Stavka and arrested Dukhonin. At the railway station in Mogilev, a mob of infuriated soldiers broke through Dukhonin's escort and killed him.

With Dukhonin's death the whole apparatus of the old army passed into Soviet hands. On 23 November at Stavka a military field staff was established under M. Ter-Arutunian and Vācietis. Their military expert was General M. D. Bonch-Bruevich, who had immediately recognized the new government and who became Chief of General Staff on 20 November.

In the Belorussian town of Minsk, the local Soviet took power on 25 October on learning that in Petrograd the revolution had begun. On

[13] J. Vacietis, *Latviesu strelnieku vesturiska nozime* (Riga, 1989), pp. 178–79; Saat and Siilivask, *Velikaia*, p. 255; *Istoriia latviiskoi SSR* (Riga, 1971), p. 427.

[14] *Bor'ba za sovetskuiu vlast' v Pribaltike* (Moscow, 1967), pp. 325–29.

the following day the Military Revolutionary Committee of the Western region and the front was established to extend Soviet power to the rest of Belorussia and the Western front. Its chairman was the Bolshevik from the Minsk Soviet, A. F. Miasnikov.

From Mogilev down to the Black Sea, however, the spread of the revolution took a different direction. The South-West front went over for the most part to the national movement which had been developing in the towns and villages of the Ukraine. This gave class antagonisms a national character and ensured that the beneficiary of the revolutionary upsurge was the Rada.

The Left Socialist Revolutionaries

Although the Left SRs had remained in the Second Congress of Soviets when the right had walked out, they had not accepted Bolshevik invitations to join the Council of People's Commissars, since they still demanded the creation a government of all socialist parties from the Bolsheviks to the Popular Socialists. In November the Left SRs formally constituted themselves into a separate party organization presided over by the venerable Mark Natanson. The First Congress was held from 19 to 28 November. In her address to the Congress on 21 November, Mariia Spiridonova claimed for it the heritage of the Social Revolutionary tradition. What had taken place in October, she believed, was only the first, the political, stage of the revolution; the second stage would be the social revolution, which would only triumph if it occurred on a world scale. And whereas the Bolsheviks had been successful in the political stage of the revolution, the limitations of their outlook would become manifest in its social stage. At the congress it was decided to enter into coalition with the Bolsheviks and, as a result of negotiations between the two parties A. L. Kolegaev became Commissar for Agriculture, P. P. Proshian for Post and Telegraph, I. Z. Steinberg for Justice, V. E. Trutovskii for Local Government and V. A. Karelin for State Properties. Spiridonova and B. D. Kamkov remained outside the government to devote their energies to building up the party organization.[15]

The Constituent Assembly

The elections to the Constituent Assembly were held between 15 and 19 November, that is, just before the SR Party formally split. The elections were by universal suffrage with a secret ballot. The turn-out was high, as much as 70 per cent in the capital cities. In the countryside participation was even higher – from 80 to 97 per cent, often with all the votes being cast for the same electoral list. In these cases the peasants would decide at the village assembly which party to vote for, and the decision would be put into effect in the voting

[15] I. N. Steinberg, *Spiridonova: Revolutionary Terrorist* (London, 1935), p. 184; S.V. Bezberezh'ev, 'Mariia Aleksandrovna Spiridonova', *Voprosy istorii* (1990, no. 9), p. 66.

booths. Peasants were accustomed to submitting to the decisions of the *mir*, and this was reflected in the way votes were cast in the villages. Returning soldiers often played a big part in the villages, by increasing local knowledge about political parties and the political situation generally.

In the 68 constituencies there was a total vote of 44,443,000. Their distribution was as in Table 9.1. The SRs received by far the largest share of the vote. The areas of their greatest success were: the central black-earth region (74.6 per cent), Siberia (74.5 per cent), the north (73.8 per cent), and the middle Volga (57.2 per cent).

Table 9.1   Elections to the Constituent Assembly, 15–19 November 1917

Party	Votes
Socialist Revolutionaries	17,864,000 (40.0%)
Bolsheviks	10,649,000 (23.9%)
Kadets	2,099,000 (4.7%)
Mensheviks	1,158,000 (2.3%)

Although the Bolsheviks' share of the vote was under 25 per cent in the country as a whole, they did a great deal better in the urban and industrial regions, where they received 36–38 per cent of the poll. In Petrograd as a whole the Bolsheviks got 45 per cent of the vote; in the working-class districts even more: Vyborg district, 70 per cent; Peterhof, 68 per cent; and Poluostrovskii, 58 per cent. In the Alexander Nevsky, Vasileostrovskii, Lesnoi, Narva, Novo-Derevensky and Okhtinskii districts, 50 per cent of the votes went to the Bolsheviks.

The Bolshevik vote was also relatively high among the troops. On the Northern and Western fronts and in the Baltic Fleet the Bolsheviks received 62.1 per cent of the vote, compared to the SRs' 25.4 per cent. In garrison towns the Bolshevik Party obtained 57 per cent of the vote. Although the Bolshevik vote was low among the peasantry as a whole, they did receive 1 million peasant votes, mostly from the north-west and the central industrial region. They tended to do well in areas where there was a high concentration of hired labour. In Livland, for example, the Bolsheviks took 71.9 per cent of the vote.

The Mensheviks polled highly only in Georgia, where they were a mass party both in the towns and in the countryside. Elsewhere their support lay mainly in small provincial towns with little industrial development, among intellectuals, artisans and small traders. In Omsk, for example, they polled 24.9 per cent of the vote, in Blagoveshchensk, 23.4 per cent and in Tambov, 17.4 per cent.

The Kadets attracted more votes than all the other non-socialist parties put together. Their support was to be found mainly in the large urban centres, and in 13 provincial towns they were the biggest party with between 43 and 48 per cent of the vote. In 32 towns, including Petrograd and Moscow, they came second. But in most areas they attracted only between 1 and 5 per cent of the voters. Even in Moscow they did not receive the support of the merchant oligarchy. Evidently it thought the Kadet Party too discredited in the eyes of the electorate and preferred to form an independent 'Trade and

Industrial Group' for which Riabushinskii, Tretiakov, Chetverikov and N. D. Morozov stood as candidates.[16]

Somewhere in the region of 410 deputies of the 715 total had assembled when the Constituent Assembly opened on 5 January 1918. Of these there were 370 SRs, 175 Bolsheviks, 40 Left SRs, 16 Mensheviks, 17 Kadets and 86 representatives of national parties and groups.[17] The session opened at 4 p.m. in the White Hall of the Tauride Palace where the Duma had met. Sverdlov opened the proceedings by reading the 'Declaration of Rights of the Working and Exploited People'. Chernov was then elected chairman. A number of speeches were then made condemning the actions of the Soviet government. At 12 a.m. an adjournment was called during which the Bolsheviks decided to read a declaration dissolving the Constituent Assembly. The declaration was duly read, but the session went on, even though the Left SRs departed at 5 a.m. depriving the meeting of a quorum. Finally, the chief of the guard, the sailor A. G. Zhelezniakov, tapped Chernov on the shoulder and told him that everyone should now leave the hall as the guard was tired. With this the Constituent Assembly ended its one and only session.

Lenin gave two main reasons for dispersing the Constituent Assembly. One was that the elections were held before the split in the SR Party took place, thus depriving the Left SRs of the opportunity to put up a separate list of candidates. This circumstance made the assembly unrepresentative of the people's will. Lenin's other argument was that a republic of Soviets was a much higher form of democracy than a republic headed by a Constituent Assembly. The same reasons were advanced for the dispersal of the Constituent Assembly by Spiridonova for the Left SRs.[18] The dispersal of the Constituent Assembly and the new constitution embodied in the 'Declaration of Rights of the Working and Exploited People' were sanctioned by the Third Congress of Soviets, which opened on 10 January.

The Bolsheviks' attitude to the Constituent Assembly was a rather cynical one. They had advocated its convocation throughout 1917, using this as a weapon against the Provisional Government. On coming to power, however, the Bolsheviks had systematically striven to undermine the Constituent Assembly's authority, being aware that they had no chance of obtaining a majority in it. The dispersal was the culmination of this policy. But that action more than any other in the early period of the Soviet regime served to discredit the Bolsheviks' democratic credentials. It not only appalled democrats of all shades within the country but it also dismayed potential allies abroad, including German socialists on whom at that very time the Soviet government was eager to make a favourable impression.

Brest-Litovsk

On 14 (27) November, the German High Command agreed to begin armistice negotiations with the Russians on 19 November (2 December). Trotsky at

---

[16] O. N. Znamenskii, *Vserossiiskoe uchreditel'noe sobranie* (Leningrad, 1976), p. 291.
[17] *Ibid.*, pp. 338–39.
[18] Steinberg, *Spiridonova*, p. 190.

once informed the Allied governments of this and invited their representatives to participate in the talks. This invitation, however, was ignored, and only the Russian delegation travelled to Brest-Litovsk to meet the German plenipotentiary, General Max Hoffmann. The Russian delegation was led by Adolf Joffe and included Kamenev, Sokolnikov, military and naval experts, and – to demonstrate the democratic character of the new Soviet regime – a worker, a peasant, a soldier and a sailor.

When the talks began on 20 November (3 December), Joffe asked that the representatives of all belligerent countries be invited to attend. Hoffmann replied that he was only authorized to conduct negotiations with the Russians but that he was entirely willing to offer conditions for a separate peace. Joffe and his delegation then went back to Petrograd to confer on the matter with Lenin and Trotsky.

When the Soviet delegation returned to Brest-Litovsk on 2 (15) December, they secured an armistice for 28 days and the undertaking that the Central Powers would transfer from the Eastern to the Western front only those troops which were already under orders to move. Somewhat surprisingly, Hoffmann also agreed to limited fraternization between the two armies and to permit the exchange of newspapers. This agreement allowed the Bolsheviks to deliver large quantities of their propaganda newspaper *Die Fackel* across the lines to the German soldiers. When Trotsky reported on the talks at Brest-Litovsk to the CEC on 8 December, he showed his audience a copy of *Die Fackel*, explaining that it was a means of conducting diplomacy directly with the German people. He stated that the Soviet position would be much better if the European peoples had risen in revolution, and if peace negotiations were being carried on not with General Hoffmann and Count Czernin but Karl Liebknecht, Clara Zetkin, Rosa Luxemburg and other German socialists.[19]

On 9 (22) December, the peace conference began at Brest-Litovsk. For these negotiations the German delegation was led by the Foreign Secretary, Baron Richard von Kühlmann, and the Austro-Hungarian one by the Foreign Minister, Count Ottokar von Czernin. Bulgaria and Turkey were also represented. On this occasion the Soviet delegation, led by Joffe, had been joined by the two Left SRs, A. A. Bitsenko and S. D. Mstislavskii.

The German High Command, represented at Brest-Litovsk by Hoffmann, was eager to end the negotiations quickly in order to be able to concentrate all available troops on the Western front as soon as possible to ensure the success of the projected spring offensive against the Allies. It also wished to extend Germany's borders to include the Livland, Kurland and Estonia as well as the Lithuanian provinces of Russia. In addition, they hoped to gain access to Ukrainian grain in order to feed the populations starved by the Allied blockade. This last objective was a compelling one for Czernin, since Austro-Hungary was desperately short of food supplies. This also prompted him to favour a quick conclusion to the negotiations.

Kühlmann, however, with an eye to Germany's bargaining position at an eventual general peace conference, was much more concerned with the presentation of his country's case. He did not wish Germany to appear

[19] Keep, *Debate*, pp. 186–88.

too hasty or too rapacious. He was prepared, therefore, to negotiate and debate with the Russians at some length, and even accepted the principles of a peace without annexations or indemnities and self-determination for nations – this much to the dismay of the German right wing and military. The Russians tried to prolong the peace talks as much as possible in the hope that revolution would break out in the countries of the Central Powers, giving them as negotiating partners Liebknecht and Rosa Luxemburg.

When Kühlmann accepted the principles of no annexations or indemnities and of self-determination, which Joffe had stated, the Soviet delegation was at first jubilant, believing that the Germans intended to remove all their armies behind their old frontiers and allow the populations of the previously occupied territories to decide their futures by plebiscite. Hoffmann, however, explained to Joffe that this was not the interpretation the Central Powers put upon the principles; since Poland, Lithuania, Kurland and Estonia had already declared their wish to secede from the Russian state, Germany did not find it possible to evacuate her troops from these areas. Disillusioned, Joffe broke off negotiations and returned with his delegation to Petrograd.[20]

By this time Lenin was beginning to lose faith in the prospect of a revolution in the West materializing soon enough to help the Soviet government in its present predicament, and now began to think it better to conclude a peace with Germany as soon as possible. Lenin's belief, however, was not widely held, and he was not influential enough to impose it on the rest of the Bolshevik Party. Trotsky attempted to sound out the Allies to see if help would be forthcoming if the Soviet State were to put up resistance to the Germans. As Britain, France and the USA had no official contact with the Soviet government, relations were maintained through unofficial agents: Bruce Lockhart, Jacques Sadoul and Raymond Robins. All three urged their respective governments to co-operate, but without success.

When negotiations resumed at Brest-Litovsk on 27 December 1917 (9 January 1918), Trotsky himself led the Soviet delegation. He was joined by Karl Radek, Stanislaw Bobinski, Peteris Stučka and Vincas Kapsukas, who acted as consultants on Polish, Baltic and Lithuanian affairs. Their function was to contest the German assertion that the populations of the occupied territories wished to detach themselves from Russia.[21] The session was also attended by a delegation from the Central Rada. In prolonged debates with Kühlmann, Trotsky rejected the German interpretation of 'self-determination', demanding that referendums should be conducted without the presence of foreign military forces.[22] Kühlmann refused to consider the evacuation of German troops, and claimed that the peoples of the occupied territories had already made their wishes known through the institutions established by the German military authorities. On 5 (18) January, Hoffmann presented the Soviet delegation with the German peace terms. These demanded the transfer to German control of Poland, Lithuania, Livland, Kurland and part of the territory inhabited by Ukrainians and Belorussians. Trotsky returned with his delegation to Petrograd to consult with his colleagues.

[20] *Ibid.*, pp. 223–30.
[21] V. Kapsukas, 'Lietuvos Bresto taikos tarybos', *Raštai* vii (Vilnius, 1964), pp. 486–87.
[22] J. W. Wheeler-Bennett, *Brest-Litovsk: The Forgotten Peace March 1918* (London, 1938), p. 157.

The issue of how the Soviet delegation ought to proceed was debated intensively in the Bolshevik Central Committee. The tactic advocated by Trotsky was summed up in the formula 'neither war nor peace'. That is, he proposed that the Russian army should be demobilized, but that the Soviet government should refuse to sign the peace treaty. Lenin considered this option to be no more than a piece of international political showmanship. He thought that the demobilization of the troops would only lead to the loss of the Estonian socialist republic. He predicted that if the Germans started to attack, the Soviet government would be forced to sign a dictated peace, and in that case it would be a worse one than that presently on offer. He was adamant, however, that Russia was in no position to fight a revolutionary war against the Germans.[23]

Bukharin was confident that if the German army did advance any farther into Russia, this would encourage the development of the international workers' movement. He was encouraged by the appearance of a strike movement in Vienna. Other members of the Central Committee were less sanguine on the prospects for international revolution and approached the question of making peace with Germany accordingly. Trotsky's tactic was carried by a small majority. In the Central Committee of the Left SR Party, Spiridonova, Kolegaev, Trutovskii and Bitsenko all favoured concluding peace with Germany in the expectation that this would further the progress of world revolution.[24]

On 28 December (10 January), however, the St Petersburg committee of the Bolshevik Party had passed a resolution calling for a revolutionary war, and on the same day the Moscow Regional Bureau headed by A. Lomov, T. V. Sapronov, I. N. Stukov and V. N. Iakovleva advocated breaking off negotiations with imperialist Germany, the immediate creation of a volunteer revolutionary army and commencement of a ruthless war against the bourgeoisie of the entire world in the cause of international socialism.[25] These views were characteristic of a current of opinion which was to be designated as 'Left Communism', whose chief representatives were Bukharin, N. Osinskii, and Radek. During the spring of 1918, the Left Communists of the Moscow Bureau published the journal *Kommunist* in which they criticized the foreign and economic policies of the party leadership. In it Bukharin first gave voice to the opinion that the concessions made to capitalism at home and abroad had caused the revolution in Russia to degenerate.

The discussions on making peace with Germany took place in the immediate aftermath of the dissolution of the Constituent Assembly, an event which produced some revulsion among socialist circles in Western Europe, and in Germany in particular. Kautsky wrote articles deploring the Bolsheviks' disregard for democratic principles. It was a propaganda reversal which weakened the Soviet hand in the peace negotiations. Lenin and Trotsky were concerned to repair the damage, and Trotsky's book *The Russian Revolution to*

---

[23] *The Bolsheviks and the October Revolution: Minutes of the Central Committee of the Russian RSDLP (bolsheviks) August 1917–February 1918* (London, 1974), pp. 174–75.

[24] A. V. Pantsov, 'Brestskii mir', *Voprosy istorii* (1990, no. 2), p. 74; Bezberezh'ev, *Spiridonova*, p. 74.

[25] K. I. Varlamov and N. A. Slamikhin, *Razoblachenie V. I. Leninym teorii i taktiki 'levykh kommunistov' (noiabr' 1917 g.–1918 g.)* (Moscow, 1964), p. 68; Pantsov, 'Brestsky mir', p. 72.

Brest-Litovsk and Lenin's *State and Revolution* were published with this in view.

The renewed peace negotiations at Brest-Litovsk on 17 January 1918 took place against a background of social unrest in Vienna and the successful advance of Soviet troops towards Kiev, the Central Rada seat. Despite the fact that the Rada controlled very little Ukrainian territory, the Central Powers concluded with it a separate peace treaty on 27 January. The agreement provided for the export to Germany and Austro-Hungary of a million tons of foodstuffs.

On the same day as the treaty with the Ukraine was concluded, Hoffmann presented a formal ultimatum to the Soviet delegation, declaring that the terms which had been offered to Russia were a *sine qua non* of a peace treaty with Germany. In response Trotsky enunciated his formulation of 'no war – no peace'. He refused to accept the German terms and declared the war at an end. He then withdrew the Soviet delegation from Brest-Litovsk in the expectation that the Central Powers' desire for peace would lead them to accept the anomalous situation.

That did not happen. Despite the opposition of Kühlmann and Czernin, Hindenburg and Ludendorff obtained the Kaiser's consent for a renewed offensive against Russia. On 18 February the German forces began their 300-kilometre advance along the entire front, meeting little or no resistance from the disintegrating Russian army. The newly formed Workers' and Peasants' Red Army was too few in numbers to be any match for the Germans. On the following day the Soviet government signalled its readiness to accept the German peace terms. The reply, consisting of new and harsher terms presented in the form of an ultimatum, was received by Lenin on the 23rd. It demanded the transfer to Germany of the entire Baltic, Poland and parts of Belorussia. Russia was obliged to evacuate the Ukraine and Finland, and to make peace with the Central Rada.

The ultimatum caused a deep division within the Bolshevik Party between those, like Bukharin, who favoured a revolutionary war, and those who agreed with Lenin that such a course of action was doomed to failure and there was no choice but to sign the humiliating peace terms. Trotsky finally sided with Lenin, and resigned as Commissar for Foreign Affairs in order to signal a new direction in Soviet policy. A delegation headed by Sokolnikov and G. V. Chicherin left for Brest-Litovsk and, demonstratively refusing to enter into any negotiations, signed the peace treaty on 3 March.

This treaty, along with the supplementary agreements concluded the following August, required Russia to renounce sovereignty over Russian Poland, Lithuania, Livland, Kurland, Estonia and the Moon Sound islands. Batum, Kars and Ardahan were to be conceded to Turkey. In addition, Russia was forced to recognize the independence of Finland, the Ukraine and Georgia, and to agree to considerable monetary reparations. Both sides undertook to refrain from conducting propaganda against each other, Russia being prohibited in particular from carrying out propaganda activities in the territories occupied by Germany and its allies.[26]

Through Lockhart, Lenin and Trotsky intimated that they might oppose

[26] Wheeler-Bennett, *Brest-Litovsk*, p. 405.

SWEDEN

FINLAND

Line of Front in
October 1917

Line of occupation by
Germany and its allies
after 3 March 1918

The 'Agreed' line, west of
which Russia renounced
all territorial rights

Narva
Petrograd

Gulf
of
Riga

Baltic Sea

Pskov

Riga

Danzig   Vilna
GERMANY

R   U

Smolensk

Moscow

S   SS   I   A

Warsaw   Brest-Litovsk

Kursk

AUSTRIA-
HUNGARY

Kiev

Kharkov

UKRAINE

Volga R.

BESSARABIA

Dnieper R.

Don R.

Caspian
Sea

ROMANIA

SERBIA

CAUCASIA

BULGARIA

Black   Sea

GREECE

TURKEY

Kars

PERSIA

0   200 miles

0   200 kilometres

The Brest-Litovsk Settlement

ratification of the treaty if they received military help from the Western powers. Lockhart recommended helping the Russians, but the War Office refused, claiming that if the Germans invaded western Siberia, the Russians would be powerless to oppose them. It considered the situation lost unless Japan acted to occupy the area in question. The Allies at this point were more afraid of Bolshevism than Germany. The treaty of Brest-Litovsk was duly ratified at the Seventh Party Congress on 6 March 1918, the congress at which the Bolshevik Party changed its name to the Russian Communist Party.[27]

On 21 February the Germans landed in Finland, routing the Red Guard and suppressing the Soviet government in Helsingfors. As German troops were now within striking distance of Petrograd, the Soviet government completed the measure contemplated by Kerensky and moved the capital to Moscow on 11 March.

The signing of the peace treaty caused serious divisions to surface within Bolshevik Party ranks. On 24 February the Moscow Regional Bureau adopted a resolution of no confidence in the Central Committee. It declared that it did not consider itself bound to comply with the conditions of the peace treaty with Germany. Similar decisions were taken by the several local party organizations throughout Russia.[28] Radek, Bobiński, Stučka and Kapsukas, who had attended the negotiations as consultants, all fiercely opposed the treaty, and all took their respective national sections of the party with them. 'Left Communism' was rife among the Polish, Ukrainian, Latvian, Lithuanian and Estonian communists. The disagreements with the party leadership, moreover, concerned not only the foreign but also the economic policies of the new government.

The majority of the Left SR Party's Central Committee, which had supported concluding peace up till the German ultimatum of 23 February, now resolutely opposed the terms. Following the ratification of the treaty, the Left SRs withdrew from the Soviet government, declaring that they did not consider themselves bound by the peace terms. Spiridonova, who continued to insist that signing the Brest-Litovsk peace had been a matter of necessity and that it was a mistake for the SRs to leave the government, found herself deeply at odds with Kamkov and most of her party. A split was only narrowly avoided.[29] Both wings, however, were able to unite in condemnation of the economic policies being pursued by the Soviet government in the spring of 1918 – the collaboration with the capitalists in industry and the collection of grain in the villages.

The New Border States

On the day before the Brest-Litovsk treaty had been signed, Soviet troops under the SR General M. A. Muraviev had overthrown the Rada and proclaimed a Ukrainian Soviet Republic in Kiev. When the Germans occupied the Ukraine they had re-established the Rada and set Field-Marshal von

[27] *Ibid.*, pp. 293-98.
[28] Varlamov and Slamikhin, *Razoblachenie*, pp. 102–103.
[29] Steinberg, *Spiridonova*, pp. 201-204.

Eichhorn the task of collecting grain supplies for the German army. This proved much more difficult than Eichhorn had anticipated, as the Ukrainian peasants resented the requisitions bitterly and threatened to reduce the area under cultivation and thus produce only enough for their own needs. When the Rada took the peasants' side, the Germans dissolved it at gun-point and, on 28 April 1918, installed in its place the more compliant and pro-German Ukrainian leader, Hetman P. P. Skoropadskii. German requisitions were continued, and the peasants responded by waging determined campaigns of partisan warfare against the forces of occupation. The Soviet government was powerless to give any help – at least openly – to the Ukrainian insurrectionaries, as this would have contravened the terms of the Brest-Litovsk treaty.

In Finland the October revolution was accompanied by a general strike, but not by any seizure of power by the Finnish socialist parties. Instead, a government was formed headed by P. Svinhufvud when the country was given independence on 18 (31) December 1917. Fearing that repressive measures would be used against them, the Social Democrats took over the largest towns – Åbo, Viipuri and Tampere – and the whole of southern Finland. They introduced workers' control in industry and took over the banks, on the example of their Russian neighbours.

The socialist government in Finland was opposed by a mixed force of Finns who had served in the Jägers Battalion of the German army and Swedish volunteers commanded by C. Mannerheim, a former general in the Russian army. The Finnish Red Guards were few in number and poorly armed. They would have been no match for Mannerheim's forces if they had not had the support of the Russians. The Soviet forces, however, had to withdraw from Finland under the terms of the Brest-Litovsk treaty.

Svinhufvud obtained the help of 20,000 German troops commanded by General Rüdiger von der Goltz. The German capture of Helsinki from the Reds took place at the beginning of April. Two weeks later Mannerheim succeeded in taking the fortress town of Tampere. He then, with German help, inflicted a decisive defeat on the Reds at Viipuri at the beginning of May. These victories were accompanied by severe reprisals against the Reds. In the months that followed, socialists continued to be hunted down and killed in the White terror that reigned throughout Finland.[30]

The sovereignty of the Baltic states was transferred from Russia to Germany by the treaty of Brest-Litovsk and the protocol signed in Berlin on 27 August 1918. The Germans then made arrangements to annex these territories but in a manner that would have the appearance of legitimacy. In April a German-controlled *Landesrat* (local assembly) was set up in Riga with the intention of forming a Baltic grand duchy comprising Latvia and Estonia, whose ruler would be the King of Prussia.[31]

In Vilna the Germans had authorized in September 1917 the convocation of a congress of Lithuanian delegates and the election of a 20-member *Taryba* or council. On 16 February 1918 the *Taryba* proclaimed an independent Lithua-

[30] V. Serge, *Year One of the Russian Revolution* (London, 1992), pp. 180–89; A. F. Upton, *The Finnish Revolution 1917–1918* (Minneapolis, MN, 1980), pp. 519–20.

[31] W. Basler, *Deutschlands Annexionspolitik in Polen und im Baltikum 1914–1918* (Berlin, 1962), pp. 321–22.

nian state, which Germany recognized on 24 March – with the proviso that there be a 'perpetual alliance between Lithuania and Germany'. On 11 July the crown of Lithuania was offered to the Duke of Urach, Wilhelm von Würtemburg, but the offer was subsequently withdrawn. An interim presidium was formed which, on 5 November, designated Augustinas Voldemaras as Prime Minister of an independent Lithuania.[32] In the eyes of the Allied powers, the Lithuanians were to remain tainted by their pro-German orientation, unlike their neighbours the Poles.

The Lithuanians had accepted the limited degree of autonomy conceded by the Germans because it offered recognition of Lithuania as a national entity, and held out the hope that genuine independence might be achieved in the future. Among the Poles, Józef Piłsudski and his followers had adopted a similar attitude towards German concessions to Polish national identity. Piłsudski had formed Polish legions to fight on the side of the Central Powers against Russia, and had accepted office in the 'Provisional Council of State' which the German occupation authorities had established in Warsaw.

An important turning-point in Polish politics had been the reorientation from the Central Powers towards the Allies. This had followed the February revolution in Russia and the establishment of the Provisional Government, which had recognized Polish unity and independence. The Allied powers could now, without offending their Russian ally, recognize the Polish National Committee in Paris as the official representative of Polish interests in Western countries. In October 1917 General Józef Haller took command of a Polish army in France, a similar force having been formed in Russia in July commanded by the former tsarist general, Józef Dowbor-Musnicki. The culmination of these developments was the publication on 8 January 1918 of President Wilson's *Fourteen Points*, of which the thirteenth spoke of an independent Polish state.

In July 1917 Piłsudski had encouraged the Polish legions to refuse to pledge loyalty to the Austrian Kaiser, leading to his imprisonment in Magdeburg castle, where he remained until November 1918. In place of the discredited Council of State, the Germans established a 'Regency Council' which was to function until such times as a Polish sovereign could be selected from the Austrian or Prussian royal families. Germany's defeat and the outbreak of the November revolution in Berlin brought an end to the German occupation of Russian Poland, as German troops were disarmed by Polish legionaries. Piłsudski emerged from his imprisonment in Magdeburg a national hero, and, taking over from the Regency Council as Provisional Head of State, established a government in Warsaw, of which Jędrzej Moraczewski, a member of the PPS, became Prime Minister.[33] Moraczewski intended to implement a democratic programme of reform on the Western model, but within two months his government was forced to resign and give way to the more right-wing one of Ignacy Paderewski, whose territorial aspirations in the east were to bring it into conflict with Soviet Russia.

[32] *Pirmasis nepriklausomos Lietuvos dešimtmetis* (London, 1955), pp. 28–32.
[33] S. Kiniewicz, *Historia Polski 1795–1918* (Warsaw, 1970), pp. 533–44.

Economic Policies

In view of the enormous importance attached to economic matters in later Soviet history, it may seem paradoxical that on coming to power in October 1917 the Bolsheviks did not have any previously defined economic programme. The reason for this was the widespread belief that none was necessary, that capitalism in its latest, imperialist stage, was spontaneously creating the rationalized and centralized structures of a socialist economy. This belief was shaken only gradually, and accounts for many of the early economic policies of the Soviet regime.

Lenin accepted the argument first put forward by Hilferding that in recent times industrial and commercial firms had united to form syndicates and trusts, and that industrial and finance capital had coalesced, thus making a small number of large banks key institutions in the economy. Since the time Hilferding had written, moreover, a further development had taken place during the war. This was State regulation of the economy introduced for military purposes. In Lenin's view it had accentuated the existing centralizing tendencies within modern capitalism, and transformed monopoly capitalism into State monopoly capitalism. This could be observed most clearly in Germany's war economy, but Lenin was able to point to the existence of coal, metal, oil and sugar syndicates in Russia, and to the fact that these had been recently co-ordinated by the war industries committees.[34]

In Lenin's view, socialism was the next step forward from State monopoly capitalism. The economic measures Lenin proposed on the eve of the Bolsheviks' accession to power were accordingly of a rather modest nature, and were concerned with encouraging processes already in operation. They were also more concerned with 'control' of the economy – that is, monitoring and regulating the economy than with actively directing or planning it. For the most part, they left property relations unchanged. Industrial and commercial undertakings would still belong to their present owners. They were:

1. the merging of all banks into a single bank with State control over its operations;
2. the nationalization of syndicates and trusts;
3. the abolition of commercial secrecy;
4. the compulsory syndication (organization in unions) of industrialists, traders and proprietors in general; and
5. the compulsory organization of the population in consumers' societies and control over these.

As Lenin explained, since the banks played a key role in modern finance capitalism, the State had only to be in possession of them to be in control of the production and distribution of all the more essential products. This would be especially the case if all the banks were merged into a single State Bank. The abolition of commercial secrecy would make economic transactions more transparent still. And because the banks were linked to the main branches of

[34] V. I. Lenin, *Polnoe sobranie sochinenii* xxxiv, p. 183.

industry and commerce to form an indivisible whole, the nationalization of the banks necessarily implied transforming the syndicates (of coal, metal, oil and sugar, etc.) into State monopolies. The branches of industry which had not yet formed syndicates would be compelled to do so in the interests of rationalisation. Consumption too, Lenin considered, would have to be regulated to some degree, since some goods were in short supply. The organization of consumers' societies, he believed, introduced elements of democracy and fairness into the rationing system.

The gradualist and evolutionary thinking on economic matters underlay the three major pieces of economic legislation passed in the first months of Soviet power. These were the CEC decrees on workers' control (14 November 1917), the creation of the Supreme Economic Council (VSNKh or Vesenkha) (2 December 1917) and the nationalization of the banks (14 December 1917).

The merging and nationalization of the banks was a high priority with the Soviet government, but this proved much more difficult than anticipated. Although the State Bank was taken over relatively early, the Soviet government was confronted by obstruction and sabotage organized by private-bank proprietors. On the eve of the Bolshevik accession to power these banks had extracted large sums of money from the State Bank and used these to finance strikes by bank clerks, civil servants, technical staffs and industrial managers. This caused immense hardship. Large numbers of engineering works closed down because there was no technical staff to co-ordinate operations. Because it was impossible to make withdrawals from the banks, no wages could be paid. Food trains arrived and were unloaded, but no one was available to organize the distribution of goods.

The strike in the capital was so effective because much of the highly trained personnel of the major industries in Petrograd were either foreigners or Russians in the service of multinational firms. There were insufficient numbers of qualified replacements to be found locally, and feverish recruiting had to be conducted in the provinces to find engineers, bank clerks and operatives of all kinds.

Attempts to utilize the banking system as a mechanism of economic accounting failed miserably. Some banks refused to divulge any information while others supplied accounts that had been concocted specially for presentation to the Soviet authorities and bore no relation to reality. By the time the decree nationalizing the private banks was promulgated by the CEC on 14 December, the economic accounting motive had been tacitly abandoned and the main objective was to break the strikes.

The nationalization of the private banks was effected by posting Red Guards at their Petrograd and Moscow branches. The measure was largely ineffective, however, and the bank strike was intensified. It was not possible to find the requisite number of qualified accountants to keep the banks open, and they remained closed until the beginning of 1918, when the money available to finance the strike ran out.[35]

Bank nationalization was accompanied by a decree annulling Russia's foreign debt. This was dictated partly by the practical consideration that the

[35] M. Philips Price, *My Reminiscences of the Russian Revolution* (London, 1921), pp. 209–12; Keep, *Debate*, pp. 205–12.

regime lacked the means to pay interest on the debt, and partly by the political motive of wishing to strike a blow at the system of finance capital. In particular it was considered to be an apt response to the Allies' refusal to take part in general peace negotiations. The measure deeply antagonized foreign governments, and increased hostility abroad towards the Bolshevik regime.[36]

The decree on workers' control was designed partly as a measure to combat sabotage by industrialists as well as one of economic regulation. Workers' control was based on the factory committees which had been in operation before the revolution. Above these were local workers' control councils, the supreme body being the All-Russian Council of Workers' Control. The decree empowered the workers to supervise industrial operations, establish output quotas and to take measures to establish production costs. In carrying out their supervisory role, the workers' control bodies would not only be able to observe what took place but also have access to the firm's books and correspondence. The rights of the proprietors, who formally retained ownership, were severely limited and depended on the decisions of the organs of workers' control.

Even when the decree was introduced in the CEC, a number of difficulties in its working had been noted. One was that workers' control was being established in the absence of any general economic plan. There was also the objection that workers and management might show more concern for their own factory than for the community as a whole. However, the decree sought to remedy this potential danger by specifying that the lower institutions of workers' control should act according to the instructions issued by the All-Russian Council of Workers' Control. A third difficulty was that the workers might interpret the decree to mean that they now owned the enterprises in which they worked, and might do with it what they wished, perhaps selling its assets or appropriating them for their own use. In the critical economic climate of the time, this was already taking place. It was also observed that the workers' control bodies, which were scattered around individual enterprises, were structured differently from trade unions, which were organized according to branch of industry. A contradiction therefore existed between the principles of workers' control and trade unionism. The trade unions, moreover, were not subordinate to the government.[37]

As originally conceived, workers' control ought to have co-existed with the capitalist economic system. Its main objective was to give the workers experience in running the economy. But from the outset economic sabotage acted as a stimulus to the nationalization of industry, as proprietors deserted their factories or starved them of resources. In these cases, too, the factory committees could not stop short at control but had to go over to the organization of production. The decree on workers' control itself generated nationalizations, since the harsh terms offered to the owners prompted many of them to disregard the new regulations. In such cases the penalty was nationalization of the enterprise.

A number of leading Bolsheviks came to advocate the systematic nationalization of enterprises and their subordination to a centralized State

---

[36] Philips Price, *Reminiscences*, pp. 209–10.
[37] Keep, *Debate*, pp. 126–27; Akhapkin, *First Decrees*, pp. 36–38.

body. Skvortsov-Stepanov thought that with the establishment of the dictatorship of the proletariat, workers' control had outgrown itself and would be
replaced by a higher form of workers' regulation of industry. In the opinion of
L. N. Kritsman, the basic idea of workers' control – the learning from the class
enemy the art of running enterprises – was Utopian. He believed the
capitalists would not agree to it, and the workers could not limit themselves
to control. In the absence of a well organized economic centre, the direction
would pass to organs of workers' control in scattered enterprises and this
would increase the disorganization. The critics of workers' control argued
that it was necessary to progress to the organized nationalization of industry
and the central direction of production.[38]

In the first six months of Soviet rule, attempts were made to implement
Lenin's idea of encouraging the creation of syndicates. Discussions with
industrialists took place on establishing joint management committees of
proprietors and workers. If an agreement was reached, the syndicates would
not be nationalized but only subjected to general regulation by the State. As a
result of the negotiations a number of syndicates appeared, mainly in light
industry.

Lenin's attempts to come to an agreement with the syndicates caused some
unease within the Bolshevik Party. The Left Communists could see a clear
parallel between Lenin's accommodation with the State capitalist syndicates
and his capitulation to the Germans at Brest-Litovsk. Bukharin thought that
the working class should not be asked to support State capitalism but to
destroy it, and that imperialism, militarism and State capitalism were all evils
which ought to be annihilated by the working class.[39]

The Left Communists believed there should be no concessions to the
capitalists. They thought that all the major enterprises should be nationalized, and the small and medium ones subordinated to the larger, or united in
unions. The management of enterprises should be in the hands of colleges
consisting of two-thirds workers and one-third technical personnel acting
under the direction of local Councils of National Economy (Sovnarkhozy).[40]

One important economic institution created in this period on the initiative
of Osinskii, a commissar of the State Bank and prominent Left Communist,
was the Supreme Council of the National Economy (Vesenkha). At its
inaugural meeting on 2 December, Osinskii explained that the decree on
workers' control had been the first step in breaking the monopoly power of
the capitalists and the State machinery. The second had been the nationalization of the banks, which had broken the sabotage of the intellectuals. Now,
however, it was necessary to counter the disruption caused by workers acting
only in the interests of their own enterprise or locality by co-ordinating the
activities of local bodies concerned with economic affairs. Vesenkha was
designed to bring about a measure of centralization within the various
economic institutions, and establish co-operation between them and the
purely political organs. It was proposed that for the moment the council

---

[38] K. Kloc and P. Marciniak, 'Zarys koncepcji przeobrazen ekonomiczno-społecznych Rosji
radzieckiej (1917–1918)', *Z pola walki* xx (1977, no. 3(79)), p. 124.
[39] *Kommunist: Ezhenedel'nyi zhurnal ekonomiki, politiki i obshchestvennosti*, ed. with intro., notes and
index by R. I. Kowalski (New York, 1990), p. 146.
[40] Kloc and Marciniak, 'Zarys koncepcji', p. 130.

should have no more than advisory powers, final decisions being left with the political Soviets.[41] The council had a number of sections and departments (fuel, metal, demobilization, finance, etc.), and presided over a hierarchy of regional and district economic Soviets (SNKh or Sovnarkhozy).

There was a structural resemblance between the Supreme Council of the National Economy and the War Industries Committees. It was in fact originally intended that the two organizations should coalesce, the WICs being renamed 'National Industrial Committees'. They were to assist in demobilizing the economy and for equipping the newly formed Red Army. Although there was agreement in principle, there was reluctance on the part of the industrial committees to merge with Vesenkha. As a result the WICs were wound up on 22 April 1918.[42]

Demobilizing industry caused additional disruption in an already chaotic economic situation. Factories producing armaments for the war effort had to be modified for the production of peacetime goods. This brought unemployment to many munitions workers and created the problem of deciding which items factories formerly on war production ought now to produce. Such decisions, however, had to be postponed with the intensification of civil war by the summer of 1918.[43]

Agrarian Policies.

If Bolshevik policies on industry were something of an improvisation in the initial period of their rule, their agricultural policies were even more so. The decree on land had incorporated the Socialist Revolutionary principle of 'socializing' the land, i.e., it abolished private ownership in land without compensation, only the holdings of ordinary peasants and ordinary Cossacks being immune from confiscation. The right to use the land was accorded to all citizens of the Russian State (without distinction of sex) desiring to cultivate it by their own labour. The employment of hired labour was not permitted.

The establishment of Soviet power in Petrograd and the promulgation of the decree on land set in motion two processes in the villages – one the creation of local Soviets and the other the confiscation of the land-owners' estates. These two processes took place practically simultaneously, and for the most part peaceably between November 1917 and February 1918. As might be expected, there was considerable local variation on how these measures were carried out. In many, but not all, cases, there was a stock-taking of estate property before confiscation took place. Sometimes the stock-taking was carried out prior to the establishment of the soviet, though in many instances it was the other way round. The election of *volost'* soviets was mostly accompanied by the dissolution of the existing *zemstvo* or land committees. But it might happen that some or all of the membership of the *zemstvo* would be elected to the soviet, or the *zemstvo* become a section of

[41] Philips Price, *Reminiscences*, pp. 213–14.
[42] M. Wilk, *Moskiewski komitet wojenno-przemysłowy 1915–1918: Studium z dziejów burżuazji rosyjskiej* (Łodź, 1972), pp. 105–107.
[43] I. I. Mints *et al.*, eds., *Istoriia SSSR* vii (Moscow, 1967), pp. 303–304.

the soviet. The village assembly, which for the most part carried out these measures, might simply declare itself to be the soviet, preserving a traditional institution under a new, modern-sounding title.[44]

In the outlying regions other patterns could be found. In some *volosts* the soviet and the *zemstvo* existed side by side; and when the correspondent of the *Manchester Guardian* visited Vologda in March 1918 he found the *zemstvo* still in sole control of the *volost*, and its members engaged in deciding how to carry out the agrarian regulations of the Provisional Government.[45]

In the central Russian provinces the stock-taking of estates came to a halt after April as the time for spring sowing approached. It was at this time that the properties surveyed were transferred to peasant use. The land which was distributed first was that on which spring crops would be sown. In the summer the meadows were divided and, in the autumn after the harvest, the distribution of fields for winter crops was carried out. But even in 1919 in some *volosts* estates were still held fully or in part by land-owners.

The Soviet government regarded the confiscation of landed estates and the distribution of the land among the peasants as the first stage in the transformation of agriculture. The next stage was to involve measures designed to point it in a socialist direction. These measures were set out in the law *On the Socialization of the Land*, which was published on 19 February 1918. As the Commissariat of Agriculture was headed at that time by Kolegaev, the law reflected the Left SR conception that the land should not belong to the State but should be available to all who worked it by their own labour. The Left SRs advocated that the land should be worked collectively by peasant communes, collectives or associations organized in collective farms or *kolkhozy*. The Bolsheviks, by contrast, favoured State ownership of the land, and believed that State capitalism should be fostered in agriculture as it was in industry. They advocated the preservation of large estates and their transformation into State farms or *sovkhozy*, where the peasants would be employed as wage labourers just as workers were in urban industry. Some traces of this conception found their way into the law on socialization through amendments introduced by Bolsheviks.[46]

In areas where the peasants were encouraged to do so by returning soldiers, who often had SR sympathies, agricultural communes were established for the collective cultivation of the land. But more often the peasants were inclined to divide up the landlords' estates and remove from them the livestock, implements and seed. As a result, the greater part of intensively cultivated farmland was reduced to the level of the primitive agriculture which surrounded it. Once divided, the land from estates did not significantly increase the holdings of individual peasant families. The newly acquired land, moreover, was often at some distance from the village, making it difficult to cultivate.

The transfer of land to the peasants served in fact to exacerbate the supply problem. In the winter and spring of 1918, there was an acute shortage of food in the consuming regions of the country. The Soviet government had

---

[44] Philips Price, *Reminiscences*, p. 265.

[45] P. N. Pershin, *Agrarnaia revoliutsiia v Rossii* i (Moscow, 1966), pp. 468–70.

[46] V. V. Kabanov, 'Osnovnoi zakon o sotsializatsii zemli', in I. M. Volkov *et al.*, eds., *Oktiabr' i sovetskoe krest'ianstvo 1917–1927* (Moscow, 1927), pp. 82–110.

inherited the monopoly in grain from the Provisional Government, and this constituted a key policy for the new regime. The grain monopoly involved the prohibition of private trade in grain and the obligatory transfer of surpluses to the State at fixed prices. The idea was to keep prices low so that everyone could afford them. But grain producers found that they could get a better price by selling illegally to private traders rather than to government agencies. 'Bagmen' bought up grain from producers and sold it in the towns at free prices. In an attempt to expedite grain collection, food detachments were sent to organize the poorer peasants against those suspected of having a surplus.

The Cheka

In an attempt to counter the sabotage of the intelligentsia, on 6 December 1917 the All-Russian Extraordinary Commission for the Struggle against Counter-Revolution and Sabotage was established. This was headed by Feliks Dzierżyński who, since the beginning of November, had been reorganizing the workers' militia; the vice-chairman was the SR V. A. Aleksandrovich. Among the more prominent members of the new commission were Józef Unszlicht and V. R. Menzhinskii and the Latvian Bolsheviks M. Lācis and J. Peterss. Although conceived as a temporary measure, the Extraordinary Commission, widely known as the 'Cheka', was to become a permanent fixture in the fabric of Soviet society.

In the first months of its existence the Cheka had only the right to carry out searches and to conduct preliminary investigations. But in February 1918 its competence was widened in connection with the German advance into the country and the increase in lawlessness. In particular, the decree drafted by Lenin and issued on 21 February, 'The Socialist Fatherland is in Danger', increased the Cheka's powers immeasurably by designating categories of people who could be shot on the spot. In the summer of 1918 as the country began to be engulfed in civil war, and no doubt with recent events in Finland in mind, the Cheka was given the right to take hostages with a view to preventing hostile action against Soviet power. Following the assassination of M. S. Uritskii and the attempt on Lenin's life in August, the Red Terror was unleashed, which claimed the lives of many innocent people.[47]

Prominent victims of the terror were the tsar and his family. Originally, following the abdication, it had been intended to send the imperial family to Britain, but the British government withdrew its offer of asylum. With the German threat to Petrograd, Nicholas and his family were moved, first to Tobolsk then to Ekaterinburg in the Urals. There they were assassinated by the local Cheka agents in July 1918 and their remains destroyed. In this way the Soviet regime tried to ensure that there could be no return to a monarchy in Russia.

---

[47] *Krasnaia kniga VChK* i (Moscow, 1989), pp. 5–7.

10

The Civil War

When Lenin and the Left Communists debated the possible consequences of concluding peace with the Germans at Brest-Litovsk, it seemed that the only choice before them was either a humiliating peace or a revolutionary war which might end in the destruction of the Soviet State or the spread of the revolution into Europe. What neither side foresaw was what in fact took place: that revulsion to the peace treaty would induce people of all walks of life to take up arms against the Bolsheviks. Lenin did not foresee that the issue of making peace with Germany was the catalyst capable of galvanizing into action anti-Bolshevik groups and currents both inside and outside the country and of bringing them together in a formidable coalition.

It is true that Lenin had spoken repeatedly of civil war in the first weeks of Soviet power, and indeed had justified early repressive measures in those terms. But this was largely rhetoric. There is no indication that Lenin had any inkling of the scale of civil war that would engulf the country. It is symptomatic that following some initial clashes with anti-Bolshevik forces on the Don, Lenin declared that the Civil War was over.[1]

A key development in the initial stages of the Civil War was that which led the Mensheviks and SRs to begin an armed struggle against the Bolsheviks. This 'democratic' opposition was a far greater threat to the Bolsheviks than any which emanated from counter-revolutionary generals. These generals had only the prospect of repeating the failed coup of Kornilov in the autumn of 1917. But a movement led by the SRs could count on popular support and the moral authority which success in the elections to the Constituent Assembly had given it. Until the spring of 1918 neither the Mensheviks nor the SRs approved of overthrowing the Bolshevik government by force. But that situation was changed by the Peace of Brest-Litovsk and the establishment of the food supply dictatorship to exact requisitions from the peasants.

The problem for the democratic parties was that they could not carry out the forcible overthrow of the Bolshevik regime if they did not have sufficient military force at their disposal. An alliance between them and military leaders such as Kornilov, Alekseev or Kaledin would have been unthinkable. The attempt by the SRs in July 1918 to recruit the Latvian riflemen to their cause failed disastrously. But in the Czecho-Slovak legion the democratic parties

---

[1] E. Mawdsley, *The Russian Civil War* (Cambridge, 1987), p. 29.

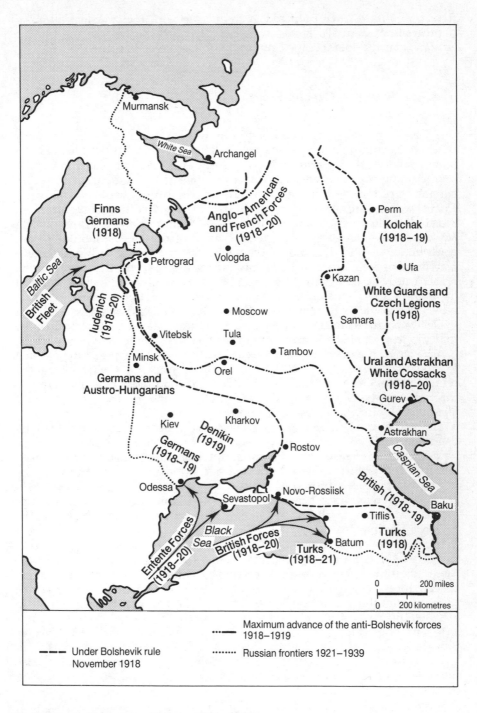

Murmansk

White Sea

Archangel

Finns
Germans
(1918)

Anglo–American
and French Forces
(1918–20)

Perm

Kolchak
(1918–19)

Baltic Sea

British
Fleet

Petrograd

Vologda

Ufa

Kazan

White Guards and
Czech Legions
(1918)

Iudenich
(1918–20)

Moscow

Samara

Vitebsk

Tula

Minsk

Tambov

Orel

Ural and Astrakhan
White Cossacks
(1918–20)

Germans and
Austro-Hungarians

Gurev

Kiev

Kharkov

Denikin
(1919)

Astrakhan

Caspian Sea

Germans
(1918–19)

Rostov

Odessa

Novo-Rossiisk

British (1918–19)

Baku

Sevastopol

Black

Sea

Tiflis

Entente Forces
(1918–20)

British Forces
(1918–20)

Turks
(1918–21)

Batum

Turks
(1918)

0   200 miles

0   200 kilometres

Maximum advance of the anti-Bolshevik forces
1918–1919

Under Bolshevik rule
November 1918

Russian frontiers 1921–1939

Civil War in European Russia 1918–1920

found a military force prepared to co-operate with them, which itself had democratic credentials. It was consequently with the help of the Czecho-Slovaks that the 'democratic counter-revolution' was launched.

The Revolt of the Czecho-Slovaks

The Czecho-Slovak legion had begun its life as a unit in the tsarist army, which had acquitted itself particularly well in the Galician offensive in 1917. It had expanded its numbers from 7,000 men in July 1917 to 30,000 in October by recruiting prisoners and deserters from the Austro-Hungarian army. The expansion of the force and its transformation into the Czecho-Slovak Army Corps was encouraged by the founder of the Czechoslovak State, Jan Masaryk, who was present in Russia in the summer and autumn of 1917. Masaryk was eager that the Czecho-Slovak Army Corps should make a contribution to the defeat of Germany in order that the Allies should be convinced of the moral case for redrawing the map of central Europe after the war. He negotiated with the French and British as well as with the Russians to have the corps transferred to France to fight on the Western front. In November some of the corps set off for France via Archangel.

Delays occurred in transporting the force while the Allies had some hope that the war against Germany might be renewed in the east. But with the conclusion of the peace negotiations at Brest-Litovsk, this possibility seemed to have disappeared so that there was no reason for the Czecho-Slovaks to remain in Russia. As it had proved difficult to send more than a token force through Archangel, it was decided to send the main force eastwards through Vladivostok and thence by sea to Europe.

This route was agreed with the Soviet government on 26 March 1918, the condition being made that the corps should surrender part of its arms and equipment. The reason for the condition was to avoid any armed clash between the Czecho-Slovak force and the Germans, which the Germans might interpret as a breach of the conditions agreed at Brest-Litovsk. The corps, which was at that time stationed in the Ukraine, made its way through Kursk and Penza to the trans-Siberian railway and started the long haul towards Vladivostok.

Mutual suspicion between the Czecho-Slovaks and local representatives of Soviet power were exacerbated by attempts to disarm the Czecho-Slovak forces thought to be carrying excessive armaments. In May the Czecho-Slovak troops rebelled at Cheliabinsk, a situation inflamed by Trotsky's order of 5 June that those Czecho-Slovaks who did not voluntarily hand over their arms would be shot on the spot.[2]

In June the scale of the Czecho-Slovak rebellion increased. The Czecho-Slovaks were able to take control of western Siberia, a considerable part of the Urals and the Volga region. By the beginning of August they had captured the towns of Samara, Barnaul, Krasnoiarsk, Cheliabinsk, Ekaterinburg,

---

[2] L. Trotsky, *How the Revolution Armed*, i trans. and annotated by B. Pearce (London, 1979), p. 282.

Omsk, Penza, Simbirsk and Kazan. In this way, the Czecho-Slovaks came to control a large section of the trans-Siberian railway, cutting off Siberia from the central provinces of Russia and preventing much-needed grain reaching the starving towns of the Russian republic.

'Komuch'

From May 1918 local SR and Menshevik organizations took part in peasant rebellions against the Soviet supply policies. In Samara and Saratov the SRs entered into agreement with the commanders of the Czecho-Slovak troops. On 8 June 1918, SR brigades supported by the Czecho-Slovaks took Samara and established the rule of the Committee of Members of the Constituent Assembly, widely known by its abbreviation 'Komuch'. In June and July Komuch extended its rule to the Volga and the Urals, and tried to exert its influence in Siberia.

Komuch intended to reconvene the Constituent Assembly and to reopen an anti-German front in the east, in this way nullifying the Brest-Litovsk treaty. It began to form its own armed forces – the People's Army – recruiting officers from the tsarist army and local peasants. Komuch attempted to implement a socialist programme but to avoid the unpopular economic measures being pursued by the Bolsheviks at that time. Komuch left the land confiscated from the land-owners in peasant hands, but did not itself continue the process of nationalizing or socializing the land. It did not impose forced requisitions on the peasants, fixed grain prices being abolished. Only those industrial and commercial firms which had been nationalized without the proper legal procedures were returned to their former owners. The Samara Soviet was allowed to continue in existence, and the Soviet of Peasants' Deputies, which had been dissolved by the Communists, was reconstituted. Nevertheless, Komuch ruled as a dictatorship and, according to one of its members, in the conditions of the Civil War was forced to shed a great deal of blood. Its security service acted as cruelly and ruthlessly as the Cheka, which the Mensheviks and SRs had deplored.[3]

Komuch was not the only government in the region. Besides those based on a national principle – that of the Bashkirs, the 'Alaş Orda' of the Kirghiz and the organization of the Turkic-Tatar peoples – there was the Siberian Regional Government at Omsk. It also had arisen as a consequence of the Czecho-Slovak revolt but, unlike Komuch, was of a conservative political complexion. In September 1918 representatives of Komuch, the Siberian Regional Government and other local organizations held a State Conference in Ufa, at which it was decided to form a united government. A Russian Provisional Government was duly constituted, which considered itself the successor to the deposed Provisional Government. A Directory of five was formed, consisting of N. D. Avksentiev (SR), General V. G. Boldyrev (SR), V. A. Vinogradov (Kadet), P. V. Volgogodskii (Kadet) and V. M. Zenzinov (SR). On 9 October

[3] V. V. Zhuravlev and N. S. Simonov, 'Prichiny i posledstviia razgona Uchreditel'nogo sobraniia', *Voprosy istorii* (1992, no. 1), p. 7.

the Directory was installed at Omsk, where it was exposed to the conservative currents of the Siberian Regional Government.

Conflict soon arose between the SRs and the more conservative groups in Omsk. These latter favoured the creation of a more authoritarian government to oppose the Bolsheviks' dictatorship. The search for a suitable candidate for dictator then began. Initially General Boldyrev was considered as a possibility, but his father had been a blacksmith and he had sympathies with the SR Party. Finally the choice fell on Rear-Admiral Kolchak, who had arrived in Siberia at the beginning of October with General Alfred Knox, the leader of the British military mission to Russia. He became War and Navy Minister in the Siberian Regional Government.

On 18 November a *coup d'état* was carried out in Omsk, establishing Kolchak as dictator. The members of the Directory were arrested, and Kolchak was raised to the rank of admiral and proclaimed 'Supreme Ruler' He at once began to reorganize his armed forces and, as early as December 1918, these were able to capture Perm and move into Soviet-held territory. In military terms the coup which brought Kolchak to power was detrimental to the Soviet government, but politically it was highly advantageous. It confirmed the Soviet government's contention that its opponents were the counter-revolutionaries, the forces of reaction.[4]

The Revolt of the Left SRs

At the Fifth Congress of Soviets, which opened on 5 July 1918 in the Bolshoi theatre in Moscow, the main topic of debate was the Peace of Brest-Litovsk. The Left SRs accused the Bolsheviks of allowing the revolution in the Ukraine to be crushed by the Germans. They demanded that the treaty be torn up and war against the Germans be recommenced. On 6 July 1918, two Left SRs, Ia. G. Bliumkin and N. A. Andreev, using forged Cheka documents, entered the German embassy in Moscow and assassinated the ambassador, Count Mirbach. The assassination was designed to provoke the Germans into resuming hostilities against the Soviet republic, and to serve as a signal for an uprising against Bolshevik rule. Left SRs captured the telegraph office and sent telegrams all over the country saying that they had seized power with the support of the workers and the troops. They managed to capture Dzierżyński, his deputy, Lācis, the chairman of the Moscow Soviet, P. G. Smidovich, and other prominent Bolsheviks.

The Soviet government was able to suppress the rebellion in Moscow and put down local risings by SRs and Anarchists throughout the country. Several SRs who had been engaged in agitation among the Red Army troops on the frontier with the Ukraine had been shot. Lenin and Trotsky hastened to the German embassy to dissociate themselves from the assassination, and to express their condolences for the Ambassador's death. Although the Germans had every reason to take reprisals against the Bolshevik regime, they were now in no position to do so, as the war was going badly for them on the Western front.

[4] H. Zand, *Z dziejów wojny domowej w Rosji* (Warsaw, 1973), p. 103.

Following the assassination of Mirbach there were mass arrests of Left SRs, and an investigation into the incident was begun by the Cheka. In the following month the Red Terror was unleashed by the Cheka following two incidents of individual terrorism. On 30 August, on leaving the Mikhelson factory after addressing the workers there, Lenin was shot and wounded by a Fania Kaplan-Royd, a Right SR. On the same day a student assassinated Uritskii, the Chairman of the Petrograd Cheka. On 31 August *Pravda* announced on its front page: 'Uritskii is dead, Lenin is wounded. With the hands of the right SRs the Allied capitalists want to behead the workers' revolution. The proletariat will reply with organized mass terror and redoubled efforts at the front . . .' Now anyone suspected of being involved in conspiracies, rebellions or White-guard organizations could be shot or imprisoned without trial. On 14 June the Mensheviks and SRs were declared counter-revolutionary parties and expelled from the Soviets.

The Red Army

During December 1917 and January 1918, the Soviet authorities took under their control the remaining institutions of the old army and elaborated plans to create new one. The decree of the Council Of People's Commissars establishing the 'Workers' and Peasants' Red Army' was issued on 15 (28) January 1918. Initially the Red Army was a volunteer force, with elected officers and wide powers given to army committees. On 19 December 1917, Trotsky had outlined the original conception of the Soviet army when, at a meeting of the CEC, he claimed that in contrast to the Germans, the Soviet State had 'a new army without chiefs, without punishments, one that is not driven forward by the officer's baton'.[5]

The event which changed completely the way the Red Army was organized was the German advance into Russia in February 1918, to which Soviet forces could offer little resistance. There was no overall command centre. Dukhonin's Stavka had been dismantled, the headquarters of the Northern and Western fronts were still in operation; and in the South-West, Antonov-Ovseenko's headquarters directed military operations in the Ukraine and on the Don. With such fragmentation of command centres, the lack of discipline among the troops, the chaotic state of provisioning and elected commanders with no training for their posts, there could be no hope of putting up any resistance to the German army.[6]

The first step towards centralizing the organization of the Red Army was the establishment on 4 March 1918 of the Supreme Military Council chaired by Trotsky, who then became Commissar for Military Affairs. This body was intended to produce combat troops by providing military training for the workers. Former officers, or 'military specialists', were invited to act as instructors in the new army. Although this took place on a comparatively small scale, it was sufficient to evoke the protests of the Left Communists. To

---

[5]   J. Keep, trans. and ed., *The Debate on Soviet Power: Minutes of the All-Russian Central Executive Committee Second Convocation, October 1917–January 1918* (Oxford, 1979), p. 235.
[6]   E. Sklianskii, *Stroitel'stvo krasnoi armii* (Moscow, 1919), p. 3.

meet the objection that 'military specialists' were an alien element in the Red Army, political commissars were assigned to the military specialists to see that the army worked in concert with the Soviet regime.[7]

By May the revolt of the Czecho-Slovaks had shown that the influx of volunteers would be insufficient to create a large enough army for the needs of the Soviet State. Moreover, the volunteer system had already demonstrated some serious disadvantages, for not only honest proletarians volunteered, but also adventurers and criminals. Compulsory conscription was introduced on 29 May for all male citizens between the ages of 18 and 40. The Red Army's numbers rose from 450,000 in the summer of 1918 to 5.5 million at the end of 1920. It became increasingly peasant in composition. In 1920, 78 per cent of Red Army soldiers were peasants, whereas only 15 per cent were workers.[8]

During July and August 1918 an energetic purge of army commanders took place, as new appointments of military specialists were made. Simultaneously the many and varied military units, institutions and formations which had sprung up were dissolved to create a united and homogeneous army.[9]

In the summer of 1918 the crisis on the Eastern front put the new organization of the Red Army to the test. In August after the fall of Kazan, Trotsky hurried in his armoured train to the nearby town of Sviazhsk. There he rallied the troops, shooting the commanding officer and the commissar, and on 10 September the Red Army was able to recapture Kazan and, two days later, Simbirsk. At Sviazhsk, Trotsky was especially impressed by the Latvian soldiers, and by the commander of the Eastern front Jukums Vācietis.

On his return to Moscow, Trotsky made some changes to the existing scheme of military organization. Since Soviet Russia was now surrounded by enemy forces and operated on internal lines of communication, there was no possibility of separating the theatre of war from other parts of the republic. The whole territory had become the rear area of the fronts. In order to bring efforts at the front into concert with those in the rear, and to co-ordinate military measures throughout the republic, on 2 September 1918 the CEC passed a resolution turning the whole country into an armed camp. A Revolutionary Military Council of the Republic, with far-reaching powers and chaired by Trotsky was established as the highest military institution. Attached to it was the field headquarters which directed military operations under the overall command of the Supreme Commander, a post to which Trotsky appointed Vācietis.[10]

By the beginning of 1919 the new system had been put into operation, and by May the organization of the fronts had been completed. The Red Army had now become a centralized and united organization, subordinate to the political control of the Communist Party. It continued, however, to be plagued with some serious problems. Large numbers of its soldiers de-

[7] Sklianskii, *Stroitel'stvo*, p. 4; F. Benvenuti, *The Bolsheviks and the Red Army 1918–1922* (Cambridge, 1988), p. 22.

[8] Sklianskii. *Stroitel'stvo*, p. 4; E. G. Gimpel'son, *Sovetskii rabochii klass 1918–1920 gg.* (Moscow, 1974), pp. 31–37.

[9] Sklianskii, *Stroitel'stvo*, p. 4.

[10] L. Trotsky, *How the Revolution Armed* i, p. 26; Benvenuti, *Bolsheviks*, p. 23.

serted, often for economic reasons. Some of the military specialists would desert to the Whites, calling into question the wisdom of utilizing their services. Front commanders felt that in practice the centre did not co-ordinate their activities and was indifferent to their difficulties. They found themselves inundated by orders from different military bodies in Moscow, and further confused by Trotsky and Podvoiskii who arrived to issue additional orders from their respective trains.[11]

The Whites

In the border regions of the former Russian Empire, the local Cossack armies refused to subordinate themselves to Soviet power and declared their loyalty to the Provisional Government. This made the Cossack leaders particularly important in the political situation which obtained at the start of the Civil War. These included General Kaledin (Don Cossacks), Colonel Dutov (Orenburg Cossacks) and Esaul G. Semenov (Baikal Cossacks). On the day the Bolsheviks came to power in Petrograd, Ataman Kaledin condemned the coup and declared his support for the existing coalition Provisional Government. This encouraged opponents of the Bolshevik regime to gather on the Don, and soon Kaledin's headquarters at Novocherkassk became the centre of oppositionist activity.

On 2 (15) November, General Alekseev arrived at Novocherkassk and began to organize a Volunteer Army, consisting initially largely of officers and cadets, to fight against the Bolsheviks. Although the army's fighting capacity was high, it had difficulty increasing its numbers beyond a few thousand and raising funds. In December Alekseev was joined by Generals Kornilov, Denikin, Lukomskii, S. L. Markov and I. P. Romanovskii, all of whom had been arrested at the time of the abortive Kornilov Affair. Kornilov became the army's military commander, while Alekseev took charge of political affairs.

Among the Russian settlers in the Don region there was increasing support for the Bolsheviks, and in November 1917 a Soviet Republic of the Don was established in Rostov. The combined force of the Volunteer Army and Kaledin's Cossacks retook Rostov on 2 December. In response to these developments, the Soviet government appointed Antonov-Ovseenko on 8 (21) December 1917 commander of the forces to combat the counter-revolutionary armies in south Russia. Two days later Antonov established his headquarters in Kharkov, and proclaimed a Soviet Ukraine in opposition to the Ukrainian Rada.

Antonov's military campaign was helped by the fact that the Cossacks had no great willingness to fight, and on 10 (23) January Kaledin's authority was undermined by the formation of a Military Revolutionary Committee of the Don Armies. Having lost the support of his troops, Kaledin committed suicide. With great rapidity, Antonov's forces captured a series of towns,

[11] 'VIII S"ezd RKP(b): Stenogramma zasedanii voennoi sektsii s"ezda 20 i 21 marta 1919 goda i zakrytogo zasedaniia s"ezda 21 marta 1919 goda', *Izvestiia TsK KPSS* (1989, no. 9), pp. 135–86.

including Rostov and Novocherkassk. On 23 March 1918 the Don Soviet Republic was proclaimed.

The Volunteer Army, however, escaped complete destruction, and on 24 February evacuated Rostov and made its way to the Kuban. It reached the Kuban on 23 March 1918 and joined up with 3,000 Kuban Cossacks. The combined force then prepared to mount an assault on Ekaterinodar, which was defended by a much stronger Soviet force. Shortly before the attack began, however, Kornilov was killed on 13 April when a shell landed on his headquarters and exploded. Command then passed to Denikin, who led an orderly retreat from Ekaterinodar back to the Don. On this occasion, as on that when the Volunteer Army withdrew from Rostov, the Soviet forces did not organize an effective pursuit, allowing their adversaries to regroup.

The campaign against Kaledin was not the only one undertaken by Soviet forces at this time. In the Ukraine they made slow but steady progress against the forces of the Ukrainian Rada. On 26 January (8 February), during the peace negotiations at Brest-Litovsk, Soviet armies occupied Kiev. Soviet forces at this time were also engaged in fighting the Orenburg Cossacks under Ataman Dutov and the Baikal Cossacks led by Ataman Grigory Semenov in the east.

The Don

When Denikin brought his Volunteer Army back to the Don, the situation there had changed radically. The Soviet regime had alienated the local population. No regard had been paid to customs, manners or faiths. Excessive severity and force had been equated with revolutionary fervour. News of such behaviour spread rapidly, and by April there was no shortage of recruits for the Volunteer Army. The Soviet regime in Novocherkassk soon fell, and a new Cossack ataman was elected. The choice fell on Krasnov, the general who had fought with Kerensky at Pulkovo heights.

Krasnov's election on 11 May came at the time when the German influence on the Don was increasing. The Central Powers hoped to exploit the growth of the White movement there and willingly supplied arms and ammunition to Krasnov. They had in him an ally, though not one so compliant, as Ataman Skoropadskii in the Ukraine. The Volunteer Army leaders, Alekseev and Denikin, remaining loyal to the Entente, would not accept German help, though they were prepared to accept German munitions channelled through Krasnov.[12]

German help allowed Krasnov to organize an army of 40,000 men by August 1918. It was not a well disciplined force, however, and the Cossack troops carried out reprisals against the peasants and workers of the Don, whom they considered to be Bolshevik supporters. At the beginning of August, Krasnov launched an attack on Tsaritsyn, a town of great strategic value, being a major railway junction on the strip of territory connecting the South and the Eastern fronts. If Krasnov had Tsaritsyn, it would then be

[12] N. E. Kakurin, *Kak srazhalas' revoliutsiia* i (Moscow, 1990), p. 24.

possible to join forces with Kolchak's armies. But the Red Army defended Tsaritsyn with great determination, and the battle for the town lasted from August 1918 until March 1919 with great losses on both sides.

Krasnov had a decisive superiority in cavalry, enabling his troops to manoeuvre quickly and attack weak points in the Soviet lines. The Red Army, however, was soon able to increase its numbers of cavalrymen, and produce outstanding cavalry commanders in B. K. Dumenko and S. M. Budienny.

The North Caucasus

The Volunteer Army did not take part in the Tsaritsyn offensive. Denikin had rejected Krasnov's proposal for a joint effort to capture Tsaritsyn and make contact with anti-Bolshevik forces in the east. He believed that an offensive in the direction of Tsaritsyn would be a strategic error. The road to Moscow lay not towards the east but directly from the south, whose populations could provide abundant reserves of Cossacks and officers willing to fight the Bolsheviks. Denikin, therefore, decided to remain in the south, and turn the Kuban into a base for the Volunteer Army. There was, moreover, the question of the alliances: Krasnov was connected with the Germans, whereas Denikin remained loyal to the Entente. In this way the two chief military forces in the south each took its own particular direction.[13]

On 23 June, the Volunteer Army, numbering some 8–9,000 men, began its second offensive into the Kuban. Although the Soviet forces were greater in number, their discipline was poor, and their resolve was undermined by the insubordination of some of their commanders. The Volunteer Army, whose numbers had swollen to some 20,000 through local recruitment, was able to capture the Kuban capital of Ekaterinodar on 16 August. Having established his secure base in the Kuban, Denikin was in a position to turn northward and begin his campaign against Moscow.

The Ukraine

After the dispersal of the Rada by the Germans in April 1918, the Ukraine was headed by the government of Hetman Skoropadskii, backed by the German military authorities. The requisitions carried out by the Germans in the countryside provoked numerous peasant uprisings. The popular movement was given political expression by Ukrainian SRs and Mensheviks. The most prominent leaders of this type were Volodymir Vynnychenko and Semen Petliura, who represented the radical wing of the Ukrainian Central Rada.

No open acts of opposition were possible in the towns because of the strict regime of military occupation, but there were a number of acts of terrorism and sabotage. On 30 July, the commander of the German forces in the Ukraine

---

[13] P. N. Miliukov, *Rossiia na perelome* i (Paris, 1927), p. 65.

General Eichhorn was assassinated by a Left Socialist Revolutionary in Kiev.

Germany's surrender to the Entente powers changed the situation. The insurrectionary movement in the Ukraine extended, and on 14 November the Rada met in Belaia Tserkov and established a Directory. The Directory army under Petliura entered Kiev on 14 December, Skoropadskii fleeing from the city in disguise.

The Directory was not the only or even the most powerful force in the Ukraine. In the countryside and in the towns, for example, were the 'Borotbisty', i.e., the Ukrainian Left SRs, who took part in the partisan battles against the German forces of occupation. Another force was the 'insurgent army' of the Anarchist, Nestor Makhno, a talented peasant partisan leader who had fought against the Germans in the Ukraine. In February 1919, Makhno allied with the Soviet forces, and the 'insurgent army' along with units led by Dybenko and N. A. Grigoriev became part of the Red Army's 1st Trans-Dniepr Division.[14]

The Bolsheviks were also an important force in the Ukraine. During the German occupation they had recruited among the workers. In the Ukraine, however, most of the proletariat was Russian – which gave the Bolsheviks an anti-Ukrainian reputation. The Ukrainian Communist Party's significance increased after the annulment of the Peace of Brest-Litovsk and the Red Army advance under Antonov-Ovseenko into the Ukraine. This was accompanied by the overthrow of the Directory and the establishment of a Ukrainian Soviet Republic. On 28 November 1919, the Provisional Workers' and Peasants' Ukrainian Government began to function. It was headed by G. L. Piatakov and consisted of K. E. Voroshilov, F. A. Artem, E. I. Kviring, V. P. Zatonskii and Iu. M. Kociubinski. It published a manifesto announcing that Soviet power in the Ukraine had been restored. By the beginning of January 1919 it had taken control of Kharkov, and on 5 February, Kiev.[15]

Intervention

The Central Powers' involvement in Russian affairs caused unease among the Allies, who sent notes of protest to the Soviet government. The Allies began to support those groups in Russia who they believed would fight against the Bolsheviks in order to restore an Eastern front against the Germans. They had seen the Czecho-Slovaks as a force which might perform this function and encouraged them to remain in Siberia. But soon the Allies came round to the view that it would be more effective to intervene in Russia directly.

The British contributed most materially to the anti-Bolshevik cause, though the Prime Minister, Lloyd-George, doubted the wisdom and efficacy of intervention. His War Minister, Churchill, on the other hand, was a fervent advocate of the anti-Bolshevik campaign. A few days after the treaty of Brest-Litovsk was signed – on 11 March 1918 – British troops landed at Murmansk, to be followed by a second contingent at Archangel in July. Their mission was

[14] V. N. Volkovinskii, 'Nestor Ivanovich Makhno', *Voprosy istorii* (1991, no. 9–10), p. 46.
[15] M. I. Kulichenko, *Bor'ba Kommunisticheskoi Partii za reshenie natsional'nogo voprosa v 1918-1920 godakh* (Khar'kov, 1963), p. 49.

not only to guard munitions supplied by the Allies but also to form an independent Russian army to continue the war against the Germans.

Britain and France had hoped that Japan would play the leading role in the creation of an Eastern front in 1918, but as early as March of that year the Japanese government made it clear that it would not be pressured into sending troops to the Urals and, in fact, was only prepared to operate in the Amur basin. An armed Japanese force landed at Vladivostok on 4 April. The Japanese were less concerned with fighting the Bolsheviks than with exploiting Siberia's economic resources. They therefore tried to prevent the Russians from establishing a unified political regime, which might be able to oppose Japanese economic penetration. The Japanese consequently gave military assistance not to Kolchak but to the Cossack atamans in the far east, such as G. M. Semenov and I. P. Kalmykov who, while formally supporting Kolchak, did much to undermine his authority.

The Americans only intervened in Russia with the greatest reluctance. It took intense pressure from the Britain and France to induce President Wilson to sanction American participation, and he may only have done so in July in the belief that by placating the Europeans on this matter he could expect their fuller co-operation at the peace conference.

After the Central Powers' surrender in November 1918 – when the need for an anti-German Eastern front had disappeared – Allied intervention in Russia entered its second phase. The withdrawal of Austro-German forces from the south of Russia, and the danger of a Red Army advance in that region, prompted the anti-Bolshevik forces in Russia to urge the Allies to come to their aid. The region had been divided by the British and French into spheres of interest, the French sphere being the Ukraine, and the British, the Caucasus. In November the British landed at Batum, and on 19 December 1918 a French division landed at Odessa.

The Eastern Front

At the beginning of his rule in Omsk, Admiral Kolchak enjoyed considerable military success. In December 1918 his armies, under Gajda and A. N. Pepelaev, took Perm, capturing 21,000 prisoners and administering a severe shock to the Soviet regime. This, however, was the last occasion on which Kolchak had help from the Czecho-Slovak troops, though the Czech commander, General R. Gajda, remained for a time in Kolchak's service. At that time Kolchak's forces were organized in three armies: the Southern, the Western and the Siberian. The Southern Army, consisting largely of Cossacks, was commanded by Ataman Dutov. The Western Army's main component was the People's Army formed by Komuch. It was badly disciplined and demoralized after its flight from the Volga in the autumn. Its commander was General M. V. Khanzhin, an old tsarist officer, who restored military discipline of the traditional type. The Siberian army, led by General Gajda, was newly formed and recruited locally.

By mid-April 1918 Kolchak's forces had broken through the Red Army's Eastern front and were making rapid progress to the west. By the end of the month they had reached Samara and Kazan. The capture of Aktiubinsk by Dutov's Cossacks cut Turkestan off from central Russia. The possibility arose of joining up with Denikin's offensive in the south and presenting the Red forces with a continuous front from which a concerted attack on the centre of Soviet power could be launched.

In May, following Kolchak's spectacular success, Generals Denikin, N. N. Iudenich and E. K. Miller recognized Kolchak as Supreme Ruler of Russia. They considered, moreover, that the domain over which Kolchak ruled was a Russia that was 'one and undivided'. For that reason when Mannerheim offered to direct his troops towards Petrograd in return for Kolchak's recognition of Finnish independence, the proposal was declined.

Kolchak's spring offensive in 1919 was to be the height of his power. For in the summer months the Red Army reorganized its forces in the east and mounted a counter-attack. The Soviet Eastern front was divided into two sectors: the northern group headed by V. I. Shorin and the southern group led by Mikhail Frunze. The southern group launched its offensive against Kolchak's Western Army on 28 April and broke through its defences at Buguruslan. On 15 May, Frunze led a new attack on the Western Army, forcing it to retreat.

The decisive operation was the battle for the town of Ufa, which lasted from 25 May to 19 June and ended with a general retreat of Kolchak's armies. Almost all of the territory Kolchak had gained in his spring offensive had been recaptured. But at this critical moment serious differences of opinion on how to proceed broke out among the commanders of the Eastern front and the leadership of the Red Army.

The Eastern front commander, S. S. Kamenev, supported by Frunze and Shorin, believed that the offensive against Kolchak's forces should be continued, taking advantage of the situation, and completely destroying Kolchak's armies. Vācietis and Trotsky disagreed; they believed that Kolchak was on the run, and that significant forces should be transferred to the Southern front, as the main threat now came from Denikin. The question was discussed by the party Central Committee on 15 June, which supported the view of the commanders of the Eastern front. The Central Committee recommended a change in command: on 8 July, Vācietis was replaced by S. S. Kamenev and Frunze became the commander of the Eastern front. There was probably an element of political manoeuvring in this controversy: S. S. Kamenev was an associate of Stalin's, and the episode provided Stalin with an opportunity to undermine Trotsky's influence.[16]

The campaign on the Eastern front continued with increased intensity. On 13 July, Zlatoust fell to the Reds, to be followed by Ekaterinburg on the following day. M. N. Tukhachevskii's forces then made their way over difficult terrain to Cheliabinsk, which they were able to capture after a major battle with heavy losses on both sides. Kolchak's armies were forced to retreat, abandoning both Cheliabinsk and Troitsk.

A factor which hastened the collapse of Kolchak's rule in Siberia was the opposition of the local population. Initially the Siberian peasantry had been

[16] J. Vācietis, *Latviešu strēlnieku vēsturiskā nozīme* (Riga, 1989), pp. 169–70; P. Kenez, *Civil War in South Russia, 1919–1920: The Defeat of the Whites* (Berkeley and Los Angeles, CA, 1977), pp. 41–43; Benvenuti, *Bolsheviks*, pp. 133–38.

willing to fight against the Bolsheviks, and recruiting in 1918 went well. But by the end of the year requisitioning had led to peasant uprisings, and these were violently suppressed by the military authorities. Entire villages were burnt. These actions and the policy of restoring the land to its former owners alienated the Siberian peasantry from Kolchak's government. During the summer of 1919, peasant partisans gave assistance to the Soviet forces.

In the middle of October 1919, the Red Army recommenced its attack and, helped by local partisans, took Omsk on 20 December 1919 and Irkutsk on 4 January 1920. On 6 January, Kolchak gave up his position of Supreme Ruler in favour of General Denikin. He appointed Ataman Semenov Commander-in-Chief of the armies in the far east and the Irkutsk military district. On 15 January, Kolchak was arrested by the Czechs and handed over to the Irkutsk Military Revolutionary Committee. After being interrogated by the Irkutsk Cheka, Kolchak was shot on 7 February 1920.[17]

The fall of Kolchak's government threatened to bring the Soviet regime in Russia into direct conflict with the Japanese in the far east. To avoid war with the Japanese ,the Soviet government agreed to create a democratic buffer state – the Far Eastern Republic. This was proclaimed on 6 April 1920 in Verkhneudinsk. This lasted until 1922, when it was incorporated into the Soviet Union.[18]

The South

In November 1918, under pressure from the Allies, the Volunteer Army and the Don Cossacks agreed to unite all anti-Soviet forces in the south in a single organization called the Armed Forces of Southern Russia (AFSR). Allied intervention in the south at this time caused the Soviet leadership grave concern, as it was anxious to defeat Krasnov at Tsaritsyn before his campaign could be supported by the Allies. In this effort the commander of the Southern front, V. M. Gittis, directed his armies towards the Don steppe, ignoring the Donbass to his right. It was in the Donbass, however, that Denikin began to concentrate his forces from the end of January 1919, following his victories in the north Caucasus.

In March 1919, Vācietis ordered a Soviet offensive in the Donbass, which began somewhat belatedly in April. Despite Trotsky's optimism about the outcome of this campaign, the Red Army's offensive was defeated and there was a threat of the whole front collapsing. Denikin was helped by the anti-Soviet rebellion of Ataman Grigorev on 7 May. By the summer of 1919, Denikin had succeeded in capturing almost the whole of Kharkov province, the whole of Ekaterinoslav province and the Crimea. On 24 June he took Kharkov, and on 30 June, Tsaritsyn. The capture of Tsaritsyn, which had withstood Krasnov's attacks for so long, gave understandable satisfaction to Denikin's supporters, and enhanced the reputation of General P. N. Wrangel, the commander of the unit who had taken it.

[17] S. V. Drokov, 'Aleksandr Vasil'evich Kolchak', *Voprosy istorii* (1991, no. 1), pp. 64–65.
[18] Miliukov, *Rossiia*, p. 160.

In July 1919, the Soviet leaders faced a crisis situation as Denikin threatened to advance towards the centre of Russia, and as progress against Kolchak in the east was being made. In these circumstances Lenin wrote his circular *Everything for the Struggle against Denikin*, in which it was recognized that the Southern front was the most important one but that forces should not be withdrawn from the east to reinforce it.

The Red Army counter-attack in August failed to turn the tide. General K. K. Mamontov's Cossacks took Tambov on the 18th, and Denikin, with the help of Petliura, captured Kiev and Odessa on the 31st. These further conquests by the Whites opened up the possibility of an offensive on Tula and Moscow, an option eagerly canvassed by Denikin's Chief of Staff, General Romanovskii. Wrangel, on the other hand, favoured going to Kolchak's help and to consolidate the territories already conquered. In the event, Denikin followed Romanovskii's advice and decided to risk advancing on Tula and Moscow.

On 12 September the decisive offensive of the AFSR in the direction of Orel–Tula began, led by Generals V. Z. Mai-Maevskii and Mamontov. By 20 September, Kursk had been taken, opening the way to Tula. Tula's capture presented a particular danger to the Soviet regime, because it was the Tula armaments industry which supplied the Red Army with a large proportion of its weapons. If this had been lost by the Reds, further fighting would have been difficult, if not impossible. Tula's defences were therefore strengthened. Between 6 and 13 October, the AFSR took Voronezh, Kalach, Kromy and Orel. This was to be the limit of the AFSR's success, which brought it within 250 miles of Moscow; from then on the White offensive was to run into difficulties.

As the military situation grew more critical for the Soviet government, on 9 October S. S. Kamenev proposed that the Southern front should attack in the direction of Kursk. On 15 October it was decided that all troops which could be spared from other fronts should be transferred to the Southern front. The Latvian riflemen and V. M. Primakov's brigade of Red Cossacks were sent there. Priority was now given to defending the Moscow–Tula region. Troops had also to be sent to defend Petrograd, which was being attacked by General Iudenich from Estonian territory.

Following preliminary operations in the region of Kromy, Orel and Voronezh, on 20 September the Red Army launched a major offensive along the Southern front towards Kursk. Denikin's forces had to retreat from Voronezh in some haste before Budienny's cavalry, leaving behind valuable military supplies. Soviet forces then fought their way through to Kursk, which was finally captured by a surprise night attack on 17–18 November. The initiative now passed to the Soviet forces, opening up the perspective for a general offensive.

As the military situation began to deteriorate for the AFSR, weaknesses in the regime Denikin had established in the territories under his control began to acquire increased importance. The peasants had initially welcomed Denikin's armies as liberators, as the Soviet regime had taken recruits and carried out requisitions. Denikin established free markets in grain, which helped the wealthy but made it more difficult for the poor to buy food. The peasants became discontented as estates were returned to their former owners, and the Denikin regime showed a marked reluctance to carry out the most modest of land reforms. There were strained relations between Denikin and the Cossacks. Denikin planned to re-establish a Russian empire that would be 'one and undivided', whereas the Cossacks wanted autonomy in a federal state. At a conference in Ekaterinodar, Denikin offended the ataman of the Kuban Cossacks, A. P. Filimonov, by impatiently demanding to know: 'Are the Cossacks for or against Russia?' Open conflict between the two sides was only avoided with difficulty.

On 19 November 1919, S. M. Budienny's Cavalry Corps became the 1 Cavalry Army. This was a symptomatic development: previously the Whites had had an absolute mastery in cavalry, thanks to which they had been able to out-manoeuvre the Red Army. That domination was lost in the battles of October and November 1919.

On 14 November 1919, the Central Committee ordered action to be speeded up in the direction of Kharkov and the Donbass. This would gain an important industrial town and also divide the the Volunteer Army from the Don Army. On 12 December Latvian riflemen and Red cavalrymen drove Denikin's forces out of Kharkov and Poltava, and on 16 December Soviet troops again entered Kiev. By the beginning of January 1920, helped by partisan action, the Donbass came under Soviet control. At the end of 1919 the Red Army attempted to regain Tsaritsyn, but at first were unable to break through Wrangel's defences. It was finally captured on 3 January 1920.

After the reverses suffered by the Volunteer Army, Wrangel replaced Mai-Maevskii as its commander. Wrangel was deeply aware of the problems of discipline that needed to be tackled. In a report he had submitted to Denikin in December 1919 he stated that the army had tried to dominate too much territory. 'Trying to be strong everywhere, we are weak everywhere . . . the morale of the army has fallen. The army has become a means of making a living. It uses local sources of supply for robbery and speculation. . . . The army has become demoralized; its soldiers have become traders and speculators.'[19] There was, however, little at this late stage which could be done about such shortcomings.

In the Ukraine, the Red Army systematically compelled what remained of the AFSR to retreat from the positions it occupied, the most stubborn battles being in the Donbass. As a result of the losses it had suffered, the Volunteer Army was reduced to the Volunteer Corps, which was now led by General A. P. Kutepov. After being defeated in the Donbass, Denikin tried to halt the Soviet offensive before Rostov and Novocherkassk. In the battles for these towns the Volunteer Corps suffered heavy casualties but were unable to prevent their capture by units of the Red Army.

The loss of Rostov and Novocherkassk destroyed any hope of recovery by the AFSR, the bulk of whose forces retreated to the Northern Caucasus. There they were able to regroup and receive reinforcements. On 21 February they managed to retake Rostov, though it was recovered by the Red Army two days later.

In February 1920, Tukhachevskii, who had replaced Shorin as the commander of the Caucasian front, launched an offensive which succeeded in

[19] R. Wojna, *W ogniu rosyjskiej wojny wewnętrznej 1918–1920* (Warsaw, 1975), p. 186.

capturing Ekaterinodar on 17 March and Novorossiisk on 27 March. Victory over the AFSR would have been complete if some of Denikin's forces had not been able to escape to the Crimea. There on 4 April Denikin resigned as head of the AFSR, to be succeeded by General Wrangel. Denikin departed from the Crimea on a British ship, spending a short time in Constantinople before sailing for France.

The Baltic

Following the military collapse of Germany in November 1918, Latvian independence was proclaimed in Riga. Jānis Čakste and Kārlis Ulmanis were elected President of the Republic and Prime Minister respectively. An Estonian Provisional Government met in Reval on 11 November and declared the independence of Estonia.[20]

At the end of 1918 the government of Soviet Russia planned an offensive by the Red Army to counter the threat of invasion from the south and to carry the revolution to Germany and Poland. This involved crossing Ukrainian and Baltic territory. To avoid the accusation of invading independent countries, Lenin decided that Soviet governments would be established in the path of the advancing Red Army.[21] On 29 November, Soviet forces under Vācietis entered Narva, and the Estland Workers' Commune was established under the leadership of Jaan Anvelt. The existing nationalist Estonian government ordered a general mobilization and, on 12 December, a British naval squadron under Admiral Sinclair arrived at Narva. On 23 December, Colonel Johan Laidoner was appointed commander-in-chief of the Estonian forces, Sinclair supplying him with weapons and two captured Soviet destroyers. In January 1919, Laidoner started a counter-offensive helped by the Russian Northern Corps under General Aleksandr Rodzianko. By February Estonia had been virtually cleared of Soviet troops.

During December 1918 Vācietis's forces advanced through Latvian territory, taking Riga on 3 January 1919. A Soviet government was established there headed by Pēteris Stučka, the Ulmanis government seeking refuge in Libau.[22] With the entry of the Red Army into Vilna on 5 January 1919, a Lithuanian Soviet government headed by Vincas Kapsukas was installed. The *Taryba* withdrew to Kaunas.

The Ulmanis government in Libau, having no armed forces of its own, was forced to seek help from the Germans. Following the Armistice, a volunteer force had been formed on Latvian territory from remnants of the German VIII Army. This 'Iron Division' was commanded by General Rüdiger von der Goltz, who had ambitions to retain the Baltic area as a sphere of German influence. In return for military assistance, the Ulmanis government agreed to grant German soldiers Latvian citizenship. Von der Goltz, however, regarded the Latvian government as little better than the Bolsheviks, and on 16 April, at

[20] Ā. Šilde, *Latvijas vēsture 1914–1940* (Stockholm, 1976), pp. 218–21.
[21] V. I. Lenin, *Polnoe sobranie sochineniy* xxxvii, p. 234.
[22] S. Kamiński, 'Wyparcie wojsk niemieckich z Estonii i Lotwy w latach 1918–1919', Part I, *Zapiski historyczne* xliii (1978), Book 1, pp. 64–71.

his instigation, the Ulmanis government was overthrown and replaced by that of the pro-German Latvian pastor, Andrieve Niedra.[23]

Von der Goltz started his offensive against the Red Army in Latvia at the beginning of March and captured Riga on 23 May, bringing down Stučka's Soviet government. Pushing northwards, von der Goltz's troops were stopped near Wenden by a combined Estonian and Latvian nationalist force. In the battle of 19–22 June, the Germans were defeated and had to retreat towards Riga.[24]

By the summer of 1919, the Allied powers had become convinced that the danger presented by the Bolsheviks had receded, and that now the greatest threat was presented by the continued German presence in the Baltic area. After repeated demands by the British, von der Goltz laid down his command and returned to Germany. He had, however, encouraged the troops of the Iron Division to enlist in the anti-Bolshevik army of P. R. Bermondt-Avalov and, ostensibly, in Russian service, to remain on both Latvian and Lithuanian territory. It took the threat of Allied sanctions against Germany for the Berlin government to order the evacuation of German troops from the Baltic. Those in Russian service, however, were now outside Germany's control.[25]

On 8 October 1919, under the pretext of trying to reach the Bolshevik front, Bermondt began an offensive in the direction of Riga. In response, the Latvian General, Jānis Balodis, deployed his troops to face the new threat and, helped by the artillery of four French destroyers, defeated the Germans, who eventually retreated to East Prussia through Lithuania. Latgale, which still remained under Bolshevik control, was cleared by Balodis with the help of Polish forces sent by Piłsudski.

Lithuanian–Polish relations were not so harmonious. The Poles regarded Vilna as their own, and were determined to claim it. As a safeguard against Polish attack, the Lithuanian Soviet Republic united with the neighbouring Belorussian Republic to form a single Soviet State, 'Litbel'.

Meanwhile the Lithuanian nationalist government in Kaunas had begun to recruit German volunteers to retake the capital, but before this could be done Polish troops under Piłsudski moved up from the south and marched on Vilna. After three days of bitter fighting, the Kapsukas government fell, and on 21 April Vilna was captured by the Poles.[26]

In November 1919, the Soviet government opened peace negotiations with Estonia, leading to a peace treaty signed in Dorpat on 2 February 1920 giving Estonia *de jure* recognition. Similar agreements between the Soviet government and the other two Baltic states followed, a treaty between Russia and Latvia being concluded on 1 August 1920, and one between Soviet Russia and Lithuania on 12 July 1920.[27]

[23] R. von der Goltz, *Meine Sendung in Finnland und im Baltikum* (Leipzig, 1920), pp. 162, 176, 185.

[24] A. Schwabe, *Histoire du peuple letton* (Stockholm, 1953), pp. 181–85.

[25] Von der Goltz, *Meine Sendung*, pp. 202, 221–23; C. L. Sullivan, 'The 1919 German Campaign in the Baltic: The Final Phase', in V. Stanley Vardys and R. J. Misiunas, *The Baltic States in Peace and War 1917–1945* (Pennsylvania, 1978), pp. 31–40.

[26] A. E. Senn, *The Emergence of Modern Lithuania* (New York, 1959), p. 105.

[27] G. von Rauch, *The Baltic States* (London, 1974), pp. 70–75.

Petrograd

In August 1918, Russian right-wing groups meeting in Pskov agreed to create, with German participation, a local military unit. This Pskov corps was formed during October. As the Germans withdrew from the area in November, the Pskov corps fought its first battles with the VII Red Army. On 26 November, Soviet forces took Pskov, compelling the corps to fall back from the town. At the end of November the corps was divided into two sections – the Northern Corps and the Southern Corps. The Southern Corps, under Prince Anatole von Lieven, went with the Germans to Latvia, where it was augmented by recruits from among Russian prisoners-of-war and Russian refugees to Germany. The Northern Corps, commanded by General Aleksandr Rodzianko, moved to Estonia, where it continued to fight against Soviet forces there under the Estonian commander-in-chief, Laidoner. Once the Red Army had been driven back from Estonian territory, however, the Russian politicians associated with the Northern Corps began to insist on independent action. In particular they wanted an offensive against Petrograd.

On 13 May, the Northern Corps commenced its offensive by capturing Iamburg. On 25 May its Estonian allies took Pskov, where subsequently the Russian commander S. N. Bulak-Balakhovich was to institute a reign of terror. Rodzianko's offensive coincided with von der Goltz's drive against Riga and Wenden, a fact which raised the Estonians' suspicions, who feared German domination of the area and who promptly ceased to help the Northern Corps.

The Soviet VII Army counter-attacked on 21 June and, after bitter fighting, stopped close to Iamburg. Pskov, however, was recaptured on 26 August with the help of the Pskov Communist Battalion and units of the Estonian Red Army.

At the end of July, General Iudenich arrived in Estonia from Helsinki and took command of the Northern Corps, which was now renamed the North-Western Army. As the British military mission to the Baltic were aware that the Iudenich's army could not succeed in its offensive on Petrograd without Estonian help, on 10 August General Frank Marsh gathered a number of local Russian politicians together and instructed them to form a democratic North-Western government which would recognize Estonian independence. The government was duly formed and the declaration made, but as neither Iudenich nor the British government considered themselves bound to honour the agreement, the exercise failed to have the desired effect on the Estonians.[28]

In October, moreover, Bermondt-Avalov, who had succeeded Lieven as commander of the Southern Corps and with whom Iudenich had agreed to form a united military force, led his armies to Latvia and Lithuania, just as von der Goltz was being forced to leave. This served to strengthen Estonian convictions that Iudenich was no real ally of theirs, and prompted them to open peace negotiation with the Soviet government.

Knowing that a Soviet–Estonian agreement would deny him the use of Estonian territory, Iudenich decided not to delay in launching his attack on

[28] Kakurin, *Kak srazhalas'*, p. 80.

Petrograd, and on 28 September units of the North-Western Army attacked unexpectedly in the direction of Luga. The main assault force attacked through Iamburg towards Gatchina. As in November 1917, the decisive battles were fought in the region of the Pulkovo heights.

There was no chance of reinforcing the VII Red Army, since all available troops were needed at that time on the Southern front against Denikin. Trotsky hurried to Petrograd on 16 October, determined to defend the city even if it meant house-to-house fighting. The Soviet forces counter-attacked on 20 October, headed by the 5th Latvian Infantry Regiment, usually reserved for guarding the Moscow Kremlin. On the 25th, Iudenich's forces were dislodged from the Pulkovo heights and on the 30th Luga and Gatchina were captured; Iamburg passed into Soviet hands on 14 November. The defeated and disintegrating North-Western Army retreated in several groups, putting up resistance here and there. After crossing the Estonian border the remains of Iudenich's armies were disarmed, and on 22 December the North-Western Army officially ceased to exist.[29]

In the course of its offensive the Red Army had taken Narva, which formed part of Estonia. This was returned to the Estonians on condition that the territory become neutral ground. Negotiations between the Soviet Russian and Estonian governments took place in Dorpat, resulting in an armistice being declared on 31 December 1919. This was followed by peace treaty between the two countries signed on 2 February 1920.

The North

In the north of Russia the same cycle of developments took place as in the east, but on a much smaller scale. The Allied landings at Murmansk and Archangel easily overthrew the feeble Soviet government that had been established there. The local anti-Bolshevik movement, however, was weak and did not manage to free itself from the tutelage of the Allies. Under their auspices, a government, headed by the veteran revolutionary N. V. Chaikovskii and consisting largely of Socialist Revolutionaries, was formed. It was thus similar in character to the Komuch government which had been established in Samara in June. It was to suffer the same fate. Over a period of time the socialist members of the government were removed and replaced by conservatives. In January 1919, Chaikovskii left Archangel and power was assumed by General Miller.

No military dictatorship was proclaimed in the north as it was in the east and south. Only on 10 February 1920 the government gave the totality of power to General Miller. But by then it had little significance, and only served to facilitate the evacuation of the Allied forces from Russia.

In the north the same situation prevailed as in other areas under White rule, and there too the authorities were just as unable to tackle the problems. There was inflation, unemployment and a breakdown of industry. The government did not succeed in winning the peasants' support. Although peasant irre-

[29] W. H. Chamberlin, *The Russian Revolution* ii (New York, 1935), p. 274.

gulars fought on the side of Miller's forces, the countryside remained overwhelmingly neutral towards the warring sides. In the towns the workers were predominantly anti-government and, as a consequence, often fell victim to repression.

Few large-scale military operations took place in the north. Attempts by Allied forces to mount offensive operations into the Russian interior were easily contained by Soviet forces. Mostly the opposing sides confined themselves to minor raids and skirmishes. There were no officer 'volunteers' in the north, and the Allies did not make appreciable progress in creating an effective Russian army.

In January 1920 the Red Army began its offensive in the north. As a number of towns fell into Soviet hands, General Miller fled from Archangel on an icebreaker on 16 February. Soviet troops entered Archangel on 21 February and Murmansk on 13 March. With these victories Soviet power was re-established in the north.

The Comintern

One condition imposed on Russia by the treaty of Brest-Litovsk was the prohibition to carry out propaganda activities in the territories occupied by Germany and its allies. The Soviet government, however, soon found a way round this restriction. It was to set up ostensibly independent communist parties in the areas in question. The first party to be established in this way was the Ukrainian Communist Party, which held its First Congress from 5 to 12 July 1918. The leaders of the new party believed that it should be an integral part of the Russian Communist Party, but for tactical considerations this should not be said openly.[30] The Belorussian Communist Party was founded on 8 August 1918; the Finnish Communist Party on 29 August 1918; the Lithuanian Communist Party on 1 October; and the Estland Communist Party on 16 November. The Latvian Social Democratic Party was renamed the Latvian Communist Party in January 1919.[31] On 16 December 1918 the two Polish parties – the PPS-Lewica and the SDKPiL – united to form the Polish Communist Party.[32] The newly formed communist parties conducted propaganda against the Germans among the local populations, and the Ukrainian party joined with local SR and Anarchist groups in carrying out partisan warfare against the occupying forces.

At the beginning of October, as the Allied victory over Germany drew near, the Soviet leadership became convinced that a revolution in Germany was in the offing. It was now essential to ensure that the activities of the national communist parties were directed towards achieving the success of the German revolution, particularly as the territory they operated in formed the 'Red bridge' connecting the Soviet Union with Germany. To co-ordinate activities of the various communist organizations, the First Conference of

[30] 'Deiatel'nost' Tsentral'nogo Komiteta partii v dokumentakh', *Izvestiia TsK KPSS* (1989, no. 3), pp. 110, 114.

[31] Kulichenko, *Bor'ba*, pp. 22–27.

[32] F. Tych, *PPS-Lewica w latach wojny 1914–1918* (Warsaw, 1960), pp. 176–78.

Communist Organizations of the Occupied Regions was held in Moscow from 19 to 24 October. It was attended by 30 communists from the territories occupied by the Germans, and was chaired by Stanisław Pestkowski from the Commissariat of Nationalities. The assembly was referred to as the 'Little International'.[33]

When Lenin addressed the delegates to the conference on 21 October, he stressed that nothing should be done to jeopardize the revolution's success in Germany. He believed in particular that the policy of partisan warfare advocated by the left wing of the Ukrainian party was potentially disastrous, and should be replaced by a campaign of peaceful propaganda. Conference delegates decided that suitable propaganda literature might be supplied by the Federation of Foreign Communists, which was attached to the Communist Party Central Committee.[34]

Between the end of November 1918 and the beginning of January 1919, Soviet republics were established in the Ukraine, Estonia, Latvia and Lithuania-Belorussia, though by February the Estonian Workers' Commune had been overthrown. From 2–6 March 1919, representatives of these now-ruling communist parties, along with members of the Federation of Foreign Communists and a sprinkling of communists from abroad, met in Moscow to hold the First Congress of the Third International – the Comintern. Altogether it was claimed that 52 delegates from 35 communist and left socialist parties, groups and organizations of 21 countries of Europe, America and Asia took part. Speakers at the congress included Bukharin, Zinoviev, Osinskii, Trotsky and Chicherin. A manifesto was adopted claiming the new International as the successor to the one founded 72 years earlier by Marx, and an Executive Committee was elected, Zinoviev becoming chairman and Radek secretary. From the beginning the organization was dominated by the Russian Communist Party. In fact, to a large extent it had evolved out of the Russian Communist Party.

The Second Congress of the Comintern opened on 19 July 1920, this time with over 200 delegates. This congress coincided with the Soviet–Polish war, and with the prospect that the Red Army might carry the revolution into Poland. Lenin was eager that the Red Army should not stop at the frontier but should carry on into Poland. Trotsky and Radek were against this idea, but Tukhachevskii, for good military reasons, was much in favour.

The most important document issued by the Second Congress was that setting forth the '21 conditions' on which parties would be admitted to the Comintern. These conditions served to ensure that each member party became a replica of the Bolshevik Party by insisting on centralization and 'iron discipline'. Parties were expected to consider themselves particular national sections of the Comintern. In preparation for the congress, Lenin had also written the pamphlet *Left Wing Communism: An Infantile Disorder*, in which he recommended that communist parties should emulate the experience of the Bolshevik Party, which through its centralization and discipline

[33] A. Deruga, 'Z dziejów ruchu rewolucyjnego na ziemiach litewsko-białoruskich w 1918 r., *Z dziejów stosunków polsko-radzieckich* xi–xii (1975), p. 306.

[34] K. L. Seleznev, 'Bol'shevistskaia agitatsiia i revoliutsionnoe dvizhenie v germanskoi armii na vostochnom fronte v 1918 g.', in V. D. Kul'bakin, ed., *Noiabr'skaia revoliutsiia v Germanii* (Moscow, 1960), pp. 295–96.

had successfully brought about the proletarian revolution in Russia. He pointed out, however, that the experience of the Bolshevik Party showed the need to compromise and avoid the mistakes of leftism. In fact in the case of the Ukraine, the Baltic territories and Hungary, the left communist policy of establishing collective and State farms had greatly impeded the extension of the revolution. And in Poland it was in the process of doing so again.

War with Poland

Soviet Russia's war with Poland in 1920 was the outcome of the complex relations which had existed between the two countries since the beginning of 1919. The new Polish republic owed its existence to the collapse during the First World War of all three partitioning powers, and to the skilful diplomacy of Józef Piłsudski who, having led Polish troops on behalf of Germany, succeeded in dissociating himself from the German war effort and enlisting the support of the Allies for the Polish cause. Piłsudski's policy towards Soviet Russia was therefore one conditioned by the need to retain the good graces of the Allies.

When Germany surrendered in November 1918 and began to evacuate the Ukraine, Belorussia and the Baltic states, the possibility arose that the Red Army would move to occupy the territories it had left. The Allies accordingly obliged the Germans not to withdraw completely until the Polish armies moved up to take their place. This happened during the first half of February 1919, though Polish legionaries were already in Vilna when Soviet forces arrived in January 1919. There was no open declaration of war on this Soviet-Polish front, but in the spring and summer of 1919, when the Soviet forces were occupied elsewhere, there was an offensive along the whole front during which the Red Army was expelled from Latgale and Vilna was captured by the Poles. This brought Piłsudski the gratitude of the young Latvian state and the bitter resentment of the Lithuanians.[35]

The peace conference at Versailles in June 1919 had determined Poland's boundaries with Germany but left those in the east undefined. A provisional frontier had been drawn by Lord Curzon, which followed the boundary of ethnic Poland. This was quite generous to Russia, since Curzon did not wish to antagonize the anti-Bolshevik forces who, he thought, might triumph. Polish political parties of the right, however, thought in terms of reconstituting the prepartition Polish Commonwealth of 1772. Piłsudski believed this unrealistic, but looked towards a federation of states – the Ukraine, Lithuania, Belorussia, Latvia and Estonia – all under Polish tutelage. To this end, Piłsudski made an agreement with the Ukrainian leader, Petliura; Piłsudski would overthrow the Soviet regime in the Ukraine and install Petliura as premier in return for a Ukrainian undertaking not to be party to any international agreements directed against Poland.[36]

From 10 February 1919, Chicherin, the Soviet Commissar of Foreign

---

[35] J. Borkowski, ed., *Rok 1920: Wojna polsko–radziecka we wspomnieniach i innych dokumentach* (Warsaw, 1990), pp. 17–18.
[36] *Ibid.*, p. 128.

Affairs, had sent the Poles a series of notes inviting them to negotiate on the boundary question and other outstanding differences. Initially the Poles had not responded, but on 27 March they replied that they were ready to enter into negotiations with Soviet Russia, but named Borisov – a town on the Soviet–Polish Belorussian front – as the proposed venue. The Poles, more-over, did not agree to a general armistice, but only to a cessation of hostilities on the Borisov sector. This suggested to the Soviet leaders that Piłsudski might use the negotiations for offensive action on the Ukrainian front. The Russians replied that they would prefer to negotiate on neutral territory, such as Estonia. This suggestion was not pursued, and on 25 April 1920 Piłsudski marched on Kiev, capturing it on 7 May.

The Soviet counter-attack soon followed. It was begun on 13 May by Tukhachevskii, whose offensive through Belorussia was halted by the Poles at Molodechno. They succeeded in doing so, however, only be withdrawing troops from the Kiev front. This was then attacked by Budienny's cavalry, which broke through the Polish lines on 5 June. A week later the Polish troops evacuated Kiev and began to retreat before the Soviet forces. A number of towns held by the Poles were taken by the Red Army, including Vilna on 14 July. This led the small Lithuanian army to intervene on the side of the Reds, who succeeded in crossing the Bug and the Niemen and in heading through Brest-Litovsk and Białystok to Warsaw.

Tukhachevskii undertook the pursuit of the Polish army to Warsaw for the strategic reason of following through his victory at Kiev.[37] It was therefore something of an afterthought when the Soviet party leadership sent leading Polish communists to set up revolutionary committees in the Polish towns captured by the Red Army. The first such committee to be constituted was the one in Białystok on 30 July. It consisted of the veteran Polish revolutionaries Feliks Dzierżyński, Julian Marchlewski, Eduard Próchniak and Feliks Kon. The manifesto issued by this committee advocated the nationalization of industry, the confiscation of landed estates and the management of these estates by committees of farm labourers.[38]

According to Marchlewski, until the arrival of the Revolutionary Commit-tee there was no one connected with the Red Army in Bialystok who could speak Polish, and nothing had been done to win over the local population. The workers, many of whom were Jewish, were quite willing to nationalize the factories and implement workers' control. The peasants, on the other hand, could see no benefit in Soviet power. This was partly because of Red Army requisitions of food, clothing and livestock but also because the Revolutionary Committee did not propose to divide up the landed estates. It advocated the Left Communist policy of converting them into State farms – the same policy which had alienated the peasants in the neighbouring Baltic states a year earlier. There was also a long-standing national antagonism between Poles and Russians, which made it unlikely that a military defeat at the hands of the Russians would be welcomed by any class of Polish society.[39]

On 25 July a Franco-British mission arrived in Warsaw to help the Poles. For the defence of Warsaw and the Polish counter-offensive, Piłsudski had as

---

[37] N. Davies, *White Eagle, Red Star: The Polish Soviet War, 1919–1920* (London, 1972), p. 208.
[38] Borkowski, *Rok 1920*, pp. 211–14.
[39] *Ibid.*, pp. 337–48.

his military adviser Marshal Foch's Chief-of-Staff, General Weygand. Although Tukhachevskii's forces were able to reach the outskirts of Warsaw, they were unable to press home their advantage through lack of reinforcements and difficulties of communication.

On 16 August Piłsudski began his counter-offensive, and was able to throw back the Soviet forces along the route they had come. Brest-Litovsk was again in Polish hands on 19 August, and Białystok on the 24th. As Soviet forces fell back from Vilna on the 25th, the city was occupied by Lithuanian units.

On 2 September peace negotiations were opened in Riga, and on 18 October an armistice was agreed between the two sides. The Soviet–Polish frontier was drawn well to the east of the Curzon line, ceding to Poland large tracts of Belorussian and Ukrainian territory. The final peace treaty between Soviet Russia and Poland was signed in Riga on 18 March 1921.

On 7 October 1920 an agreement, sponsored by the League of Nations, was signed at Suvalki between Poland and Lithuania establishing the boundary between them, Vilna being on the Lithuanian side. Two days later, however, Polish troops under General Lucjan Żeligowski invaded the Vilna region and retained it for Poland.[40]

Wrangel and the Crimea

After the hurried evacuation of what remained of the Volunteer Army – some 20,000 volunteers and 12,000 Cossacks – to the Crimea, General Wrangel set about trying to correct some of the mistakes made by Denikin. Although he himself was an aristocrat with decidedly conservative views, he believed that a programme of reform was necessary to win support for the White cause. He called this 'a leftist policy in rightist hands'. With the help of the former tsarist minister, A. V. Krivoshein, he elaborated an agrarian reform designed to give land to the peasants in return for long-term compensation to the land-owners. Although far beyond anything conceded by other White leaders, the agrarian programme did not excite the local peasantry.[41]

Wrangel also tried to modify Denikin's insistence on a Russia 'united and undivided' in order to cultivate allies among the non-Russian nationalities. He tried (unsuccessfully) to enlist the help of Piłsudski and Makhno. Wrangel's request for co-operation was not only rejected by Makhno but Makhno also hanged Wrangel's emissary and published Wrangel's letter and his own reply.

Wrangel was also concerned to rebuild his armed forces and to restore discipline among them. This was achieved during March–April 1920. Initially Wrangel was dependent on foreign aid to equip his troops. This came mainly from the French, who recognized his government on 10 August, the British refusing to support any further military action by the Whites.

Between June and September 1920, Wrangel launched three successive military operations. The first of these commenced on 6 June, during the

[40] W. Jędrejewicz, *Kronika życia Józefa Piłsudskiego* i (London, 1986), p. 525.
[41] Miliukov, *Rossiia*, pp. 222–29.

Soviet–Polish war, and succeeded in establishing a base in the northern Tauride. The Red Army was forced to retreat, and the local peasantry initially welcomed Wrangel's forces. These forces, however, began to loot the peasantry in the territory they controlled, just as Denikin's troops had done previously, and quickly lost the population's sympathy.

In his second offensive during the latter half of August Wrangel tried once again to gain control of the 'Vendee of the Russian revolution', the Cossack regions of the Don, Kuban and Terek. He hoped his operation would be accompanied by a Cossack rebellion, but in the event this did not materialize, and his landing failed to achieve its objective.

On 14 September, Wrangel's forces began a new offensive, this time into the Ukraine, in the hope of joining up with the Polish armies. The moment was opportune because the Red Army was occupied on the Polish front and was suffering defeat at the hands of the Poles. Wrangel's forces succeeded in gaining control of a large expanse of territory but, on 18 October, the armistice was signed between Russia and Poland, making it possible for Russia to transfer troops, including Budienny's 1st Cavalry Army, from the Polish to the Southern front, on which Frunze had launched a counter-offensive against Wrangel.

The Red Armies encircled Wrangel's forces on the northern Tauride inflicting enormous casualties. Those who managed to escape from the encirclement fled in disorder towards the Crimea. The Red Army fought its way through the isthmus of Perekop on 8–9 November in pursuit of the remnants of Wrangel's armies. By a special order issued on 13 November, Wrangel dissolved the AFSR. It only remained for him to organize the evacuation of his troops. The 140,000 or so men left on 127 vessels were to become émigrés in Bulgaria, Serbia, Greece, Prinkipo, Lemnos, Cyprus or Egypt. Most of those who left at that time never saw their country again.

The Character of the Civil War

What was the Civil War fought about? It was certainly not the issue of collaboration with the Germans, which initially united opposition to their rule. Krasnov was soon receiving aid directly from the Germans, and passing it on to Alekseev and Denikin indirectly. Iudenich's North-Western Army collaborated with von der Goltz. There was nothing inherently anti-German about the White movement.

Nor was the Civil War one of democracy against dictatorship. All the White governments either began as dictatorships or quickly became dictatorships. Moderate socialist governments, such as Komuch or the Chaikovskii government in the north, were rapidly swept away. This pattern itself, however, is instructive. It reflects the fact that socialism, democracy and liberal principles were the concerns primarily of the Russian intelligentsia, a minority group in the country. While the Provisional Government had existed, it had appeared that democratic principles enjoyed wide acceptance, but in the aftermath of the Bolshevik accession to power, more elemental forces began to be unleashed.

The most far-reaching measure the Bolsheviks introduced, the one which changed the social structure of the country, was the decree on land. This was a measure that, with the stroke of a pen, deprived the land-owning class of its wealth, its privileged status and a way of life it had enjoyed for many generations. The land-owners were never likely to submit meekly to the provisions of the decree on land and, when the opportunity arose, they fought tooth and nail to keep their land and the power it brought with it. The Civil War was the last episode in the struggle between the Russian land-owners and the peasantry to determine who should control the land.

It is important to establish what the Civil War was fought about, because then one is in a better position to judge why the Reds were able to win. One reason historians usually advance is that the Whites made the mistake of not offering the peasants land to win over their loyalties. That proposition implies that, in return for a military victory, the Whites would have been prepared to see some part of the land go to the peasants. But then what use would the military victory have been, if the objective of the fighting had been conceded?

One has to remember, too, that the Reds were not able to take full advantage of the land factor because, during the Civil War, they were advocating collectivized forms of agriculture, and these had no appeal to the peasants. Soviet requisitioning policy also served to alienate peasant support. Symptomatic of the qualified support of the peasants for the Soviet regime was the declaration they commonly made that they supported the Bolsheviks but not the Communists. In other words, they approved of the decree on land but not the subsequent policies.

The Reds were able to benefit from the antipathy of the various national-alities of the former Russian Empire towards the Whites, who were centralists and opponents of national autonomy. This factor was important in protecting the approaches to Petrograd from the Baltic region and diminishing the threat presented by the North-Western Army.

Historians often mention the strategic advantage enjoyed by the Reds in having internal lines of communication, while their adversaries were posi-tioned at various points on the periphery. But this had its negative side. It obliged the Soviet forces to fight on four fronts, the North, South, East and West, with no secure rear. Each opponent, on the other hand, could operate on a single front, and with no danger of being attacked from the rear or the flanks. The Whites, moreover, had the advantage of receiving military supplies from the Allies, though the latter helped very little in the actual fighting.

Whatever geographical or political factors might have weighed in their favour, the Reds still had to achieve superiority on the battlefield. That they were able to do this testifies to their success in building the Red Army as an effective fighting force. Probably because of its novelty and its spirit of improvisation, the Red Army offered a 'career open to talents' for military commanders. Frunze and Budienny were among those who rose to promi-nence as Red Army commanders in the Civil War. Ironically, it was Trotsky who accomplished what Guchkov had striven for so long to achieve.

11

War Communism

The economic system which was in operation from the summer of 1918 to the beginning of 1921 was referred to retrospectively as 'war communism'. The term was first used by Alexander Bogdanov in a pamphlet entitled *Questions of Socialism*, written in 1917 and published in the following year. It was taken up by Lenin in his article, 'The tax in kind', written in 1921 to introduce the New Economic Policy initiated at the start of that year. At the Eleventh Party Congress in December, 'war communism' was a term used in speeches by Trotsky, E. A. Preobrazhenskii, D. B. Riazanov and V. M. Molotov. As in Lenin's case, the speakers employed the expression in the context of justifying the New Economic Policy, and contrasting it favourably with the economic policies of the preceding period. It has always been a matter of controversy whether 'war communism' arose out of the exigencies of war and collapse or whether it was introduced deliberately as the implementation of communist ideology, later being ascribed to the necessities of war when its failure became manifest.

In this connection Bogdanov's pamphlet in which the term 'war communism' first appeared is of considerable significance. It takes the form of a polemic against those socialists who, following Hilferding, believed that the prerequisites for socialism had been created within capitalism, and that the war economies of the belligerent countries – Germany's in particular – were the point of culmination of this process, and formed the basis for emerging socialist economies. This, as Bogdanov noted, was a belief held by many Russian socialists. He himself had never held it, considering it to be a mirage arising from the general hopelessness of the times, but one essential to expose for what it was.

Bogdanov argued that the war economies were steps not in the direction of socialism but of an authoritarian and bureaucratic system which he called 'war communism'. The driving force behind the creation of 'war communism' was the diminishing supply of foodstuffs and other necessities caused by the economic disruption of war. Its dynamic was the logic of distribution, not – as in other social systems – of production. Shortages required rationing and the fixing of prices. This brought in its train the need to control production, which implied centralization and the organization of branches of industry in trusts. Directly connected with the regulation of production was the State obligation to work and the extension of military forms of organization to the working classes of society.[1]

---

[1] A. A. Bogdanov, *Voprosy sotsializma: Raboty raznykh let* (Moscow, 1990), pp. 335-44.

Bogdanov's sketch of 'war communism', written in 1917, contains most of the salient features of the actual system which emerged in the three years which followed. The accuracy of his prediction reinforces his argument that the economic system which he described would have come about in any case, given the circumstances, and had nothing whatsoever to do with socialist or any other kind of ideology. Bogdanov's pamphlet, however, is also valuable in that it documents the fact that most of his socialist contemporaries did indeed think that the measures being implemented were ones of a socialist or communist kind. The necessity which they perceived was not so much the dictates of war as the inevitability of the historical process.[2]

The Economic Environment

The shortages, which Bogdanov saw as the driving force behind 'war communism', became extremely acute during the Civil War. Then vast areas of the country were controlled by forces hostile to the Soviet government. The loss of territory in this way affected both agriculture and industry. The occupation of the Ukraine, the Volga basin and Siberia deprived the Soviet State of its main grain-growing areas. In the same way the Soviet State was deprived of a considerable part of its resources of raw materials and fuel for its industries. Russia lost the regions which formerly had supplied 90 per cent of its coal, 85 per cent of its iron ore and 75 per cent of its iron and steel. The oil from the fields at Baku became inaccessible when British forces occupied the area. The supply of cotton from Turkestan and Transcaucasia was halted, causing severe disruption to the textile industry.[3]

Particularly serious was the British naval blockade imposed along the Baltic coast. This was because Russia had relied heavily on foreign imports for even its most basic agricultural implements – spades, axes, scythes, sickles, etc. As imports of these items ceased, the agricultural productivity fell. The shortage of industrial goods which the peasants needed, moreover, deprived the Soviet government of goods to exchange for agricultural produce. With nothing to gain in return, the peasants were understandably reluctant to part with their crops.

Because Russian industry had traditionally been dependent on foreign investment and expertise, the withdrawal of external support caused it to regress considerably. The most technically advanced industries in Russia were usually branches of foreign firms, and the curtailment of economic relations with the external world could eliminate those branches of industry completely. Russia had at that time, for example, no native electrical industry; appliances were assembled in Russian factories from components imported from abroad. When the blockade was imposed these imports ceased, leaving Russia to improvise as best it could in the use of electrical energy.[4]

[2]   On early Soviet evaluations of war communism, see A. Nove, *An Economic History of the USSR 1917–1991* (Harmondsworth, 1992), pp. 73–75.

[3]   E. G. Gimpel'son, *'Voennyi kommunizm'. Politika, praktika, ideologiia* (Moscow, 1973), pp. 45–46.

[4]   V. P. Miliutin, *Istoriia ekonomicheskogo razvitiia SSSR (1917–1927)* (Moscow-Leningrad, 1929), p. 202.

Lack of fuel and raw materials caused a sharp decline in industrial production. According to a census carried out on 31 August 1918, 38 per cent of industrial enterprises were idle. In the following year the position deteriorated further. After four years of war, railway transport in Russia was in a catastrophic state. The number of locomotives and waggons had been reduced three or fourfold compared with pre-war levels. The volume of railway traffic was only 23 per cent in 1918 of what it had been in 1913. By 1919, moreover, half of all railway traffic was being devoted to military purposes.

To fight a war in these circumstances the Soviet State had to mobilize all the material and human resources it had available. The country was turned into an armed camp whose slogan was 'Everything for the war!' This was reflected in the organizational methods of the whole State apparatus, as strict centralism and command structures were introduced. In the economic field these appeared first of all in the sphere of food supplies, since hunger was the initial threat to the Soviet State.

Industry

The summer of 1918 opened up a new phase in Soviet economic policy. Until then the government had tried to put into practice the widely held opinion among socialists that the structures of finance capitalism – the banks and cartels – would provide the ready-made foundation for a socialist economy. The corollary of that opinion was that no fundamental economic transformations were necessary or appropriate. By the summer of 1918 the policy of 'State capitalism' had become increasingly difficult to sustain, and there was growing pressure for the wholesale nationalization of the major industries.

Several factors pushed the government in this direction. The strike by the bank employees had dashed any hopes of using the financial institutions to monitor and regulate the economy. The strike destroyed a key element in Lenin's prerevolutionary vision of how the socialist economy would develop. A similar factor was the widespread refusal of industrialists and managers to co-operate in the implementation of workers' control. The penalty, moreover, for non-compliance with the decree on workers' control was the confiscation and nationalization of enterprises. In this way the number of enterprises in State ownership was increased. Some factories were nationalized by the workers themselves, by local Soviets or by local Councils of the National Economy (Sovnarkhozy). This took place despite repeated prohibitions by the government to do so. Fear that proprietors might close down their factories prompted workers or local economic institutions to take matters into their own hands in an effort to keep them in operation.

Nor was there ever a complete consensus of opinion within the Bolshevik Party on the correctness of the 'State capitalist' policy. Bukharin and other Left Communists saw State capitalism, with its use of capitalist structures and its collaboration with businessmen and managers, as a betrayal of revolutionary principles. They advocated in its place the nationalization of industry and its organization by the workers themselves. The Left Communists, therefore, looked with approval on the acts of nationalization that were taking place on the workers' initiative.

The widespread nationalization of industrial firms in the summer of 1918 had little to do with economic necessity; the motivation was more of a political nature. On 28 June 1918, the Council of People's Commissars issued a decree nationalizing all the major enterprises in industry and transport. This included all firms with capital of a million or more rubles. The stimulus for this mass nationalization was the sale of Russian firms to German subjects. The Soviet government expected to be presented with a demand from the German ambassador stating that certain factories which were not yet nationalized had been sold to German citizens and were therefore exempt from the decrees of the Supreme Council of the National Economy. Before this could be done, Vesenkha compiled a list of firms to become State property and published them in *Izvestiia*.[5]

Vesenkha had at that time no means of running all the newly nationalized factories now in its jurisdiction. Accordingly, the decree rented back the factories to their former owners at no cost. It was expected that the former owners would continue to finance the enterprises and to draw income from them. The firms would be subject to supervision and regulation by Vesenkha and to monitoring by workers' control. They could at any time be taken out of temporary use by the former owners and transferred to the management of the appropriate section of Vesenkha. This was done for the most part during the spring of 1919.[6]

The acute shortages of fuel and raw materials and the consequent need by the State to control resources as far as possible led to the steady extension of the number and types of firms nationalized. By the first quarter of 1919, most of the major firms in central Russia had been nationalized. In the months that followed, medium-sized and even some smaller enterprises were also taken into state control. However, some small firms and even some medium-sized ones, representing 8–10 per cent of the total, were still in private hands at the end of the Civil War.

The extension of State control of industry was accompanied by changes in the way industry was run. The various enterprises were no longer simply subject to monitoring as, for example, by the institutions of workers' control; increasingly the functioning of the enterprises was dictated by Vesenkha. The running of industry also became much more centralized, as Vesenkha now acquired the role of the single centre to which all branches of the economy were subordinated.

Vesenkha had both production sections dealing with a particular branch of industry – fuel, metal, chemicals, etc. – and functional departments – economic policy, finance and accounting, management, etc. – dealing with these matters in relation to the various branches of industry. Regional Sovnarkhozy had a similar structure. The growing number of firms passing under its control caused Vesenkha to create more specialized divisions concerned with running enterprises of a particular category. These divisions took the form of 'central committees' or 'chief administrations' (*glavki*) and

[5] M. Philips Price, *My Reminiscences of the Russian Revolution* (London, 1921), pp. 285–86.
[6] *Natsionalizatsiia promyshlennosti i organizatsiia sotsialisticheskogo proizvodstva v Petrograde (1917–1920)* i (Leningrad, 1958), p. xi.

were subordinated either to the production sections or directly to Vesenkha's presidium.[7]

In the autumn of 1918 there were 18 *glavki*. By the end of 1920 there were 52. They laid down the purpose and plans of enterprises, arranged their supplies of raw materials and fuel, and undertook the distribution of their products.

The merging of all the firms in a given industry into a single conglomerate gave the immediate advantage of being able to gain control of existing stocks of finished goods and make them available for distribution. It also made it possible to move stocks of raw materials and fuel from one enterprise to another, concentrating them in the most efficient and best equipped enterprises, in this way maximizing the limited resources available.

The system of *glavki* naturally worked most effectively in its initial phase, when it was mostly employed in distributing and redistributing goods and resources. Its limitations became quickly apparent when it actually began to attempt the organization of production. This involved amassing all the necessary machinery, components, materials, fuel, labour, etc., some of which would fall within the sphere of competence of other *glavki*. As responsibility for arranging suppliers was not in the hands of the individual enterprise but of the chief administration for the whole industry, this could be an enormously cumbersome and prolonged procedure.

The organization of the enterprises within *glavki* was hierarchical and bureaucratic. Decisions were made at the centre and handed down to the individual firms. There was no provision made for initiatives from below, or for any input from the workers in management. There were no material incentives in the individual firms to work efficiently.[8]

At best the *glavki* system gave rationalization within industries but not between industries. The co-ordinating institution for the economy as a whole was Vesenkha, but the processing of orders, their distribution to the appropriate *glavki*, the procurement of the necessary resources for their fulfilment within the given timescale, etc., was well beyond Vesenkha's capacities. As a result, the *glavki* operated in an autonomous way, without regard for each other. Thus, in some factories supplies accumulated; in others there was a shortage.[9]

As the system did not act spontaneously to iron out imbalances and difficulties, it required constant intervention by State functionaries to keep it in operation. The growth of a bureaucracy was one important by-product of the industrial structures of 'war communism'. Another characteristic consequence of the cumbersome procedures of the *glavki* system was the constant resort to the free market for items the State sector could not supply or could only provide with great difficulty. In this way the *glavki* system not only maintained the private sector in the economy but may also even have helped generate that private sector.

---

[7] *Ibid.*, pp. xv–xvi.
[8] Gimpel'son, *Voennyi Kommunizm*, p. 53.
[9] S. Malle, *The Economic Organization of War Communism 1918-1921* (Cambridge, 1985), pp. 232–33.

Agriculture

Long before the Bolsheviks came to power, hunger in the towns had prompted the workers to go to the countryside and offer industrial goods to the peasants in exchange for grain. This 'commodity exchange', however, could be no more than a very partial solution to the food crisis. This was because it only satisfied local needs – and that only temporarily. It dissipated the small amount of industrial goods which the government had at its disposal, and it gave these goods to those peasants who had accumulated stocks of grain, to the *kulaks* whom the government viewed as the group deliberately withholding grain supplies. The government took the view that if 'commodity exchange' were to take place, it should be on a centralized, all-State basis, and that the industrial goods should not be given to individuals but to local institutions to distribute among the poorer peasants. It was hoped that these poorer peasants would then put pressure on those who had a surplus of grain to sell it to the government.[10]

Centralized commodity exchange, however, did not succeed in making the peasants surrender their grain. By a decree of 9 May 1918, the government established a 'food-supply dictatorship', by which war was declared on the agrarian bourgeoisie and the village poor were organized in the 'struggle for bread'.

The government believed that in the grain producing provinces there were still stocks of grain from the harvests of 1916 and 1917, but that these were in the hands of *kulaks* and wealthy peasants. The wealthy peasants only parted with their grain to bagmen and speculators for inflated prices, quite indifferent to those dying of hunger in poorer provinces and in the towns. In Lenin's opinion the only option was to counter the force of the wealthy peasants with the force of the poorer ones. He advocated leaving not a pound of grain in the hands of the *kulaks* except that necessary for seed and subsistence until the next harvest. Those who did not surrender their surpluses were to be declared 'enemies of the people', imprisoned for no less than 10 years and be driven for ever from their communes. He called upon those peasants who had no surpluses of grain to struggle ruthlessly against those who had.[11]

On 11 June 1918, the government set up 'committees of the poor peasantry' or *kombedy*. The *kombedy* were to work out the amount of grain which each family could keep for its own use, and how much it had to deliver to the State. They were to aid the local food organizations by removing surplus grain from the *kulaks* and the rich peasants, and distributing in the villages such industrial goods as were available. Contingents of workers were dispatched into the countryside to help in the grain collections and to give support to the *kombedy*.

The policy of using *kombedy* to requisition grain did not produce the desired results. It was based on a mistaken conception of the structure and mechanics of peasant society. It assumed that the village contained the same class divisions as urban society, and that the poor would naturally unite against

[10] M. I. Davydov, *Bor'ba za khleb* (Moscow, 1971), pp. 64–67.
[11] *Dekrety Sovetskoi vlasti* iii (Moscow, 1957), pp. 261–66.

the rich. The policy did not take into account the traditional solidarity of the *mir*. The poorer peasants were more likely to uphold the unity of the peasant community than to disrupt it by entering into conflict with its most prudent and respected members. In any case, the comparative wealth of those peasant households with a grain surplus was less likely to come from exploiting their neighbours than from keeping the family together, and so preserving relatively large plots of land.[12]

Peasants had little enthusiasm for forming *kombedy*, considering them socially divisive. As a result, *kombedy* were often composed of non-peasants and they were also likely to attract a criminal element, which saw its chance to rob the peasants of their property. The peasants tended to conceal what stocks of grain they might have and to resist the collection agencies by force. In response to a peasant rebellion in August 1918, Lenin advocated publicly hanging a hundred recalcitrant peasants as an example to others.[13]

Even where the *kombedy* were successful in requisitioning foodstuffs, there was still no guarantee that these would reach their destination. The shortage of transport condemned some of the grain to rot at the collection points. The *kombedy* had no resources to feed the livestock it requisitioned, so it was often simply slaughtered and eaten. Much of what was requisitioned, moreover, was diverted to the private market and sold at free prices. The *kombedy* were abolished by a decree promulgated on 2 December 1918.[14]

Early in the following year a more effective method of grain collection was elaborated. The problem with the existing method was that it could only collect the amount of grain the government agencies happened to find in the peasants' possession. From this, in accordance with the regulations, a certain quantity had to be left with the producers for food and seed for the next harvest. Once this quantity had been deducted, what remained was the surplus that could be requisitioned. Since the peasants did their best to conceal their harvests and to minimize what could be considered as surplus, this was a rather haphazard process, and the amount of foodstuffs collected fell far short of what was required to feed the Red Army and the urban population. A decree promulgated on 11 January 1919 got round this problem by standing the procedure on its head. The amount of grain and fodder required was first of all established, and it was this which determined the quantities of agricultural produce which was to be requisitioned from the peasantry at the fixed prices.

This apportioning of compulsory requisitions or *prodrazverstka*, gave a great deal of discretion to the Commissariat of Food. It decided, in accordance with the size of the harvest, the amount of available reserves and the quotas required, which provinces were to be subject to the requisitions and what amount of grain and fodder was to be collected. The decree envisaged that some of the grain requisitioned would be distributed to those among the local

[12] P. Scheibert, *Lenin an der Macht: Das russische Volk in der Revolution 1918–1922* (Weinheim, 1984), pp. 108, 133.

[13] L. Lih, *Bread and Authority in Russia* (Berkeley, CA, 1990), pp. 176–77; O. Figes, *Peasant Russia, Civil War: The Volga Countryside in Revolution* (Oxford, 1989), p. 99, 190–93; *Komsomol'skaia pravda*, 12 February 1992.

[14] Scheibert, *Lenin*, pp. 122–26; L. Kritsman, *Geroicheskii period velikoi russkoi revoliutsii* (Moscow, 1925), p. 65; Figes, *Peasant Russia*, pp. 253–55.

peasant population who had insufficient to feed themselves. In fact, as Lenin admitted in 1921, much grain that was necessary to sustain the peasants was removed to fulfil the quotas that had been set.[15] There was always a temptation by the government to set requirements higher than was neces-sary on the assumption that not all the grain would be collected.

Prodrazverstka was applied first of all to grain but was later extended to other agricultural produce such as meat, butter and potatoes. The methods of *prodrazverstka* were traditional and well tried ones which had been used in pre-revolutionary times by both the tsarist government and land-owners. The particular imposition was handed over to the peasants to fulfil, and it was then up to the peasant institutions to determine which families would contribute what amount of the total. *Prodrazverstka* therefore had the ad-vantage that it was a mechanism that capitalized on the workings of the peasant commune.[16]

The disadvantage of *prodrazverstka* was that it maintained fixed prices and the State monopoly in grain. Nor was there any suggestion that the grain surrendered would be compensated for by a commensurate supply of industrial goods. In this way the peasantry was compelled to subsidize the Soviet war effort. There was no material incentive for the peasants to hand over their produce, beyond the concession that if they had surrendered 70 per cent by June they would be excused paying their taxes for that year – the taxes, of course, being demanded in agricultural produce. On the other hand, those peasants who avoided the requisitions were threatened with the confiscation of their property and imprisonment.[17] The method was never-theless quite successful as the amount of grain the State succeeded in collecting increased considerably after its introduction.

Despite the Supply Commissar, A. D. Tsiurupa's, contention that *prodraz-verstka* provided the peasant with an incentive to increase his sown area, since more would be left to him after he had delivered his quota to the State,[18] the amount of land under cultivation had declined significantly by the autumn of 1920. This was probably less as a means of resistance to State requisitions than as a response to the shortage of labour and implements. A contemporary observer reports how at that time instead of ploughing with ploughshares, peasants were scratching the surface of the ground with burnt staves, and instead of harrowing with steel-spiked harrows were brushing the ground with light constructions of wooden spikes bound together with twigs.[19] As a means of encouraging increased production, a decree issued in December 1920 obliged the peasants to sow an area in accordance with a plan as their duty to the State. Rewards were offered to peasants who obtained the best results by carrying out the plan and raised productivity by making improve-ments to the land.[20]

Despite the fall in productivity, the government continued to demand food deliveries from the peasants, even when the signs of famine had become clear.

[15] V. I. Lenin, *Polnoe sobranie sochinenii* xliii, p. 219.
[16] Figes, *Peasant Russia*, p. 100.
[17] *Dekrety Sovetskoi vlasti* iv, pp. 292–94.
[18] Lih, *Bread*, p. 184.
[19] A. Ransome, *The Crisis in Russia* (London, 1922), p. 22.
[20] Gimpel'son, *Voennyi Kommunizm*, p. 84.

Collection officials were apt to exceed their authority by demanding un-authorized deliveries of foodstuffs. And the surrender of grain to the State was no guarantee that units of the Red Army would not descend on the village and simply requisition whatever supplies they needed. The despera-tion and resentment of the peasants gave rise to a series of uprisings all over Russia towards the end of the Civil War. Their most common slogan was 'Long live the Bolsheviks; down with the Communists'.[21]

In the long term the Soviet government aimed at the replacement of small-scale peasant agriculture by large-scale collective farming, and the unifica-tion of the collective farms into a single organization, subordinate to an overall economic plan. The workers on these farms would be brought together in a single labour army, on the model of workers in the industrial sector.[22]

Material incentives were offered to peasants as an inducement to form agricultural collectives. These collectives were of two main types. State farms were subordinated to the Commissariat of Agriculture and were established on former landed estates. Their members tended to be landless peasants and former urban workers. Collective farms, on the other hand, were associations of peasants who had opted to farm the land at their disposal by pooling their resources. Neither type, however, was very successful in its economic performance; and such collectives were resented by the peasants of the surrounding area, as the land they occupied was lost to peasant agriculture.[23]

Trade and Finance

As a result of economic disruption and the shortages that went with it, money steadily lost its ability to purchase goods. The printing presses were unable to keep pace with the demand for paper money, as inflation drastically reduced its value. In 1918, 33,676 million rubles were put into circulation; in 1919, 163,689 million rubles; in 1920, 943,581.7 million rubles; and in the first quarter of 1921, 518,086.6 million rubles. Besides the money issued by the government, local authorities made good the deficit in currency by issuing money substitutes, with and without the consent of the central government. In this situation the banking and credit system ceased to function.[24]

The decline in the value of money led to what was termed at the time the 'naturalization' of the economy, that is, to payments of all kinds being made in goods rather than in money. Increasingly wages were paid in kind, as money wages very quickly fell behind prices on the free market.

A system of rationing according to classes was introduced. Consumers were placed in four categories:

1. Workers engaged in heavy manual labour and 'Red soldiers'.
2. Workers engaged in light forms of manual labour.

---

[21] Figes, *Peasant Russia*, pp. 270–72.
[22] *Zemledelie v Sovetskoi Rossii: Sbornik statei k s"ezdu sovetov* (Moscow, 1919), p. 11.
[23] Figes, *Peasant Russia*, pp. 298–303.
[24] J. Ciepielewski, *Historia społeczno-ekonomiczna Związku Radzieckiego* (Warsaw, 1974), p. 147.

3. Employees of government institutions and private enterprises, and members of the free professions.
4. Capitalists, landlords and 'parasites'.

Money was dispensed with in transactions between enterprises to reduce the requirement for paper money. These simply became accounting procedures, though still in monetary units. When, however, State enterprises had to resort to the private market for the items they needed, such accounts were paid in money. There was thus a paradoxical situation that while there was a strong tendency towards the elimination of money altogether in the economy, there remained important areas where money was necessary and where there was a constant demand for increasing quantities of paper currency.

The Soviet government was very little dismayed by the hyper-inflation and the 'naturalization' of the economy. The Communist leadership was inclined to view these developments in an optimistic light, taking the view that they were an indication that the economy was heading in the direction of a moneyless, socialist economy. The economist, Preobrazhenskii, was a notable advocate of this point of view, regarding the printing presses producing devalued currency as the 'machine-gun which attacked the bourgeois regime in the rear'.[25] Certainly, one effect of the inflation was to dispossess the former moneyed classes whose wealth was destroyed by the depreciation of the currency.

For the supplies of grain surrendered to the State, the peasants were supposed to receive industrial goods in return. But because of the contraction of industry the Soviet government did not have enough goods to give in exchange. Most industrial goods went to the Red Army: in 1919–20 the army received 70–100 per cent of the total output of cotton fabrics, 90 per cent of men's boots, 60 per cent of sugar and 100 per cent of tobacco. In order to be able to dispose of what industrial goods there were, the Soviet government, by a decree of 21 November 1918, established for itself a monopoly in the trade of most industrial goods.[26]

The scope for private trade was steadily reduced. The prohibition on the trade in grain was confirmed in May 1918 as part of the 'food dictatorship'. Subsequently State monopolies were extended to almost all articles of personal consumption, and private trade in these rationed goods was regarded as a State crime. Even the trade by 'bagmen' (individuals who brought agricultural produce to sell or barter in the towns) was declared illegal and subject to strict penalties. Detachments of the Cheka were employed to search trains destined for towns and to arrest any suspected bagmen they found. Only the produce of handicraft industries was permitted.

Despite efforts to restrict it severely, private trade persisted throughout the period of war communism. The supply system was so inefficient in providing the people with everyday necessities that they were forced to use the Sukharevka market in Moscow and its equivalent in other towns. Not only individuals but also industrial firms and even government institutions had to resort to the private market. Nevertheless, small traders were constantly

[25] M. Dobb, *Soviet Economic Development since 1917* (London, 1966), p. 122.
[26] Gimpel'son, *Voennyi Kommunizm*, p. 38.

rounded up by the Cheka and their stocks of goods confiscated. Major trading concerns, however, could afford to bribe Cheka officials and continue to conduct business unimpeded.[27]

Efforts to eliminate private trading served to increase bureaucratic practices. According to Arthur Ransome, writing in 1919, in order to prevent speculation in articles of clothing, it was necessary to prove that any purchases were for personal use. Thus, if someone needed a new suit of clothes, he would go in his rags to his house committee and satisfy them that he really needed new clothing for himself, He was then given a certificate confirming his right to buy a suit. This he could then do if he had the money, and if he could find a suit to buy.[28]

A similar bureaucratic saga of an attempt to buy a load of coal is related by C. E. Bechhofer. Bechhofer's experience was not in the Soviet republic, however, but in Denikin's Russia.[29] It illustrates the fact that similar conditions of scarcity gave rise to similar bureaucratic methods, irrespective of any ideological considerations.

Labour

Labour, especially skilled labour, was one of the resources that had to be husbanded as carefully as possible to ensure the maximum benefit from its use. The universal obligation to work was introduced, putting into practice the dictum 'He who does not work neither shall he eat'. There was an obligation to work on every able-bodied person between the ages of 16 and 50. Instead of internal passports, workbooks were issued and workers were placed in categories according to the kind of work they did. This determined what kind of rations they received. Only by obtaining a workbook would people be entitled to receive a ration and to travel about the country.

The closure of factories through lack of resources or through the rationalization of production carried out by the *glavki* created considerable unemployment. Neither the Red Army nor the expansion of war industries from the summer of 1918 could absorb all of the million and a half registered unemployed at that time. With the agreement of the trade unions, the first to be laid off were those unskilled workers who had come to work in industry during the war. Some of them went back to rural areas where the food crisis was less severe; some went to join the food detachments and requisition food from the peasants. The process reversed the dilution of the working class that had taken place during the war, and led to an increased concentration in the towns of the skilled cadre workers, a high proportion of whom were educated and politically aware.[30] Some of these, at least, however, like Kaiurov and Chugurin, who had been prominent in the February revolution, were lost to industry by being deployed in political campaigns, and becoming in effect Soviet functionaries.

[27] A. Berkman, *The Bolshevik Myth* (London, 1989), p. 65.
[28] A. Ransome, *Six Weeks in Russia* (London, 1919), p. 18.
[29] C. E. Bechhofer, *In Denikin's Russia and the Caucasus 1919–1920* (London, 1921), p. 85.
[30] E. G. Gimpel'son, *Sovetskii rabochii klass 1918–1920 gg.* (Moscow, 1974), pp. 26–31.

As conditions in the towns deteriorated and food became more difficult to obtain, a great many workers left their workplaces and returned to the countryside. This was possible because very few of them had severed completely the links with their villages. Russian workers in general were not 'proletarians'; it could not be said of them that they had no alternative but to earn their living by wage labour. The majority had the option of returning, when times became hard, to their native villages to find food and shelter. The ability to do this obviated the need for a comprehensive system of social security. Alexandra Kollontai's Commissariat of Social Security in fact did very little during the Civil War period to support workers in need.

Economic necessity did not chain Russian workers to their factories, as was the case in countries of Western Europe. This created difficulties of two kinds for the Soviet regime. The first was how to retain the labour needed to keep industry going, even when remaining in the factories demanded a personal sacrifice from the workers. The second difficulty was that since the workers had a foot both in the towns and the countryside, they were well placed to bring in agricultural produce to the towns and sell it at free-market prices. In this way they helped remove an element of economic necessity from the peasants to part with their grain to the State at the fixed prices offered.

The workers had to be forced by a form of non-economic compulsion to stay in the factories. The question of imposing labour discipline became all-important. In 1919 Bukharin gave an indication of the kind of moral blackmail that was deployed against industrial workers when he asserted that every worker should be inculcated with the idea that any slackness or carelessness was treason to the common cause of the working class. The workers' own organizations, the trade unions, were expected to help the Soviet government by keeping the workers in the factories and seeing to it that they worked to the best of their abilities. The Soviet government argued repeatedly that this could not be regarded as exploitation of the workers because the Soviet State acted in the workers' best interests. It was after all the 'dictatorship of the proletariat', and the proletariat could hardly exploit itself.

The militarization of labour was first introduced in industries connected with defence. In November 1918 it was extended to the railways, and in March 1919 to the river and maritime fleets. At the beginning of 1920 a new form of militarization of labour was introduced. The idea was elaborated by Trotsky, who saw it as a logical extension of the universal labour obligation. Trotsky argued that the principle of 'free labour' was a liberal-capitalist one, and meant only the freedom to be exploited. In a socialist society, on the other hand, where the objective of labour was overcoming the external physical conditions which were hostile to human existence, everyone was obliged to participate in the production of material values, and to do this in the most rational way within the framework of a general economic plan.

In the difficult transition period to socialism Soviet Russia was currently experiencing, Trotsky believed, a degree of compulsion was necessary, especially towards the more backward elements among the peasantry and the working class itself. The more backward the social group, the more compulsion was required. He thought that the best way to apply this compulsion was to extend the methods of the Red Army to the sphere of labour organization, making modifications where necessary.

One form of the militarization of labour advocated by Trotsky was the creation of labour armies. Instead of being demobilized, military units no longer required for fighting would be deployed as industrial labour. Trotsky foresaw, however, that his militarization policy was likely to meet opposition from the workers, who would see in it a revival of the methods employed by Arakcheev in the days of Alexander I. He therefore advocated a campaign to combat 'trade-union prejudices' and to explain the necessity and the progressive character of the coalescence of the organization of labour and the organization of defence in a socialist society. This conception was accepted by the Ninth Party Congress in March–April 1920. Clearly at that time the party concurred with Trotsky in regarding the militarisation of labour as a permanent feature of the Soviet regime.[31]

Ideology

When in the spring of 1919 the recently renamed Russian Communist Party drew up its new programme, it was in a position to align its earlier prognostications about revolution with the actual experience of taking power and running the country for almost a year and a half. Bukharin was an active participant in formulating the new programme and, along with Preobrazhenskii he wrote a popular commentary on the programme entitled *The ABC of Communism*, which appeared in 1920. In that same year Bukharin also published his major theoretical work on 'war communism', *The Economics of the Transition Period*, which took up some important issues raised in *The ABC*.

Bukharin was an especially significant commentator on 'war communism' because, in 1915, he had written the article 'The world economy and imperialism', which had discussed how he believed the socialist order would emerge from recent developments in capitalism. A comparison of this article with Bukharin's writings in 1919–20 gives an insight into how his thinking, as well as that of his contemporaries, had evolved over the revolutionary period.

During the war the consensus among socialist writers had been that by creating monopolies, syndicates and trusts, finance capital had laid the foundations of a centralized and regulated socialist economy. This idea is reflected in 'The world economy and imperialism', Bukharin arguing that the processes of centralization and organization in finance capitalism had formed 'the prerequisites for an organized socialist economy'.[32] On the eve of taking power, Lenin had expressed the belief that the banks and syndicates of the capitalist system were the apparatus necessary to bring about socialism. Indeed, according to Lenin, 'without the big banks socialism would be impossible'.[33] This expectation, however, was frustrated, first by the sabotage of the bank employees and then by the hyper-inflation. Under these

---

[31] L. D. Trotsky, *K istorii russkoi revoliutsii* (Moscow, 1990), pp. 151–58; V. F. Buldakov and V. V. Kabanov, ' "Voennyi kommunizm": ideologiia i obshchestvennoe razvitie', *Voprosy istorii* (1990, no. 3), pp. 46–47.

[32] N. I. Bukharin, *Problemy teorii i praktiki sotsializma* (Moscow, 1989), p. 53.

[33] V. I. Lenin, *Polnoe sobranie sochinenii* xxxiv, p. 307.

circumstances there was no hope of exercising any kind of control over the economy through the banking and credit system.

When, therefore, the party programme was drafted the section on finance capital mentioned only that in recent times free competition had given way to monopoly, and that the anarchy of the market had been replaced by regulation. The proposition that this might form the prerequisites for a socialist economy was not enunciated. Only a few traces of the idea that finance capitalism provided the economic basis for socialism are to be found in *The ABC of Communism* as, for example, the statement that 'the centralisation of industry only becomes possible when the centralisation of capital has reached a certain stage'.[34]

The Economics of the Transition Period was Bukharin's fullest and most systematic treatment of 'war communism'. Whereas *The ABC* had largely avoided the question of what the relationship was between finance capitalism and the socialist economy, *The Economics of the Transition Period* treated this as the central problem to be addressed. The novelty of Bukharin's approach in this work was that it asserted that the continuity between capitalist and socialist economic institutions had been destroyed by the revolution.

Bukharin referred specifically to Hilferding's conception that socialism matured within the capitalist system, and that the seizure of the six largest banks would give the proletariat control over a nation's entire industry. This, Bukharin pointed out, had not proved to be the case. For the banks controlled industry through the credit and monetary systems, and it was precisely these things which had collapsed in the wake of the revolution. Similarly, in the past, the maturity of the capitalist system for socialism had been seen – as it had been in *The ABC* by Bukharin and Preobrazhenskii – in terms of its degree of concentration and centralization. But, Bukharin now argued, experience had shown that it was just this centralized apparatus of capitalism which disintegrated in the process of revolution, and consequently it could not serve as the basis for the new social order.

Bukharin's position was that any genuine proletarian revolution would bring with it the disintegration of the existing capitalist economic structures. The resulting economic disruption was therefore what he termed 'negative expanded reproduction' – an expression he had based on Marx's term 'expanded reproduction' which signified the extension and intensification of capitalist relations. In 'negative expanded reproduction' the capitalist system was resolved into its component parts. Socialism would require to be consciously built, by putting together a new combination of the elements that had constituted the capitalist system.

According to Bukharin, in the transition period from capitalism to socialism objective economic processes would be replaced by 'non-economic compulsion'. The proletarian State would use coercion for such purposes as requisitioning grain supplies from the peasants and imposing taxation in kind upon them. A system of universal compulsory labour would be required; and whereas under capitalism this would mean the enslavement of the workers, under the conditions of the dictatorship of the proletariat it

[34] N. I. Bukharin and E. A. Preobrazhensky, *The ABC of Communism* (Harmondsworth, 1969), p. 209.

would signify no more than self-organization by the workers. In fact, in Bukharin's presentation, the main features of 'war communism' were given a theoretical justification.

Bukharin concluded his book by accounting for the Russian revolution in the context of the inter-related world economic system. The component parts of this system, Bukharin believed, were joined together like the links of a chain, so that when a crisis occurred it would inevitably assume the character of a world crisis.

Bukharin posed the question: 'With which links was this collapse bound to begin?' His answer was: 'It stands to reason that it was bound to begin precisely with those links which were most weakly organized in a capitalist way'. Here Bukharin argued that in countries which were advanced economically the State's political power fused with the economic institutions of finance capital, and that this combined force presented tremendous resistance to the workers' movement. It was for this reason, Bukharin concluded, that 'the collapse of the world capitalist system began with the weakest national economic systems, with the least highly developed State-capitalist organizations'.[35]

Opposite this passage in Bukharin's book Lenin noted: 'untrue: with the moderately weak. Without a certain level of capitalism nothing would have happened here in Russia'.[36] The famous phrase 'The chain of imperialism broke at its weakest link' is, therefore, a paraphrase of Bukharin's argument. And obviously it was not a conception with which Lenin agreed. Nevertheless 'The chain of imperialism broke at its weakest link' has become one of the most famous 'Lenin' quotations. According to some scholars it was in this conception that Lenin's theory of revolution consisted.

---

[35] Bukharin, *Problemy*, p. 171.
[36] *Leninskii sbornik* xi, (Moscow-Leningrad, 1929), p. 397.

12

Oppositions

The Trade-Union Debate

The Reds achieved military victory in the Civil War, but at a great cost both in terms of loss of life, and of placing enormous strains on the country's economy and society. As long as the Civil War continued, these tensions were contained, but as the war came to an end they began to erupt in a wave of discontent which swept the country. In the countryside there were peasant uprisings as a response to the government's requisition policies and the attempts to impose collectivist forms of agriculture. In August the provinces of Tambov and Voronezh were engulfed by the peasant rebellion led by A. S. Antonov. There were similar uprisings in the Ukraine and in the Volga region. These manifestations of peasant discontent were declared by the Soviet authorities to be inspired by *kulaks* or 'White Guards' and put down by military force.

Even sympathetic visitors to Soviet Russia in 1920 were struck by the harshness of the regime and its unwillingness to countenance any kind of opposition. It had become bureaucratic, enmeshed in red tape, and involved in corruption and privilege. Members of the Bolshevik Central Committee had now given themselves the entitlement to a special 'Kremlin ration' so that they could enjoy white bread, rice, butter, meat and wine. Bukharin and Chicherin were among those who retained a Spartan life style. Delegations of foreign socialists were treated to sumptuous banquets, well aware that in the Moscow streets people died of hunger.[1] During the Civil War the Communist Party's power had grown enormously. The actions of the Socialist Revolutionaries and the Mensheviks in taking up arms against the Soviet regime allowed the Bolsheviks to class them as counter-revolutionary and exclude them in the middle of 1918 from the Soviets. The further political activity of these parties was on Communist terms. The elimination of any competition from other socialist parties established the monopoly of political power by the Communist Party and completed the process begun in October 1917.[2]

By the spring of 1919, the CEC had lost all power to the Central Committee of the Communist Party. At the Eighth Party Congress the process of political centralization was carried further by the delegation of some of the Central

[1] V. Brovkin, ed. and trans., *Dear Comrades: Menshevik Reports on the Bolshevik Revolution and Civil War* (Stanford, CA, 1991), p. 210.
[2] L. Schapiro, *The Origin of the Communist Autocracy* (2nd edn), (London, 1977), pp. 151–52.

Committee's functions to three bodies appointed by it. These were the Political Bureau (Politburo), the Organization Bureau (Orgburo) and the Secretariat. In this way the Politburo became the effective decision-making body. According to Osinskii, the Politburo of five people decided all the most important questions, while the plenary session of the Central Committee met for general conversation.[3]

The Orgburo also consisted of five people, its function being the appointment and removal of party members from important posts, initially with the approval of the Politburo. The Secretariat, which was later to supersede the Politburo as the important seat of power, had the function of keeping track of which party members were actual or potential oppositionists and replacing them with those willing to carry through the official policies of the day. The Secretariat was presided over by Sverdlov until his death in 1919. He was replaced by N. N. Krestinskii, who proved unequal to the task of rooting out oppositionists, and in 1920 the Secretariat was reinforced by the addition of L. P. Serebriakov and Preobrazhenskii, who, like Krestinskii, were supporters of Trotsky.

As a measure against the growth of bureaucracy and red tape, the Eighth Party Congress created a new commissariat, that of the Workers' and Peasants' Inspection (Rabkrin). This was headed by Stalin under whom, according to Trotsky, it soon became 'a hotbed of political intrigue'. At any rate, it made insufficient headway in the campaign against bureaucracy to impress the oppositionists.[4]

The proletariat, whom the Soviet regime claimed to represent, emerged from the Civil War in a particularly enfeebled state. Those workers who remained in industry were poorly paid, under-nourished, poorly housed and frequent victims of the typhus and cholera epidemics which swept the country during the Civil War years. The workers identified themselves less and less with the Communist Party, seeing the trade unions as organizations which were more likely to represent their interests.

The trade unions, however, had evolved more towards safeguarding production than the interests of the workers. In January 1918 at the First Congress of Trade Unions, it had been decided to merge the factory committees with the trade unions. Henceforth the factory committee became the factory branch of the trade union. A year later the Second Congress of Trade Unions resolved to unite all workers in a given enterprise in a single trade union, and to strengthen the production principle of the unions.

During the Civil War, trade-union membership increased, despite the decreasing number of industrial workers. This was because the Second Congress of Trade Unions had made union membership compulsory. Since the unions had become responsible for labour discipline, it was essential that every worker should be a union member. The Mensheviks, who still maintained a foothold in the trade unions, deplored their tendency to become adjuncts of the State and the Bolshevik Party, and advocated trade-union independence.

The close association between the State and the trade unions, on the other

[3] L. Trotsky, *Stalin* ii (London, 1969), p. 151.
[4] *Ibid.*, pp. 152–33.

hand, had the effect of investing the trade unions with some State functions, not only at the centre but also at the factory-committee level. They were involved in appointing managers of enterprises and in some management functions. Often the trade unions' activities encroached on and duplicated the functions of factory management. Tensions and conflicts were apt to result.

On 25 August 1919, the question of the relations between the institutions of Vesenkha and the trade unions was discussed at a session of the Presidium of Vesenkha. This arose in connection with the fact that the Central Committee of the Union of Metal Workers, chaired by Shliapnikov, had attempted to appoint the management of some enterprises in the industry. Rejecting such claims as illegal, Vesenkha drew up a set of guidelines, reserving for itself all management functions. Some trade unions, however, continued to demand that trade unions be given the power to run industry. Shliapnikov, for one, believed that all the rights and functions in the sphere of production ought to belong to the trade unions.

Trotsky, on the other hand, thought that for the sake of efficiency the trade unions should not be divorced from the State but should be gradually merged with State institutions. This doctrine emerged following Trotsky's appointment to the Commissariat of Transport in March 1920. He had been charged with trying to remedy the desperate situation on the railways, as the transport system was threatened with complete breakdown, which in turn would have incalculable economic consequences.

In tackling the country's transport problems, Trotsky found that – as he had foreseen when elaborating his plans for the militarization of labour – one of the obstacles he confronted was the interference of the railwaymen's union. The People's Commissariat of Transport had modelled its institutions on those of the Red Army. They were run not by committees, as in other commissariats, but by individuals, who tended to be professional transport specialists. Each was shadowed by a commissar – exactly as military commanders were. And just as the Red Army had its Chief Political Administration of the Revolutionary Council of the Republic, so the Commissariat of Transport had its own Chief Political Administration – Glavpolitput. This institution was created by Trotsky in March 1920 and its function was to root out slackness and indiscipline on the railways by the imposition of harsh penalties on all who were found guilty. Trotsky did not enlist the services of the railwaymen's union in this campaign but by-passed it. When the railwaymen's union objected, the Central Committee of the Communist Party decided to depose the leadership of the railwaymen's union and replace it with a new committee, known as Tsektran.[5]

When the Fifth Conference of Trade Unions met in Moscow from 2–6 November 1920, Trotsky urged that the duplication of responsibility between the trade unions and the administrative organs, which had given rise to so much confusion, should be eliminated. This could only be done by the transformation of the trade unions into production unions. If the leaders of the unions objected, they would be 'shaken up' in the same way as the transport unions had been shaken up by the imposition of military methods.

The prospect of the Tsektran model being extended to other trade unions

<hr/>

[5] L. Kritsman, *Geroicheskii period velikoi russkoi revoliutsii* (Moscow, 1925), pp. 104–105.

alarmed Communist trade unionists, prompting them to dissociate themselves from Trotsky's ideas. The Latvian trade unionist, Janis Rudzutaks, led the campaign, saying that the military methods proposed by Trotsky were sheer nonsense and nothing more than a bureaucratic ploy. Rudzutaks condemned especially the attachment of political sections to the trade unions, arguing that these would either replace the trade unions entirely or be absorbed within the trade-union structure. The conference ended by endorsing the theses proposed by Rudzutaks, which formed the basis for the position of the Central Committee majority. The debate on the trade unions which followed threatened to create a serious split within the Bolshevik Party, and placed Lenin and Trotsky on opposite sides of a deep ideological divide.[6] At the same time, Shliapnikov and other members of the Workers' Opposition were also putting forward a view on the subject of the trade unions. Trotsky and the Workers' Opposition represented the opposite ends of a political spectrum. Whereas Trotsky wanted the trade unions to become part of the State apparatus, Shliapnikov wanted the organs of the State to become part of the trade unions. The Workers' Opposition demanded that the ruling institution of the economy should be the 'All-Russian Congress of Producers'. Provincial, regional and district producers' councils would be elected from below. It also demanded that there should be a unified economic plan for the rational utilization of economic resources and the distribution of goods. It demanded that a plan be drawn up for achieving the productive levels of 1913 within a set number of years. On immediate practical issues, the Workers' Opposition sought the equalization of wages, free distribution of food and basic necessities to all workers, and the gradual replacement of money payments by payments in kind.[7]

Aleksandra Kollontai put the theoretical case for the Workers' Opposition in a pamphlet distributed to party members during the Tenth Party Congress in 1921. Kollontai's pamphlet, *The Workers' Opposition*, is significant as an early analysis of the bureaucratic degeneration of the Soviet state. The root causes of this she considered to be the influence of bourgeois specialists. This influence had stifled the workers' initiative and left them passive and apathetic. Kollontai called for a return to the elective principle, eliminating bureaucracy by making all officials answerable to the public at large. She advocated greater openness within the party, freedom of expression and greater democracy. She also called on the party to purge itself of non-proletarian elements, and make itself truly a workers' party. Kollontai reminded her readers of Marx's dictum that 'the liberation of the working class was the task of the working class itself', a principle which directly contradicted Lenin's conception of what the Communist Party ought to be.[8]

Like the Workers' Opposition, the Democratic Centralist group believed that greater rights should be given to the trade unions in the running of the economy. The Democratic Centralists consisted mainly of long-standing

[6] P. A. Garvi, *Professional'nye soiuzy v Rossii v pervye gody revoliutsii (1917–1921)* (New York, 1981), pp. 86–87.

[7] *O roli professional'nykh soiuzov v proizvodstve* (Moscow, 1921), pp. 59–61.

[8] M. P. Kim, ed., *Lenin i kul'turnaia revoliutsiia: Khronika sobytii (1917-1923 gg.)* (Moscow, 1972), pp. 250–58; A. Kollontai, *Selected Writings of Aleksandra Kollontai*, trans. with an introduction and commentaries by A. Holt (London, 1977), p. 191.

members of the Bolshevik Party, such as Osinskii and Sapronov, who had been Left Communists in 1918. They thought that after it had come to power, the party had betrayed its own democratic ideals, as set out in Lenin's *State and Revolution*. They opposed the bureaucratic centralism of Lenin's Central Committee and advocated greater freedom within the party, insisting that every important question should be discussed by the party rank-and-file before decisions were taken. They believed that the Central Committee should not manage the party but should only give it general direction. Thus, while the Democratic Centralists upheld the Leninist principle of party organization and only criticized individual shortcomings, the Workers' Opposition questioned the very theoretical basis on which the Bolshevik Party was constructed.[9]

Lenin's position on the trade unions was an intermediate one between Trotsky's and Shliapnikov's. He argued that Trotsky was mistaken in thinking that the trade unions did not need to defend the workers because the State was a 'workers' State'. In Lenin's opinion, the existing Soviet State was such that the entire organized proletariat had to defend itself. 'We must,' Lenin stated 'use these workers' organizations for the defence of the workers from their state and for the defence by the workers of our state.' This position was set out in the 'Platform of the Ten' on 14 January 1921, signed by Lenin, Zinoviev, Stalin, M. P. Tomskii, Kalinin, Rudzutaks, S. A. Lozovskii, Petrovskii and Artem. This was to be the approach to the trade-union question adopted by the Tenth Party Congress in March 1921. Bukharin initially had held a position midway between Trotsky and Lenin, but latterly allied completely with Trotsky.

Kronstadt

Coinciding with the fourth anniversary of the February revolution of 1917, a rebellion broke out at the naval base in Kronstadt. The character of this uprising and the ruthlessness of its suppression gave a clear indication that the democratic ideals which had inspired the February revolution had been abandoned by the Communist government. In this sense the Kronstadt rebellion marks the end of what has been called 'the heroic period of the Russian revolution'.

To some degree the origins of the Kronstadt mutiny were analogous to the debate on the trade unions. Like the Red Army and the Commissariat of Transport, the navy had its political section – 'Pubalt'. This was felt by the sailors to be a bureaucratic and authoritarian organization, and at the Second Conference of Communist Sailors of the Baltic Fleet on 25 February 1921, several speakers demanded the abolition of political sections in the navy, a demand which was to re-emerge in the course of the Kronstadt rebellion.

In mid-February industrial unrest evoked by economic hardship broke out in Moscow. Factory meetings were succeeded by strikes and demonstrations, as workers took to the streets to demand 'free trade', higher rations and the

[9]   A. Ciliga, *The Russian Enigma* (London, 1979), pp. 274–77.

abolition of grain requisitions. The industrial unrest quickly spread to Petrograd, where a number of large factories, including the Putilov works, came out on strike between 23 and 28 February. The workers demanded winter clothing and a more regular issue of rations. Besides these economic demands, proclamations appeared putting forward more political ones, such as the liberation of all arrested socialists, freedom of speech, press and assembly for all workers and free election of factory committees.[10]

On 24 February, the Petrograd Committee of the Communist Party, headed by Zinoviev, organized a defence committee consisting of Lashevich, a member of the Military Revolutionary Council of the Republic, N. M. Antselovich, a member of the Council of Trade Unions, and D. N. Avrov, the commander of the Petrograd military district. The Defence Committee ordered every city district to set up its own 'revolutionary *troika*' to prevent the spread of disturbances. On the same day martial law was proclaimed throughout the city, with an 11 p.m. curfew imposed, and all gatherings on the streets prohibited at any time. Arrests of strikers multiplied, and several trade unions were dissolved, their members being turned over to the Cheka.

On 26 February the crews of the two battleships the *Petropavlovsk* and the *Sevastopol*, held an emergency meeting and decided to send a delegation to Petrograd to find out what was happening in the city. It visited a number of factories, at that time surrounded by troops and military cadets. On the 28th, the sailors returned to Kronstadt and reported what they had seen. In sympathy with the grievances of the Petrograd strikers, and aghast at how the latter were being treated by the authorities, the crew of the *Petropavlovsk*, presided over by the naval clerk S. M. Petrichenko, voted for a resolution containing a number of significant demands. There were as follows:

1. In view of the fact that the present Soviets no longer expressed the will of the workers and peasants, immediately to hold new elections by secret ballot, the pre-election campaign to have full freedom of agitation among the workers and peasants.
2. To establish freedom of speech and of the press for workers and peasants, for the Anarchists, and for left socialist parties.
3. To secure freedom of assembly for trade unions and peasant organizations.
4. To call a non-party conference of the workers, soldiers and sailors of Petrograd, Kronstadt and the Petrograd province no later than 10 March 1921.
5. To liberate all political prisoners of the socialist parties, as well as all workers, peasants, soldiers and sailors imprisoned in connection with the labour and peasant movements.
6. To elect a commission to review the cases of those held in prison and concentration camps.
7. To abolish all political sections in the armed forces, because no political party should be given special privileges for the propagation of its ideas, or receive the financial support of the government for such purposes.

[10] P. Avrich, *Kronstadt 1921* (Princeton, NJ, 1970), pp. 37–45.

Instead of the political sections there should be established educational and cultural commissions, locally elected and financed by the government.

8. To abolish immediately all the road-blocks set up between town and countryside.

9. To equalize the rations of all workers, with the exception of those employed in trades injurious to health.

10. To abolish the Communist combat detachments in all units of the army, as well as the Communist guards kept on duty in factories. Should such guards be required, they should be appointed in the army from the ranks, and in the factories according to the judgement of the workers.

11. To give the peasants full freedom of action in regard to their land, and also the right to keep cattle, on condition that the peasants manage with their own means; that is, without employing hired labour.

12. To request all branches of the army, as well as military trainees, to concur in the resolutions.

13. To demand that the press give proper publicity to the resolution;

14. To appoint an itinerant bureau of control.

15. To permit free handicraft production by one's own efforts.[11]

The resolution passed by the Kronstadt sailors constitutes an indictment of the Soviet regime at that time. It predicates a country in which there were not the most elementary civil rights. There was no freedom of assembly, speech or of the press. There was a political system in which one party had a monopoly of power and expression. It was a system which did not reflect the will of the people, and one which allowed imprisonment for political reasons without trial.

The Kronstadt rebels were, however, not purists in the matter of political pluralism or civil rights. They championed only working people and socialist parties, not people as a whole or political parties in general. This was an attitude the Kronstadters shared with all those who had advocated a government of all the socialist parties back in the autumn of 1917. But the converse of this circumstance is that the Kronstadt resolution is a document embodying socialist assumptions. Many of the ideas it contained were ones earlier subscribed to by the Bolshevik Party. That it no longer did so was no doubt a reason why Communist leaders in the spring of 1921 found the Kronstadt uprising so subversive. The Kronstadt sailors, moreover, were a group of people who had been in the forefront of the Russian revolutionary movement in the tumultuous year of 1917.

It is also significant that the resolution so little reflects the sectional interests of the Kronstadt sailors but expresses the grievances of all the working people among Russia's population – the peasants and the workers especially. It was a condemnation of the 'war communist' system and the Communist Party's system of rule.

Some of the demands in the resolution could have been conceded by the Communist government, and in fact some key economic points were about to be conceded at the Tenth Party Congress, when the war communist system

---

[11] *Pravda o Kronshtadte* (Prague, 1921), p. 47.

was abandoned. But those demands which attacked the Communist monopoly of political power could not have been met without the collapse of the existing regime. This was an important factor in the way the Soviet government chose to deal with the Kronstadt rebels.

On 1 March a mass meeting of sailors, soldiers and workers took place on Kronstadt's Anchor Square. It was attended by 12,000–15,000 people. It was presided over by P. D. Vasiliev, the Communist chairman of the Kronstadt Soviet. Kalinin, the chairman of the CEC, and N. N. Kuzmin, the commissar of the Baltic Fleet, had been invited to speak. Kalinin, Kuzmin and others who tried to defend the Soviet regime, were heckled and shouted down. The officials were followed, however, by speakers from among the sailors, who were deeply critical of current economic policies. One sailor, P. Perepelkin from the *Sevastopol*, read the resolution adopted the day before on the *Petropavlovsk* and asked that it be voted upon. The resolution was carried by an overwhelming majority, only the small number of Communists present voting against. Perepelkin ended his speech by calling upon his audience to make arrangements for holding new elections to the Kronstadt Soviet, as advocated in the resolution. This suggestion of Perepelkin's was adopted, it being decided that the various military units and organizations should meet the next day to choose delegates to discuss the new elections.

On 2 March meetings took place throughout Kronstadt. With the exception of the Communists present, these meetings approved the *Petropavlovsk* resolution and elected their respective delegates. The delegates' meeting which took place in the School of Marine Engineering was again chaired by Petrichenko. Both Kuzmin and Vasiliev spoke in defence of the policies of the Soviet regime, warning that the Communist Party would not relinquish power without a fight. As there was a fear that Kronstadt might come under a military attack by the Soviet authorities, it was decided to establish a Provisional Revolutionary Committee with Petrichenko as chairman to administer the town and the fortress.

The Committee's first actions were to take precautions against Communist reprisals. This was done by arresting Kuzmin, Vasiliev, the ships' commissars and other leading figures in the local Communist party. Many other Communists fled from Kronstadt to avoid being captured, though the Provisional Revolutionary Committee only intended to hold some Communists in custody, not to threaten their lives. The fugitives, however, spread the rumour that a revolt was taking place in Kronstadt inspired by White Guards and led by a general, A. N. Kozlovskii. The Kozlovskii in question, an artillery specialist, along with other officers of the Kronstadt garrison, decided at this time to put their services at the disposal of the Provisional Revolutionary Committee.[12]

In its first proclamation the Provisional Revolutionary Committee stated that it was concerned to avoid bloodshed and that its aim was, through the joint efforts of town and fortress, to create the proper conditions for elections to the new Soviet. Later in the day the committee sent armed detachments to

[12] Kozlovskii's account, dated 13 October 1921, is reproduced in V. A. Smolin, ed., 'Kronshtadt v 1921 godu: Novye dokumenty', *Russkoe proshloe* (1991, no. 2), pp. 351–52.

occupy the arsenals, the telephone exchange, food depots, power plants, Cheka headquarters and other strategic points. By midnight the whole of Kronstadt had been secured for the rebels.

The Provisional Revolutionary Committee appreciated the value of publicity. Copies of the *Petropavlovsk* resolution were taken to the mainland and distributed in Oranienbaum, Petrograd, and other towns in the vicinity. On 3 March, the committee began to publish a daily newspaper, *Bulletin of the Provisional Revolutionary Committee of Sailors, Red Armymen and Workers of the Town of Kronstadt*,[13] which was to appear without interruption until the 16th, the day preceding the final assault on Kronstadt.

The Communists, for their part, tried to discredit the Kronstadt mutiny in every way possible. They called it a White Guard plot, inspired by foreign powers. It was alleged that Kuzmin had been brutally handled during his captivity in Kronstadt, and had been lucky to escape summary execution. Although the Russian émigrés were delighted when they received news of the Kronstadt rebellion, there is no evidence whatever that they had been involved in its organization. And, as Victor Serge verified in a conversation with Kuzmin himself, no harm had come to Kuzmin while in custody on the *Petropavlovsk*. He and the other Communist captives were treated absolutely correctly.[14] The official press studiously avoided making any examination of what the causes of the rebellion were and concealed any criticisms that were made of the Soviet regime.

On 3 March, the Soviet government issued an ultimatum calling on the Kronstadters to end their rebellion, free the arrested Communists and surrender the ringleaders to the government. A government aeroplane dropped leaflets on Kronstadt stating that Zinoviev's Defence Committee had arrested and imprisoned the families of Kronstadt sailors as hostages for the safety of Kuzmin and Vasiliev. The leaflet threatened that if any harm came to the two officials, the hostages would pay for it with their lives. The Provisional Revolutionary Committee replied with a radio message insisting on the liberation of the hostages, and announcing that the committee itself would not take reprisals against the families of Communists in Kronstadt, as it considered such methods shameful and degrading.

This exchange was followed on the 5th by an ultimatum from Trotsky demanding that the arrested commissars and other representatives of the government be released forthwith. Only those who surrendered unconditionally might count on the mercy of the Soviet Republic. At the same time Trotsky announced that he was issuing orders to prepare to quell the mutiny and subdue the mutineers by force of arms.[15]

If this declaration had little chance of calming passions in Kronstadt, the ultimatum issued by Zinoviev's Defence Committee on the same day had even less. It reminded its readers what had happened to Wrangel's forces, who were dying like flies of hunger and disease, and threatened that the same fate awaited the Kronstadt mutineers as well unless they surrendered within

---

[13] *Izvestiia Vremennogo Revoliutsionnogo Komiteta Matrosov, Krasnoarmeitsev i Rabochikh gor. Kronshtadta.*

[14] V. Serge, *Memoirs of a Revolutionary 1901–1941*, trans. and ed. P. Sedgwick, (Oxford, 1963), pp. 126–27.

[15] *Pravda o Kronshtadte*, p. 73.

24 hours. If they did, they would be pardoned; but if they resisted, they would 'be shot like partridges'.[16]

Alarmed at the prospect of military action being taken against the Kronstadt rebels, some Russian and foreign Anarchists in Moscow, including Victor Serge, Emma Goldman and Alexander Berkman, offered to mediate in the conflict. The offer was received indulgently by Zinoviev, but the mediation attempt ended in failure. The Petrograd Soviet proposed to send representatives to Kronstadt to look into the differences between the Kronstadters and the Soviet government. The Kronstadters, however, suspected this to be a trap, and put forward their own counter-proposal. This agreed to receive a Soviet delegation but suggested that this delegation should be supplemented by delegates freely elected by the factories and military units of Petrograd in elections monitored by representatives from Kronstadt. This response effectively undermined the only attempt at mediation between the two sides.

On 5 March, Tukhachevskii was put in charge of the military forces in Petrograd, replacing Avrov on Zinoviev's defence committee. On the evening of 7 March he began military operations against Kronstadt. Artillery battles preceded the Red Army's attempts to storm Kronstadt across the ice. This first attack, however, was beaten back by the artillery and machine-gun fire of the Kronstadt rebels.

In the days that followed, Tukhachevskii brought up reinforcements of infantry and artillery. Attacks on Kronstadt were kept up day and night, exhausting the defenders, of whom there were only some 3,800. There was great urgency on Tukhachevskii's part to capture the naval base before the ice melted, which would make an infantry attack on Kronstadt impossible. Through constant firing, the Kronstadt artillery became unusable. Both food and ammunition ran out, as no help from outside was given to the Kronstadt defenders. Contrary to the rebels' expectations, the movement did not spread to Petrograd and other working-class centres. The authorities had foreseen this danger and made sufficient economic concessions to prevent it. On 16–17 March, Tukhachevskii launched his final assault and through superiority in numbers and armaments, was able to take Kronstadt after bitter fighting.[17]

Before Kronstadt fell, Petrichenko and other members of the Provisional Revolutionary Committee escaped to Terijoki in Finland. Kozlovskii and other military specialists who had co-operated with the committee also fled. On 20 March, 13 of the rebels were tried and shot. Several hundred more were shot without trial in Kronstadt. The remainder were transferred to Cheka prisons on the mainland, where they were shot in small batches over the succeeding months.[18]

To the Anarchists Berkman, Goldman and Serge, the suppression of the Kronstadt rebellion marked a turning-point in the Russian revolution, to which they had originally been extremely sympathetic. It seemed to them that the great ideas of 1917, which had enabled the Bolshevik Party to win over the peasant masses, the army, the working class, as well as the radical intelligentsia, were quite clearly dead. Serge believed that while Kronstadt had

[16] Avrich, *Kronstadt 1921*, p. 146.
[17] *Ibid.*, pp. 149–54.
[18] *Ibid.*, p. 215.

right on its side, the Soviet government had no choice but to suppress the insurrection. His reasoning was that victory for the Kronstadters would mean disaster for the country. If the Bolshevik dictatorship fell, it would be a short step to chaos, and through chaos to a peasant rising, the massacre of the Communists, the return of the émigrés and the establishment of an anti-proletarian dictatorship. For Serge the choice was between two evils.[19]

The Tenth Party Congress

The Tenth Party Congress, which took place from 8 to 16 March, proceeded under the shadow of the Kronstadt mutiny. Many delegates from the congress were mobilized to take part in the assault on the island fortress. Prominent among these were members of the oppositions, the Workers' Opposition and the Democratic Centralists, who were anxious to demonstrate their loyalty to the regime.[20]

Despite their efforts to dissociate themselves from the events at Kronstadt, at the congress the oppositions were linked to the Kronstadt mutiny. Both in their different ways had challenged the legitimacy of the Communist regime by their denial that the ruling Communist Party expressed the interests of the working class. The Communist leaders' response was not to examine how it was that the interests of the party and those of the workers had parted company but to assert that neither the Kronstadt rebels nor the Workers' Opposition were authentic working-class movements.

This tactic had already been employed with regard to the Kronstadt rebellion. From the outset it had been classed as a White Guard plot, a conspiracy by the interventionist powers, a scheme by the Mensheviks and SRs – everything except what it was – a rebellion by ordinary sailors against the Communist Party's policies. The tactic had prompted the Kronstadt rebels to publish in their *Bulletin* the names of all the members of the Provisional Revolutionary Committee, together with their occupations, to demonstrate the plebeian character of their movement.[21]

In his speech at the congress on 9 March, Shliapnikov cast doubt on the proletarian composition of the Communist Party. He claimed that it was degenerating, that recently its social composition had changed radically, that there had been an influx into it of an alien petty-bourgeois element. The proportion of workers in the party had sharply declined. Shliapnikov pointed out that in the Petrograd party, iron and steel workers constituted only 2 per cent of the membership; for Moscow the corresponding figure was 4 per cent. This indicated, he said, a massive exodus of the working class from the party, which was becoming increasingly alienated from the proletariat.

At the congress session on 11 March, Bukharin denied that the Workers' Opposition was indeed an opposition by the workers; it was, he asserted, in reality a peasants' opposition. It was precisely peasant ideology which

[19] Serge, *Memoirs*, p. 129.
[20] *Ibid.*, p. 130.
[21] *Pravda o Kronshtadte*, pp. 131, 158.

accounted for the erroneous views of the Workers' Opposition. This ideology did not take into account the differences in outlook that existed between the peasantry and the working class and between different strata within the working class. It overlooked the differences between the advanced elements in the working class and the mass of workers who were barely distinguished from peasants. The principle of absolute democracy advocated by both the Workers' Opposition and the Democratic Centralist group would ensure the domination of peasant interests over those of the most advanced sections of the working class. This, Bukharin contended, was what would be achieved by the Workers' Opposition's conception of a general 'Congress of Producers'. He thought that the Kronstadt uprising inspired by General Kozlovskii and the SRs was a lesser danger to the Soviet State than the petty-bourgeois infection that had manifested itself like gangrene in the strikes that had preceded the rebellion in Moscow and Petrograd.[22]

Bukharin's argument was rather ingenious. It was able to discount the manifestations of worker discontent with the Soviet regime by classing them as 'petty-bourgeois'. The advanced workers – the true proletarians – supported the Soviet regime. (Because they supported the Soviet regime they showed themselves to be advanced.) Pure democracy was, therefore, undesirable because it could only drown the minority of advanced workers in the mass of petty-bourgeois workers influenced by peasant ideology.

The degree of democracy one could permit, Bukharin argued, depended on how advanced a given section of the population was. Thus, the maximum degree of democracy was found in the Communist Party, as the organization of the most advanced elements within the most advanced class. The extent of democracy diminished in less advanced organizations and was permitted least of all in the army. In this argument a special role was attributed to the working class, one in keeping with the case Lenin had made in *What Is To Be Done?* back in 1902.

Of course, Bukharin admitted, the advanced ruling party ought on occasion to make concessions to the more backward sections of the population. And this it was now doing; it was going to replace the *prodrazverstka* with a tax in kind. Here Bukharin was referring to the most important economic change introduced at the Tenth Party Congress. It was in fact the end of war communism and the introduction of the New Economic Policy (NEP). Bukharin spoke of this measure as a concession to the more backward elements of the population who were demanding freedom of trade. He described it as 'a kind of peasant Brest-Litovsk'. Clearly, Lenin, Bukharin and other members of the Soviet government thought of NEP on its introduction as a retreat from the set of policies, which taken as a whole, they now began to characterize retrospectively as 'war communism'.

The replacement of the *prodrazverstka* by a tax in kind was a measure which had been proposed for some months, but until then strenuously resisted by the Soviet government. It meant that the peasants now had to pay a tax in grain or other agricultural produce to the State, but after payment of the tax they could do with any stocks they had left as they thought fit. They could use the grain to feed themselves, increase their cultivated area or to exchange for

---

[22] *Desiatyi s"ezd RKP(b)* (Moscow, 1963), pp. 223–25.

industrial goods. They were also allowed to sell the additional grain on the free market.[23] This last concession prepared the ground for the return of the freedom of trade and the dismantling of the war communist system.[24]

On the question of the trade unions, the Tenth Party Congress gave its overwhelming support to Lenin's 'Platform of the Ten'. During the congress, Lenin took steps to consolidate his victory by ensuring that supporters of the platform would be in control of the party apparatus. At that time, the secretariat was in the hands of Krestinskii, Serebriakov and Preobrazhenskii – all allies of Trotsky. On the evening of 9 March, therefore, Lenin assembled some trusted delegates and with them drew up a list of approved candidates for the Central Committee. He intended that two-thirds of the Central Committee should consist of supporters of the Platform of the Ten, while the remaining third of the places should be apportioned among the representatives of Trotsky's platform, the Workers' Opposition and the Democratic Centralists. Lenin mentioned in particular that Krestinskii, Serebriakov and Preobrazhenskii should not be elected to the Central Committee, but that he thought that Shliapnikov and I. I. Kutuzov from the Workers' Opposition and Sapronov from the Democratic Centralists ought to be elected. By including some oppositionists in the Central Committee Lenin hoped to ensure that these groups were not alienated from the regime, and that they would be bound by the collective decisions of the Central Committee. As they could always be out-voted, their presence would not constitute any danger.[25]

But, as an additional safeguard, Lenin thought it prudent to pass a resolution at the congress condemning fractionalism, dissolve all existing fractions and declare fractional activity incompatible with party membership. He believed that provision should be made for expelling even a member of the Central Committee if that member was involved in fractional activities. This would, however, require a two-thirds majority of members and candidate members of the Central Committee.

On the last day of the congress, Lenin produced two resolutions – 'On party unity' and 'On the Syndicalist and Anarchist deviation in our party'. The first of these resolutions contained the proposal to outlaw fractionalism, as Lenin had planned previously. But as a concession to the opposition groups, it included in addition the undertaking that the party would in the future take measures to respond to the points these groups had made, such as purging the party of non-proletarian and unreliable elements, combating bureaucratic practices and developing democracy and workers' initiative. The second resolution echoed the arguments Bukharin had advanced against the Workers' Opposition, by pointing out that the concept of 'producer' confused proletarians with non-proletarians and small commodity producers. Lenin was emphatic that Marxism taught that only the Communist Party was capable of organizing a vanguard of the proletariat that would be able to withstand the vacillations of the petty-bourgeois element which predominated in Russian conditions. To deny this, Lenin considered, was a syndicalist and anarchist deviation.[26]

[23] *Resheniia partii i pravitel'stva po khoziaistvennym voprosam* i (Moscow, 1967), pp. 200–202.
[24] A. Nove, *An Economic History of the USSR 1917–1991* (Harmondsworth, 1992), p. 79.
[25] A. I. Mikoian, *Mysli i vospominaniia o Lenine* (Moscow, 1970), pp. 136–38.
[26] V. I. Lenin, *Polnoe sobranie sochinenii* xliii, pp. 98–111.

The resolutions, which were approved by the congress, had the effect of reinforcing Lenin's doctrine on the leading role of the party, lessening the scope for intra-party disagreements and setting in motion the practice of party purges. All of these consequences were destined to make a contribution to the emergence during the 1920s of the system which was to become associated with the name of Stalin.

The Russian Revolution in Retrospect

The Revolution in Russian History

What kind of revolution took place in Russia? In what ways did it change Russian society? That these questions have no simple answers reflects the complexity and uniqueness of Russia's historical development.

The most characteristic feature of Russian society in modern times was that its peasant population had preserved the traditional commune, a group identity largely coinciding with the village. The peasant commune was itself the product of historical development, and had its own distinctive collectivist dynamic. It was still highly resilient well into the twentieth century, and was quite capable of adapting itself to new conditions and taking on new forms, while retaining its egalitarian ethic. The most serious threat to the commune was the economic individualism of the capitalist system, which was making significant inroads into Russian society in the nineteenth and twentieth centuries. One fundamental aspect of the Russian revolution was its rejection of capitalist individualism in favour of traditional collectivist and egalitarian attitudes and practices. The revolution thus served to reinforce Russia's national peculiarities *vis-à-vis* the West.

The strains caused by the introduction of market relations into traditional collectivist society formed the background to a number of social conflicts throughout the Russian Empire. The most long standing of these was that between landlords and peasants for the land. The peasants had never recognized the right of the land-owners to own the land as private property, and believed that all land without exception should be at the disposal of the commune for division among its members.

The development of a money economy, encouraged by the agrarian reform of 1861, added a new dimension to the struggle between landlord and peasant. On the one hand, it threatened the privileged position of the landed aristocracy by undermining their economic security and making them more dependent on the government for support. On the other hand, it added urgency to the peasants' claim for more land to support themselves in the new economic climate, particularly with the increase in the peasant population, which put ever more pressure on land resources.

The peasants' need to raise money both to meet their obligations to the State and to buy consumer goods led many of them to seek work in the towns. In this way, they contributed to the formation of the capitalist economic order, and also became involved in another social conflict – that between capitalists and workers. Although this clash of interests might appear to be the class struggle between labour and capital familiar in the West, this was only partly the case. Both the working class and the indigenous bourgeoisie in Russia were very new groups in society. The working class retained the collectivist outlook and behaviour of the peasants. The Russian business community was a small minority in an environment generally hostile to private enterprise. It consisted of two groups: one centred in Moscow, which had evolved out of the indigenous merchantry, and one based in St Petersburg, largely composed of the representatives of foreign firms which had set up business in Russia.

There was conflict not only between workers and capitalists but also between capitalists and land-owners. The extension of the market system in Russia was a threat to most land-owners, whose estates were poorly adapted to an environment of economic competition, in which they became indebted or were forced to sell their properties. The capitalists, on the other hand, saw the landed nobility as a social group which perpetuated the anti-business climate in the country, and which prevented the representatives of commerce and industry enjoying a political influence commensurate with their economic power.

Of the two groups of capitalists, the Moscow merchants had the more far-reaching political ambitions, while the St Petersburg group, connected with foreign firms, was more inclined to seek accommodation with the existing regime. The differences in political attitude caused friction between the two business communities, and prevented their effective co-operation.

These social and economic tensions were complicated by national and religious ones. In some cases national and religious identities were closely related, as exemplified by the Poles, the Jews and the Moslem peoples, all of whom suffered discrimination in the Russian Empire. However, secular forms of national self-identity had also begun to manifest themselves in the latter half of the nineteenth century, often influenced by the national movements in Western Europe. They were directed at achieving at least a measure of cultural autonomy within the Russian Empire. These movements were seldom internally homogeneous and often saw each other as the main adversary rather than the Russian autocracy.

In 1905, the conflicts and tensions within Russian society erupted into a revolution which threatened to bring down the autocratic regime. One important reason they did not do so was that the government made enough concessions to win over the most moderate sections of the opposition. The opportunity to form a stable constitutional regime was lost, however, because the tsar and his entourage were determined to maintain the autocracy. The more conservative elements in the government regarded the concessions made in 1905 as a tactical manoeuvre, and believed they should be revoked now that the crisis was over. It had long been the practice in Russian politics that the government would grant concessions only when it was forced to do so through the weakness of its position, and would see no reason to concede anything when it was in a position of strength.

When Russia became involved in the First World War, the traditional pattern of Russian politics soon asserted itself: success in the war favoured the government, while defeat was exploited by the opposition to pressure the government into making concessions. The revolutionary movement, which had been subdued when hostilities began, reasserted itself by 1916, fuelled by the privations of war. The workers' discontent escalated unexpectedly at the end of February 1917, overthrowing the autocracy and leaving the Provisional Government and the Soviet in power.

It might have been possible for the two institutions in combination to form a stable regime in the country since there was not only competition between them but also mutual dependence. Why did this not happen? Weaknesses stemmed from the liberal values upheld in varying degrees by both the Provisional Government and the Soviet, since these values were not shared by the population at large. As one of its chief priorities, the government implemented measures to dismantle the tsarist apparatus of oppression. At the same time it issued legislation to extend civil rights to wide sections of the population. Nevertheless, it resolved to leave any substantive reforms to be decided by the Constituent Assembly. This was an unavoidable decision by a government which was dedicated to the principle of the rule of law. For the Provisional Government it was important not simply that the population should be able to achieve its aspirations but that these aspirations should be achieved in an orderly and legitimate way.

For the population of the Russian Empire, however, the pace of change was far more important than the procedures by which it came about. Most looked on the Provisional Government's insistence on legal procedures as pointless bureaucratic formalities. Workers, peasants and national groups increasingly took matters into their own hands, and acted in defiance of official prohibitions. They were able to do so with impunity because early Provisional Government legislation had removed any sanctions that could be deployed in support of the law, and the new civil rights legislation could be utilized to oppose government policies.

In any case, there were few sections of Russian society which could afford to wait patiently for the convocation of the Constituent Assembly. The Provisional Government's continuation of the war, and the economic disruption brought about by this policy, caused enormous hardship, impelling peasants and workers to find their own solutions to the problems of peace, bread and land. The economic consequences of the war acted as a powerful stimulus behind the social movements of 1917, and were the influence determining the form these movements took.

The Bolshevik Party had not been a major political force during the first months of 1917. It had occupied a position on the margins of political events on the extreme left wing. Unlike the Mensheviks and the Socialist Revolutionaries, it had not been involved in any of the coalition governments, and in fact the Bolshevik leader, Lenin, had rejected any co-operation with the Provisional Government in principle. By the autumn of 1917 the Bolsheviks' position on the sidelines worked in their favour as they had not been tainted with the failures of the Provisional Government. Lenin urged that the Bolshevik Party take power, firm in the belief that once in government the pressing economic problems could be solved by radical, socialist policies. The popular appeal of the Bolsheviks in October was that they offered a programme of peace, bread and land – precisely those things the Provisional Government had so signally failed to deliver.

When the Bolsheviks came to power, they immediately issued decrees on peace, land reform and workers' control in industry. The measures were widely popular when they were introduced, but all were abandoned with the onset of the Civil War. The Bolsheviks came to power without a coherent economic strategy, as they believed none was necessary. In this assumption they were mistaken; and as early experience showed, their theoretical studies had given them a very poor understanding of how the Russian wartime economy actually operated.

In response to economic disruption, shortages and speculation, the Bolshevik government had to extend and intensify the measures previously resorted to by the Provisional Government and by the tsarist regime before it. These were to maintain a monopoly of grain and other goods of prime necessity and to operate a rationing system. The centralized control of industrial undertakings which this entailed encouraged widespread nationalization by the Bolshevik government. The elimination of market relations and the diminution of money transactions which accompanied these policies encouraged many in the Bolshevik Party to view them as features of an emergent socialist economy.

Resistance to the Bolshevik policies, especially the land-owners' opposition to the agrarian policy, precipitated the Civil War, in the course of which the Bolsheviks succeeded in consolidating their hold on the country. During the Civil War the changes which the 1917 revolution had initiated were assimilated by Russian society at large, altering its structure considerably in comparison with what it had been before the First World War.

The biggest change that had taken place was that, though some individual estates managed to survive, the formerly powerful land-owner class had been eliminated. The peasants had emerged victorious in the centuries-old struggle for the land – at least for the time being. The threat to traditional collectivism posed by separators from the commune had also been overcome, and the *mir* was left to function unimpeded.

A second important change was that the business communities had disappeared. Neither the indigenous Moscow merchant entrepreneurs nor the representatives of foreign investment remained. This business community had always constituted a small minority in the country, operating in a generally hostile environment. It very easily fell victim to the upheavals of the revolutionary era. With the elimination of the country's entrepreneurs and the reversal of the Stolypin reform, the way was decisively barred to any further development of capitalist relations.

The autocratic form of government had been eliminated by the revolution, along with the land-owning class with which it was closely associated. The most economically powerful as well as the most numerous class was now the peasantry, particularly as it had attracted many former industrial workers to its ranks during the Civil War. This predominance, however, was not translated into political power. The running of the country was in the hands of a group of radical intelligentsia, which maintained its position not through its numbers or its economic power but by compulsion. It made use of the same kind of repressive structures the tsarist government had employed to maintain the supremacy of the land-owning aristocracy. In many cases the institutions used were the same. This kind of continuity, in conjunction with a heavily centralized economic apparatus, helped create the bureaucratic organization characteristic of the Soviet regime.

The result of the revolution was to simplify social relations in Russia, arrest the development towards a market system and perpetuate in the country the kind of economic organization that had been common to most of the belligerent countries during the war. To provide itself with legitimacy, the new ruling élite placed the changes the Russian revolution had wrought within the framework of socialist theory. It was in this form that the Russian revolution was evaluated abroad.

Contrary to their rhetoric, the Bolsheviks did not put into practice ideas inspired by Karl Marx. For in the last decade of his life, Marx had studied how capital had begun to circulate in Russia, and had come to the conclusion that the process might be arrested by a timely revolution, and that a socialist system might be established founded on the peasant commune. In the 1880s, however, Plekhanov had, for polemical purposes, attributed to Marx the opinion that all countries had to pass through the same historical stages, Russia being no exception in this respect.

The doctrine of historical development which Plekhanov propounded implied that the socialist revolution in Russia could only come about some time in the distant future, when capitalism had run its course. Russia's economic backwardness suggested that the socialist revolution there would come after revolutions in the more developed European countries. Shortly before and during the First World War, however, various writers inspired by Marx's economics pointed to a pattern of world economic integration, which suggested that socialism in all countries might be achieved at approximately the same time. They thought that the structures of a socialist system were being created by the monopolies and trusts characteristic of finance capital. As some of these monopolies and trusts could be observed in Russia, it encouraged Lenin and other members of the Bolshevik Party to believe that Russia, like the rest of Europe, was ripe for socialist revolution.

Soon after coming to power the Bolshevik leaders discovered that their expectations had been mistaken. They found that the economic disruption in Russia was not the sign of an emergent socialist system but simply the collapse of the existing one. Nor did the revolution spread immediately throughout Europe. These discoveries brought with them not simply practical but also theoretical difficulties for the Bolsheviks. They were deprived of the ideological justification for having taken power in October. The last tenuous connection with Marx's ideas had been broken. The response of the Bolsheviks was not to abandon their claim to continuity with Marx, but to improvise a new theoretical framework, presenting the policies they were forced to adopt in Marxist terms. The only element of Marx's thinking which remained in this endeavour was the terminology.

The Russian Revolution in Historical Writing

The way in which the Bolsheviks subordinated Marxist ideology to their current political objectives is paralleled by the manner in which they presented the history of their own accession to power. This too was significant in legitimizing Bolshevik rule in Russia, and from its very inception the Soviet regime established a firm control over how the history of the Russian revolution was written. As the political situation in which this legitimacy had to be established changed considerably in the first years of the Soviet regime, the history of the Russian revolution had to be adjusted to meet these needs. This created the impression that early Soviet historical writing on the Russian revolution showed a variety of interpretations which later disappeared in the Stalin era. An awareness of how the history of the Russian revolution was written in the early years of the Soviet regime and the purposes it served allows one to evaluate critically the source materials which emanated from the Soviet Union at that time, and helps explain how some early Western conceptions of the Russian revolution came about.

The Bolsheviks' adversaries, the émigré writers, had political motivations too, which were reflected in the works they produced on the Russian revolution. In many respects, the revolution's battles continued to be fought on the pages of historical publications. The Soviet and the émigré interpretations not only diverged but also inter-related and complemented each other on key issues. Convergence of opinion of this type was a powerful influence on Western historical writing.

The political struggles in the Soviet Union in the Stalin era left their mark on how the Russian revolution was interpreted, and affected the availability of materials. Similarly, the long process of dismantling the Stalinist system had important repercussions on the manner in which episodes of the Russian revolution were presented. Historians have to reckon with this ideological dimension in their subject of study. In order to allow for bias in the sources, they have first to know what the bias is.

Early Soviet Writing on the Russian Revolution

The book which set the precedent for how Soviet historical writing on the Russian revolution was to function was Trotsky's short work *The Russian Revolution to Brest-Litovsk*. It was written in the spring of 1918, while the author was taking part in the peace negotiations at Brest-Litovsk.[1] Trotsky's book was written with a German audience in mind. It was designed to present the acquisition of power by the Bolsheviks in the best possible light in the hope that it would encourage the German workers to make a revolution in their own country.

Trotsky had to reckon with the fact that the response to the October revolution in the German socialist press had been generally unfavourable. Kautsky in particular had accused the Bolsheviks of establishing a dictator-

[1] L. Trotsky, *My Life* (New York, 1970), p. 370.

ship over the workers and peasants, of infringing democratic principles and of refusing to broaden the base of their government by including in it representatives of other political parties. In his book, Trotsky set out to answer these charges. He tried to show that the Bolsheviks had not carried out a coup behind the backs of the Russian people but had done everything possible to involve the other socialist parties in the new Soviet government.

The need to show that Kautsky's criticism of the Bolsheviks was misplaced strongly influenced Trotsky's presentation of the October revolution. Trotsky contended that the popularity of the Bolshevik Party after the Kornilov rebellion would have brought it to power through the elections to the Second Congress of Soviets. But since Kerensky and his associates intended to prevent the convocation of the congress by armed force, the Bolsheviks and their allies had formed a Military Revolutionary Committee to monitor troop movements in and out of Petrograd. A series of offensive measures initiated by Kerensky had prompted the MRC to capture the Winter Palace and arrest the members of the Provisional Government. Although the Bolsheviks had made every effort to involve the Mensheviks and Socialist Revolutionaries in the new government, these parties had refused to co-operate with the Bolsheviks, leaving the latter to take power on their own.[2]

In this presentation of events there was no point at which the Bolsheviks took the offensive. They had come to power only as a response to the threat of force by their opponents. It was the latter who had disrupted the democratic process because they, unlike the Bolsheviks, did not enjoy popular support.

Before the formation of the Comintern in 1919, conducting revolutionary propaganda abroad was the responsibility of Trotsky's Commissariat of Foreign Affairs. In December 1917 there was attached to the Commissariat a Department of International Revolutionary Propaganda specially for this purpose. The department had various foreign language sections staffed by Bolsheviks who had lived abroad and by foreigners enlisted to help the Bolshevik cause. For a time the American journalist John Reed was in charge of the English language section. After the signing of the Treaty of Brest-Litovsk and the banning of revolutionary propaganda abroad, the department was given the more innocuous title of the Department of Foreign Political Literature.[3]

With the onset of the Civil War and the intervention the activities of the Department of Political Literature were extended. Propaganda was now produced to be directed at the foreign troops fighting in Russia. The English language section of the department was reinforced by foreigners who supported the Soviet regime and disapproved of the intervention. These included the journalist on the *Manchester Guardian*, M. Philips Price and the writer, Arthur Ransome.[4]

The most celebrated work to emerge from this period was John Reed's *Ten Days That Shook the World*. This book was issued by a socialist publisher in the USA, but its political orientation and its interpretation of the Russian

[2] L. Trotsky, 'The Russian Revolution', *The Essential Trotsky* (London, 1963), pp. 62–74.

[3] E. Homberger and J. Biggart, eds., *John Reed and the Russian Revolution: Uncollected Articles, Letters and Speeches on Russia, 1917–1920* (London, 1992), pp 146, 165.

[4] A. S. Iakushevskii, *Propagandistskaia rabota bol'shevikov sredi voisk interventov v 1918–1920 gg.* (Moscow, 1963), p. 118.

revolution were products of Trotsky's Department of Foreign Political Literature. Reed's account of how the Bolshevik Party came to power follows closely Trotsky's version in *The Russian Revolution to Brest-Litovsk*. In Reed's book there is no abrupt seizure of power by the Bolsheviks. There is instead the claim that had their opponents allowed matters to take their course, the Bolsheviks would have taken power by due electoral process. It was only the threat that troops would be sent into Petrograd to prevent the convocation of the Soviet Congress which forced the Bolsheviks to take defensive measures in the form of establishing a Military Revolutionary Committee to control troop movements. Reed is emphatic that the initiative to take power did not come from the Bolshevik Party but from the workers, who demanded that the Bolsheviks take action. They reluctantly did so, and despite efforts to involve other socialist parties in government, they found themselves in power alone. Reed reinforced his picture of the Bolsheviks as reluctant revolutionaries by stressing their amateurishness as politicians and their lack of experience in government.[5]

Up to 1920 the interpretation of the Russian revolution promoted by the Soviet regime was one which tried to convey that the acquisition of power by the Bolsheviks had been in response to the demands of the people; it had not been conspiratorial, well organized or planned in advance. This interpretation was to change radically in 1920 and was associated with the establishment of Istpart, an institution created to disseminate the new presentation of the Russian revolution.

Istpart

By 1920 the tide had turned in favour of the Reds in the Civil War. The Soviet regime no longer felt itself on the defensive but poised to carry the revolution into Western Europe. The Comintern, established the previous year, acquired increased importance, and within it the Russian Communist Party was predominant. It could claim to have shown the world how to make a successful workers' revolution. The Russian communists were consequently in a position to hold up this revolution as a model to be followed. These changed circumstances called for a new interpretation of the revolution, and from 1920 onwards there emerged a version of events which contrasted sharply with that Trotsky had put forward two years earlier.

This new interpretation held that the October revolution had been organized and led by the Bolshevik Party. It was now maintained that because of the way the party was organized – its centralization and discipline – and because it operated according to Marxist principles, it had been able to lead the Russian working class in an armed insurrection which had overthrown the rule of the capitalist government and established the dictatorship of the proletariat. This interpretation was first put forward in Lenin's pamphlet *Left Wing Communism, An Infantile Disorder*, which was distributed among the delegates to the Second Congress of the Comintern in

---

[5] J. Reed, *Ten Days That Shook the World* (London, 1961), p. 30.

the summer of 1920. It was now a matter of aligning historical writing with political doctrine.

Lenin's pamphlet was designed to convey to socialists throughout the world that if they wished to bring about a socialist revolution like the one in Russia, they would have to establish parties modelled on the Bolshevik Party. The idea contained quite a few assumptions about what the Russian revolution had been. It implied that the revolution had been socialist; that Russia had been a capitalist country, and that political power in 1917 had been in the hands of the capitalist class. It also implied that the revolution in Russia was something which could be replicated in other countries and that, therefore, it embodied nothing in its essentials that was specifically Russian. But most significant of all was the assumption that the October revolution had been brought about not by the Bolshevik promises of peace, bread and land in the autumn of 1917, but by Bolshevik methods of party organization, by the principles Lenin had first elaborated in his book *What Is To Be Done?* published in 1902. In this way the October revolution became a vindication of Lenin's ideas. By linking his ideas so unobtrusively but effectively to a major event, Lenin ensured that posterity would look on him as the architect of the Russian revolution.[6]

To propagate his ideas on the Russian revolution Lenin caused a 'Commission on the History of the Russian Communist Party and the October Revolution' to be established in August 1920. The organization was popularly known as 'Istpart'. The functions of Istpart were formally defined in a decree of 21 September 1920. These were: 'the collection, editing and publishing of materials relating to the history of the October revolution and the Russian Communist Party.' The decree went on to stress that anyone who was in possession of any of these materials was obliged to surrender them to the commission. This was empowered to demand any such materials from institutions or private persons and, if required, could call upon the Soviet authorities to enforce its demands.[7] In this way Istpart was able to establish within the country a virtual monopoly on materials relating to the history of the Russian revolution.

Istpart organizations were established throughout the country to ensure that local histories of the revolution accorded with the interpretation approved by the centre. Istpart also had a national dimension, which was present almost from the commission's inception. On 22 September 1920 – that is, a month after the establishment of Istpart – the leadership of the Latvian Communist Party in Russia decided to set up a Commission for the History of the Communist Party of Latvia. This was headed by Peteris Stučka and was modelled on Istpart. In fact it was soon christened 'Latistpart'. The Latvian commission worked closely with Istpart and co-ordinated its activities with the central organization so that historical interpretations elaborated by the central Istpart were handed down to its Latvian counterpart.

In 1925 the Latvian organization was joined by commissions for the history of the Estonian Communist Party, the Lithuanian Communist Party, the revolutionary movement in Finland and the revolutionary movement in

---

[6] V. I. Lenin, *Polnoe sobranie sochinenii* xli, pp. 3–8.
[7] *Proletarskaia revoliutsiia* (1930, no. 5), p. 165.

Poland. This organizational structure ensured that although studies of national Communist parties and revolutionary movements were devolved to Communist historians of those nations, the official Soviet doctrine was still followed.[8]

Lenin's new presentation of the Russian revolution had rendered Trotsky's *Russian Revolution to Brest-Litovsk* out of date. A new authoritative work setting out the accepted doctrine was required. Again the responsibility fell to Trotsky. In May 1922 he was requested by the Central Committee to edit a book on the history of the October revolution to be written by the deputy director of the agitation and propaganda department of the Central Committee, Ia. A. Iakovlev. The result was a short pamphlet entitled *On the Historical Significance of October*.[9]

Trotsky and Iakovlev's pamphlet was an important one because it gave overall shape to the Soviet version of the 1917 revolution, since it dealt not only with the October but also the February revolution. This was, in fact the first Soviet work to deal with the February revolution. This had not been mentioned in either Trotsky's 1918 pamphlet or John Reed's book, where the main attention had been focused on the events of October 1917. Although Lenin had not been concerned with the February revolution in *Left Wing Communism, An Infantile Disorder*, the argument he had presented there contained implications for the way in which the February revolution required to be treated. For if the success of the October revolution had been brought about by the organization and leadership of the Bolshevik Party, what could one say about a revolution in which power had passed to the bourgeoisie, to the Provisional Government? Clearly from this revolution leadership and organization had to be lacking. This was in fact the argument put forward by Trotsky and Iakovlev.

On the Historical Significance of October drew a sharp contrast between the February and October revolutions. Whereas the latter was well planned and directed, the former was spontaneous and unprepared. In terms of the level of organization, February and October represented two ends of a spectrum. Whereas in February virtually no organization or leadership had been present, in October the elements of organization and leadership reached their highest level. This was the picture of 1917 presented by all general accounts produced in the period, and the version supported by any documentary publications or memoir literature which appeared in the decade between 1920 and 1930.

The memoirs of A. G. Shliapnikov, who had been the Bolshevik leader in Petrograd during the days of the February revolution, constituted something of an exception. Published between 1923 and 1931, Shliapnikov's memoirs provided a detailed account of what he had done and observed in the February revolution, and it was Shliapnikov's impression that the 'underground parties had carried on a very intensive preparation for what was later known as the February revolution'.[10] Shliapnikov probably succeeded in getting his book past Istpart because, although a dissident – a leader of the

[8] A. K. Biron and M. F. Biron, *Stanovlenie sovetskoi istoriografii Latvii* (Riga, 1981), pp. 28–37.
[9] L. Trotsky, *The Essential Trotsky* (London, 1963), pp. 194–95; Ia. A. Iakovlev, *Ob istoricheskom smysle Oktiabria* (Moscow, 1922).
[10] A. G. Shliapnikov, 'O knige N. Sukhanova', *Pechat' i revoliutsiia* iv (1923), p. 47.

'Workers' Opposition' – he was still a member of the Central Committee. He had great difficulty in getting his book published, and soon after it appeared it was subjected to a campaign of abuse, the main accusation being that it exaggerated the degree of organization in the February revolution.

An important function of Istpart was publishing Lenin's collected works. These began to appear from 1920 onwards, and the enterprise had the co-operation of Lenin himself. By 1924 collected editions of Trotsky's, Zinoviev's and Kamenev's writings had begun to appear and some of their individual writings were republished, such as Trotsky's book *1905*.

The publishing of collected works served two overlapping functions. The first was that by structuring their studies around them, historians would be able to interpret events of recent history in a way which accorded with the views of the party leadership. This applied primarily to Lenin's works. By structuring events around Lenin's writings one inevitably produced a version of history which demonstrated the correctness of Lenin's views. The logic of this method was to lead eventually to the history of the Bolshevik Party and the revolution becoming a kind of commentary on Lenin's ideas. The second consideration was that it increased considerably the standing and prestige of the party leaders honoured by having a collected edition of their works. This consideration meant that any items which would tend to detract from the standing of a given party leader would be omitted from his published works.

The purpose of providing a ready-made historical interpretation to follow would, of course, only succeed if all the writings of the party leaders maintained a certain unanimity. And giving prestige to party leaders was only possible if the collected works in question did not contain criticisms of each other. Until 1924, by a judicious choice of what to publish and in what order, Istpart succeeded in maintaining the requisite appearance of unity. But in that year the arrangements were disrupted by the publication of Trotsky's 'Lessons of October' as the introductory essay to the volume of his collected works covering the period of the Russian revolution. He used the essay in his political struggle against Zinoviev and Kamenev.

The assumption contained in 'Lessons of October' was that one's political status depended on the part one had played in the revolution. When Trotsky disparaged Zinoviev and Kamenev's roles in 1917 he thereby undermined their present political standing. This connection between making a significant contribution to the success of the October revolution and occupying a leading position in the party had been a principle upheld by Istpart. For if the party's legitimacy to rule stemmed from its ability to carry out a revolution, then it was logical to expect that the actual people in power would be those who had led that revolution.

This meant that people who were prominent in the party leadership in the early 1920s were held to have played an important part in the October revolution or in the revolutionary movement more generally. On the other hand, those who had genuinely played major roles in the revolution but were not party leaders would not necessarily have their contributions recognized. A major figure in the Russian revolutionary movement like Alexander Bogdanov, who was an adversary of Lenin, was not mentioned in historical works at all.

Thus to be recognized as having played an important part in the October revolution was not a statement of fact but a sign of official approval. Trotsky was a beneficiary of these honorific attributions before 1924, when Stalin attributed a leading part in the October revolution to him in November 1918. After 1924 the machinery went into reverse in Trotsky's case and, in keeping with the regime's disfavour, he was denied any significant part in bringing about the October revolution.

The anti-Trotsky campaign which followed the publication of 'Lessons of October' was a major landmark in Soviet historical writing because it brought to the surface the political use to which the history of the October revolution was being put. Now that Trotsky had become an opponent of the Soviet leadership, Stalin, Bukharin, Zinoviev, Kamenev and others wrote articles denying that Trotsky had played any special part in the October revolution.[11] When Zinoviev and Kamenev allied with Trotsky in 1926 their opposition to the seizure of power in 1917 was recalled and emphasized. Trotsky, on the other hand, now became anxious to stress that in the October days Kamenev at least had been by his side in the headquarters of the Military Revolutionary Committee.[12]

Stalin's Influence

The involvement of historical questions in the political struggles of the 1920s served to devalue historical scholarship in the Soviet Union. More and more areas of historical study acquired a political significance as they were used as ideological ammunition by the Soviet leadership or by one or other of the political groupings. This situation provided the opportunity for Stalin to exert his influence over all historical writing between 1930 and 1934. The old division between subjects falling into the province of Istpart and the rest of historical study disappeared. From then on all areas of history became subject to Stalin's control.

An important landmark in the imposition of Stalin's will on Soviet historical writing was the letter he sent to the journal *Proletarskaia revoliutsiia* in 1931, outlawing the discussion of certain historical topics which he held to be 'axiomatic truths'.[13] The culmination of the process was reached in 1939 with the publication of the *Short Course of the History of the Russian Communist Party (bolsheviks)*, which contained Stalin's version of the revolution and the revolutionary movement, and which all historians of the period were obliged to follow.

One of the first changes Stalin made to the way the Russian revolution was written about in the 1930s was to make his own role more prominent. Accounts of the February revolution no longer pointed out his defensist position on the war. Stalin changed the interpretation of the February revolution completely by insisting that it had been organized and led by the Bolshevik Party, just as the October revolution had been. From 1930 onwards, Shliapnikov's account of the February days was denounced for having diminished the part played by the Bolsheviks.

[11] 'Vokrug stat'i L. D. Trotskogo "Uroki Oktiabtia"', *Izvestiia TsK KPSS* (1991, no. 7), pp. 158–77.
[12] L. Trotsky, *The Stalin School of Falsification* (New York, 1962), p. 14.
[13] J. Stalin, *Problems of Leninism* (Moscow, 1953), pp. 482–97.

Stalin's reign of terror claimed as victims many participants in the Russian revolution. As 'enemies of the people' these men and women could not be referred to by Soviet historians as only those currently in favour with Stalin might be mentioned. Although the phenomenon was particularly noticeable under Stalin, the practice had been initiated by Istpart in the early 1920s. It resulted in several episodes of the Russian revolution being written about by historians without the names of specific individuals being referred to. An example of this was the treatment of the February revolution, in which very few of the Bolsheviks involved were named, since most of them had perished in Stalin's purges.

In the mid-1930s Stalin used his power over historical writing to align the presentation of pre-revolutionary Russian history with his own theoretical writings. The effect of this adjustment was to eliminate the Russian bourgeoisie from the historical record of the Russian revolution. Stalin wished this done because existing historical interpretations conflicted with the presuppositions of the pamphlet he had written in 1924, *The Foundations of Leninism*, in which he set out his theory of 'socialism in one country'.

He had done this in the guise of developing ideas which had been put forward by Lenin. A key question in Stalin's essay was why a socialist revolution had been possible in Russia. The answer, Stalin asserted, was contained in the dictum which he wrongly attributed to Lenin, that 'the chain of imperialism broke at its weakest link'. Stalin clearly intended that the pre-revolutionary Russian economy should be regarded as being at a low level of development. This had not been the usual interpretation of Russian economic history during the 1920s, which had maintained that before the revolution significant industrial development had taken place. The growth of industry and trade was associated with the development of an indigenous Russian bourgeoisie, on which some important works had been published.[14]

From 1934 it became official doctrine that before the revolution, Russian industrial development had been minimal, and that Russian capitalism had been dependent on Western European capital. This, in Stalin's view, explained Russia's 'semi-colonial status'.[15] Ironically, the same view of Russian economic development was held by Trotsky, who used it to support his theory of 'permanent revolution'. The argument advanced in his *History of the Russian Revolution* was that the weakness of the Russian bourgeoisie ensured that the proletariat would assume the leadership over the peasantry and that the revolution in Russia would be a socialist one.[16]

Trotsky's *History of the Russian Revolution*

Trotsky's *History of the Russian Revolution* appeared just at the time when Soviet historical writing was being subjected to Stalin's direct control. The

[14] Among these few, but important, works were: P. A. Berlin, *Russkaia burzhuaziia v staroe i novoe vremia* (Moscow, 1922); B. B. Grave, *Burzhuaziia nakanune fevral'skoi revoliutsii* (Moscow-Leningrad, 1927); B. B. Grave, *K istorii klassovoi bor'by v Rossii* (Moscow-Leningrad, 1926).
[15] I. V. Stalin, *Sochineniia*, ed. R. McNeal (Stanford, CA, 1967), p. 39.
[16] L. Trotsky, *The History of the Russian Revolution* (London, 1934), pp. 25–37.

first volume was published in Berlin in 1931, and Volumes 2 and 3 followed in 1933. Trotsky's book was the first comprehensive historical work on the 1917 revolution, either in the West or the Soviet Union.

The interpretation of 1917 in Trotsky's *History of the Russian Revolution* is markedly different from that in *The Russian Revolution to Brest-Litovsk*. In the *History* the October revolution is held to be a well planned and organized uprising by the Bolshevik Party. The pattern of 1917 as a whole in Trotsky's book corresponds closely to that in Iakovlev's 1922 pamphlet *On the Historical Significance of October*, in that it presents a contrast between the spontaneity of the February revolution and the planned character of October. This pattern was utilized by Trotsky to point up the lessons he wanted his readers to draw from his book.

What Trotsky did not say explicitly, but is obvious from the most cursory perusal, is that his *History* was a polemical work. It was a reaction to the anti-Trotsky campaign carried on in the Soviet Union after 1924 when Trotsky published his *Lessons of October*. The book reflects the kind of attack made on him at that time. These were the following:

1. That Trotsky played no special part in the October revolution; that his capacity had only been that of chairman of the Petrograd Soviet. He was accused of having obstructed the October uprising.
2. That he was an anti-Leninist. This charge was important after 1924, when the cult of Lenin had begun to develop.
3. That Trotsky's ideas were heretical. It was held that the theory of 'permanent revolution' contradicted the conception of 'socialism in one country' which, according to Stalin, originated with Lenin.

Trotsky designed his history of the 1917 revolution to counter these charges and to turn the tables on his opponents. He tried to show that not only was he, Trotsky, the best Leninist, but that he was the *only* Leninist, since the 'Old Bolsheviks' had found themselves in opposition to Lenin at every critical juncture. Trotsky also argued that Lenin had never accepted the idea of 'socialism in one country' and indeed in April 1917 had come round to accepting the Trotskyist theory of 'permanent revolution'.

One of the episodes of 1917 which Trotsky's account highlights is Lenin's return to Petrograd in April when he presented his *April Theses* to the Bolshevik Party, setting out what he considered its future policies ought to be. Trotsky maintains that at this point Lenin found himself isolated in the Bolshevik Party, but that the ideas put forward by Trotsky at that same time in New York were identical to Lenin's. A comparison of the relevant documents, however, shows this not to be the case.

The other key episode in Trotsky's history is mid-October 1917 when, according to Trotsky, Lenin's call for an armed uprising was resisted by most members of the Bolshevik leadership, and only he gave Lenin his full support. Trotsky did not make it clear exactly what he had done in October events, but he quoted the testimonial literature written in the early years of the Soviet regime to the effect that he had played a considerable role in the October revolution. He implied that what these testimonials said was the historical truth.

Trotsky's book is misleading because it uses sources selectively to prove its point and gives an impression of events not supported by the evidence. The reliance of Trotsky's method of argumentation on materials produced by Istpart in the early 1920s has the implication that these materials are trustworthy and objective. In this way, the purpose of the Istpart organization is obscured, making it difficult for historians to evaluate the reliability of its publications.

The influence of Trotsky's *History* is so great on Western historical scholarship because historians outside the Soviet Union began to write about the Russian revolution only after Trotsky's book was published. During the 1920s in the West, memoir and documentary literature had mainly been published, including of course John Reed's *Ten Days That Shook the World*. The first major work of Western historical scholarship on the Russian revolution was William Chamberlin's *History of the Russian Revolution*, which appeared in 1936 – that is after the publication of Trotsky's *History*. One may readily observe that Chamberlin had read Trotsky's book and been influenced by it, as were all subsequent students of the Russian revolution in the West.

First-Hand Accounts of the Revolution Produced outside the Soviet Union

Both Trotsky and Chamberlin were able to draw on works on the Russian revolution written by participants in the events and published outside the Soviet Union. These writings lay beyond the control of the Soviet authorities and provided independent testimony on the Russian revolution. How different were these accounts from those produced in the Soviet Union, which followed the dictates of party politics?

One of the most important primary sources for the events of 1917 is a non-Soviet work written inside the Soviet Union: N. N. Sukhanov's *Notes on the Russian Revolution*. Sukhanov's book is a remarkably detailed treatment of the subject, and it contains a wealth of information collected by someone who was both a talented writer and a close observer of the events. His seven-volume book of memoirs was published in 1922 and 1923 by Z. I. Gzhebin, an associate of Gorky's, who was contracted by the Soviet government to produce books in Berlin for sale in Russia. The terms of the contract gave the Soviet government some control over what books Gzhebin published, though disagreemants between the two sides indicate that this control was not as full as the Soviet government would have liked.[17] The ambiguity of the relationship between Gzhebin and the Soviet government means that one cannot unreservedly class Sukhanov as a writer whose work was published outside the Soviet Union.

When Sukhanov began to write his reminiscences in 1918 he made no secret of what he was doing, and the Soviet leadership was well aware of the enterprise. His only conflict with the Soviet authorities seems to have been over his treatment of the July days. Sukhanov had the distinct impression that the Bolsheviks were planning to seize power at that time, and Trotsky warned him through Lunacharsky against following that particular interpretation.

[17] 'Iz perepiski A. M. Gor'kogo', *Izvestiia TsK KPSS* (1991, no. 6), pp. 152–56.

Not only did Sukhanov persist in his version of events but he also published Trotsky's objections as well.[18]

In the main, however, Sukhanov's presentation of 1917 did not diverge markedly from the official Soviet version of the time. He described a February revolution for which all the political parties had been unprepared, and an October revolution which had been planned by the Bolshevik Party in his own flat while he himself was absent. On these key events his memoirs did not contradict Istpart doctrine. This probably accounts for the equanimity with which the Soviet authorities viewed the appearance of Sukhanov's book.

Nevertheless, one of the few reviews Sukhanov's book received in the Soviet Union was an unfavourable one, and that was by Shliapnikov, who held that the underground political parties had in fact provided leadership in the February days. Shliapnikov pointed out that Sukhanov was not himself involved in the political underground, and was not in a position to know what it had done. Sukhanov had only joined the revolution on 27 February, after the decisive battles had been fought, so that it would seem to him that the upsurge was spontaneous.[19]

Shliapnikov's comments are helpful in indicating an essential characteristic of Sukhanov's view of 1917. Sukhanov had limited himself to recounting what he himself witnessed at the time. He does not investigate what might have been the actual state of affairs, even though he had the opportunity to do so by asking how other participants remembered what had taken place. Sukhanov's is the viewpoint of an eye-witness, and in this capacity his recollections gave accounts of the February and the October revolutions which coincided with official presentations of these events.

One of the earliest non-Soviet accounts of the Russian revolution was Miliukov's. Although Miliukov was hostile to the seizure of power by the Bolsheviks, he was in no doubt that the October revolution had been planned and organized by them.

Miliukov began to write his history of the Russian revolution in the spring of 1918 soon after helping to establish the Volunteer Army. The section of this book dealing with the October revolution was published in Sofia in 1921. His treatment of the period simultaneously condemns the Bolsheviks and justifies Kornilov. He states as a fact that the Bolsheviks were planning to stage an uprising on 29 August. Kornilov anticipated this action and, in accordance with the wishes of the Provisional Government, sent troops to quell the Bolshevik revolt. The Bolsheviks, however, cancelled their proposed action, placing Kornilov in the awkward position of attacking not the Bolsheviks but the Provisional Government. The Bolsheviks, however, did not cancel their plans altogether, but only postponed them until after the suppression of the Kornilov movement.[20]

Miliukov's was not an account of the October revolution which was suggested by the available evidence but one dictated by political considerations. It had the effect of crediting the Bolsheviks with 'very competent

[18] N. N. Sukhanov, *The Russian Revolution 1917*, ed., abridged and trans. J. Carmichael (Oxford, 1955), pp. 480–81.
[19] Shliapnikov, 'O knige N. Sukhanova'.
[20] P. N. Miliukov, *The Russian Revolution, Vol. 1: The Revolution Divided: Spring 1917*, ed. R. Stites, trans. T. Stites and R. Stites (Gulf Breeze, FL, 1978), p. 166.

leadership'. Miliukov may have looked on this leadership unfavourably, but he did not dispute that the Bolsheviks had organized a successful *coup d'état* to overthrow the Provisional Government. In this respect his version of events coincided with Istpart's.

Miliukov challenged the legitimacy of the Bolshevik seizure of power by asserting that it had been encouraged and supported by the Germans. The accusation of German support had been made against the Bolsheviks during 1917, and was to be repeated by other émigré historians of the Russian revolution. The implication was that the October revolution was something imported from outside and had not properly been a part of Russian history. In this way he suggested that Bolshevik rule was not the legitimate outcome of Russian historical development.

The doctrine of the German origins of the October revolution had the effect of impoverishing émigré writing on the subject. For if the revolution had originated in Berlin, there was little point in examining the tensions within Russian society. Émigré writers accordingly tended to ignore social problems. Miliukov's book, for example, is almost exclusively taken up with political history; workers, peasants and the army receive very little attention. Nor does Miliukov deal at any great length with the part played by the Russian business circles in bringing about the overthrow of the autocracy. These were aspects of the Russian revolution studied by historians in the Soviet Union during the 1920s.[21]

Kerensky's version of the October revolution was similar to Miliukov's in that it maintained that the Bolsheviks had carried out a *coup d'état* against the Provisional Government, and that they had been in league with the Germans in doing so. The difference was that Kerensky held Kornilov and his associates responsible for creating the circumstances which had made the Bolshevik coup possible.

In emigration, Kerensky never ceased to look for evidence to support his contention that Kornilov had been involved in a plot against the Provisional Government in 1917. The first book Kerensky published on the Russian revolution was his account of the Kornilov Affair in 1918. It was Kerensky's researches of this kind which kept alive interest in the contribution of the business community to the history of 1917.

With the passage of time, more and more material on the subject became available, particularly when the memoirs of Alexander Guchkov were serialized in the Parisian newspaper *Poslednie novosti* during August and September 1936.[22] The series prompted comments from A. I. Putilov, S. N. Tretiakov and others, which threw new and substantial light on the Kornilov Affair. Because of Stalin's doctrine on Russian economic development, which discouraged historical studies on the business community, the new materials could not be used by Soviet historians until the late 1950s. By that time Stalin had died and the process of de-Stalinization had been set in motion.

---

[21] Important works of this type were A. Pankratova, *Fabzavkomy Rossii v bor'be za sotsialisticheskuiu fabriku* (Moscow, 1923); S. M. Dubrovskii, *Krest'ianstvo v 1917 godu* (Moscow-Leningrad, 1927).

[22] *Voprosy istorii* (1991, no. 7–8), pp. 191–200.

The Impact of De-Stalinization and *Glasnost'* on Soviet Historical Writing

The attempts of Soviet historians to dismantle the Stalinist legacy began in the wake of N. S. Khrushchev's 'secret speech' at the Twentieth Party Congress in 1956. This turned out to be a very difficult and lengthy process. It was interrupted by Khrushchev's deposition in 1964 and was resumed only 20 years later with the accession to power of M. S. Gorbachev.

It was a relatively easy matter to remove the grosser Stalinist distortions connected with the 'cult of personality'. Stalin's ubiquitous presence in every event of note in modern Russian and Soviet history was quickly and easily discontinued. After 1956 Stalin joined the vast numbers of people who had simply disappeared from history. It was much more difficult to return historical studies in the Soviet Union to something like normality and to restore credibility to historical scholarship.

The consignment of Stalin to the ranks of the 'non-people' meant that the old rules of Soviet historiography still applied: mention of a given historical figure implied approval. Stalin's victims – 'enemies of the people' – could not be mentioned. Their writings could not be quoted or works which mentioned them could not be referred to. These rules were to remain in operation until the end of the 1980s.

Khrushchev set in motion the machinery to reduce the numbers of the 'enemies of the people' and rehabilitate many of those who had been participants in the Russian revolution and revolutionary movement, a group which had been devastated by Stalin's reign of terror. These rehabilitations made it possible once again to populate the history of the Russian revolution with actual historical figures. They could be written about and have their writings published. As a result historical research on the revolution could be undertaken.

But the Khrushchev rehabilitations were selective. By no means everyone who had fallen victim to Stalin could be mentioned by historians. Some important names were still prohibited. These included Bukharin, A. I. Rykov, M. P. Tomskii, Zinoviev, Kamenev and, of course, Trotsky. Thus, although historical research on the Russian revolution was recommenced under Khrushchev, it could not be other than patchy and incomplete.

Khrushchev himself wanted to take the process of rehabilitation further, but he was resisted by the more conservative elements within the party, especially those who had been in power in the Stalin era and shared the guilt for the crimes committed. Even the attempts to take the study of history out of the Stalinist mould met with stern resistance from those who saw their political positions threatened by Khrushchev's campaign of de-Stalinization. The history of the Russian revolution could not be dissociated from current power struggles.

Nevertheless, in the new climate created after the Twentieth Party Congress it became possible for Soviet historians to question Stalin's doctrine that Russia's pre-revolutionary economy had stood at a low level of development, and that Russia had been a 'semi-colony' of the Western powers. Articles of this kind began to appear as early as 1956 in the journal *Voprosy istorii* (*Questions of History*). The position that the tsarist economy had been well developed before the First World War, however, did not become the new orthodoxy. The opposite point of view was still held, and could be argued not only out of Stalinist conservatism but also because it was a view arrived at by a scholarly consideration of the evidence.

The aspect of the Russian revolution around which most controversy raged in the 1950s was the question of the theory and tactics of the Bolshevik leaders in Petrograd on the eve of Lenin's return in April 1917. This was a key issue for Trotsky's interpretation of the Russian revolution, and had been a pivotal question in the Stalinization of historical writing, and it was to be one again in the process of de-Stalinization.

In the March 1956 issue of *Voprosy istorii* the journal's deputy editor, E. N. Burdzhalov, published an article entitled 'The Tactics of the Bolsheviks in March and April 1917'.[23] In it he drew attention to the fact that the question of the policies pursued by the Bolshevik Party in the first weeks after the February revolution until Lenin's return to Petrograd in April had been treated fleetingly and erroneously in recent Soviet works. In a number of works including, Burdzhalov confessed, some of his own, it had been maintained that before Lenin's return Stalin, Molotov and others had advocated a policy of no confidence in the Provisional Government, opposition to continuing the war and condemnation of the 'defensists'.

Burdzhalov's article was not merely a contribution to scholarship; it was a political act designed to promote the de-Stalinization policies initiated by the Twentieth Party Congress. As such it was resented by the more conservative sections of the Soviet establishment, and a bitter campaign was launched against Burdzhalov and the editorial board of *Voprosy istorii*. In 1957 Burdzhalov was removed from his post as deputy editor, and a less adventurous editorial board was installed.

The charge made against Burdzhalov was that his approach lacked *partiinost'*, commitment to party principles; that he had slipped into 'objectivism'. This accusation had at its root a deep dilemma for Soviet historical writing. For even when one removed the distortions to the historical record perpetrated by Stalin there still could be no question of historians being allowed to follow the direction indicated by what evidence they had at their disposal. How the history of the Russian revolution was written still had to legitimize the role of the party and follow the interpretation that would show the party in the desired light. This was the inescapable concomitant of Leninism, an ideology which based itself on a supposed historical fact: that the party had led the Russian proletariat to power by overthrowing the bourgeoisie. This interpretation had to be safeguarded from all possible historical investigation; it was too important to leave to historians.

Even after Khrushchev's fall in 1964 and the establishment of the more cautious Brezhnev regime, Soviet historical scholarship continued to develop. During the Brezhnev years many historical works were published containing, if not novel interpretations, then at least much useful factual information. Some fine studies in Russian social history were published during the 1960s and 1970s. There was certainly no return to the intellectual barrenness of the Stalin era. Though on the face of it there was ideological conformity, in reality

[23] E. N. Burdzhalov, 'O taktike bol'shevikov v marte-aprele 1917 goda', *Voprosy istorii* (1956, no. 4), pp. 000.

this had a mostly formal character. In the introductions to their books authors would pay some perfunctory tribute to the classics of Marxism–Leninism, and then for the remainder of the work concentrate on empirical detail. This provided important material for Western historians, and they in their turn probably had a beneficial effect on the level of Soviet scholarship in the period. It is worth noting that it was in the Brezhnev era that Western scholarship on the history of the Russian revolution began to expand rapidly.

The policy of *glasnost'* which was initiated when Gorbachev became General Secretary of the party in 1985 continued the processes begun in the Khrushchev era. More non-persons were rehabilitated, prominent among them being Bukharin, whose ideas on the use of the market in a socialist economy accorded with the reforms Gorbachev planned to introduce. Although not rehabilitated, Trotsky could now be mentioned and some of his writings were republished. A spirit of increased candidness pervaded the historical journals, and some documents relating to the history of the Bolshevik Party were published for the first time.

A great deal of material published in the Soviet Union as a result of *glasnost'* was not really new. One such category of materials was the works of Russian authors hitherto proscribed – Bukharin, Sukhanov, Khrushchev, Trotsky – which were already known to Western scholars at least. The other category comprised translations of works by Western scholars, which made use of the flawed materials emanating from the Soviet Union.

The abortive coup in August 1991 had some fundamental implications for access to archival sources on the Russian revolution. Following that event, the Communist Party lost its hold on State power and was replaced by a government dedicated to breaking continuity with the Communist past. The Communist Party lost control of its archives, and these now became in principle open to scholars both inside and outside Russia. New possibilities were thereby opened up for the study of the Russian revolution and of the Soviet period in general.

There are nevertheless two compelling reasons why the study of Soviet historical writing on the revolution retains its importance for historians.

One arises from the fact that Soviet attitudes to historical events are reflected in some of the archival materials themselves. The other is that the opening of archives does not compel historians to put out of their minds all the partial and flawed versions of events they have assimilated from earlier publications. Rather, there is the danger that new materials might be interpreted in the light of the imperfect existing consensus. Only through an awareness of the precise limitations of existing sources can best use be made of the new material which becomes available.

Select Bibliography

Primary Sources in English

Akhapkin, Yu., ed., *First Decrees of Soviet Power*, London, 1970.

Bechhofer, C. E. *In Denikin's Russia and the Caucasus 1919–1920*, London, 1921.

Berkman, A. *The Bolshevik Myth*, London, 1989.

Bone, A., trans., *The Bolsheviks and the October Revolution: Minutes of the Central Committee of the Russian RSDLP (bolsheviks) August 1917–February 1918*, London, 1974.

Brovkin, V. N., ed. and trans., *Dear Comrades: Menshevik Reports on the Bolshevik Revolution and Civil War*, Stanford, CA, 1991.

Browder, R. P. and Kerensky, A. F., eds., *The Russian Provisional Government 1917*, 3 vols., Stanford, CA, 1961.

Buchanan, M. *The Dissolution of an Empire*, London, 1932.

Buchanan, Sir G. *My Mission to Russia and Other Diplomatic Memories*, 2 vols., London, 1923.

Bukharin, N. I. and Preobrazhensky, E. A. *The ABC of Communism*, Harmondsworth, 1969.

Bunyan, J. and Fisher, H. H., eds., *The Bolshevik Revolution, 1917–18: Documents and Materials*, Stanford, CA, 1934.

Bunyan, J. ed., *Intervention, Civil War, and Communism in Russia*, New York, 1936.

Daniels, R. V., ed., *A Documentary History of Communism*, 2 vols., Vermont, 1984.

Denikin, A. I. *The Russian Turmoil*, London, 1922.

Francis, D. R. *Russia from the American Embassy*, New York, 1921.

Golder, F. A., ed., *Documents of Russian History 1914–1917*, Gloucester, MA, 1927.

Goldman, E. *My Disillusionment in Russia*, New York, 1923.

Gorky, M. *Untimely Thoughts: Essays on Revolution, Culture and the Bolsheviks, 1917–18*, London, 1968.

Got'e, I. V. *Time of Troubles: The Diary of Iury Vladimirovich Got'e*, trans., ed. and introduced by T. Emmons, London, 1988.

Hard, W. *Raymond Robins' Own Story*, New York, 1920.

Homberger, E. and Biggart, J., eds., *John Reed and the Russian Revolution: Uncollected Articles, Letters and Speeches on Russia, 1917–1920*, London, 1992.

Ilyin-Genevsky, A. F. *From the February Revolution to the October Revolution 1917*, London, 1932.

Keep, J. trans. and ed., *The Debate on Soviet Power: Minutes of the All-Russian Central Executive Committee Second Convocation, October 1917–January 1918*, Oxford, 1979.

Kerensky, A. *The Prelude to Bolshevism: The Kornilov Rebellion*, London, 1919.

Kerensky, A. *The Catastrophe*, New York, 1927.

Kerensky, A. *Russia and History's Turning Point*, New York, 1965.

Knox, Major-General Sir A. *With the Russian Army, 1914–1917*, 2 vols., London, 1921.

Kollontai, A. *Selected Writings of Aleksandra Kollontai*, trans. with an introduction and commentaries by A. Holt, London, 1977.

Lenin, V. I. *Collected Works*, 45 vols., Moscow, 1960–70.

Leroy-Beaulieu, A. *The Empire of the Tsars and the Russians*, New York, 1902.

Lockhart, R. H. B. *Memoirs of a British Agent*, London, 1932.

MacIlhone, R., ed., *Petrograd, October, 1917: Reminiscences*, Moscow, 1957.

McCauley, M., ed., *Octobrists to Bolsheviks 1905–1917*, London, 1984.

Mohrenschildt, D. von, ed., *The Russian Revolution: Contemporary Accounts*, Oxford, 1971.

Mstislavskii, S. M. *Five Days which Transformed Russia*, trans. E. K. Zelensky, introduced by W. G. Rosenberg, London, 1988.

Nabokov, V. D. *V. D. Nabokov and the Russian Provisional Government*, New Haven, CT and London, 1976.

Philips Price, M. *My Reminiscences of the Russian Revolution*, London, 1921.

Ransome, A. *Six Weeks in Russia in 1919*, London, 1919.

Ransome, A. *The Crisis in Russia*, London, 1922.

Reed, J. *Ten Days That Shook the World*, New York, 1919.

Riddell, J., ed., *Founding the Communist International: Proceedings of the First Congress, March 1919*, New York, 1987.

Russell, B. *The Practice and Theory of Bolshevism*, London, 1920.

Sack, A. J. *The Birth of Russian Democracy*, New York, 1918.

Serge, V. *Memoirs of a Revolutionary 1901–1941*, trans. and ed. P. Sedgwick, Oxford, 1963.

Shlyapnikov, A. *On the Eve of 1917*, trans. R. Chappell, London, 1982.

Snowden, Mrs P. *Through Bolshevik Russia*, London, 1920.

Sukhanov, N. N. *The Russian Revolution 1917*, ed., abridged and trans. by J. Carmichael, Oxford, 1955.

Tengoborski, M. L. de *Commentaries on the Productive Forces of Russia*, 2 vols., London, 1856.

Williams, A. R. *Through the Russian Revolution*, Moscow, 1967.

Secondary Sources in English

Abraham, R. *Alexander Kerensky: The First Love of the Revolution*, London, 1987.

Antsiferov, A. N. *et al. Russian Agriculture during the War*, New Haven, CT, 1930.

Atkinson, D. *The End of the Russian Land Commune 1905–1930*, Stanford, CA, 1983.

Avrich, P. *Kronstadt 1921*, Princeton, NJ, 1970.

Bartlett, R., ed., *Land Commune and Peasant Community in Russia: Communal Forms in Imperial and Early Soviet Society*, London, 1990.

Benvenuti, F. *The Bolsheviks and the Red Army 1918–1922*, Cambridge, 1988.

Bilmanis, A. *A History of Latvia*, Princeton, NJ, 1951.

Bonnell, V. E. *The Russian Worker: Life and Labor under the Tsarist Regime*, Berkeley, CA, 1983.

Brinton, M. *The Bolsheviks and Workers' Control*, London, 1970.

Carr, E. H. *The Bolshevik Revolution*, 3 vols., London, 1950–53.

Carr, E. H. *The Russian Revolution from Lenin to Stalin 1917–29*, London, 1979.

Chamberlin, W. H. *The Russian Revolution*, 2 vols., New York, 1935.

Chernov, V. *The Great Russian Revolution*, New Haven, CT, 1936.

Cohen, S. S. *Bukharin and the Bolshevik Revolution: A Political Biography 1888–1938*, New York, 1973.

Daniels, R. *The Conscience of the Revolution*, Cambridge, MA, 1960.

Daniels, R. *Red October: the Bolshevik Revolution of 1917*, London, 1968.

Dobb, M. *Soviet Economic Development since 1917*, London, 1966.

Eklof, B. and Frank, S. P. *The World of the Russian Peasant: Post-Emancipation Culture and Society*, London, 1990.

Emmons, T. *The Formation of Political Parties and the First National Elections in Russia*, Cambridge, MA, 1983.

Ezergailis, A. *The 1917 Revolution in Latvia*, New York and London, 1974.

Ezergailis, A. *The Latvian Impact on the Bolshevik Revolution*, New York, 1983.

Figes, O. *Peasant Russia, Civil War: The Volga Countryside in Revolution*, Oxford, 1989.

Fitzpatrick, S. *The Russian Revolution*, Oxford, 1982.

Florinsky, M. T. *The End of the Russian Empire*, New Haven, CT, 1931.

Florinsky, M. T. *Russia: A History and an Interpretation*, 2 vols., New York, 1960.

Frankel, E. R. *et al.* eds., *Revolution in Russia: Reassessments of 1917*, Cambridge, 1992.

Gatrell, P. *The Tsarist Economy 1850–1917*, London, 1986.

Gill, G. J. *Peasants and Government in the Russian Revolution*, London, 1979.

Golovine, N. N. *The Russian Army in the World War*, New Haven, CT, 1931.

Hasegawa, T. *The February Revolution*, Seattle, WA, and London, 1981.

Heenan, L. E. *Russian Democracy's Fatal Blunder: The Summer Offensive of 1917*, New York, 1987.

Homberger, E. *John Reed*, Manchester, 1990.

Hosking, G. *The Russian Constitutional Experiment: Government and Duma, 1907–1914*, Cambridge, 1973.

Hosking, G. *A History of the Soviet Union*, London, 1985.

Hunczak, T. ed., *The Ukraine, 1917–1921*, Cambridge, MA, 1977.

Johnson, R. E. *Peasant and Proletarian: The Working Class of Moscow in the Late Nineteenth Century*, Leicester, 1979.

Kaiser, D. H. ed., *The Workers' Revolution in Russia: The View from Below*, Cambridge, 1987.

Katkov, G. *Russia 1917: The February Revolution*, London, 1967.

Katkov, G. *The Kornilov Affair*, London, 1980.

Keep, J., ed., *Contemporary History in the Soviet Mirror*, London, 1964.

Keep, J. *The Russian Revolution: a Study in Mass Mobilization*, London, 1976.

Koenker, D. P. *Moscow Workers and the 1917 Revolution*, Princeton, NJ, 1981.

Koenker, D. P. and Rosenberg, W. G. *Strikes and Revolution in Russia, 1917*, Princeton, NJ, 1989.

Leggett, G. *The Cheka: Lenin's Political Police*, Oxford, 1981.

Lih, L. *Bread and Authority in Russia*, Berkeley, CA, 1990.

Lincoln, W. B. *Red Victory: A History of the Russian Civil War*, New York, 1989.

Malle, S. *The Economic Organization of War Communism 1918–1921*, Cambridge, 1985.

Mawdsley, E. *The Russian Revolution and the Baltic Fleet*, London, 1978.

Mawdsley, E. *The Russian Civil War*, Cambridge, 1987.

Maynard, Sir J. *The Russian Peasant and Other Studies*, London, 1942.

McKean, R. B. *The Russian Constitutional Monarchy, 1907–17*, London, 1977.

McKean, R. B. *St Petersburg Between the Revolutions*, New Haven, CT, 1990.

Medvedev, R. *The October Revolution*, trans. G. Saunders, London, 1979.

Miliukov, P. N. *The Russian Revolution, Vol. 1: The Revolution Divided: Spring 1917*, ed. by R. Stites, trans. T. and R. Stites, Gulf Breeze, FL, 1978.

Miliukov, P. N. *The Russian Revolution, Vol. 2: Kornilov or Lenin? – Summer 1917*, ed., trans. and with an introduction by G. M. Hamburg, Gulf Breeze, FL, 1984.

Miliukov, P. N. *The Russian Revolution, Vol. 3: The Agony of the Provisional Government*, ed., trans. and with an introduction by G. M. Hamburg, Gulf Breeze, FL, 1987.

Munck, J. L. *The Kornilov Revolt: A Critical Examination of Sources and Research*, Aarhus, 1987.

Nove, A. *An Economic History of the USSR 1917–1991*, Harmondsworth, 1992.

Owen, T. C. *Capitalism and Politics in Russia: A Social History of the Moscow Merchants, 1855–1905*, Cambridge, 1981.

Pares, B. *The Fall of the Russian Monarchy*, London, 1939.

Pinchuk, B-C. *The Octobrists in the Third Duma 1907–1912*, Washington DC, 1974.

Pipes, R., ed., *Revolutionary Russia: A Symposium*, Cambridge, MA, 1968.

Pipes, R. *The Russian Revolution 1899–1919*, London, 1990.

Rabinowitch, A. *Prelude to Revolution*, Bloomington, IN, 1968.

Rabinowitch, A. *The Bolsheviks Come to Power*, London, 1979.

Radkey, O. H. *The Agrarian Foes of Bolshevism*, New York, 1958.

Rieber, A. J. *Merchants and Entrepreneurs in Imperial Russia*, Chapel Hill, NC, 1982.

Rigby, T. H. *Lenin's Government: Sovnarkom 1917–1922*, Cambridge, 1979.

Rosenberg, W. G. *Liberals in the Russian Revolution*, Princeton, NJ, 1974.

Sarkisyanz, M. *A Modern History of Transcaucasian Armenia*, Nagpur, 1975.

Schapiro, L. *The Communist Party of the Soviet Union*, London, 1963.

Schapiro, L. *The Origin of the Communist Autocracy* (2nd edn), London, 1977.

Schapiro, L. *1917: The Russian Revolutions and the Origins of Present-Day Communism*, London, 1984.

Serge, V. *Year One of the Russian Revolution*, trans. and ed. by P. Sedgwick, London, 1992.

Siegelbaum, L. H. *The Politics of Industrial Mobilisation in Russia, 1914–17*, London, 1983.
Sirianni, C. *Workers' Control and Socialist Democracy*, London, 1982.
Smith, S. A. *Red Petrograd: Revolution in the Factories, 1917–18*, Cambridge, 1983.
Stone, N. *The Eastern Front 1914–1917*, London, 1975.
Tokmakoff, G. P. A. *Stolypin and the Third Duma*, Lanham, 1981.
Ulam, A. *Lenin and the Bolsheviks*, London, 1965.
Upton, A. F. *The Finnish Revolution 1917–1918*, Minneapolis, MN, 1980.
Wade, R. *The Russian Search for Peace: February–October 1917*, Stanford, CA, 1969.
Wandycz, P. S. *Soviet–Polish Relations 1917–1921*, Cambridge, MA, 1969.
Wheeler-Bennett, J. W. *Brest-Litovsk: The Forgotten Peace March 1918*, London, 1938.
Wildman, A. K. *The Making of a Workers' Revolution: Russian Social Democracy, 1891–1903*, Chicago, 1967.
Wildman, A. K. *The End of the Russian Imperial Army*, vol. i, Princeton, NJ, 1980; vol. ii, Princeton, NJ, 1987.
Williams, B. *The Russian Revolution 1917–1921*, Oxford, 1987.
Williams, H. W. *Russia of the Russians*, London, 1920.

Primary Sources in Russian and Other Languages

Mints, I. I. *et al.*, eds., *Fabrichno-zavodskie komitety Petrograda v 1917 godu. Protokoly*, Moscow, 1979.
Amosov, P. N. *et al.*, eds., *Oktiabr'skaia revoliutsiia i fabzavkomy*, 2 vols., Moscow, 1927.
Anet, C. *La révolution russe*, Paris, 1918.
Balk, A. P. 'Gibel' tsarskogo Petrograda: Fevral'skaia revoliutsiia glazami gradonachal'nika A. P. Balka', *Russkoe proshloe*, 1991, no.1 .
Bogdanov, A. A. *Voprosy sotsializma: raboty raznykh let*, Moscow, 1990.
Borkowski, J., ed., *Rok 1920: Wojna polsko–radziecka we wspomnieniach i innych dokumentach*, Warsaw, 1990.
Bukharin, N. I. *Problemy teorii i praktiki sotsializma*, Moscow, 1989.
Buryshkin, P. *Moskva kupecheskaia*, New York, 1954.
Denikin, A. I. *Ocherki russkoi smuty*, 5 vols., Paris, 1921–26.
Galperina, B. D., ed., 'Petrogradskii sovet rabochikh i soldatskikh deputatov v aprele 1917 goda', *Voprosy istorii*, 1990, no. 4.
Gavrilov, I. G. 'Na vyborgskoi storone v 1914–1917 gg.', *Krasnaia letopis'*, 1927, no. 2.
Giatsintov, E. N. 'Tragediia russkoi armii v 1917 godu', *Russkoe proshloe*, 1991, no. 1.
Goldenveizer, A. A. 'Iz kievskikh vospominanii (1917–1921)', *Arkhiv russkoi revoliutsii*, 1922, vi.
Golikov, G. P. *et al.*, eds., *Vospominaniia o Vladimire Il'iche Lenine*, 5 vols., Moscow, 1968.

Grave, B. B. *Burzhuaziia nakanune fevral'skoi revoliutsii*, Moscow-Leningrad, 1927.

Guchkov, A. I. 'Vospominaniia', *Poslednie novosti*, 1936, August 12, 15, 19, 23, 26, 30, September 2, 6, 9, 13, 16, 20, 23, 27, 30.

Guchkov, A. I. 'A. I. Guchkov rasskazyvaet', *Voprosy istorii*, 1991, no. 7–8, no. 9–10, no. 12.

Hahlweg, W., ed., *Lenins Rückkehr nach Russland, 1917: Die deutschen Akten*, Leiden, 1957.

Haxthausen, A. von, *Studien über die innern Zustände, das Volksleben und insbesondere die ländlichen Einrichtungen Russlands*, vols i and ii, Hannover, 1847, vol. iii, Berlin 1852.

Kaiurov, V. N. 'Shest' dnei fevral'skoi revoliutsii', *Proletarskaia revoliutsiia*, 1923, no. 1.

Kak sovershilas' velikaia russkaia revoliutsiia: Podrobnoe opisanie istoricheskikh sobytii za period vremeni s 23 fevralia po 4 marta 1917 g., Petrograd, 1917.

Kapsukas, V. 'Lietuvos Bresto taikos tarybos', *Raštai*, vol. vii, Vilnius, 1964.

Kniazev, G. A. 'Iz zapisnoi knizhki russkogo intelligenta za vremia voiny i revoliutsii 1915–1922', *Russkoe proshloe*, 1991, no. 2.

Kommunist: Ezhenedel'nyi zhurnal ekonomiki, politiki i obshchestvennosti, ed. with introduction, notes and index by R. I. Kowalski, New York, 1990.

Krasnaia kniga VChK, 2 vols., Moscow, 1989.

Lieven, W., *Das rote Russland*, Berlin, 1918.

Miliukov, P. N. *God bor'by*, St Petersburg, 1907.

Miliukov, P. N. *Tri popytki*, Paris, 1921.

Miliukov, P. N. *Vospominaniia (1859–1917)*, New York, 1955.

O roli professional'nykh soiuzov v proizvodstve, Moscow, 1921.

Oldenbourg, S. *Le coup d'état bolchéviste*, Paris, 1929.

Paléologue, M. *La Russie des tsars pendant la grande guerre*, 3 vols., Paris, 1921–22.

Piłsudski, J. *Rok 1920*, London, 1987.

Pirmasis nepriklausomos Lietuvos dešimtmetis, London, 1955.

Pokrovskii, M. N. and Iakovlev, Ia. A. *Krest'ianskoe dvizhenie v 1917 godu*, Moscow-Leningrad, 1927.

Posse, V. A. 'Ot Fevralia do Bresta (vospominaniia)', *Russkoe proshloe*, 1991, no. 1.

Posse, V. A. 'V gody grazhdanskoi voiny', *Russkoe proshloe*, 1991, no. 2.

Pravda o Kronshtadte, Prague, 1921.

Resheniia partii i pravitel'stva po khoziaistvennym voprosam, vol. i, Moscow, 1967.

Sadoul, J. *Notes sur la révolution bolchévique*, Paris, 1919.

Scheibert, P. ed., *Die russischen politischen Parteien von 1905 bis 1917. Ein Dokumentationsband*, Darmstadt, 1983.

Shakhovskoi, V. N. 'Sic transit gloria mundi', Paris, 1952.

Shliapnikov, A. G. 'Fevral'skie dni v Peterburge', *Proletarskaia revoliutsiia*, 1923, no. 1.

Shliapnikov, A. G. *Semnadtsatyi god*, 4 vols., Moscow-Leningrad, 1923–31.

Shliapnikov, A. G. *Kanun semnadtsatogo goda*, Moscow, 1992.

Sidorov, A. L., ed., *Ekonomicheskoe polozhenie Rossii nakanune Velikoi Oktiabr'skoi sotsialisticheskoi revoliutsii: Dokumenty i materialy*, 3 vols., Moscow-Leningrad, 1957.

Smirnov, A. F., ed., *Oktiabr' v Petrograde*, Moscow, 1987.
Smolin, V. A. ed. 'Kronshtadt v 1921 godu: Novye dokumenty', *Russkoe proshloe*, 1991, no. 2.
Stankevich, V. B. *Vospominaniia 1914–1919*, Berlin, 1920.
Stolypin, P. A. *Nam nuzhna velikaia Rossiia*, Moscow, 1991.
Sukhomlinov, V. *Vospominaniia*, Berlin, 1924.
Trotsky, L. D. *et al.* 'Vospominaniia ob Oktiabr'skom perevorote', *Proletarskaia revoliutsiia*, 1922, no. 10.
Trotsky, L. D. *Moia zhizn'*, 2 vols., Moscow, 1990.
Tsereteli, I. G. *Vospominaniia o fevral'skoi revoliutsii*, 2 vols., Paris–The Hague, 1963.
Ustrialov, N. V. 'Belyi Omsk (Dnevnik kolchakovtsa)', *Russkoe proshloe*, 1991, no. 2.
Vācietis, J. *Latviešu strēlnieku vēsturiskā nozīme*, Riga, 1989.
Velikaia Oktiabr'skaia sotsialisticheskaia revoliutsiia, Moscow, 1957.
Vtoroi s"ezd Kommunisticheskoi partii (bol'shevikov) Ukrainy. 17–22 oktiabria 1918 goda. Protokoly, Kiev, 1991.

Secondary Sources in Russian and Other Languages

Anfimov, A. M. *Rossiiskaia derevnia v gody pervoi mirovoi voiny*, Moscow, 1962.
Anfimov, A. M. *Krest'ianskoe khoziaistvo Evropeiskoi Rossii 1881–1904*, Moscow, 1980.
Anweiler, O. *Die Rätebewegung in Russland 1905–1921*, Leiden, 1958.
Arutiunian, A. O. *Kavkazskii front 1914–1917 gg.*, Yerevan, 1971.
Avdeev, N. *Revoliutsiia 1917 goda (Khronika sobytii)*, vols. i and ii, Moscow-Petrograd, 1923.
Avrekh, A. Ia. *Tsarizm i tret'eiun'skaia sistema*, Moscow, 1966.
Avrekh, A. Ia. *Stolypin i tret'ia duma*, Moscow, 1968.
Avrekh, A. Ia. 'Progressizm i problema sozdaniia partii "nastoiashchei" burzhuazii',*Voprosy istorii*, 1980, no. 9.
Avrekh, A. Ia. *Masony i revoliutsiia*, Moscow, 1990.
Baklanova, I. A. *Rabochie Petrograda v period mirnogo razvitiia revoliutsii (mart–iiun' 1917 g.)*, Leningrad, 1978.
Basler, W. *Deutschlands Annexionspolitik in Polen und im Baltikum 1914–1918*, Berlin, 1962.
Bazylow, L. *Ostatnie lata Rosji carskiej: Rządy Stolypina*, Warsaw, 1972.
Bazylow, L. *Dzieje Rosji 1801–1917*, Warsaw, 1977.
Bazylow, L. *Obalenie caratu*, Warsaw, 1977.
Bazylow, L. and Sobczak, J., eds., *Encyklopedia Rewolucji Październikowej*, Warsaw, 1977.
Bezberezh'ev, S. V. 'Mariia Aleksandrovna Spiridonova', *Voprosy istorii*, 1990, no.9.
Biron, A. K. and Biron, M. F. *Stanovlenie sovetskoi istoriografii Latvii*, Riga, 1981.
Bor'ba za ustanovlenie i uprochenie sovetskoi vlasti, Moscow, 1962.
Buldakov, V. F. and Kabanov, V. V. '"Voennyi kommunizm": ideologiia i obshchestvennoe razvitie', *Voprosy istorii*, 1990, no. 3.

Burdzhalov, E. N. *Vtoraia russkaia revoliutsiia*, Moscow, 1967.

Čepėnas, P. *Naujųjų laikų Lietuvos istorija*, Chicago, 1976.

Chermenskii, E. D. *IV Gosudarstvennaia duma i sverzhenie tsarizma v Rossii*, Moscow, 1976.

Ciepielewski, J. *Historia społeczno-ekonomiczna Związku Radzieckiego*, Warsaw, 1974.

Dauge, P. P. *Stučkas dzive un darbs*, Riga, 1958.

Diakin, V. S. *Russkaia burzhuaziia i tsarizm v gody pervoi mirovoi voiny*, Leningrad, 1967.

Diakin, V. S. *Samoderzhavie, burzhuaziia i dvorianstvo v 1907–1911 gg.*, Leningrad, 1978.

Diakin, V.S. *Burzhuaziia, dvorianstvo i tsarizm v 1911–1914 gg.*, Leningrad, 1988.

Drokov, S.V. 'Aleksandr Vasil'evich Kolchak', *Voprosy istorii*, 1991, no. 1.

Dubrovskii, S. M. *Krest'ianstvo v 1917 godu*, Moscow-Leningrad, 1927.

Dubrovskii, S. M. *Krest'ianskoe dvizhenie v revoliutsii 1905–1907 gg.*, Moscow, 1956.

Dubrovskii, S. M. *Stolypinskaia zemel'naia reforma*, Moscow, 1963.

Dubrovskii, S. M. *Sel'skoe khoziaistvo i krest'ianstvo v period imperializma*, Moscow, 1975.

Erykalov, E. F. *Oktiabr'skoe vooruzhennoe vosstanie v Petrograde*, Leningrad, 1966.

Freidlin, B. M. *Ocherki istorii rabochego dvizheniia v Rossii v 1917 g.*, Moscow, 1967.

Frenkin, M. *Russkaia armiia i revoliutsiia 1917–1918*, Munich, 1978.

Ganelin, R. Sh. and Shepelev, L. E. 'Predprinimatel'skie organizatsii v Petrograde v 1917 g.', in *Oktiabr'skoe vooruzhennoe vosstanie v Petrograde*, Moscow-Leningrad, 1957, pp. 259–317.

Gaponenko, L. S. *Rabochii klass Rossii v 1917 godu*, Moscow, 1970.

Garvi, P. A. *Professional'nye soiuzy v Rossii v pervye gody revoliutsii (1917–1921)*, New York, 1981.

Gavrilov, L. M. *Soldatskie komitety v Oktiabr'skoi revoliutsii*, Moscow, 1983.

Germanis, U. *Oberst Vacietis und die lettischen Schützen im Weltkrieg und in der Oktoberrevolution*, Stockholm, 1974.

Gimpel'son, E. G. 'Voennyi kommunizm'. *Politika, praktika, ideologiia*, Moscow, 1973.

Gimpel'son, E. G. *Sovetskii rabochii klass 1918–1920 gg.*, Moscow, 1974.

Golovin, N. N. *Rossiiskaia kontr-revoliutsiia v 1917–1918 gg.*, Tallinn, 1937.

Gorinov, M. M. and Tsakunov, S. V. 'Leninskaia kontseptsiia NEPa: Stanovlenie i razvitie', *Voprosy istorii*, 1990, no. 4.

Gorodetskii, E. N. *Sovetskaia istoriografiia velikogo Oktiabria*, Moscow, 1981.

Gostynska, W. *Stosunki polsko–radzieckie 1918–1919*, Warsaw, 1972.

Grave, B. B. *K istorii klassovoi bor'by v Rossii*, Moscow-Leningrad, 1926.

Grille, D. *Lenins Rivale: Bogdanov und seine Philosophie*, Cologne, 1966.

Hayit, B. *Turkistan zwischen Russland und China*, Amsterdam, 1971.

Hildermeier, M. *Die Sozialrevolutionäre Partei Russlands: Agrarsozialismus und Modernisierung im Zarenreich (1900–1914)*, Cologne–Vienna, 1978.

Itkin, M. L. 'Tsentry fabrichno-zavodskikh komitetov Rossii v 1917 godu', *Voprosy istorii*, 1974, no. 2.

Kabanov, V. V. 'Oktiabr'skaia revoliutsiia i krest'ianskaia obshchina', *Istoricheskie zapiski*, 1984, no. 111.

Kakurin, N. E. *Kak srazhalas' revoliutsiia*, 2 vols., Moscow, 1990.

Karpov, N. *Agrarnaia politika Stolypina*, Leningrad, 1925.

Khromov, P. A. *Ekonomicheskoe razvitie Rossii v XIX–XX vekakh 1800–1917*, Moscow, 1950.

Kim, M. P. ed. *Lenin i kul'turnaia revoliutsiia: Khronika sobytii (1917–1923 gg.)*, Moscow, 1972.

Komin, V. V. *Bankrotstvo burzhuaznykh i melkoburzhuaznykh partii Rossii v period podgotovki i pobedy velikoi Oktiabr'skoi Sotsialisticheskoi revoliutsii*, Moscow, 1965.

Korelin, A. P. *Dvorianstvo v poreformennoi Rossii 1861–1904 gg.*, Moscow, 1979.

Kormanowa, Żanna, Walentyna Najdus, *Historia Polski*, vol. iii, part 5, Warsaw, 1974.

Kostrikin, V. I. *Zemel'nye komitety v 1917 godu*, Moscow, 1975.

Kovalevskii, M. M. *Le régime économique de la Russie*, Paris, 1898.

Kovalevskii, M. M. *La crise russe*, Paris, 1906.

Kritsman, L. *Geroichesky period velikoi russkoi revoliutsii*, Moscow, 1925.

Kruus, H. *Grundriss der Geschichte des estnischen Volkes*, Tartu, 1932.

Kulichenko, M. I. *Bor'ba Kommunisticheskoi Partii za reshenie natsional'nogo voprosa v 1918–1920 godakh*, Khar'kov, 1963.

Köörna, A. *Suure sotsialistliku oktobrirevolutsiooni majanduslikud eeldused Eestis*, Tallinn, 1961.

Larin, I. and Kritzman, L. *Wirtschaftsleben und wirtschaftlicher Aufbau in Sowjet–Russland 1917–1920*, Hamburg, 1921.

Laverychev, V. Ia. 'Vserossiiskii soiuz torgovli i promyshlennosti', *Istoricheskie zapiski*, 1961, no. 70.

Maliavskii, A. D. *Krest'ianskoe dvizhenie v Rossii v 1917 g. Mart-Oktiabr'*, Moscow, 1981.

Mel'gunov, S. *Na puti k dvortsovomu perevorotu*, Paris, 1931.

Mett, I. *La commune de Cronstadt*, Paris, 1938.

Miliukov, P. N. *Rossiia na perelome*, 2 vols., Paris, 1927.

Miliukov, P. N. *Histoire de Russie*, vol. iii, Paris, 1933.

Miliutin, V. P. *Istoriia ekonomicheskogo razvitiia SSSR (1917–1927)*, Moscow-Leningrad, 1929.

Miller, V. I. *Soldatskie komitety russkoi armii v 1917 g.*, Moscow, 1974.

Mints, I. I., ed., *Lenin i Oktiabr'skoe vooruzhennoe vosstanie v Petrograde*, Moscow, 1964.

Mints, I. I. *et al.* eds., *Bor'ba za sovetskuiu vlast' v Pribaltike*, Moscow, 1967.

Mints, I. I. *et al.* eds., *Sverzhenie samoderzhaviia: Sbornik statei*, Moscow, 1970.

Ochmański, J. *Historia Litwy*, Wrocław, 1967.

Pantsov, A. V. 'Brestskii mir', *Voprosy istorii*, 1990, no. 2.

Pantsov, A. V. 'Lev Davydovich Trotskii', *Voprosy istorii*, 1990, no. 5.

Pershin, P. N. *Agrarnaia revoliutsiia v Rossii*, 2 vols., Moscow, 1966.

Pirumova, N. M. *Zemskoe liberal'noe dvizhenie*, Moscow, 1977.

Pokrovskii. M. N. *Ocherki russkogo revoliutsionnogo dvizheniia XIX–XX vv.*, Moscow, 1924.

Polivanov, O. A. 'TsIK Sovetov nakanune Petrogradskogo vooruzhennogo vosstaniia', *Voprosy istorii*, 1992, no. 2–3.

Preyer, W. D. *Die russische Agrarreform*, Jena, 1914.

Rakitin, A. B. *V. A. Antonov-Ovseenko*, Leningrad, 1989.

Razgon, A. I. *VTsIK Sovetov v pervye mesiatsy diktatury proletariata*, Moscow, 1977.

Rittikh, A. A. *Krest'ianskoe zemlepol'zovaniie*, St Petersburg, 1903.

Rostunov, I. I. *Russkii front pervoi mirovoi voiny*, Moscow, 1976

Ruban, N. V. *Oktiabr'skaia revoliutsiia i krakh men'shevizma*, Moscow, 1968.

Rubinshtein, N. 'Vneshniaia politika kerenshchiny', in *Ocherki istorii oktiabr'skoi revoliutsii*, vol. i, Moscow-Leningrad, 1927.

Saat, J. and Siilivask, K. *Velikaia Oktiabr'skaia sotsialisticheskaia revoliutsiia v Estonii*, Tallinn, 1977.

Shestakov, A. V. *Bor'ba sel'skikh rabochikh v revoliutsii 1905–1907 gg.*, Moscow-Leningrad, 1930.

Siilivask, K. *Revolutsioon, kodusõda ja välisriikide interventsioon Eestis (1917–1920)*, Tallinn, 1977.

Šilde, Ā. *Latvijas vēsture 1914–1940*, Stockholm, 1976.

Sivolapova, G. F. 'S"ezd Sovetov Severnoi oblasti v 1917 g.', *Istoricheskie zapiski*, 1980, no. 105.

Slonimskii, A. G. *Katastrofa russkogo liberalizma*, Dushanbe, 1975.

Sobczak, J. *Pierwsze dni rewolucji: kronika 6 XI–3 XII 1917 r.*, Warsaw, 1977.

Startsev, V. I. *Russkaia burzhuaziia i samoderzhavie v 1905-1917 gg.*, Leningrad, 1977.

Startsev, V. I. *Vnutrenniaia politika Vremennogo pravitel'stva*, Leningrad, 1980.

Startsev, V. I. *Krakh kerenshchiny*, Leningrad, 1982.

Suprunenko, M. I. *et al.*, eds., *Istoriia ukrains'koi RSR*, vol. v, Kiev, 1977.

Taigro, Ü. *Eesti Töörahva Kommuun*, Tallinn, 1957.

Temkin, Ia. G. *Tsimmerval'd–Kintal'*, Moscow, 1967.

Temkin, Ia. G. *Ot vtorogo k tret'emu internatsionalu*, Moscow, 1978.

Trapeznikov, S. P. *Leninizm i agrarno-krest'ianskii vopros*, 2 vols., Moscow, 1967.

Trotsky, L. D. *K istorii russkoi revoliutsii*, Moscow, 1990.

Trotsky, L. D. *Stalin*, 2 vols., Moscow, 1990.

Tych, F. *PPS-Lewica w latach wojny 1914–1918*, Warsaw, 1960.

Vaitkevičius, B. *Socialistinė revoliucija Lietuvoje 1918–1919 metais*, Vilnius, 1967.

Valk, S. N. and Ganelin, R. Sh., *et al. Oktiabr'skoe vooruzhennoe vosstanie: Semnadtsatyi god v Petrograde*, 2 vols., Leningrad, 1967.

Varlamov, K. I. and Slamikhin, N. A. *Razoblachenie V.I. Leninym teorii i taktiki 'levykh kommunistov' (noiabr' 1917 g.–1918 g.)*, Moscow, 1964.

Vasiukov, V. S. *Vneshniaia politika Vremennogo pravitel'stva*, Moscow, 1966.

Volkovinskii, V. N. 'Nestor Ivanovich Makhno', *Voprosy istorii*, 1991, no. 9–10.

Volobuev, P. V. *Ekonomicheskaia politika Vremennogo pravitel'stva*, Moscow, 1962.

Volobuev, P. V. *Proletariat i burzhuaziia Rossii v 1917 g.*, Moscow, 1964.

Wilk, M. *Moskiewski komitet wojenno-przemysłowy 1915–1918: Studium z dziejów burżuazji rosyjskiej*, Łódź, 1972.

Wojna, R. *W ogniu rosyjskiej wojny wewnętrznej 1918–1920*, Warsaw, 1975.

Zand, H. *Z dziejów wojny domowej w Rosji*, Warsaw, 1973.

Zhuravlev, V. V. and Simonov, N. S 'Prichiny i posledstviia razgona Uchreditel'nogo sobraniia', *Voprosy istorii*, 1992, no. 1.

Znamenskii, O. N. *Iul'skii krizis 1917 goda*, Moscow-Leningrad, 1964.
Znamenskii, O. N. *Vserossiiskoe uchreditel'noe sobranie*, Leningrad, 1976.
Zyrianov, P. N. 'Zemel'no-raspredelitel'naia deiatel'nost' krestian'skoi
   obshchiny v 1907–1914 gg., *Istoricheskie zapiski*, 1988, no. 116.
Zyrianov, P. N. 'Petr Arkad'evich Stolypin', *Voprosy istorii*, 1990, no. 6.

Biographical Notes

Alekseev, Mikhail Vasilevich (1857–1918) General; Chief-of-Staff to Nicholas II 1915–17; Supreme Commander-in-Chief, March–May 1917; Chief-of-Staff to Kerensky, September–October 1917; organizer of the Volunteer Army, 1918.

Antonov-Ovseenko, Vladimir Aleksandrovich (1884–1939) Graduate of St Petersburg Military Engineering Academy; participant in 1905 revolution; organized capture of Winter Palace, October 1917; commander of the Ukrainian front, 1919.

Avksent'ev, Nikolai Dmitrievich (1878–1943) Prominent SR; Chairman of All-Russian Congress of Peasants' Soviets, 1917; Minister of the Interior, July–September 1917; Chairman, Democratic Conference and Pre-Parliament, 1917; Chairman, Ufa Directorate, 1918; emigrated.

Bazarov, Vladimir Aleksandrovich (1874–1939) Economist and philosopher; associate of A. A. Bogdanov; in 1917 belonged to group of Social Democrat Internationalists grouped round Gorky's newspaper *Novaia zhizn'*.

Berkman, Alexander (1870–1936) American Jewish anarchist of Russian origin; deported from the USA along with Emma Goldman in 1919 for anti-war activities; returned to Russia and worked for the Bolshevik regime; left Russia at the end of 1921.

Bobiński, Stanisław (1882–1935) Member of SDKPiL; adviser on Polish affairs to the Soviet delegation at the peace negotiations at Brest-Litovsk.

Bogdanov [Malinovsky], Aleksandr Aleksandrovich (1873–1928) Philosopher, doctor and economist; founder member of the RSDLP; after the 1905 revolution an opponent of Lenin; leader of Proletkult movement, 1918; denied the socialist character of War Communism.

Brusilov, Aleksei Alekseevich (1853–1926) General; Commander-in-Chief SW front, March 1916–May 1917; Supreme Commander, May–July 1917; served in Red Army.

Budienny, Semen Mikhailovich (1883–1973) Peasant family; drafted into the army in 1903; served in cavalry as an NCO; fought in Russo-Japanese and First World Wars; delegate in regimental and divisional committees, summer 1917; formed a cavalry unit to combat Whites on the Don, February 1918; second in command of I Socialist Peasants' Cavalry Regiment, June–September 1918; Commander of I Cavalry Army, November 1919–October 1923; Marshal of the Soviet Union, 1935.

Bukharin, Nikolai Ivanovich (1888–1938) Native of Moscow; son of schoolteacher; member of RSDLP from 1906; participant in 1905 revolution in Moscow; emigrated to Germany, 1911; published *The World Economy and Imperialism*, 1915; emigration in New York and editor of *Novyi mir*, 1916; returned to Moscow, May 1917; member of Bolshevik CC, August 1917; participant in October revolution in Moscow; Left Communist, 1918; editor of *Pravda*, 1918–29; organizer of Comintern, 1919; along with E. A. Preobrazhensky published *The ABC of Communism*, 1919; published *Economics of the Transition Period*, 1920; upholder of NEP and opponent of Stalin's collectivization of agriculture; author of numerous works on socialist theory.

Čakste, Jānis (1859–1927) Latvian; son of landlord; law graduate of Moscow University, 1886; practised law in Mitau; member of I Duma; President of Latvia, 1922–27.

Chernov [Gardenin], Viktor Mikhailovich (1876–1952) One of the founders and the leading theoretician of the SR Party; during the First World War an internationalist; Minister of Agriculture, May–August 1917; Chairman of Constituent Assembly; emigrated, 1921.

Chkheidze, Nikolai Semenovich (1864–1926) Menshevik leader; member of III and IV Dumas; member of Duma Provisional Committee; Chairman of Petrograd Soviet, February–August 1917; Chairman of CEC; emigrated to France, 1921; committed suicide.

Chugurin, Ivan Dmitrevich (1883–1947) Native of Sormovo; joined RSDLP, 1902; participant in 1905 uprising in Sormovo; student at Lenin's party school at Longjumeau, 1910; worker at Promet, then Aivaz, factories, 1916–17; member of Bolshevik Vyborg and Petersburg Committees; leader of food detachment in Kazan province, 1918; political commissar in V Army, 1918–19; member of Moscow Cheka, 1919; Chairman of Saratov Soviet, 1919; Chairman of Siberian coal industry, 1919; Chairman of coal-mining industry in Donbass, 1920; Deputy Director of Sormovo Factory, 1921; Director of Northern Shipyard in Leningrad, 1924.

Dan [Gurvich], Fedor Ilich (1871–1947) Leading Menshevik defensist; advocate of coalition government; vice-chairman of CEC and chief editor of *Izvestiia*, 1917; exiled abroad, 1922.

Daniševskis, Jūlijs Kārlis (1884–1938) Latvian; farmer's son; joined Latvian Social Democratic Party in Mitau, 1900; participant in 1905 revolution; arrested and exiled to Siberia, 1914; member of Moscow Soviet, 1917; editor of the Latvian newspaper *Cina* and the Russian newspaper *Okopnaia pravda*; during Civil War, member of the Revolutionary Military Council of the Republic; worked in Soviet economic institutions, 1920s and 1930s.

Denikin, Anton Ivanovich (1872–1947) General; Commander-in-Chief of the SW front, 1917; Commander of the Volunteer Army and the Armed Forces of the South of Russia, 1918–20; emigrated.

Dukhonin, Nikolai Nikolaevich (1876–1917) Chief of Staff to the Supreme Commander-in-Chief, November 1917; Supreme Commander from 1 November 1917; dismissed by Lenin for refusal to enter into negotiations with the Germans; killed by soldiers at Mogilev, 20 November 1917.

Durnovo, Petr Nikolaevich (1844–1915) Graduate of Military-Judicial Academy, 1872; civil servant in Ministry of Justice; police official in Ministry of the Interior, 1881–93; Deputy Minister of the Interior, 1900–1905; Minister of the Interior in Witte's Cabinet, October 1905; member of the State Council, 1906; opponent of Stolypin; advocate of German orientation in Russia's foreign policy.

Dybenko, Pavel Efimovich (1889–1938) Peasant recruit to Baltic Fleet, 1911; joined Bolsheviks, 1911; member of Helsingfors Soviet and leader of Tsentrobalt, 1917; member of Petrograd MRC; People's Commissar for the Navy.

Dzierżyński, Feliks (1877–1926) Of Polish gentry parentage from Vilna province; founder member of SDKPiL, 1899; repeatedly imprisoned and exiled for revolutionary activities; imprisoned in Moscow, 1916; released February 1917; member of Bolshevik CC, 1917; Chairman of Cheka, 7 December 1917.

Efremov, Ivan Nikolaev (1866–1932) Land-owner and politician; member of I, III and IV Dumas; founder member of Progressist party; initiator of Progressive Bloc, 1915; left Progressist Party to found Radical Democratic Party, 1917; served as Minister of Social Security in the Second Coalition Cabinet of the Provisional Government; emigrated to Switzerland.

Frunze, Mikhail Vasilevich (1885–1925) Son of medical orderly of Moldavian origin; joined Bolsheviks, 1904; led strike of textile workers in Ivanovo-Voznesensk, 1905; arrested and sentenced to death, 1907; headed Bolshevik underground organization in Minsk, 1916; Military Commissar in Ivanovo-Voznesensk and Iaroslavl, 1918; Commander of IV Army on eastern front, January 1919; Commander of Southern Group of Eastern front, April 1919; Commander of eastern front, July 1919; Commander of Turkestan front, August 1919; Commander of Southern front, September 1920; Commander of armies of Ukraine and Crimea, December 1920; author of many works on military science.

Gorky Maxim [Aleksei Maksimovich Peshkov] (1868–1936) Russian author and playwright; native of Nizhny Novgorod; closely connected with revolutionary movement; adherent of Alexander Bogdanov's group, 1907–12; publisher of *Novaia zhizn'*, 1917; opponent of Bolshevik seizure of power.

Guchkov, Aleksandr Ivanovich (1862–1936) Moscow merchant family; history graduate of Moscow University, 1885; studied history and philosophy at the universities of Berlin and Heidelberg; charity work in Russia for famine victims, 1892–93; member of Moscow City Council, 1897; fought on the side of the Boers against the British in South Africa, 1900; organizer for Red Cross during Russo-Japanese War, 1904; founder member and leader of Octobrist Party, 1905; member of III Duma; Duma Chairman, 1910–11; Chairman of Central War Industries Committee, 1915–17; Minister of War and Navy in Provisional Government; resigned 2 May 1917; emigrated in 1918.

Gvozdev, Kuzma Antonovich (1883–?) Son of Kuban peasant; member of SR Party until 1907, then joined Mensheviks; advocate of 'defensism'; leader of Workers' Group in the Central War Industries Committee, 1915; member of Executive Committee of Petrograd Soviet, 1917; Minister of Labour in Provisional Government; after 1918 worked in Soviet workers' organizations.

Haxthausen, August Franz Ludwig Maria Freiherr von (1792–1866) Folklorist and adherent of the Romantic movement in Germany; student of agrarian relations, arguing against the extension of capitalism to agriculture and advocating the restitution of social organization based on hierarchical estates; at the invitation of Nicholas I travelled in Russia, spring 1843–summer 1844; account of journey published in *Studien über die inneren Zustände, das Volksleben und insbesondere die ländlichen Einrichtungen Rußlands* published between 1847 and 1852.

Hilferding, Rudolf (1877–1941) Native of Vienna; medical graduate of Vienna University, 1901; joined Social Democratic movement and worked on Kautsky's *Die Neue Zeit*, 1902; editor of the SPD newspaper *Vorwärts*; published *Das Finanzkapital*, 1910; drafted into the Austro-Hungarian Army as an army doctor; Finance Minister in Weimar Republic, 1923 and 1928; emigrated to France, 1933; murdered by Gestapo in Paris, 1941.

Hrushevskyi, Mykhailo (1866–1934) Ukrainian historian and politician; Chairman of the Ukrainian Central Rada, 1917; emigrated, 1919; returned to academic life in Kiev, 1924.

Ilin-Zhenevskii, Aleksandr Fedorovich (1894–1941) Publicist and historian of the workers' movement; joined Bolsheviks, 1912; editor of the Bolshevik newspapers *Volna, Golos pravdy* and *Soldatskaia pravda*, 1917; commissar of MRC; from 1923, Director of the Leningrad section of Istpart.

Iudenich, Nikolai Nikolaevich (1862–1933) Commander of Caucasian Army, 1915; Commander-in-Chief of Caucasian front, 1915–17; Commander of NW Army, 1918; led unsuccessful offensives on Petrograd, 1919; emigrated.

Joffe, Adolf Abramovich (1833–1927) Member of RSDLP; member of Mezhraionka; joined Bolsheviks, 1917; member of Soviet delegation to the peace negotiations at Brest-Litovsk; led Soviet delegation in peace negotiations with Poland at Riga, 1921; member of Trotskyist opposition; committed suicide.

Kaiurov, Vasily Nikolaevich (1876–1936) Born in Simbirsk province; joined RSDLP, 1899; joined Bolsheviks, 1903; member of Sormovo and Nizhny Novgorod committees of Bolshevik Party; participant in 1905 revolution in Sormovo; leading figure in Bolshevik underground in Petrograd, 1912–17; organizer of strike movement during February revolution in Petrograd; leading member of Vyborg District Soviet; Military Commissar to V Army on Eastern front during Civil War; Chairman of the Siberian Regional Commission of the Central Control Commission on purging the party; worker in the Lenin Institute and party archives in Moscow, 1926; member of M. N. Riutin's anti-Stalin group, the Union of Marxist-Leninists, 1932; arrested and exiled to Bashkiria, where he died.

Kaledin, Aleksei Maksimovich (1861–1918) Commander of VIII Army on SW front during the First World War; elected Ataman of Don Cossacks, June 1917; organizer of anti-Bolshevik forces in the south of Russia, December 1917; committed suicide, 11 February 1918.

Kamenev, Sergei Sergeevich (1881–1936) Career officer in the Russian Army; achieved rank of colonel in the First World War; joined Red Army, 1918; Commander of eastern front, September 1918; Supreme Commander of the Armed Forces of the Soviet Union, 8 July 1919–28 April 1924.

Kamenev [Rosenfeld], Lev Borisovich (1883–1936) Born in Moscow, son of railway engineer; went to school in Vilna; studied at Moscow University; joined RSDLP, 1901; joined Bolsheviks, 1903; exiled to Siberia, 1915; member of Bolshevik CC, April 1917; member of Soviet CEC, July 1917; opposed armed uprising by Bolsheviks, October 1917; Chairman of CEC, 26 October–16 November 1917; Chairman of Moscow Soviet, 1918–26; member of Politburo, 1919–25; participant in anti-Trotsky campaign, 1923–24; allied with Trotsky, 1926–27; expelled from the party, 1927; broke with Trotsky and readmitted to the party, 1928; expelled in connection with the Riutin platform, 1932; readmitted to the party, 1933; arrested following Kirov's assassination, 1934; defendant at show trial and executed, 1936.

Kamkov [Katz] Boris Davidovich (1885–1938) Left Socialist Revolutionary leader; opponent of Brest-Litovsk peace; imprisoned for three years as organizer of Count Mirbach's assassination and the SR uprising in Moscow.

Kartashev, Anton Vladimirovich (1875–1960) Ecclesiastical historian; member of Kadet Party; Ober-Procurator of the Holy Synod in the Provisional Government, July–August, 1917; Minister of Religious Affairs, August–October, 1917; settled in Finland, 1919; connected with North-Western Government created during Iudenich's offensive on Petrograd; emigrated to Paris; Chairman of Russian National Committee, 1921–25.

Kautsky, Karl (1854–1938) Leading theoretician of the German Social Democratic Party and the II International; born in Prague; editor of the SDP's theoretical journal *Die Neue Zeit*, 1883–1917; until 1910 a prominent critic of Eduard Bernstein's revisionism; during the First World War denied that the conflict between the imperialist powers would necessarily culminate in socialism; critic of Bolshevik rule in Russia.

Kerensky, Aleksandr Fedorovich (1881–1970) Law graduate of St Petersburg University, 1904; frequently acted for the defence in trials of revolutionaries; member of IV Duma, 1912; chairman of Trudovik fraction; member of Provisional Committee of the Duma, February 1917; vice-chairman of the Petrograd Soviet, 2 March 1917; Minister of Justice in the Provisional Government; Minister of War and Navy, May–June 1917; Prime Minister, 8 July 1917; Supreme Commander-in-Chief and Head of Directorate following the Kornilov rebellion; emigrated to France, 1918; moved to USA, 1940.

Kingissepp, Viktor (1888–1922) Estonian; native of Ösel (Saaremaa) Island; working-class family; joined RSDLP, 1906; political activist in St Petersburg and Reval, 1907–14; military service on Caucasian front, 1916; after February revolution returned to Estonia and headed the Bolshevik organization; leading member of MRC attached to Executive Committee of Soviet of Estland Region, 22 October 1917; arrested and shot by Estonian police.

Khatisian [Khatisov], Alexander (1876–1945) Mayor of Tiflis, 1910–17; member of Kadet Party; joined Dashnaktsutiun in 1917; Minister of Foreign Affairs, then President of the Armenian government, 1918–20; settled in Paris; Chairman of the League of Nations Committee for Armenian Refugees.

Kolchak, Aleksander Vasilevich (1873–1920) Commander of the Black Sea Fleet, 1916; War Minister in Russian Provisional Government in Omsk,

November 1918; declared 'Supreme Ruler' following *coup d'état* on 18 November; left Omsk, November 1919; captured by Czechoslovaks and shot by Soviet authorities at Irkutsk on 4 January 1920.

Kolegaev, Andrei Lukich (1887–1937) Joined SR Party, leading Left SR, 1917; 1906; Commissar for Agriculture in Soviet Government, December 1917–March 1918; joined Bolshevik Party, November 1918; organized provisioning on Southern front during Civil War.

Kollontai, Aleksandra Mikhailovna (1872–1952) Daughter of tsarist general; connected with revolutionary movement from 1890s; joined Mensheviks, 1906; in emigration, 1908–17; joined Bolsheviks in 1915; member of CC; Commissar for Social Security in Soviet Government; Left Communist and resigned from Government, 1918; led the Women's Section of the CC (*Zhenotdel*), 1920; leader of Workers' Opposition; from 1920s held a number of diplomatic posts.

Konovalov, Aleksandr Ivanovich (1875–1948) Politician and member of Moscow business community; leader of the Progressist party; member of IV Duma; vice-chairman of Central War Industries Committee, 1915–17; member of Duma Provisional Committee; founder member of All-Russian Union of Trade and Industry, 1917; Minister of Trade and Industry in the Provisional Government, March–July 1917; returned to the same post as a representative of the Kadet Party in September 1917; emigrated to USA.

Kornilov, Lavr Georgevich (1870–1918) General; born in Kazakhstan, the son of a Cossack officer; career officer in tsarist army; military attaché in China, 1907–11; during the First World War commanded infantry division; captured by Austrians, April 1915; escaped, July 1916; Commander of Petrograd Military District, March 1917; commander of VIII Army, May 1917; Commander of SW front, July 1917; appointed Supreme Commander-in-Chief, 18 July 1917; 27 August dismissed by Kerensky; arrested by General Alekseev and imprisoned at Bykhov, 2 September 1917; escaped to Novocherkassk, where he participated in forming the Volunteer Army; killed during attack on Ekaterinodar, 13 April 1918.

Kozlovskii, Aleksandr Nikolaevich (1861–1940) General; joined Red Army in 1918; from December 1920 Commander of artillery forces in Kronstadt, where he joined the rebellion in 1921; after the defeat of the uprising he fled to Finland, where he spent the rest of his life.

Kozłowski, Mieczysław (1876–1927) Native of Vilna; son of schoolteacher; founder member of SDKPiL; practised law in St Petersburg, 1907–17; SDKPiL delegate to the Petrograd Soviet and member of Executive Committee, March 1917; People's Commissar of Justice in Lithuanian–Belorussian Soviet Government, January–April 1919.

Krasnov, Petr Nikolaevich (1869–1947) General; Commander of III Cavalry Corps, August 1917; Commander of pro-Kerensky forces in advance on Petrograd, 26–31 October 1917; taken prisoner at Pulkovo and released on word of honour not to continue opposition to revolution; elected Ataman of Don Cossack Armies, May 1918; with German help conducted unsuccessful offensive against Tsaritsyn; subordinated his forces to Denikin's command, January 1919; emigrated to Germany, February 1919; during the Second World War co-operated with Germans; captured and shot by Soviet authorities.

Krestinskii, Nikolai Nikolaevich (1883–1938) Son of a high-school teacher; born in Mogilev; joined RSDLP in Vilna, 1903; graduated from St Petersburg University and began to practise law, 1907; exiled to Ekaterinburg, 1914; member of Bolshevik Ekaterinburg Regional Committee, 1917; Chief Commissar of the State Bank; People's Commissar of Finance, 1918–22; secretary of the Bolshevik CC, December 1919–March 1921; during Brest-Litovsk peace negotiations a Left Communist; a supporter of Trotsky in the trade-union debate.

Krupskaia, Nadezhda Konstantinovna (1869–1939) Lenin's wife; daughter of Volhynian nobleman; schoolteacher, 1891–96; member of St Petersburg Union of Struggle for the Liberation of the Working Class; joined RSDLP, 1898; member of Bolshevik Vyborg District Committee, 1917; served in Commissariat of Education.

Krylenko, Nikolai Vasilevich (1885–1938) Son of civil servant; joined RSDLP, 1904; studied history and law at St Petersburg University; party organizer in Moscow, 1915; arrested and sent to front, 1916; member of soldiers' committees on SW front; organizer of Congress of Soviets of the Northern Region; member of Petrograd MRC, October 1917; member of People's Commissariat of Army and Navy Affairs; Supreme Commander-in-Chief, 9 November 1917.

Krymov, Aleksandr Mikhailovich (1871–1917) General; from April 1917 Commander III Cavalry Corps, which he led against Petrograd during the Kornilov mutiny; committed suicide on 31 August 1917.

Kutler, Nikolai Nikolaevich (1859–1924) Director of department in Ministry of Finance, 1899–1904; Deputy Minister of the Interior, 1904–1905; Director of agrarian and agricultural affairs under Witte and drafter of land reform envisaging compulsory alienation of private land, 1905–1906; official disapproval of the proposed reform forced resignation; joined Kadets, 1906; member of II and III Dumas; Chairman, Council of Congresses of Industry and Trade, 1917; Petrograd delegate to the Constituent Assembly, 1917; briefly arrested for anti-Soviet activities, December 1917; employed in Commissariat of Finance; member of the board of State Bank, 1922.

Kuz'min, Nikolai Nikolaevich (1883–1939) Graduate of St Petersburg University; joined RSDLP in 1903; Commissar in various units of the Red Army, then Commissar of Baltic Fleet; during Kronstadt rebellion imprisoned for 16 days by the rebels.

Lazimir [Laasimir], Paul (1891–1920) Estonian; son of professional NCO; military medical orderly; Left SR, 1917; member of Executive Committee of Petrograd Soviet; vice-chairman of Military Department and Chairman of the Soldiers' Section of the Petrograd Soviet; first Chairman of MRC; joined Bolsheviks, 1918; died of typhus.

Lednicki, Aleksander (1866–1934) Native of Minsk; peasant family; law graduate of Moscow University; member of Kadet Party, 1906–16; member of I Duma, 1906; founder of Polish Committee to Help War Victims in Moscow; Chairman of the Provisional Government's Liquidation Commission for the Affairs of the Kingdom of Poland, March 1917; representative of the Regency Council to the Soviet Government, January 1918; returned to Poland, October 1918.

Lenin [Ulianov], Vladimir Ilich (1870–1924) Born in Simbirsk; son of school inspector; law graduate of St Petersburg University; founded Union of Struggle for the Liberation of the Working Class, 1895; arrested and exiled to Siberia, 1895; in emigration, 1900; editor of *Iskra*, 1900–1903; published *What Is To Be Done?*; led Bolshevik wing of RSDLP, formed at II Congress, 1903; returned to Russia in November 1905; again in emigration, 1907–17; advocated turning the world war into a civil war; with German help returned to Russia, 3 April 1917; delivered *April Theses* setting out Bolshevik tactics – no support for the war, no support for the Provisional Government and the transfer of State power to the Soviets; following the July Days in hiding in Finland; after the failure of the Kornilov revolt, an advocate of armed uprising; elected Chairman of Council of People's Commissars, 26 October 1917; advocate of immediate peace with Germany; shot and wounded by SR terrorist, 30 August 1918; organizer of Comintern, March 1919; framer of economic, social, military, nationality and cultural policies in the first years of Soviet regime; prolific writer on politics, economics and philosophy.

Lockhart, Robert Hamilton Bruce (1887–1970) Born in Anstruther, Fife; son of schoolmaster; educated at Fettes College, Edinburgh; acting British Consul-General in Russia, 1912–17; head of special mission to Russia to establish unofficial relations between Britain and Soviet Russia, 1918; arrested and detained on suspicion of espionage; exchanged for Litvinov; commercial secretary in Prague, 1919; left Foreign Service, 1922.

Lunacharskiiy, Anatoly Vasilevich (1875–1933) Born in Poltava; son of civil servant; studied philosophy in Zurich; returned to Russia, 1897; imprisoned and exiled for participation in 1905 revolution, contributing to a number of Bolshevik newspapers; emigrated, 1906; published *Religion and Socialism*, 1908; associated with Trotsky's *Nashe slovo* during the First World War; returned to Russia, May 1917; joined Bolshevik Party along with Mezhraionka; member of Petrograd MRC; Commissar of Education, October 1917–29.

Lvov, Georgy Evgenevich Prince (1861–1925) Large-scale land-owner; member of the Moscow Committee of the Progressist Party; Chairman of the Union of Towns and Zemstvos.

Lvov, Vladimir Nikolaevich (1872–1935) Land-owner; member of III and IV Dumas; Ober-Procurator of the Holy Synod in the Provisional Government, 2 March–24 July.

Makhno, Nestor Ivanovich (1888–1935) Born in Guliai Pole in the Ekaterinoslav province; Ukrainian peasant family; member of local anarchist group, 1906–1908; arrested with other members of the group, 1908; sentenced to death, but reprieved because of his youth; released from prison, March 1917; Chairman of Guliai Pole Soviet, August 1917; campaigned against Central Rada, Kaledin's Cossacks, German forces of occupation and Skoropadskii's troops, 1917–18; brigade Commander in Red Army, February 1919; unjustly accused by Red Army High Command of opening font to Denikin's forces, May 1919; attacked Red Army units, July 1919; headed peasant rebellion against Denikin's rule in Ukraine, August–September 1920; combatted Red Army in the Ukraine, 1920; allied with Soviet forces against Wrangel, October 1920; harried by the Red

Army, crossed into Rumania, August 1921; arrested and tried in Poland for banditry, 1923; settled in Paris, 1924; author of memoirs.

Marx, Karl (1818–83) Influential German thinker in the tradition of Fichte, Schelling and Hegel; from 1844 onwards worked on a book to be entitled *The Critique of Political Economy*, designed to integrate philosophy with economics; only parts of the incomplete project were published – *Capital* Volume I during Marx's lifetime, and *Capital* Volumes II and III post-humously by his friend, Friedrich Engels.

Mickevičius-Kapsukas, Vincas (1880–1935) Lithuanian; peasant family; studied political economy and philosophy at Berne University, 1902–1904; joined Lithuanian Social Democratic Party, 1903; participant in 1905 revolution in Lithuania; arrested and sentenced to eight years hard labour, 1907; escaped from Siberia, 1913; lived in Kraków, 1914; moved to Bellshill, Scotland and edited the newspapers *Rankpelnis* and *Socialdemok-ratas*; moved to Philadelphia, USA and edited *Naujoji gadynė*; returned to Russia and joined Bolsheviks, 1917; Commissar of Lithuanian Affairs in Commissariat of Nationalities, December 1917; participant in peace nego-tiations at Brest-Litovsk, 1918; Premier of Lithuanian Soviet Republic, 1918–19; prolific writer on politics, history and philosophy.

Miliukov, Pavel Nikolaevich (1859–1943) Born in Moscow; son of architect; history graduate of Moscow University, 1882; lecturer in Russian History at Moscow University, 1886–95; founder member of Kadet Party, 1905; Chairman of Kadet Party and editor of its newspaper *Rech'*; member of III and IV Dumas; Minister of Foreign Affairs in the Provisional Govern-ment; resigned 2 May 1917; helped found the Volunteer Army, 1918; emigrated to England, 1920; moved to Paris, 1921; author of numerous works on Russian history and politics.

Nekrasov, Nikolai Vissarionovich (1879–1940) Leader of the left wing of the Kadet Party; member of the III and IV Dumas; member of the Duma Provisional Committee, 1917; Minister of Transport in Provisional Govern-ment; member of Radical Democratic Party, July 1917; Governor General of Finland, September–October 1917; administrative and teaching work in the Soviet Union, 1920s and 1930s.

Pētersons, Kārlis (1877–1926) Latvian; peasant family background; joined revolutionary movement in Riga in 1890s; belonged to the Marxist-influ-enced 'Jauna Strava' (New Current) movement; Riga, then Libau corre-spondent of *Dienas Lapa*; drafted into army and served in the Latvian Rifle Reserve Regiment, 1916; member of Iskolastrel and editorial board of *Brīvais Strēlnieks*; member of Petrograd MRC; military Commissar in Latvian Rifle division, April 1918.

Peterss, Jēkabs (1886–1938) Latvian; born in peasant family; participant in 1905 revolution; emigrated to England, 1909; member of London Latvian Social Democratic Group and British Socialist Party; returned to Russia after February revolution; Latvian Social Democratic Party propagandist in XII Army; editor of *Ciņa*; member of Petrograd MRC; member of Cheka leadership; member of Workers' and Peasants' Inspectorate, 1924–30.

Petrichenko, Stepan Maksimovich (1892–?) Born into a Kaluga peasant family; joined navy in 1914, where he served as a clerk; during the Kronstadt mutiny in March 1921 head of Provisional Revolutionary

Committee; fled to Finland; in Prague published the book *The Truth about Kronstadt*; recruited by Soviet Intelligence in 1927; returned to the Soviet Union in 1945; disappeared.

Piłsudski, Józef (1867–1935) Pole; minor gentry family; educated in Vilna; founder member of the Polish Socialist Party (PPS); Commander of I Brigade of Polish Legions, 1914–16; Chief of military department of Provisional Council of State, 1917; interned by Germans in Magdeburg; released, November 1918; head of Polish army and State, 14 November 1918–9 December 1922; conducted war with Soviet Russia, 1919–20; 1923 withdrew from politics; premier of Poland with dictatorial powers, May 1926–35.

Plekhanov, Georgy Valentinovich (1856–1918) Born in the village of Gudalovka in Tambov province; son of a minor land-owner; educated at Voronezh Military School and the SPb Mining Institute, 1868–76; joined Bakininist anarchist group of 'Rebels', which later merged with 'Land and Liberty', 1876; on Land and Liberty's split into 'People's Will' and 'Black Repartition', Plekhanov became a founder member of Black Repartition; forced to emigrate to Switzerland, 1880; translated *Communist Manifesto* into Russian; founder member of 'Liberation of Labour', 1883; published *Socialism and the Political Struggle*, 1883; published *Our Differences*, a book criticizing 'People's Will' and calling its members 'Narodniks', 1885; participated in founding Congress of Second International, 1889; published *The Development of the Monist View of History*, 1895; editor of *Iskra*, along with Lenin, Martov and others, 1901; adopted Menshevik position, 1904; participant in Fifth Congress of RSDLP, 1907; editor of pro-war *Edinstvo*, 1914; arrived in Petrograd, 13 April 1917; died in Finland.

Preobrazhenskii, Evgeny Aleksandrovich (1886–1937) Born in Bolkhovo, Orel province; son of a priest; joined the RSDLP, 1903; participant in the December 1905 uprising in Moscow; party organizer in the Urals, 1906–1908; arrested and exiled to Siberia, 1909–17; participant in October revolution in the Urals; Left Communist, 1918; member of commission to draft the new party programme, 1919; joint author with Bukharin of *The ABC of Communism*; member of Party Secretariat, 1920; signatory of the left oppositionist 'Platform of the 46', 1923; author of *The New Economics*, introducing the concept of 'primitive socialist accumulation', 1924; expelled from the party several times, 1927–35; arrested and shot.

Purishkevich, Vladimir Mitrofanovich (1870–1920) Leader of the extreme right in II, III and IV Dumas; founder member of the Union of Russian People and the Union of the Archangel Mikhail; participant in the assassination of Rasputin.

Putilov, Aleksei Ivanovich (1866–?) Law graduate of St Petersburg University, 1889; civil servant in Ministry of the Interior and Ministry of Finance; close associate of Witte; Deputy Minister of Finance and Director of the Nobles' and Peasants' Land Banks, 1905; retired from civil service; elected director of the Russo-Chinese Bank; Chairman of the board of Russo-Asiatic Bank, 1910; Chairman or board member of about 50; joint owner of Stakheev-Batolin concern; owner of Putilov steel works, Petrograd; delegate of the Council of Congresses of Industry and Trade to Pre-Parliament; emigrated to France after the Bolsheviks came to power.

Rabchinskii, Ivan Vasilevich (1879–1950) Born in Kiev province; son of railway worker; railway telegraph operator in St Petersburg; railwaymen's delegate to St Petersburg Soviet, 1905; worker in Reval War Industries Committee, 1915–17; member of Executive Committee of Reval Soviet; member of Reval Bolshevik leadership; initiator of Congress of Soviets of the Northern Region; Chairman of MRC of Estland; deputy commissar of Post and Telegraph; deputy chairman of mining section of Vesenkha, 1919–20; editor of technical publications, 1920s; Director of Institute of Applied Minerology, 1930s.

Rasputin, Grigory Efimovich (1872–1916) Son of Siberian peasant; adopted views of Khlysty sect; introduced at court, 1907; acquired great influence over the tsarina and the tsar; assassinated, 16 December 1916.

Reed, John (1887–1920) Born in Portland, Oregon, USA; graduated from Harvard University, 1910; author of *Insurgent Mexico*, 1914; opposed American involvement in the First World War; visited Russia on assignment for *Metropolitan Magazine*, 1915; arrived in Russia on assignment for *The Masses*, August 1917; worked in the Bureau for International Propaganda, November 1917; left Russia, January 1918; completed *Ten Days that Shook the World*, January, 1919; returned to Russia, October 1919; delegate to the Second Congress of the Comintern and elected to its Central Committee; died in Moscow.

Riabushinskii, Pavel Pavlovich (1871–1924). Banker and industrialist; from 1912 an organizer of the Progressist Party, and publisher of its newspaper *Utro Rossy* (*Morning Russia*). In 1915 initiator of the War Industries Committees; member of the Central Committee and Chairman of the Moscow WIC.

Rodzianko, Mikhail Vladimirovich (1859–1924) Land-owner; Octobrist; member of III and IV Dumas; Chairman of IV Duma; Chairman of Duma Provisional Committee, 1917; emigrated, 1920.

Rudzutaks, Jānis (1887–1938) Latvian; son of farm labourer; member of Latvian Social Democratic Party, 1903; participant in 1905 revolution in Riga; imprisoned in Riga and Moscow, 1909–17; secretary of the Textile Workers' Union; Chairman of the All-Russian Transport Workers' Union; General Secretary of the All-Russian Central Council of Trade Unions; member of the CC and Politburo, 1920–37.

Ruzskii, Nikolai Vladimirovich (1854–1918) Commander-in-Chief of Northern front, August–December, 1915, July 1916–April 1917; retired in the summer of 1917; killed by Red Army soldiers in Piatigorsk.

Rykov, Aleksei Ivanovich (1881–1938) Born in Saratov; peasant family; studied law at Kazan University; joined the RSDLP, 1898; political organizer in Moscow, St Petersburg and Odessa; participant in the 1905 revolution in Moscow; repeatedly imprisoned and exiled; freed from exile in Narym by the February revolution; member of Moscow Soviet; People's Commissar for Internal Affairs; Chairman of Vesenkha, April 1918–February 1924; 'extraordinary representative of the Council of Labour and Defence for the provisioning of the Red Army and the Navy'; Chairman of the Council of People's Commissars (in succession to Lenin), 1924; associated with the Right Opposition, late 1920s; expelled from the party, 1937; arrested and shot.

Savinkov, Boris Viktorovich (1879–1925) Joined SR Party, 1903; member of

SR 'Combat Organization', 1903–1906; involved in assassinations of Plehve and Grand Duke Sergei; served as volunteer in French army in the First World War; returned to Russia, April 1917; appointed Commissar of VII Army on SW front; assistant War Minister, July–August 1917; participant in Kornilov Affair, August 1917; participant in Kerensky and Krasnov's offensive on Petrograd, October 1917; founder of Volunteer Army, 1918; organizer of anti-Soviet committee in Warsaw, 1920–21; arrested and imprisoned by Soviet authorities, 1924; committed suicide.

Shliapnikov, Aleksandr Gavrilovich (1885–1937) Native of Vladimir province; working-class family; joined RSDLP, 1901; member of St Petersburg Committee of RSDLP, 1907; worker in France, England and Germany, 1908–14; returned to Russia, April 1914; member of RSDLP CC, 1915; founder member of CC Russian Bureau, 1916; founder member of St Petersburg Soviet, February 1917; Chairman of All-Russian Union of Metal-Workers, 1917; member Petrograd MRC; Commissar of Labour, 26 October 1917; leader of the Workers' Opposition, 1920–22; member of the Bolshevik CC, 1921–22; expelled from party, 1933; shot.

Spiridonova, Mariia Aleksandrovna (1884–1941) Born in Tambov; family of minor nobility; joined SR Party while still at school in Tambov, 1901; attempted to assassinate the governor of Tambov, G. N. Luzhenovsky, as a reprisal for his brutal suppression of local peasant disturbances, 1906; initial sentence of death commuted to indeterminate imprisonment; released in March 1917; joined left wing of the SR Party; founder member of Left SR Party, November 1917; advocate of Left SR coalition with Bolsheviks; supporter of Brest-Litovsk peace until April 1918; arrested following assassination of Mirbach, 8 July 1918; released December 1918; repeatedly arrested and imprisoned and exiled, 1919–38; condemned to death by military tribunal in 1941.

Stalin [Jugashvili], Iosif Vissarionovich (1879–1953) Born in Gori, Georgia; son of cobbler; educated at seminary in Tiflis; joined Social Democrats, 1898; political organizer in Transcaucasia; member of Bolshevik CC and editor of *Pravda*, 1912; repeatedly imprisoned and exiled; returned to Petrograd from Siberia, 12 March 1917; member of Petrograd MRC; Commissar for Nationality Affairs, 1917–22; member of the Revolutionary Military Council of the Republic during Civil War; member of Politburo, 1919–52; General Secretary of CC of Communist Party, April 1922; member of Comintern Executive Committee, 1925–43; initiator of collectivization of agriculture, 1929; author of letter to *Proletarskaia revoliutsiia* outlawing discussion of many historical questions, 1931; initiator of mass imprisonment and execution of perceived 'enemies of the people', especially in 1937–38; Supreme Commander of the Armed Forces of the USSR, 1941–45.

Stolypin, Petr Arkadievich (1862–1911) Noble land-owning family; attended school in Vilna; studied mathematics and natural sciences at St Petersburg University, 1881–85; served in Ministry of State Domains, 1885–89; served in Ministry of the Interior; and as marshal of the Kovno district nobility; marshal of Kovno province nobility, 1899; Governor of Grodno, 1902; Governor of Saratov, 1903–1906; Minister of the Interior and Chairman of the Council of Ministers, 1906–11; assassinated by D. G. Bogrov in Kiev.

Stučka, Pēteris (1865–1932) Latvian; peasant family; studied law at St

Petersburg University; practised law in Riga, 1893; leading member of Marxist-influenced 'Jauna strāva' (New Current) movement and editor of its newspaper *Dienas Lapa*, 1888–97; founder member of Latvian Social Democratic Party; advocate of union with Bolshevik Party; member of Petrograd Soviet Executive Committee, 1917; member of Petrograd MRC; People's Commissar of Justice, November 1917; member of Soviet delegation at Brest-Litovsk peace negotiations; President of Latvian Soviet Government, December 1918–January 1920; Deputy People's Commissar of Justice, 1919–23; Chairman of the RSFSR Supreme Court; author of many works on socialist legal theory.

Sukhanov [Gimmer], Nikolai Nikolaevich (1882–1940) Born in Moscow; family of impoverished nobility; graduated from Moscow High School and went to Paris to study at the Higher School of Social Sciences, founded by the Russian sociologist M. M. Kovalevsky, 1902; returned to Russia, joined the SR Party and enrolled at Moscow University, 1903; arrested and imprisoned, 1904; released and took part in the December uprising in Moscow, 1905; exiled to Archangel province, 1910; released and returned to St Petersburg, 1913; editor of *Sovremennik*, 1914; editor of *Letopis*, an anti-war paper financed by Gorky, 1915–17; member of Executive Committee of the Petrograd Soviet, February 1917; joined Mensheviks, May 1917; contributor to Gorky's newspaper *Novaia zhizn*, 1917; member of CEC, 1917–18; opponent of Brest-Litovsk peace and critic of early policies of Bolsheviks, 1918; along with other Mensheviks expelled from CEC, June 1918; wrote *Notes on the Revolution*, 1918–21; left Mensheviks and applied (unsuccessfully) to join Bolshevik Party, 1923; edited Soviet economic journals, 1924–25; arrested on charge of belonging to underground Menshevik organization, 1930; exiled to Tobolsk, 1935; arrested on new charges, 1937; condemned to death and shot.

Tereshchenko, Mikhail Ivanovich (1888–1956) Land-owner, financier and industrialist; non-party liberal close to the Progressists; Chairman of Kiev War Industries Committee, 1915–17; Minister of Finance in the Provisional Government, 2 March–5 May 1917; Minister of Foreign Affairs, 6 May–October 1917; emigrated to England.

Tomskii [Efremov], Mikhail Pavlovich (1880–1936) Working-class family; joined Bolshevik Party, 1904; trade-union organizer; member of Reval Soviet, 1905; imprisoned and exiled to Tomsk; returned to Petrograd, 1917; elected to leadership of Union of Metal workers; secretary, then Chairman of All-Russian Council of Trade Unions; sided with Lenin in trade-union debate, 1920; member of Politburo, 1922; sided with Bukharin and Rykov against Stalin, 1928; committed suicide.

Tret'akov, Sergei Nikolaevich (1882–1944) Moscow merchant family; Chairman of Moscow Stock Exchange; member of the Council of Congresses of Industry and Trade; member of CWIC, 1915–17; founder member of All-Russian Union of Trade and Industry, March 1917; member of CC of Kadet Party, summer 1917; Chairman of Provisional Government's Economic Council and Main Economic Committee; Minister of Trade and Industry in Kolchak's government; emigrated, 1920.

Trotsky [Bronstein], Lev Davydovich (1879–1940) Born in Kherson province; Jewish peasant family; founder member of Southern-Russia

Workers' Union in Nikolaev, 1896–98; exiled to Siberia; escaped and joined Lenin in London, 1902; delegate of Siberian Social Democrats at II Congress of RSDLP, 1903, at which he sided with Martov against Lenin; returned to Russia, beginning of 1905; Chairman of the St Petersburg Soviet, 27 November–3 December 1905; arrested and exiled to Siberia; escaped abroad; during the First World War edited the newspaper *Nashe slovo* in Paris; deported from France for anti-war agitation; editor of New York newspaper *Novyi mir*, 1916; after February revolution set out for Russia, but detained in Halifax, Canada; arrived in Petrograd, 5 May 1917; along with Mezhraionka joined the Bolshevik Party, July 1917; arrested and imprisoned, 23 July 1917; elected member of Bolshevik CC, August 1917; released from prison, 2 September; elected Chairman of Petrograd Soviet, 25 September; supervised the activities of MRC, 24–25 October; Commissar for Foreign Affairs, 26 October 1917–24 February 1918; leader of Soviet delegation at Brest-Litovsk peace negotiations; Commissar for Military Affairs, 14 March 1918; Chairman of Revolutionary Military Council of the Republic, 2 September 1918; member of Comintern Executive Committee; Commissar for Transport, 1920; critic of centralization of power in the party, 1923; author of *Lessons of October*, 1924; joined by Zinoviev and Kamenev in 'United Opposition', 1926–27; expelled from party, 1927; exiled to Alma Ata, 1928; deported to Prinkipo, 1929; published *My Life*, 1930; published *History of the Russian Revolution*, 1931–33; moved to Norway, 1935–37; settled in Mexico, 1937; assassinated by Stalin agent, 20 August 1940.

Tsereteli, Irakli (1881–1959) Born in Kutaisi, Georgia; son of writer; entered Moscow University law faculty, 1900; exiled to Siberia, 1901; returned to Tiflis and joined RSDLP, 1903; sided with the Mensheviks against Lenin; studied in Berlin and Geneva, 1904; elected to II Duma, 1906; on the Duma's dissolution on 3 June 1907 put on trial and exiled to Siberia; during the war, formed a group which opposed both unconditional defensism and defeatism – a current known as 'Siberian Zimmerwaldism'; returned to Petrograd, 21 March 1917; member of CEC; Minister of Post and Telegraph in Provisional Government, May–July 1917; acting Minister of Interior, July 1917; moved to Georgia, 1918; emigrated to France, 1921; emigrated to USA, 1940; died in New York.

Tukhachevskii, Mikhail Nikolaevich (1893–1937) Son of minor land-owner in Smolensk province; graduated from military academy and commissioned into Semenov guards regiment, 1914; served in the First World War as second lieutenant; joined Red Army, April 1918; commanded I Army on Eastern front, June 1918–January 1919; second in command of Southern front fighting against Don Cossacks, January–March 1919; Commander of Southern front in war against the Poles, April 1920–March 1921; Commander of VII Army deployed against Kronstadt rebels, March 1921; Commander of armies sent to crush peasant uprising in Tambov, May 1921; appointed Director of Red Army Military Academy, August 1921; Chief of Red Army Staff, 1924; leading Soviet military theoretician; accused of treason and shot.

Ulmanis, Kārlis (1877–1942) Latvian; son of land-owner; agronomy graduate of Nebraska University; returned to Russia, 1913; President of Latvia, 1918–21; held posts of President and Minister of Foreign Affairs, 1925–40.

Uritskii, Mosei Salomonovich (1873–1918) Born in the Ukraine, son of a Jewish merchant; studied law at Kiev University; joined Mensheviks, 1903; participant in 1905 revolution in St Petersburg; emigrated, 1914; returned to Russia after the February revolution and joined Mezhraionka, then accepted into Bolshevik Party; member of Bolshevik CC; member of Petrograd MRC; Left Communist, 1918; Chairman of the Petrograd Cheka; assassinated by SR terrorist, 30 August 1918.

Vācietis, Jukums (1873–1938) Latvian; peasant family; graduate of St Petersburg General Staff Academy, 1909; Commander of V Zemgale Latvian Rifle Regiment; supporter of Soviet power, October 1917; on orders of MEC of XII Army captured Walk; appointed Commander of Latvian Rifle Soviet Division, 13 April 1918; suppressed Left SR uprising in Moscow, 6–7 July; Commander of eastern front, July–September 1918; led defence of Kazan, August 1918; Supreme Commander of the Armed Forces of the RSFSR, 6 September 1918–8 July 1919; member of Military Revolutionary Council of the Republic, August 1919–21; professor of Red Army Military Academy from 1922.

Verkhovskii, Aleksandr Ivanovich (1886–1938) General; Commander of Moscow Military District, 3 July 1917; War Minister in the Provisional Government, 30 August–20 October 1917; emigrated to Finland, 1918; returned to Russia and joined Red Army, February 1919; instructor in Red Army Military Academy, 1921–30.

Voldemaras, Augustinas (1883–1942) Lithuanian; history graduate of St Petersburg University, 1909; member of Taryba, 1918; Premier of Lithuanian government, November 1918.

Volodarskii [Goldstein], Moisei Markovich (1891–1918) Born in Volhynia province; son of Jewish artisan; member of Bund, 1905; emigrated to USA, 1913; returned to Petrograd, May 1917 and joined Mezhraionka organization; elected member of the St Petersburg Committee of the Bolshevik Party; Commissar for press, propaganda and agitation; assassinated by SR.

Witte, Sergei Iul'evich (1849–1915) Born in Tiflis; family of Russified Baltic Germans; mathematics graduate of Odessa University, 1870; civil servant in Odessa specializing in railway and transport matters, 1871–77; member of organization to counter the revolutionary activities of 'People's Will', 1881; author of articles opposing the extension of capitalism in Russia, 1883; Director of the railways department in the Ministry of Finance, 1889; Minister of Transport, 1892; Minister of Finance, August 1892–1903; advocate of utilizing foreign capital to develop industry in Russia; Chairman of the Council of Ministers, 1903; advocate of replacing peasant communal land-ownership with individual holdings, 1904; sponsor of October Manifesto, 1905; leader of Russian delegation at peace talks with Japanese in Portsmouth, USA, 1905; resigned from government, April 1906; author of memoirs.

Wrangel, Petr Nikolaevich (1878–1928) General; family of Baltic German nobility; graduate of Mining Institute, 1901; graduate of General Staff Academy, 1910; took part in Russo-Japanese and First World Wars; joined Volunteer Army, August 1918; Commander of cavalry formations, 1919;

Commander of Volunteer Army, December 1919–January 1920; Supreme Commander-in-Chief Armed Forces of the South of Russia (Russian Army), 4 April–13 November 1920; emigrated.

Yčas, Martynas (1885–1941) Lithuanian; law graduate of Tomsk University, 1911; Kadet member of IV Duma; Chairman of Lithuanian Refugee Committee, 1914–17; Minister of Finance in Lithuanian government.

Zenzinov, Vladimir Mikhailovich (1880–1953) Native of Moscow; wealthy family; studied at Berlin, Heidelberg and Halle Universities; returned to Russia, 1904; arrested and exiled, 1905; founder member of SR party and member of its CC; during First World War a defensist; member of Petrograd Soviet Executive Committee, 1917; editor of *Delo naroda*; member of the Ufa Directory, 1918; emigrated, 1920.

Zinoviev [Radomyslsky], Grigory Evseevich (1883–1936) Born in Elizavetgrad, Kherson province; joined RSDLP, 1901; studied at Berne University, 1904; returned to Russia and became a political organizer in St Petersburg, 1905; attended V Congress in London and elected to the CC, 1907; arrested, released and emigrated to Geneva, 1908; during the First World War wrote several joint works with Lenin; returned to Petrograd with Lenin, April 1917; opposed armed uprising, October 1917; Chairman of the Petrograd Soviet, December 1917–January 1926; Chairman of Comintern, March 1919–October 1926; participant in anti-Trotsky campaign, 1923–24; allied with Trotsky, 1926–27; expelled from the party, 1927; broke with Trotsky and readmitted to the party, 1928; expelled in connection with the Riutin platform, 1932; readmitted to the party, 1933; arrested following Kirov's assassination, 1934; defendant at show trial and executed, 1936.

Index